THE COMPLETE GUIDE TO GAME AUDIO

For Comp
Sound De

794.
8
MAR

ballymoney
nrc
northern regional college

Learning Resource Centre

ers

Aar

CMP Books
CMP Media LLC
1601 West 23rd Street, Suite 200
Lawrence, Kansas 66046
USA

Editor:	Michelle O'Neal
Layout Design & Production:	Michelle O'Neal
Cover Art Design:	Michael Striler
Cover Layout Design:	Damien Castaneda

Distributed in the U.S. and Canada by:
Publishers Group West
1700 Fourth Street
Berkeley, CA 94710
1-800-788-3123

ISBN-13: 978-1-57820-083-2
ISBN-10: 1-57820-083-0

"Aspiring sound designers and composers regularly ask me what it takes to break into this industry. Now I can say read *The Complete Guide to Game Audio!*"
— **Darryl S. Duncan**, President & CEO, GameBeat, Inc.

"An exhaustive and indispensable resource for game audio from initial concept to cashing the royalty checks."
— **Jennifer Olsen**, Senior Editor, *Game Developer* magazine

"A fountainhead of valuable insight, this book thoroughly demystifies the art of game music and sound like no other."
— **Jon Holland**, game composer and sound designer

"Finally, a comprehensive guide for anyone interested in game audio!"
— **Mark Temple**, game producer and President, Enemy Technology

"Aaron is truly a game audio expert and a great teacher. This book will help anyone aspiring to succeed in the biz."
— **Jack Buser**, Computer and Game Initiative Engineer, Dolby Laboratories

"This impressive guide is a great resource for anyone just starting out in the business, as well as professionals already working in the industry."
— **Keith Arem**, game composer, sound designer and President, PCB Productions

"If you're considering game audio creation as a profession, or just curious about how it's done... BUY THIS BOOK NOW!"
— **Tommy Tallarico**, game composer and President, Tommy Tallarico Studios

"Aaron Marks' experience and insight into the inner workings of the game audio world make this book an invaluable resource."
— **Greg O'Conner Read**, founder and editor, Music4Games.net

"A 'must have' book for anyone considering a career in game audio."
— **Will Davis**, game composer, sound designer, and President, Audio-Development Ltd., United Kingdom

"This will surely become the bible of any up and coming sound designer or composer wanting to work on video games."
— **Joey Kuras**, sound designer, Tommy Tallarico Studios

"Kudos to Marks for his candid look into the industry, and the processes behind technique and creativity behind new digital media."
— **Tim Rideout**, musician/composer, Canada

"Somebody gag this guy! He's giving away all our secrets!"
— **Chance Thomas**, game composer and President, HUGEsound

Dedicated with love and affection to
my wife, Cynthia, and daughter, Kristina;
the two greatest girls in the world.

Without their generosity and understanding,
this book could not have been written.

TABLE OF CONTENTS

CHAPTER 3: Getting Organized and Ready for Business 45

CHAPTER 8: Creating Music for Games..... 187

Foreword

For the past 10 years, I've had the privilege to be involved in one of the most fascinating and dynamic professions around. Composing, creating, and producing sound for video games is a challenging entertainment career — every bit as exciting as working in the film or television industry. The games industry is a diverse and changing world, and this book can be your passport to a rewarding and fruitful career.

People often ask me how I got started in the games industry. Being a game composer or sound designer isn't the most well-known profession, so how does someone actually get started? Well, the first rule of thumb is… you gotta love games!

Defender, Tempest, Berserk, Asteroids, Choplifter, Battle Zone, Phoenix, Sinistar, Dragon's Lair, Spy Hunter — these were the glorious programs that shaped my early life growing up. Sure my education revolved around math, social studies, English, and all the usual school requirements, but video games influenced me in ways that no class ever did. Video games opened my eyes to new worlds, new ideas, and especially new sounds.

As a child, I remember seeing "Tron" in the theatre, and thinking how amazing it would be to live in a universe of video games. My wish was soon answered when my father brought home an Apple II computer for the family. I quickly realized that this new machine was much better equipped as a home game machine than a mere family word processor.

As I got older, I became involved in synthesizers and bands, and discovered I could combine my love of computers with my love of music. Throughout high school, much to my parent's dismay, I would drag our family computer to my local band gigs and sequence live on stage. After high school, I went on to earn a Bachelor's degree in Audio Engineering and Electronic Music Synthesis — which perfectly integrated my passion for computers with music and recording. I was offered my first record deal my freshman year of school, and I signed a recording contract with my band Contagion on Capitol Records during my senior year of college.

Even on tour, I couldn't escape my passion for games. One of my fondest memories from our 1992 North American tour was playing Street Fighter in the back of the tour bus between cities.

One concert, we even hooked our Nintendo to the other band's video projection wall and played a match during their concert performance.

When I returned from the tour, I decided to make my introduction into the game industry by approaching a local developer in Los Angeles. After quickly learning the ropes with early console development, I was approached by Virgin Interactive to become their in-house staff composer. Within a year, I was promoted to their Director of Audio and began supervising all music and sound for Virgin's internal and external titles. Directing audio for one of the largest game publishers in the United States and Europe gave me a fantastic first-hand education, and a wonderful working experience in one of the fastest growing industries of its time. In 1999, I decided it was finally time to establish a dedicated, interactive audio company and started PCB Productions, to focus on high-end game audio. Since starting my own facility, I have had the great opportunity to work with some of the industries finest developers and publishers. Over the past two years, some of my more recognized titles include: Tony Hawk Pro Skater 2, Tony Hawk Pro Skater 3, Ridge Racer 64, Thrill Kill, Disney's Emperor's New Groove, Spiderman 2, Draconus, X-Men2 and many, many others.

The Industry Now

The games industry can be a very exciting and dynamic place for musicians and sound designers. Through sound and music, a game can completely immerse a player in another universe or reality. The creative freedom to manipulate moods and environments is limited only by the technical capabilities of the machine and a musician's imagination.

While being creatively liberating, interactive game audio can also be technically demanding. Scoring and designing audio for games can often be much more challenging than motion pictures. This is due to the simple fact that games are, by nature, non-linear. An example of this can be simply demonstrated by a car passing the camera. In a film or television program, where the picture is established and consistent, the image of the car pass-by is a linear, time-established scene that can be scored, synchronized, recorded, and mixed by a sound designer or musician. By contrast, in a 3-dimensional game environment, there can be *hundreds* of variables that determine how and where the car exists within a 3D space. Because a player can view the car from a multitude of angles, the sound must be capable of being manipulated to match the image from any viewpoint. A simple car sound may need to be looped, layered, panned, pitch shifted, downsampled, and format converted — just to accommodate a simple car pass sound.

One other obvious difference from films is that an audio designer typically doesn't always "mix" the sounds in a game because all games require each sound to be individually manipulated and programmed within the code. In a game environment, there may be hundreds of pieces of dialog, music, ambience, and Foley sound effects — each with their own volume, pitch, and positioning within the 3D environment. It is generally up to the programmer's code to determine how these will be mixed real-time in the game. (It's no wonder that even the most amazing sound effect or piece of music can be utterly annoying, if it is played incorrectly or too repetitively in a game!) It is important that audio designers learn as much about how their sounds will be *implemented*, as how their sounds will be *created*. Having a strong understanding of game mechanics, programming techniques, and platform limitations will make your life much easier.

Until recently, software sound design had not been recognized as a well-regarded, well-paid industry profession — mainly due to the lack of game *system* fidelity. In the past, PC speakers and console systems had limited audio fidelity and kept the resolution of sound to a minimum. In recent years, there has been a strong effort to enhance sound for games, and next generation systems and speakers have made great strides to address memory and bandwidth for audio. Dolby encoding, DVD drives, surround sound speakers, and increased memory have given sound professionals a new field to play on.

One fascinating aspect about the games industry is that its technology changes constantly. With every new technological development, enhanced software package, or hardware device, each new game title tries to out-perform the previous one. As technology improves by leaps and bounds each year, every game title attempts to implement new ways of making games faster, bigger, and louder than before. For an audio professional, this means constantly adapting to new recording techniques and establishing new compositional methods to keep up with an ever-evolving industry.

Because the games industry tends to be a "hit-driven" business, many titles these days are based on major motion picture properties, allowing game players to interact with worlds originally created for the silver screen. Almost every box office hit will spawn multiple interactive games based on the property. This is also true for well-known superheroes, comic books, sports teams, racing cars... you name it. For a game audio engineer and composer, this often means working on prestigious titles — sometimes working with star talent and being involved with big Hollywood productions.

Another interesting observation about the games industry is the youthful age of its creators. In most companies, the average age of game development teams ranges from 20–40 years old. This is not an industry of children, but rather a generation of people who grew up playing games, and chose to deviate from a "normal" career route. Up until recently, a career in the games industry was seen as a low wage job for kids. However, in recent years, the games industry has yielded higher profits than the music and film industries combined. Because most musicians and audio designers already know the struggles of justifying their careers, the game environment is a great place to fit in…and never have to wear a tie.

Given the relative youth of the industry, the game community is unfortunately void of experienced role models. There are not many well-known game professionals who stand as an example of how to make a living in games. Sure, Bill Gates is an inspiration for computer entrepreneurs everywhere, but there aren't many game audio professionals who lead the road for future generations.

The Complete Guide to Game Audio serves as that role model for game audio and is a great resource for anyone looking to enter this fascinating industry. New and old engineers alike will find this book as a strong reference tool to understand the boundaries of the interactive arena and how to survive in it. This sure would have been useful when I was getting started! Good luck with your future projects, and I look forward to playing one of your games soon!

Keith Arem
PCB Productions
Game composer/sound designer

About the Author

Music had always been a part of Aaron Marks' life. But it wasn't until 1995, when his overgrown hobby became On Your Mark Music Productions, that he began selling it to the world. He began with the local radio and television scene, composing jingles and scoring Public Service Announcements with eventual sights on Hollywood. Instead he fell headfirst into the games industry, where his sound design talents also exploded, leading him to music and sound effects credits on a PlayStation 2 game, five CD-ROM game projects, 60 on-line casino games, eight touch screen arcade games, and numerous multimedia projects. He continues to pursue fame and fortune while also sidelining as a writer of game music and audio interests for *Game Developer Magazine*, Gamasutra.com, and Music4Games.

The Author's Gameography:

ESPN MSL Extra Time	Konami Computer Entertainment of America. Music cues and sound bank programming for this PlayStation 2 soccer title.
Bloxx, Shanghai Express, Palm Reader, Zillionaire, LoveOMeter, Mezmerized, Kubis, Slide 'Em	uWink, Inc. Sound effects and music cues for these touch screen arcade games.
Online casino/arcade game sound effects and music	Flipside.com, VirtualVegas.com, PrizeCentral.com, iWin.com. Currently completed 60 individual Java based games for these extremely popular free web sites.
The Many Faces of Go Deluxe	Smart Games. Sound effects for this CD-ROM strategy game.
1st Earth Battalion	Enemy Technology (Developer). Musical score, sound effects and narratives for this upcoming space strategy game.
Hardwood Solitaire II	Silvercreek Entertainment (Developer). Sound effects.

The Author's Gameography:

Hardwood Hearts	Silvercreek Entertainment (Developer). Sound effects. Finalist at 2nd Annual IGF held at GDC.
Fallen Heroes	A&B Entertainment (Developer), ionos, inc (Publisher). Sound Effects and character narratives for this currently unreleased CD-ROM title.
SC3	A&B Entertainment (Developer), ionos, inc (Publisher). Musical score, sound effects and character narratives for this currently unreleased CD-ROM title.

Acknowledgments

It would have been nearly impossible to write a book of this scope without the help and inspiration of many remarkable people. I'd like to give special thanks and recognition to the many teams and individuals who helped keep my facts straight and the proverbial nose to the grindstone.

A Heartfelt "Thank You" to:

My family (all of the Marks', Sartors, Rodgers, and Van Cleaves), Alex Dunne, David Tractenberg, Mark Temple, Michael Striler, Lou Ellero, Pete Bernard, Jon Holland, Keith Arem, Jamey Scott, Todd Fay, Tommy Tallarico, Joey Kuras, Chance Thomas, Tim Larkin, Greg Rahn, Will Davis, Stephen Rippy, Darryl Duncan, Chris Rickwood, Brian Tuey, Jennifer Olsen, Steve Trushar, Glen Stafford, Terry Bratcher, Jack Buser, John Griffin, Jon Hoffberg, Jon Jones, Mark DeLoura, Paul Temme, Michelle O'Neal, Matt Kelsey, Dan Huebner, Unkhakook, Scott Selfon, Brian Schmidt, Michael Henry, Nicola Tomljanovich, Greg O'Connor-Read, Kevin McMullan, Murray Allen, Christian Anderson, Lee Moyer, Lori Solomon, and Joe Encarnacion.

Thanks also to:

Dolby Labs, Cakewalk, Sonic Foundry, Syntrillium, SoCal TRACON, *Game Developer Magazine*, Gamasutra, Music4Games, NFG, Ensemble Studios, and the game companies who have given me the chance to not only prove myself but to gain the wisdom to teach others.

And to all of the many others I'm sure I forgot. Your contributions were all very much appreciated!

CHAPTER 1
An Introduction to Game Audio

1.1 Insert Quarter Here

They say a journey begins with a first step, followed by another and another. Regardless of whether you are already many miles down the road or are just about to take that first step, this book is designed with you in mind. Working in the multi-billion dollar game industry as an audio content provider is a challenging and rewarding avenue — best traveled with a useful guidebook in hand. My thanks to you for bringing this particular one along.

There are as many reasons as there are individuals for wanting to work in the games domain. Doing something you enjoy, creating games which millions will play and experience, *and* getting a paycheck for it, are undoubtedly given most often. Another motivation, perhaps, is the mystique and prestige associated with it. Most of the world is practically computer illiterate and those of us who can get inside "the box" and make it do incredible things holds a high place in our society. We like to be that kind of person.

There are countless job descriptions within the industry: programmer, artist, animator, game designer, producer, etc. But the ones which probably led you to pick up this book are titles such as: composer, musician, sound designer, or audio content provider. These are the jobs that bring us the kind of satisfaction we crave — creating music and getting paid to do it. It will also give us another way to get our music "out there" and maybe even receive a Grammy Award in the process, getting us the needed recognition and acceptance from our family and friends who thought being a musician was a "waste of time" and might even serve as a stepping stone to another career such as film. There are endless possibilities for meeting your personal and professional goals as a game score composer and sound designer. And it's not such a bad career either.

Music had always seemed to be a part of my life and like everyone else, I had big dreams. I just didn't have a clue as to the "what" or "how" part of it though. I did know how to spend money, however, and as my abilities and interests grew, so did the number of instruments and recording gear in my inventory. So much, in fact, that my wife became concerned with the excessive outflow. The foot was brought down with a thud and a new challenge was posed. I could not buy any more "gear" unless I made money with it, and after that, this little hobby of mine was to remain self-sufficient.

Originally, local television and radio seemed to hold some promise but as I jumped into that chaos with both feet, I soon realized the competition was fierce and little 'ol me was just a tadpole in a piranha-infested sea. Out of necessity, my strategy widened and diversification became fundamental. I looked into composing for music libraries, local video production companies, and multimedia. I had to have more gear, after all.

I soon learned just how these other businesses worked. They all wanted grand, original orchestral scores, á la John Williams, but only wanted to pay $200 for them. Considering the amount of time and effort you need to pursue this course, there was no way to see any return on the investment. It became painfully obvious that even though I was still overwhelmed by the urge to sell my music to someone, this was not the way to go about it.

Figure 1.1 The constant pursuit of more gear is great motivation for selling your music to the games industry.

(Photo courtesy of AMC Studios.)

I didn't naturally move to video games. I was still playing the original Nintendo at this point and didn't consider the noise I was hearing to be music. And I'm sure nobody was making any money for those simple compositions either.

But when scoring for video games finally did run up and slap me across the face, I realized my perceptions of this strange, new world were woefully distorted. The gaming world has advanced far beyond what I had imagined and the music had become utterly fantastic! And to top it off, I discovered some game composers were making $50,000+ per game for just a month or so of work. Now I was interested!

Thus began an incredible journey — making money selling my brand of noise, realizing my goals and my dreams, raising my "hobby" to a successful business and most importantly, bringing peace and harmony to the home front. But, because I knew absolutely nothing about the business, it took a couple years to struggle into it, learn the ropes, and find my niche before I began to realize success.

That, in a nutshell, is the purpose of this book:

• to educate you,

• to help you decide if this industry is right for you, and

• to give you the knowledge to take the gaming world by storm.

My experiences have given me a certain view of this unique industry and this is what I intend to share with you. If I can provide you the assistance to hit the ground running and save a couple years in the process, my objectives have been fulfilled. So, sit down, hang on, and enjoy the ride.

1.2 The Bleeps and Bloops of Yesteryear

In 1971, video games made their grand entrance with the game 'Computer Space.' While it isn't as well remembered as some, society took to this new form of entertainment, plunking down stacks of quarters at a time. A year later, Atari's Pong, took its place in history. This console game was uncomplicated by today's standards; its few sounds were simple, single tone, electronically-generated bleeps. Atari's home entertainment offering in 1975 brought 'Pong' into our homes, but it wasn't until 1977 that the Atari 2600 game system brought a slightly improved presentation of sound.

As the thirst for these games grew, so did the technology and the search for increased stimulation was set into high gear. Various methods and audio processors where applied to aurally satisfy the game player and keep them coming back. In 1979, Mattel presented their Intellivision system, offering a sound generator capable of three-part harmony. Atari answered back in 1982 with their 5200 platform and a dedicated audio processor called Pokey. The Pokey chip used four separate channels which controlled the pitch, volume, and distortion values of each, allowing a four-piece virtual band to perform for the first time.

From here on out, almost every new game system had more audio resources to draw from. The original Nintendo Entertainment System (NES) in 1985 used five channels of monophonic sound. Sega's introduction in 1986 brought three monophonic sound generators using four octaves each into the ring. By 1989, the NEC Turbo Grafx brought six voices with stereo output and the Sega Genesis with 10 voices — both with a later add-on which allowed for CD quality audio. At last, we were getting to enjoy some music and sound the way it was meant to be heard. Audio processors continued to improve, adapting synthesizer chips, 16-bit processors, more voices, more memory, better compression and decompression algorithms, and even internal effects processors.

But far away from the consoles and dedicated gaming platforms, the personal computer was beginning to show its potential. Initially, the sound quality was no better than the early console games — the generated bleeps played back through an even more horrendous sounding internal speaker. Memory space was always an issue and the considerations for audio were last in a very long line. As a response to the almost hopeless situation, sound cards were developed with small synthesizer chips built in which allowed very small message files (encoded with triggers similar to the roll on a player piano) which told the device what sounds to play and when to play them. The sound bank consisted of 128 sounds with the capability to play a total of 16 notes at a time. This use of the MIDI (Musical Instrument Digital Interface) standard gave us some hope. The tinny, cheesy sounds that early cards produced were a far cry from the real thing, but at least the compositions were becoming better and more complex and musicians were replacing program-mers at an increasing rate.

The computer sound file, such as today's .wav and .aiff files, initially utilized a compression algorithm which enabled real recorded sounds to be played back in the .voc format. This gave a musician the ability to track music in a studio using traditional recording methods and then con-vert to the required sound file format. The sound quality wasn't much better than the MIDI music being expelled; initial sample rates of 11 kHz, 8-bit mono were hardly even AM radio quality, but at least the composer wasn't restricted to the sound palette which came with the hardware. Sound designers benefited, as well, allowing their creativity to literally explode. The stage was set, ready for the next level and beyond.

1.3 Where Sound is Now

Today, game audio has evolved to an art form of its own. Game music quality, the release of stand-alone game music CDs and their potential for a Grammy Award has, at last, brought game music composition on par with the television and film industries. Who would have ever thought this even possible 30 years ago? Game music has made a quantum leap forward and we not only have the talents of game composers to thank, but the entire game industry for their continued support and for the technological advancements of audio hardware.

While 22 kHz, 16- or 8-bit sounds are still in use, these audio properties are slowly being replaced with 44.1 kHz, 16-bit stereo (CD quality audio) as the standard. Storage space, mem-ory, and faster processors continue to improve and the increase in audio file size has kept pace. Larger file sizes equal better sounding audio and CD quality audio takes up a lot of space.

The previous, popular MIDI music standard has come close to falling by the wayside as the demanding public has expressed their disappointment with it. Internal instruments gradually became better as sound card manufacturers included high-grade synthesizer chips, but because this quality differed greatly between manufacturers, what sounded good on one card sounded like a train wreck on another. This lack of consistency may bring MIDI's eventual downfall in gaming, but advancements still hold potential to keep it alive a while longer. The advent of Down-Loadable Sounds (DLS) and newer sound cards, has sparked recent renewed interest in the MIDI standard and may be its saving grace. Games can now make use of "sound fonts" which are loaded into a sound card's internal memory and triggered by standard sequenced data. This idea has been used in cartridge games with much success to enable a game to have its own audio personality, instead of using the exact sounds every other game is using. The beauty of this is that composers and sound designers can pick and choose their own sounds instead of being stuck with what the sound card manufacturer has installed. The developer can bypass sys-tem RAM and use the sound cards circuitry and benefit from the very small MIDI file sizes. Cur-rently, a composer would only be able to use any of the standard 128 general MIDI sounds loaded on a sound card and, typically, most of those go unused. By loading a new bank of sound fonts before game play, all 128 sounds can be used, if needed, to make the audio a much more interesting experience.

There are still a few games in development which use the older MIDI music standard for those computer owners who have older equipment. High quality audio can put extreme demands on a system; MIDI does not. Savvy game developers make these considerations to sell more games and keep an eye on their bottom line.

Overall, the general trend shows a continued movement towards improved sound quality. Arcade games have more speakers, sub-woofers, and better playback devices. Home gaming consoles have stereo outputs and additional sound controls built in. PCs include upgraded audio hardware as standard and stream-quality audio straight from the disk. Game developers understand the impact of superior music compositions and film quality sound effects and their increased sound budgets allow them to hire veteran audio professionals to make this all happen. Composers and sound designers are even brought in earlier in the development cycle — as part of the design team — instead of as an afterthought during the final phases of production. Eventually, video games will be more like interactive movies where the psychological effects of music and sound will be dominant.

The new frontier at present day is the Web. If history is any indication, as games move onto the Internet, the same wants and need will apply. Current use of sound is restricted mostly to small sound file sizes and MIDI music. Web games, at the moment, are using audio properties as low as 8 kHz, 8-bit mono and compressed file formats do nothing to enhance the sound. Java and Shockwave

Figure 1.2 A studio at Dolby Labs in San Francisco, where surround sound equipment and techniques are designed and tested.

Flash games are designed to load quickly and the smaller the sound file, the better. Some Web game designers opt to leave out audio all together or reuse one or two sounds for everything — reminding me of the early days of video game design. Keep an eye on the broadband wave, and as it becomes faster, audio quality will follow the same path.

1.4 *Where Sound is Going*

The future holds some incredible offerings for game audio — your imagination, the only limiting factor. Picture yourself surrounded fully by sound, where game play relies heavily on your sense of hearing. Walking down a dark corridor in a first person shooter, hearing your footsteps below you, environmental sounds coming from air ducts and doorways, suddenly, you hear a noise behind and to your left, you turn to be confronted by a ghastly beast who wants you for lunch. You fire your weapon, the sound reverberating, shell casings tinkling on the floor, and the creature falls to the ground with a thud. That is going to be some serious entertainment! Sound will be as important as your eyesight in this new virtual world. The name of the game is *total absorption*, and you, as a composer or sound designer, will help set the stage.

Some form of surround sound will likely become prevalent; Dolby Digital, DTS, or perhaps another unknown format, with multiple audio channels intended to envelope a player into the experience. There is much in the works to make this a reality — deciding on a standard; getting the hardware designers, game developers, composers, and sound creators all on board; and getting the game player fired up to go out and buy the new equipment. But with any new format idea, it takes a couple of years to see its full potential. But it is definitely on its way.

Interactive audio is another concept making headway into games. For years, developers and sound gurus have been pondering ways to make playing a video game more like experiencing a movie. With film, all music and sound effects are post production elements which are added after all the visual elements are created. As a movie plays, the linear soundtrack follows along, setting the appropriate mood for each scene — building tension or tugging at your heartstrings. However, most video games aren't predictable in that sense and a music score cannot anticipate what will happen next to a player. Audio presentation methods are being developed to interact with what the player is *experiencing*; whether they are casually exploring a game level or locked in heated battle with an opponent, the music will change accordingly. This will enable a developer to have more control over the game player's experience and mood and to create a fully involved experience. The results will be incredible.

It's a given: computers will continue to get faster, and as the hardware improves, the gaming experience will follow close behind. And it is only obvious that game audio will be right there to take advantage of it all. The DVD format, with storage space of 4.8 gb, appears to be on the road to replace the CD. With this, all audio will be at least 44.1 kHz, 16-bit stereo. And as audio technology grows to a standard of 96 kHz, 24-bit, surround, there will be room to accommodate. The sound quality will be incredible, right there in the "audiophile" range, which in turn, will drive the need for better recording methods, equipment, extremely talented composers and sound designers, and the accompanying elevated audio budgets.

1.5 *Chances of Finding Work*

With the current and future state of game audio, you can imagine the need for skilled audio craftsmen to provide content. What are your chances? With the hundreds of game companies worldwide and the constant flow of games into production, your chances are very good. We are in an exciting time in this industry, with continually evolving technology taking the whole game experience to new heights and the public constantly hungry for more. Together they will feed the development of bigger and better games and audio will become vital in that total experience.

In any issue of *Games Business Magazine*, there are pages full of games in production. The issue I grabbed randomly lists 320 current games in the making and these were only from the major game development companies which report to this magazine. Add more than 10 times that amount unreported and from smaller developers. If that still doesn't give you the full picture, drop in on any E3 (Electronic Entertainment Expo) show and wander the floor for awhile. After one day, you still won't have seen the number of games making their way to the marketplace. Somewhere in that cacophony of lights and sound is a game in need of its own audio identity which you can provide. Walk into any major computer software retailer and gander at the row upon row of game boxes on display. Head off to your local arcade and take in all the coin-op game consoles vying for your attention. Search the internet for online Shockwave Flash and Java games. You'll never find them all! Are you getting the picture yet?

The game industry is HUGE and there is always work for those who are good enough, persistent enough, and lucky enough to be in the right place at the right time.

1.6 The Rewards

Providing audio for games can be a unique challenge and sometimes a job well done can be reward in itself. But satisfaction alone cannot put food on your table or buy the new gear you have to have. While the money can be quite good, and often is, there are other enticements which make composing for games a worthwhile endeavor.

You've all heard the statement, "the perfect job is being able to take what you enjoy doing and make a living at it." I couldn't agree more. The one constant throughout my life has always been music, and to me, it makes perfect sense to pursue it as a career. There is no greater reward than following your passion and getting someone to pay you to do it.

Jamey Scott, in-house composer and sound designer for Presto Studios in San Diego, California, is a perfect example. He has some serious formal music training and experience and has worked on several projects including Compton's Interactive Encyclopedia, Compton's Interactive Children's Bible Stories, MGM Babes in Toyland Interactive CD, Presto's Gundam 0079, and The Journeyman Project III — Legacy of Time, and could basically write his own ticket in the game world. But, instead, he prefers his in-house position and the steady paycheck it brings. As an alternative to the chaos of marketing and worrying where the next job is coming from, Jamey prefers the comfort and security of working in-house, which in turn, allows him to focus solely on his craft. "For me, being an in-house composer and sound designer working with a team, I am more focused on the creation of the art," says Jamey. His particular reward is having steady work and doing something he loves.

Believe it or not, there are actually people who aren't in this business for the money. They can pursue their passion for music in a creative and supportive setting and earn a living in the process. It might seem crazy now, but a few years as a contractor might just change your mind about in-house work. Don't thumb your nose just yet.

1.6.1 Fame

In Japan, game score composers have attained "rock star" status among their appreciative public. Rabid fans flock in mass to see appearances of their favorite video game stars and sales of video game soundtracks continue to top the charts, driving a whole other aspect to the industry.

The fame and glory of being a recording artist is quite well known to us in the United States and game score composers and musicians are standing poised to take advantage of this type of notoriety too. We don't share the spotlight with "name brand" artists and we don't have hordes of screaming fans, but we do have a sort of recognition that feeds our egos and drives us to do more and to do it better. Eventually, as the popularity of game soundtracks grows and as the public becomes more aware of our existence, fans bases will develop, and the fame that many seek, will be close at hand.

How many times have you seen "music by Bobby Prince, composer for DOOM" on a box cover? Talk about fame! Everyone in the industry knows who Bobby Prince is and the whole trade is benefiting as composers are being used as selling points. Bobby's stock goes up as more game companies just "gotta have him." He's done other games such as Wolfenstein 3D, Duke Nukem 3D, DemonStar, Axis and Allies, among others and while he rides high on his string of hits, the fame endures. I'll take luck over skill any day and Bobby just may have been in the right place at the right time getting involved with a hit game like DOOM. The music was pretty darned good too.

And how about George Sanger, aka The Fatman? Having spent many years in Texas, I can appreciate the grand Texas-style way of doing things and George has it down pat. He's done a stable full of games like The 7th Guest, The 11th Hour, Wing Commander, Might and Magic III, Total Recall, Star Trek III, NASCAR Racing, Putt Putt Saves the Zoo, ATF, and over 130 other games since 1983 — bringing his own panache and flair to the gaming industry. Along with Team Fat, he has composed some truly innovative and absolutely memorable game scores. I'm sure every kid in America under the age of 15 has heard his music and could even sing along with some of the themes. Not only does his 10-gallon hat and grandiose compositions cause him stand out, his magazine columns and efforts in joining the gaming forces at his yearly Project BBQ make him hard to ignore. Everyone knows who the Fatman is. That's not such bad notoriety.

There are varied degrees of "famous" and depending on what you may be seeking, you can find it in the gaming world. Whether it is acclaim within the industry for your work ethic and superior audio product, nationwide fame as a game score composer playing your music to thousands of screaming fans, releasing a hit soundtrack CD, or even being known by the kids on your block as the person who makes "cool tunes" for video games, they are all worthwhile places to be and have their own distinct rewards. Not only is it great to be recognized by your peers in the industry, but it is hard to beat that warm and fuzzy feeling having touched a young teenager's life and inspiring them to learn or appreciate music. It's all right here — ready and waiting.

1.6.2 Fortune

Making a living doing what you love and the corresponding notoriety are enough reward for some, but let's face it, one of the real reasons composers and musicians become involved with the gaming world is the potential to earn their fortune. The movers, shakers, and deal makers are the ones making things happen in this occupation and their business tenacity has made them financially well off.

When game music began and the programmers were slowly replaced by composers, the miniscule income was almost hardly worth the effort. But as game budgets skyrocketed into the millions of dollars, composers started to get their share by creating extremely appropriate, thought provoking, and well-crafted music with professional musicians and the occasional symphony orchestra to boot. There are very busy composers out there who earn $50–60,000 for an hour or hour and a half's worth of music per game and some of them do up to 30 games a year! Do the math; there is some serious cash potential. And that isn't even all of it — there is also:

- earnings from royalties and soundtrack releases,
- fees for the same music on different game platforms (SKUs), and
- money from licensing in commercials, television shows, and movies (ancillary rights).

The sky is wide open. If you have negotiated a good deal and signed a contract with a big developer, the potential to have income from simultaneous sources, all from the same music score, can really make a difference.

Fortune has indeed smiled upon several game composers. They all possess similar traits and have made games very exciting with their musical offerings. Their deal-making skills, reputation for providing quality, on-schedule audio, and stature within the industry have all contributed to their on-going success.

Tommy Tallarico has lived one of my favorite success stories. His tenaciousness and drive has taken him from working two full-time jobs, 16 hours a day, and literally living on the beach when he first moved to California in 1991 to a mogul living in a bazillion room estate with a Lamborghini, among others, parked in his garage. His deal-making skills and excitement for what he does are legendary and composing music for over 150 games and four game soundtrack releases has secured his place at the top. He even hosts a weekly TV show, "Electric Playground." Throughout the book I'll be sharing with you much of Tommy's deal-making prowess, sample contracts, and ideas that have helped make him so successful. .

GAME COMPOSERS AT WORK

Tommy Tallarico of Tommy Tallarico Studios

How do you go about scoring for a project? "The best thing for me is to just play the game with no sound and just wait for stuff to start coming to me. Then I go into my studio (upstairs) and figure out the notes on the keyboard that were dancing around in my head seconds before. Sometimes when there needs to be something done quick and the game or level isn't complete, I'll work off of storyboards. As far as style of music is concerned, every company is different; it's usually decided by the designer or the producer or the programmer or the product manager or the marketing department or the president of the company or the test department or the janitor or even sometimes the musician?!?! Seriously though, there have been times when people have come to me with a very complete style they have in mind, 'Can we have the rhythm section of Prodigy, the sounds of The Chemical Brothers, the feel of Nine Inch Nails, oh yeah, and the guitar sound of Waylon Jennings?'. Most of the time, they just give me the project and say to do what you think is best. I give them my ideas and if they like them, they hire me; if they think or feel that I'm way off base, then they don't but that hasn't really happened too much though. Usually the companies will give me storyboards of the game or other music CDs that captures the style they think would work. The best is when I can just sit down and play the game with no music and figure out what I think the best style for that particular level is."

When do you tend to be most creative? "I set up my studio in my house. All the guys who work for me also have been set-up at their own places. Doing this allows us all to work on our stuff whenever we want or feel like. For the most part, though, nighttime seems to be the most creatively productive for me."

What skills do other composers need to get into the games business? Can you share any secrets? "As far as being a successful audio designer is this industry, I think determination and talent are the two biggest assets you can have.

Learn the in's and out's of the hardware platform you are working on. Know what you can get away with technically and then sit down with the programmers to find out the best way to accomplish what your trying to achieve. A lot of times projects are just given to the audio guys and they are told what to do. If they were involved from the beginning, they would be able to technically achieve more things.

From a musically creative standpoint, I would say listen to lots of movie soundtracks to get a vibe of what people are used to hearing in certain situations. For example, if you are working on a pirate level, go and find every pirate movie you can to get ideas and elements to incorporate in with your own style. When I worked with the Hungarian National Symphony Orchestra and the Budapest Chamber Choir for Evil Dead last year, I wanted a very haunting yet adventurous evil vibe. So, I listened to Carl Orff's 'Carmina Burana' and the soundtracks for The Omen and Conan the Barbarian. It really helped me a lot.

From a sound design creative standpoint, I would say it's always best to combine pre-existing sound libraries and going out and recording/editing your own sounds. Many sound designers sometimes use sound libraries too much. Sound libraries are great for certain things, but not for everything. Libraries are also great for layering in with sounds you've created.

Another secret is to try and do something that has never been done before. When I first took on Tony Hawk Skateboarding, no one had any idea it was going to be as popular as it was. I liked it because there had never been a good sounding skateboarding game EVER! I really like the 'challenge' part of the job. In the early days, I think mostly what I did was to give players the kind of music they wanted to hear. I remember playing games and thinking, 'This music sucks! It sounds like a merry-go-round tune or some childish bleeps and blips.'

Figure 1.3 Tommy Tallarico in his studio loft surrounded by essential tools of the trade.

Why weren't people doing rock, pop, blues, orchestral, dance, techno, etc.? No one had ever really heard a real guitar in a video game until the early '90's.

Another thing I started doing was to introduce lots of musical samples right into the cartridge MIDI files. Back in the old days on the Sega Genesis, people would use the sample chip to play a scratchy voice sample ('FIGHT') or use it to intro the company name ('SEGA'). I decided: why not have that sample channel be playing as much as possible? I had convinced programmers that if they gave me enough space, I would make the Genesis sound like no one has ever heard. So I used kick drum and snare drum samples, guitar and horn hits, singing voices, etc., right in the music. On top of that, I would use as many real sampled sound effects as I could. By prioritizing every sound in the game, I was able to constantly have the sample chip playing without any recognizable drop out when other things took priority. If you go back and listen to a game like Earthworm Jim or Aladdin, you'll hear samples going off all the time. No one ever really did that.

Over the last few years, I've been saying 'WOW!'. Usually followed by a 'Damn, I wanted to do that!'. A lot of times the game has to be the right kind of game in order for it to have great music. So sometimes the music or project finds you. I remember the first time I played Parappa the Rapper where they used multiple streams going on at the same time to get the instruments to fall out or layer depending on how well you were doing. I had just finished working on Treasures of the Deep and we were kinda doing the same thing, but not to the same extent. I was actually really blown away that it worked as well as it did in Parappa! Until you actually do something like that, you're never entirely sure how it's going to come off within the game.

Be willing to go out on a limb or chart new territory when the opportunity presents itself. Sometimes it can really pay off!"

1.7 Let's Go Get 'em

Creating audio for games is an incredible ride and if you stick with it long enough and have your act together, you'll eventually have something to show off to all your friends. Who knows, you may even win a Grammy to adorn your mantelpiece. Appendix A goes into detail about this coveted award and what we need to do as game composers to make it a reality — it's not as easy as simply showing up to the party, you know. This industry has much to offer, so, if you're ready, let's move on to the meat and potatoes.

CHAPTER 2
Essential Skill Sets and Tools

2.1 Important Skills

Now that you have been properly motivated to consider the game world a place to sell your music and the creative flame inside you has been turned up a notch, let's check out the important skills and equipment you will need to work and thrive in this industry.

I think it is probably safe to assume that you have either done some composing or play a musical instrument (or two) and you might even have much of the equipment already. If not, I welcome you into our world and applaud you for doing your homework.

The practicing one-man band seems to be the working method of choice for most game composers. By not having to rely on anyone else, the process becomes streamlined and more gets done. You can stay focused for longer periods of time and compose scores without interruption. Unless I'm using a specific musician for their sound or for something I am not capable of doing, I never have to wait for anyone to show up — because I am already there! And you can work when you are at your most creative; perfect for the night-owl or the morning person.

There are also many music "teams" within audio production houses, who have specific duties and skill sets which complement a project. Even in that atmosphere, it is advantageous to everyone if you are familiar with the other functions of a production.

2.1.1 Attitude

Attitude plays a big part in this business and is the one thing which can set you apart or destroy your chances all together. The very first game job I got (I found out later) was because of my attitude. I had absolutely no experience composing for games or doing sound design, and while it initially factored into the developer's decision, my confidence and positive attitude is what got me the gig. Because it seemed to work the first time, it has become a permanent fixture in my sales pitch.

Your passion and drive will certainly be enough to get you started, but no matter how much you already know, or think you know, there will always be more to learn along the way. Always remain receptive to new ideas and concepts. Technology improvements are rapid and by keeping up with the latest, you put yourself in a good position to take advantage of it. It's always nice to say "Yeah, I'm familiar with that," rather than admitting your ignorance. Sometimes it can mean winning or losing a contract.

2.1.2 Business Sense

As the one-man show, you can expect to wear many hats: the composer, musician, engineer, producer, technician, sound designer, voice talent, salesman, marketing director, secretary, accountant, janitor – hey, wait a minute! Where did the music go? Unfortunately, composing music and sound design comes into play less than 25% of the time and maybe only around 5% if you are just starting out. You have to remember you are in business; you are selling a product and all the rules and strategies come into play here. Being successful means being business savvy and remaining focused on your "product." Until you've attained success and can hire a staff of assistants to provide your business needs, you will not be able to just sit at your piano and write. Then again, who wants to do that all the time anyway? A little hard work and dedication on your own behalf makes your efforts even that much more rewarding. Take some time and study how a business operates and you'll be miles ahead of anyone who muddles through it blindly.

2.1.3 Marketing

Another critical skill, absolutely unrelated to creating audio, is the ability to market yourself. It doesn't matter one iota if you were a child prodigy, mastering every instrument before you were 8-years-old, and have the abilities of a world class composer if no one knows you exist. You can't just open the doors to your business and expect customers to flood into your studio and the phone to ring off the hook — unless you've spent some quality time beforehand, making sure the right people are aware of your existence. And once they know about you, make sure you properly entice them to buy your product. All this is part of marketing.

Marketing is as old as business itself; the more you know and use, the more work you will have. You will find yourself spending a majority of your time planning and implementing ways to get customers in the door, constantly changing strategies and ideas as you go, searching for the most effective method that brings in the most money for the effort. And you thought you were going to spend all your time composing and creating sound effects! But this too can be an exciting challenge. There are very successful people who specialize in marketing and it may initially seem overwhelming to you. But once you get the hang of it, it becomes second nature and lots of fun.

Later in Chapter 4, I'll spend more time on this subject with some very basic marketing concepts and strategies geared towards your efforts in the game world. If you can't wait, go ahead and flip there now. But come back soon, I'm going to get back to music stuff now.

2.1.4 Music Skills

The key piece of the puzzle is your skills as a composer, musician, engineer, producer, and technician and is probably what you've been waiting to hear. Nowadays, most music is done in the composer's home or project studio forcing us into the "jack of all trades" role. It is paramount that you are familiar, if not an expert, at all of these tasks. Keeping the creative process unhindered and free-flowing is fundamental to composing. Nothing ruins your creativity faster than having to stop to troubleshoot or look something up in a manual. The more you know now, the better.

Musicianship

Your musicianship should be well-practiced and solid as a rock. Sequencers and multi-track recording software can enhance these abilities and fix mistakes but trust me, building upon a solid foundation will save you much headache in the end.

Figure 2.1 Guitar virtuoso Jon Jones laying guitar tracks for Konami's ESPN MSL Extra Time PlayStation 2 game.

I also recommend that regardless of your instrument of choice, become proficient on the keyboard. The MIDI keyboard, next to the computer, is essential equipment which has the capability to access all other MIDI instruments in your arsenal. It is a focal point by which you can control other keyboards, sound modules, samplers, electronic drums, and even start and stop your computer recording software by. This workhorse is in constant use and a must to master.

The keyboard, as a musical instrument, can be highly expressive — nearly unlimited sounds can be played from one. Musically speaking, this knowledge and power is inspiring, but too much of one direction can become stale and characterless.

If you are already a keyboardist, pick up the drums or guitar — anything other than the keys and learn to play. It will open up another world, and give you a better understanding of how music works plus another instrument to compose on. Styles can vary widely when composing on piano for one tune and guitar for another. Your outlook will always be fresh and the music will reflect positively.

Another advantage will be self-sufficiency. While I enjoy composing and playing with other musicians, it saves time not having to wait for a player to show, enabling you to get your work done faster. The clock is running and busy production schedules are not always flexible enough to accommodate. Most composers in the game industry are multi-instrumentalists — having become so out of necessity.

Creativity/Compositional Skills

Never written a song? Then this might not be the business for you. Game music is designed to create a specific mood and audio "feel" for the accompanying virtual world and it is something you should be able to pinpoint exactly within the first couple of tries. While you may be strongest in one particular style of music, consider studying and composing in a variety of others as well. All games are not just techno or other upbeat rhythmic compositions only there as background clutter. They serve a definite purpose and are skillfully mastered to absorb the player fully into the experience.

You might be lucky enough to find work composing in "your" style, but I prefer to diversify and have more potential jobs available. Techno is the latest trend, but orchestral, rock, pop, sports, hill-billy, children's, religious, and so on are just as legitimate and paying just as well. There are even games which include music in many styles on the same project. You want a developer or publisher to rely solely on *you* for their musical needs and not have to seek out anyone else. One-stop shopping is convenient for them; good business for you.

Practice composing short pieces in various styles as a creative drill. This will increase your repertoire while simultaneously adding more variety to your demo reel. Game composers Brian Tuey and Leo Sartwell of Thunder Soundscapes constantly push their creative envelopes and have some fun in the process. They will opt for an approach previously undiscovered and see what happens. This has helped their creativity tremendously by exploring avenues they hadn't previously considered. Try composing "Egyptian surf music" or "Heavy Metal Monk Chants" and see where it leads you. It's really not as far off as you think. Developers often have some crazy ideas and your creativity will be appreciated and rewarded.

Writing for games is not like writing for your own album release. You will not have the luxury of time — composing and recording only when the "mood" strikes you. Like any other fast-paced adventure such as writing for commercials, weekly TV shows, and film, you must be able to turn your creativity on like a faucet. It must be an immediate reaction, ready to go at a moment's notice. If you wait for the elusive muse to show herself, the rapidly approaching deadline will come and go and you'll be left looking foolish. You do not want to be the one person the project is waiting on. Time is money and any delay could mean wasted funds for the developer and publisher who are counting on you. If you are used to composing only when you *feel* like it, fight the urge, write when you don't feel particularly creative, pretend you have a looming deadline — just do it. As you mature in this business, you'll discover it gets easier and easier to turn on the switch. The problem then becomes turning it off and knowing when a piece is done; the curse of being a perfectionist, I guess.

Engineering Skills

Know thy equipment and software inside and out! Study the manuals, try new techniques in your spare time, and know their strengths and weakness. Waiting until you are recording a project is too late to figure out how to use your gear. Losing a sound in the maze of electronics

Figure 2.2 Engineers should be very familiar with their gear, in order to keep the creativity moving in a forward direction.

can lead to some extensive delays and may tamper with your mindset at the most inopportune time.

Practice your engineering skills. Know how to get the best sound from your instruments, and have the EQ and effects processor settings memorized. Standardize and streamline the process, if you can, by leaving the same instruments plugged into the same channels on your mixer and fight the urge to change it. It will save you substantial time to be able to grab the right knob or fader without having to think about it during a session.

The marketing departments at every equipment and software manufacturer are hard at work enticing you to buy their latest and greatest products. If you are a recording facility and have rich, demanding clients who love to spend money, you have a legitimate need to buy the newest gear. But, if you are a project studio only recording your music, you might not. My general philosophy is to buy only the gear that will make me more *competitive* and *profitable*; not buy gear because I've "got to have it." By remaining solidly on the trailing edge of technology, I don't have to constantly relearn new equipment and software. Instead, I keep and maintain what works for my composing and recording methods. It's not that I refuse to upgrade, because I do from time to time, I just don't do it unless it satisfies both of my requirements. By staying with familiar gear, I'm able to work without constantly thinking about technical issues and disrupting the creative process.

Recently, I had a project with a new game company requiring me to add sound effects to their animation files. The game was still in development and they were trying to add an audio personality to their movies and have something to show their investors at the same time. Unfortunately, the software they were using was completely new and the learning curve was steeper than normal for me. What would have been a two or three day sound design project, became a five day undertaking because they also required me to add sounds to the animation files myself. After day two, I called the company who developed this "tool" directly and discovered I could not layer sounds on various tracks as it advertised, but had to do a composite on a single track instead. No problem, except there was no reference to synchronize to and a stopwatch was unreliable when the animations bogged down or skipped frames. A trusty calculator and a lot of trial-and-error finally did the trick, but not after a couple added days to the production cycle and much grumbling. A new program, without all the bugs fixed and no one available who had any experience with it, brought a normally speedy sound design process down to near gridlock. A great lesson when introducing something new into your process. Beware.

Familiarity with your equipment will make your job easier and I cannot stress its importance enough. Consider audio engineering courses at your local college, volunteering yourself and studio to record demos for local bands, remixing your old tunes — all in the name of keeping your ears open and staying on top of your game. A skill without practice becomes a hindrance. Suddenly, I'm a philosopher.

Producer Skills

As the proverbial one-man band, you are also acting as producer. When producing other band projects, it's easier to remain objective because you are not emotionally attached to the music as a musician would be. In this case, you would have the luxury of focusing on the overall picture, keeping it on track, motivating and evoking heartfelt performances from the musicians, and sheltering them from any outside influences which might disrupt their creativity. It is indeed a job in itself.

When producing your own music, the line becomes blurred and may not always be the best situation unless you can take a step back and maintain your objectivity. This is almost an acquired skill — obtained slowly and painfully through years of experience — but it is something you should strive for in your quest.

You cannot fall in love with your music. Because this is a "work for hire" situation, you have been commissioned to write a score which will enhance the overall game project and that must always be your first priority. You are creating for the project, not for yourself. If a producer asks you to take out a passage of the music and it happens to be your favorite part, you must be able to detach yourself and make the change. Remember, none of this is personal, although you might be inclined to feel that way. It is strictly business and it demands objectivity from everyone involved.

Another producer function which must be considered is the knowledge of how the music and/or sound effects will interact in the soundscape. During the development process, there are particular questions to ask, designed to gain an overall understanding of what sonic activities are present in a game. If separate narration is to play over particular music, it should be considered and the final mix of the music should have a "hole" in that frequency range to accommodate the voice-over. Otherwise, the programmer may decrease the music volume to compensate — perhaps degrading the entire audio moment. The same thing with sound effects. If there are heavy explosions in the lower frequency range, then the music should have less bass end so the most important sounds are heard. It can be a lot to consider, but an on-the-ball producer can make all the difference. If you do intend to release the game's music as a CD soundtrack, the music will have to stand on its own. You'll probably need two different mixes entirely to make this happen.

Technical Knowledge

Another skill set which goes hand-in-hand with musical and engineering know-how is solid "technical" abilities. You can fudge on this and get away with hiring outside help, but you'll be increasing overhead and traveling further away from your goal of becoming self-sufficient. You've probably been picking up more than you think repairing and troubleshooting your way to successful recording sessions. You'll have gathered basic skills in

- tracking down a faulty patch cord and soldering it back together,
- successfully splicing together a complicated MIDI set-up and having it work,
- understanding and synchronizing difference pieces of equipment,
- integrating your computer into the recording process by yourself,

and so on. There is a myriad of complicated, specialized equipment which needs to somehow all work together and if you can make it happen with only minor assistance, you have already established a satisfactory technical foundation.

2.1.5 Computer Knowledge

In this day and age, it is nearly impossible to compose music and design sound effects for video games without having a computer. Plus, how do you expect to know what is going on without playing a game or two yourself? The first word in "computer games" is computer. Know thy computer!

A developer is considering you as the sound contractor on a big game project and, after the non-disclosure agreement is signed, sends you a beta version of the game to load on your computer for a look-see. What do you think your chances are going to be if you can't get the program to work on your machine? Sometimes, it takes a bit of finessing and coaxing to get a game to work and if you can't do it, the developer sure won't have the time to. This is a severe case and highly simplified, of course, but the truth is, a developer is already extremely busy getting their game to market, and they prefer to deal with the path of least resistance. I've even been told by several developers they would never consider hiring anyone unless that individual possessed solid computer skills. Adept computer literacy is a good thing and will keep you from being knocked out of the competition.

Music making today is centered almost entirely around the computer. Sequencing programs, multi-track recording programs, sound editing programs, effects processing plug-ins, notation and accompaniment software, samplers, and so forth are studio mainstays and you've got to know how to make them all work correctly. If you can install sound cards, MIDI cards, or digital recording cards on your own, that is a big plus. No one knows your system better than you, unless you have a trusted computer guru at the ready to serve your needs. On-the-spot troubleshooting can save the day.

Much of the sound design process is done on a computer — from initial recordings to the editing process to conversions to the final playback format. It definitely pays to be knowledgeable and unafraid in this frontier. The more you know and understand about it, the better off you will be.

GAME COMPOSERS AT WORK

Will Davis of Will Davis Audio Development

Describe your thought process for scoring. "The primary goal is to simply create audio the client wants. The trick is to work within the parameters of the project and create audio that has the desired effect on the player and also fits in with the vision of the designers. At the end of the day, the audio is just part of a greater  whole; it has to 'feel' right. Everything I create for a game is easily changeable which allows the audio to adapt to modifications to the project with a minimum of fuss. There is little point in wasting time or money."

Are there any particular secrets to your creativity? "Not really; it's pretty simple. Music is just a note, a bit of a gap, another note, and so on until it's finished. Coming up with ideas and themes is the easy bit. It's the tidying up and getting the production to sound and feel right that takes the time."

When do you find you are most creative? "Any time except early in the morning; I'm a night person at heart. Which is fine as it fits in with the American company's office hours anyway."

Is there a typical workday for you? "Hmm, I get up when I wake up, which is much better than trying to get up before I'm awake, which I've tried on occasion. But I then spend several hours blindly fumbling around the kitchen desperately trying to make coffee. If I'm doing a CGB project, I'll just grab the laptop and find somewhere nice to sit and work — which in the summer is normally the beach. If it's a full blown CD score, then it's into the studio and work away until I run out of coffee."

2.1.6 Sound Design

Another important skill which will serve you well in the gaming industry is sound design. You may not realize it, but as a musician, you already have the foundation. All it takes is some fine tuning and finesse to make it another profitable part of your business.

Consider the creation of a sound effect to be like a mini musical composition. You first choose the 'sounds' which will work best to reach your end goal. You cut, paste, layer, EQ, pan, fade, add some effects processing, do a final mix, and voilà, instant sound effect. You build a musical piece the same way. Well, it's practically the same — except the choice of instrumentation is slightly different and instead of the final mix being minutes long, it's seconds long.

For those of you who create your own keyboard patches or samples, these are the same skills sound designers use on a daily basis. They don't always use everyday sounds or sound effects libraries, they also use keyboards and tone generators and manipulate them to create the effect they are looking for. It's the same thing when you develop your own original keyboard patches. You're a sound designer too! Keep that in mind.

"Diversify and thrive" is a business axiom which applies well to game audio folks. You don't have to create music for video games solely; keep your options open and also consider jobs composing for multimedia, video, radio, TV, and film. You have a valued skill — don't waste it on one medium. The same goes with your sound design talents. By becoming proficient as a sound designer, you've just doubled the amount of jobs you can do in games. Game developers almost expect a composer to double as the sound designer as well or to at least have someone on their team who acts in that capacity. They see it in this way: you have a tape recorder and a microphone, so you must be able to do sound effects too. Ridiculous, I know, but that is the misconception the wise have capitalized on. There is no reason you can't take advantage of this also.

Another great reason to have "sound designer" on you resume is to make yourself (and your audio production house) a developer's or client's one-stop shop. The game development process is already complex and the fewer people producers have to explain their vision to, the better. They would much rather hire one person, keeping things simple. They know that any time anything audio is needed, they can call you. By making yourself and your company that much more attractive, you have opened up the world of possibilities — whether you prefer to work as a contractor or a full-service, in-house audio authority.

2.1.7 Voice-Overs

As the person with the tape recorder and microphone, you might be assigned yet another task for your already overflowing "to do" list. Did you know you can be expected to not only be able to audition and hire character actors and voice-over talent but direct and record them too? You've already got your finger on the pulse of the musician's world, why not voice talent? "But all I wanted to be was a game score composer," you say. Sure, but you'd be wasting another opportunity to make some money and giving the developer a reason to look elsewhere to take care of their audio needs. You already possess the skills needed to make great recordings and you can probably motivate your artists into some dazzling performances. With a little bit of patience and practice, you can develop an expert approach to this line of work.

Needed a hot guitarist for a recent project of yours? Where did you go to find them? Did you try word-of-mouth, the newspaper, or a talent agency? Where would you go for voice talent? Try the same places. You could even try your local radio and television stations to contact people who do all the commercial voice-overs. Jon St. John, radio personality in San Diego, California, is also the voice of Duke Nukem and many other voices in Half Life — Opposing Forces, Twisted Metal 4, The Sonic Adventure Game, NBA Shootout, Ken Griffey Jr. Baseball, and others. Voice acting is what he does and he does it very well. Just because they hold a certain "celebrity" status on TV or radio is no reason to be intimidated by them. They are normal people looking for work, so introduce yourself and make them part of your network. You'll never know when they could come in handy.

Talent agencies are another great source and are not as complex to deal with as you might think. Let them know your criteria and they arrange auditions for you. You sift through audio or video tapes or even sit patiently while they perform for you in person. Pick your favorite and set up a recording session. Fairly easy and it will only cost you between $250–500 for the voice talent (which you've already included in your contract for the job, so it isn't coming out of your pocket.) We are in the profession of hiring talent on occasion, so learn to do it well. You have probably been through all this with musicians so you are equipped with the knowledge to make it happen. While this particular skill won't make or break your game scoring career, it will make you much more appealing to your clients.

Many game composers and sound designers act as their *own* voice talent. When a deadline is looming and you have to wait for talent to show up, this type of stress can easily disappear by becoming your own readily-available voice actor.

As a creative entity in music, your mind is already geared towards performance and I'd be willing to bet you have plenty of "funny voices" in your repertoire that could be taken advantage of. And with creative use of EQ, effects, and some pitch shift, you can make a man sound like a woman and vice versa. I've been a pesky gremlin, a goblin, a seductive Russian female agent, a barrel-chested gladiator, a southern steamboat captain, a racetrack announcer, a card dealer, a fashion designer complete with lisp, a fighter pilot, an air traffic controller, a cowboy, a game show host, a king, a queen, a geek, an orc, an elf, dog, cat, parrot, frog, rabbit, fish, and even a regular guy. I have borrowed from my high school drama days, and have taken my impatience and a microphone to add another sideline to the job that, frankly, I'm having an awful lot of fun with. I got into this industry to do music, but have remained open to all the possibilities. Creativity can pay off in many ways.

2.1.8 Industry Knowledge

The only thing left on this long list of essential skills to make you competitive in this foreign land is knowledge of the gaming industry itself and how it works. It is a world unto itself and far from your comfort zone as a musician. If you already possess some solid business sense, you are another step ahead of the crowd, but knowing when and where to strike in games is key.

Do research.   Talk to any friends or acquaintances who are in the industry — find out how their companies work, who to talk with to get the jobs, and most importantly, how they do what they do. Talk to other game composers, sound designers, and voice talent. These people have plenty of knowledge and are willing to share much of it. Don't expect them to give you the names and phone numbers of clients they have fought hard for, but they will usually discuss the process and the technicalities. Most are very open and friendly.

Be a sponge.   Absorb everything. Be on the alert for any information about the games business. Subscribe to a few magazines like: *PC Gamer, Computer Gaming World, Computer Games Magazine,* and *Game Informer Magazine* (for the consumer side). Try magazines like *Games Business* for the business side. *Game Developer Magazine* is a good bet for the "how to," down-and-dirty, technical side. Of course, get on the web. There are many sites available free of charge which are full of great information. Gamasutra (www.gamasutra.com) is a superb resource for industry information and job leads. See Chapter 4 for more.

Every time you walk into a retail outlet, check out the video game aisles, pick up boxes, and research the companies who are making these products. Buy a few. Don't be shy. They're a tax write-off for your business now. You can't expect to do audio for games if you aren't familiar with the major titles, what technology is being used, and what types of sounds they are making.

Rent games from your local video stores. No one said this was going to be all work now, did they? You can have fun on occasion.

The point is: be educated about the industry. It is in constant motion as smaller companies are taken over by larger ones, and companies disappear one week to spring up somewhere else under a new name the next. A producer you worked with on one project may have jumped ship to another company or even started his own. By keeping your finger on the pulse of gaming, you can guarantee your survival and flourish. Evolution is constant. Education is paramount. Know thy business.

2.2 Tools of the Trade

Musical arsenals vary greatly with each composer. Some prefer a minimalist approach, to keep technology from interfering with the process and allowing them to create truly unencumbered art. Others have to possess all the latest and greatest gadgets and gizmos, computer wizardry, and plug-in noise making boxes — preferring to let technology drive the creative course. Both extremes produce appropriate game scores which serve the virtual experience well. Most of us, however, are somewhere in the middle. The trick is finding what works best for *you*; whether it be leading the pack, using up-to-the-minute hardware on the leading edge, or working comfortably with the tried-and-true on the trailing edge. There are advantages and disadvantages to both.

Composer set-ups

Keep an eye open throughout the book for the "Tools of the Trade" sections on various composers' set-ups and gear lists that answer the question: what do the people who are doing this every day **really** use? Examine their audio tools, find the trends, and discover what everyone else is using to do today's great game audio.

By purchasing equipment and software the second it hits the store shelves, you are guaranteed to have the newest possible technologies at your disposal. With the highest sample and bit rates at your command, your music has the potential to be pristine and an example of sonic perfection. And based on your equipment inventory, you are also more likely to be able to handle jobs that utilize these technologies. Because most of us usually wait until a job requires a specific piece of gear before we incur the expense, you may have the advantage by already owning and being familiar with it. But don't let this belief be the most influential force in your business.

There is always something newer and better on the market. By the time you've pain-stakingly purchased what you thought was the best piece of equipment, something else has been introduced that is leaner and meaner. You will quickly go broke with this mindset.

Another disadvantage that can become quite frustrating happens when you buy that great "gotta have" piece of gear, get it back to the studio, and realize it won't interface with your existing set-up. Back to the store you go only to find that no one has developed yet, or even thought of, the cable or box you need to make it work. Or maybe you get lucky. But then you get it back, plug it in, and discover some horrendous software bug has stopped you cold. Give the manufacturer a couple months to develop a patch, box it back up, and send it to the factory for them to fix. Think I'm being a bit extreme? Not at all. It's happened to me and many others I've met.

The trailing edge of technology is not a bad place to be with most equipment. The manufacturers have had plenty of time to work out the kinks and have received plenty of feedback from consumers about which features they feel are useful. When the next version does appear, you know you are working with technology that has been on the market for some time and has been upgraded with some very convenient features. Not a bad trade-off for some patience and disciplined spending.

What about the constant learning curve required with the continuous flow of new equipment through your doors? It would be much different if you were running a full-blown recording studio, but as the sole composer and business proprietor, no one has that kind of time to spend learning and relearning. As your studio set-up becomes second nature and with familiar parts at your fingertips, very little effort is needed to find or record the sound you're looking for. Streamlining your composing and recording processes will keep you efficient as you work to move your product out the door.

Why have I been pushing this line of reasoning? I want you to keep these points in mind as we go through the list of absolutely essential equipment. I will cover: the basics, the bare bones setup, the nice-to-have kind of gear, and what established game composers are using themselves to do the job. You can get this venture off the ground with very little, but as money starts coming in, it will be very tempting to spend it on toys which will do nothing for your bottom line or your success. Trust me on this. It's easy to get carried away.

Buy only what will make you competitive and only what will make you money.

Assuming you own an instrument or two and have some kind of medium to capture them, believe it or not, you could almost get by with this as is. If you have the ability to get music to a developer in a polished form, you are in the game. But most developers don't have the time or the expertise to convert your tape to their required final format. It's up to you and probably best that way. You are the "ears" of a development team and have more years of experience in the audio arena. You know what the music is supposed to sound like and what noise was designed into it. By delivering material in its final format, you can almost relax, knowing the audio is sounding its best.

TOOLS OF THE TRADE

Chris Rickwood, Composer/Sound Designer, Rickwood Music

Chris' studio is basically a composition studio with the bare minimums. While he is capable of producing everything he needs through samplers and software, he will go to a professional recording studio to record acoustic instruments as the need arises. The home studio is just a way of creating sketches as quickly as possible, but there is no replacement for getting live, professional players to record your hard-labored scores.

Computer: Custom-built Pentium III 500 Mhz, 128 MB memory, 8 GB system drive, 30 GB (7200 RPM) audio drive, Dell 19" monitor, Echo Gina Audio Interface

Software: Cakewalk Pro Audio 9, Sonic Foundry Sound Forge® 5.0

Multi-track: Cakewalk Pro Audio 9

Monitor system: Mackie 1402 VLZ, Event 20/20 bas monitors

Mixdown: Mixdowns are completely digital inside the PC

Sound modules: Roland Alpha Juno 2 keyboard (old but reliable), EMU E4 sampler fully loaded, Alesis QSR (usually for quick sketches), Yamaha DX100, Alesis SR-16, EMU XL-1, Gigasampler (on its way)

Instruments: Ibanez Electric Guitar, Takamine Acoustic Guitar

---

2.2.1 Computers

You will need a computer for many tasks; it is an indispensable part of every studio nowadays. As the brain of your operation, it not only accomplishes your administrative tasks such as word

Figure 2.3 A typical computer audio workstation.

processing, email, internet access, accounting, and so on, but is used extensively in the creative music making and sound design process. MIDI sequencing, sound editing, multi-track recording, mastering, CD duplication, and so forth are all vital activities which center around this appliance. You cannot get by without it.

The software you purchase will ultimately drive the minimum requirements of the computer you use. For MIDI sequencing or basic sound editing programs, consider

- a Pentium 133 mHz with 8 MB RAM,
- the Apple 2e, Quadra series computers, or
- the PowerMac 7100 and 8100.

If you have one in a closet somewhere, pull it out, dust it off, and put it back to work. But if you want to spare some frustrations and a lot of finger-tapping while files process, I recommend starting off with at least

- a Pentium II (or AMD K6) 300 mHz with 32 MB RAM and 6 GB hard drive,
- an Apple G3,
- or basic iMac.

If you can afford it, go as high as you can with a Pentium III or IV, a beefed-up iMac, or Apple G4, and load it to the gills with RAM and the largest hard drives you can get your hands on. Audio files tend to be large and gobble up storage space at an incredible rate.

Make sure you have a reliable archival system as well — a CD-R or Zip drive will work well but because you'll have the tendency to be burning audio disks anyway, a CD-R will cover both.

Regardless of what you buy to do the work, make sure it is a system that will carry you for at least a couple of years. Upgrading computer systems can be a lifetime process, so at some point, you need to just stop the cycle and do your job until you absolutely *need* to make another purchase. Drive that baby until it won't go no more.

A word about hard drives

Recording music in real time to a hard drive can tax any system. One way to ensure flawless recording is to have a high-speed drive or one which is rated for A/V use. Look for rotation speeds of 7,200 rpm or more. I did have some luck with a 5,400 rpm drive, but never felt totally comfortable using it for audio data. Stay away from bargain brands; look for reliable product names which have a proven track record. Don't skimp on the quality of this type of storage medium. It will be getting plenty of hard use in its life and a failure will shut you down. Seagate, Maxtor, Fujitsu, Western Digital, and Quantum are solid bets. Dedicated hard drive storage systems are also available like Glyph Technology's rack-mounted units, designed specifically for audio use. An even better bet.

An extremely fast internet connection is something else you should consider when putting together your studio computer. A 56k modem is the minimum requirement, but consider either a T1 line, DSL, or cable modem. One of the great things about this job is that you don't have to actually be on site at the developer's office. As long as the final audio work is presented in the correct format, that's pretty much all they care about. Delivery is typically across the internet and when files sizes are 11 MB per minute of audio, it's not uncommon to send off files of 100 MB or more. After staying up all night to send a measly 10 MB file from a 14.4k modem, I went out and bought the fastest connection I could find. I haven't regretted the decision even once.

2.2.2 Interfaces

Having a computer is almost worthless without the appropriate interfaces which connect to your gear. You could compose and do sound effects entirely on a computer. Using loop, notation, or sequencing programs which play on software-based synthesizers and samplers, you can make some great game audio. There are a few composers who do, but the majority like to have this as just another option. Interfaces with your electronic instruments and recording gear will greatly expand your possibilities.

You will need a appropriate sound card — one which sounds good without adding noise and one with all the plugs you need to easily get audio in and out of your computer cleanly. Nowadays, it is possible to find a decent sound card which not only has analog audio inputs and outputs, but digital as well. I recommend having one with the digital I/O option, which can route sound to and from your digital mixing board, digital recorder, or instruments. By keeping sound in the digital domain, you are avoiding any unwanted discoloration from needless conversions back and forth from analog to digital storage — preserving the audio as you originally intended. On the PC side, higher-end cards, like the SoundBlaster Platinum, Digidesign Audiomedia, and Event Electronics Gina or Layla cards are superb. Mac owners can use the proprietary sound card or the MOTU 2408 or its equivalent for multiple inputs.

Some type of MIDI interface is also required between your computer and electronics devices. Selected sound cards have MIDI capabilities but only on a limited basis — usually with only one MIDI in and one MIDI out giving you 16 channels of information. As a basic set-up, this is workable, but for your eventual growth, a further investment of $50 will secure a separate MIDI card with two in and outs, for 32 channels. MidiMan makes great cards for the PC and Mac with 1×1, 2×2, and 4×4 options. This can seriously increase your MIDI capability and overall system control and performance. Their USB equivalents are also solid bets.

2.2.3 Software

With a solid computer system ready to go, let's now talk about the software which will help us put together our audio product. I don't currently endorse any particular software but am extremely familiar with the programs in use at my facility, so I might occasionally lean in that direction. This is your bread and butter, so in the end, you'll need to decide on the right combination for your needs.

The companion CD-ROM includes a few examples and demo programs available to suit your needs. It is by no means inclusive of every product on the market and due to size and other constraints, we couldn't get even close to including them all. I have included a number of programs which other composers and sound designers use but keep in mind, there are also many less expensive and less traveled programs available which will do the trick. There are many companies with a web presence who have demos and fully-functional programs available for download on their websites. Keep an eye open and be sure to check them out. You may just find a gem.

2.2.4 Sequencers

Sequencing software is a must when dealing with instruments using the MIDI standard. Every professional keyboard, sampler, sound module, and electronic drum kit utilizes this interface along with many types of outboard gear like sound effects and guitar processors. By having an appropriate MIDI interface between your computer and gear, you will be able to act as the one-man show — having control over your entire set-up with the touch of a button.

Several sequencing programs are available — some simple and others incredibly advanced with integrating multi-track audio options and plug-ins. If you aren't familiar with these, I suggest starting out basic (and inexpensive) then build up as you become proficient. Cakewalk, Steinberg Cubase, Mark of the Unicorn Digital Performer, and Emagic Logic are mainstream with good track records and many years of experience behind them. The one you choose depends on you though. You'll find that over the years, you will gravitate towards software you are comfortable with regardless of what other people may say and for me it was Cakewalk. As my needs grew, so did the complexity and features of the software and I've not had a reason to go elsewhere. That old, comfortable shoe still fits. I'm pretty sure if I'd started out with any other program, I'd being saying the same thing about it as well. It's hard to go wrong as long as the tool helps you in your creation process.

2.2.5 Multi-track Systems

Music constructed using several instruments and sounds are recorded onto some form of multi-track system, whether it is a tape- or software-based medium. By recording each instrument to its own "track," more total control is afforded during mix down phases. Although it is certainly plausible to record using "virtual" MIDI tracks, there are many occasions when the addition of non-MIDI instruments — like guitar, live drums, and vocals — help break up the mechanical feel of the music and humanize it. When creating sound effects though, software-based multi-track systems allow the best all-around options.

Multi-track software is not absolutely essential if you have the capability of a multi-track tape machine, but it still comes in very useful for music and sound design. Pro Tools is a favorite for some, but there is also an amount who dislike it with identical fervor. Steinberg's Cubase VST or Nuendo, Cakewalk's SONAR, and Sonic Foundry's Vegas Video are other solid programs which fulfill the multi-track mission. Again, it comes down to personal

Figure 2.4 Steinberg's multi-track audio and MIDI powerhouse, Nuendo.

preference and budget. You can get by without it so don't beat yourself up if the budget doesn't allow for it yet.

Nuendo and SONAR are two powerful programs at different ends of the price spectrum. Nuendo is Steinberg's high-priced, no-holds-barred software version of the professional Digital Audio Workstation (DAW). Combined with multi-track audio and MIDI production, its strengths are:

- automated and surround mixing,
- use of internal virtual instruments, and
- a very neat little feature which let's you undo any edit at any time during the production, even if it was 100 edits ago.

This is a very professional-looking program — reminiscent of a large studio mixing console with more plug-in processor support than you can shake a stick at. It is a great program if you want to spend the money.

If you still want the power of combined audio and MIDI production without the large expense, try Cakewalk's SONAR. This incredible program takes their expertise in MIDI production to an entirely new level, adding

- unlimited audio tracks,
- internal virtual instruments and DownLoadable Sound Fonts (DLS),
- advanced loop production tools,
- real-time effects plug-ins, and
- tons of extras.

This program has quite a bit to offer. Vegas Video is strictly a digital audio production tool so if you require MIDI support, one of these programs will do you well.

For quite some time, I had been doing sound design with a no-frills sound editing program. I would layer, cut, paste, and expend much time in trial and error — forging new sounds in the stereo and mono realm. I was quite happy until I met a fellow sound designer using Pro Tools. My jaw hit the floor when he showed me the awesome capabilities of creating sound effects in a multi-track atmosphere. Instead of the old "hope and pray" method, this was indeed nirvana. By having each layer of sound on a different track, you have complete control and as

Figure 2.5 Cakewalk's latest MIDI and audio production application, SONAR.

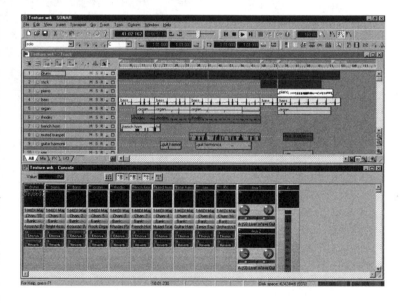

the layers become thicker, you can go back and tweak by individually equalizing, panning, fading, and processing them to your heart's content. And most of the programs are non-destructive meaning they leave the original sounds untouched. Only during playback and final rendering do the plug-in effects assist to produce the end product.

Since that time, I haven't looked back and do all of my sound effects creation in multi-track. After they are rendered, I polish them up in my sound editing program for their final stop before delivery.

2.2.6 Sound Editors

Sound files cannot be manipulated in the computer domain without a strong sound editing program. If you don't have anything else, make sure you definitely have one of these. In fact, I'd say it is virtually impossible to work in the games industry without one. Once music is created, it has to be translated into an acceptable computer format for playback within a game. It can also ensure it sounds its best with EQ, volume, compression, effects, and many other features. By supplementing what you hear, this visual method will show you any dead space before or after the sound, any peaks which may distort, and the overall loudness of the sound. This can come in handy when keeping file sizes down. Silence takes up the same amount of space as noise, plus, when you see a sound as a solid, square block of color, you may reconsider the mix with more dynamics.

One of the more popular sound editing programs is Sonic Foundry's Sound Forge®. Others which you might also consider: Cool Edit, Digital Performer, Wavelab, or GoldWave.

Having a solid main editing program will make life easier for you in the end, so don't scrimp if you can help it. Also consider having several programs available to keep your ideas fresh and to take advantage of each program's better features. I initially didn't consider the shareware version of GoldWave to be worth my time until another sound designer mentioned it had a great Doppler effect. Now I use it exclusively for that one effect. There are a couple of these available on the companion CD-ROM. Give them a look.

Figure 2.6 Sonic Foundry's capable audio editing software, Sound Forge®.

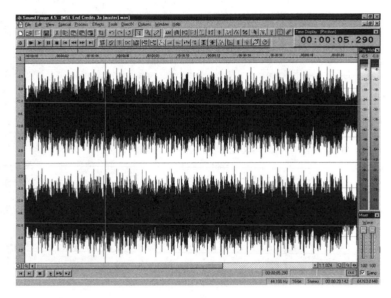

2.2.7 Mastering

Mastering software is mainly designed with CD production in mind and if you plan on releasing any of your game soundtracks, this will come in handy. When producing music for games, this type of software — while not used exclusively in the creative process — has a few features which are practical. Before I submit music in its final format, I'll run it all through my mastering software, ensuring consistent volume levels, adding crossfades to those cues which will run together, and adding any last compression or final touches. I'm mainly concerned with the overall picture, making sure the music sounds like it came from the same place, written for the same game, and that they work well together. Video games can jump from menu screens to action to cinematics to credits fairly rapidly, so the music for each can often be heard by the user in close succession. I want to make sure they all are of equal volume and sound quality — none sticking out or calling attention to itself. The music should be there to enhance the game, not take it over. Programs available include Sonic Foundry's CD Architect, Wavelab, Steinberg Mastering, and T-Racks 24.

2.2.8 Plug-ins

You can never have enough effect processors in your hardware arsenal or enough effect plug-ins for your software set-up. The manipulation of sound is what keeps things interesting to our ears and there are literally hundreds of plug-ins which add their own brand of flavoring to the mix. Many of the previously mentioned programs come with several plug-ins pre-loaded, giving you the option to add reverb, chorus, flange, or other effects to your sounds. The problem with these included effects is that everyone else has them too. By adding other plug-ins, you guarantee a distinct sound to your mixes that are fresh and stand out in the sonic crowd.

Of course, the manufacturers of these add-ons know this and have priced them accordingly. So, to keep you out of the poor house, only buy what you really need and what will make you competitive. (I know, I've said it before.) You can find plug-ins in any music catalog that sells software, as well as music stores and your online retailers.

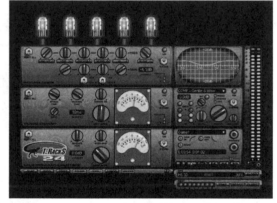

Figure 2.7 IK Multimedia Production's analog mastering software, T-Racks 24.

2.2.9 Loop Software

Other "nice-to-have" programs which help computer game score writing are those which utilize loop libraries. Originally, I wasn't too keen on them — thinking they'd eventually replace composers with programmers just to save a buck or two. But then I heard the so-called "music" these non-musicians were coming up with and I relaxed. The musicianship of these prerecorded tracks are typically good, but the arrangements are what give away their amateurish production. There is much a true musician can do with these tools to make them sound great.

The Sonic Foundry's ACID™ series — with an abundance of loop libraries in varied styles — can turn some wicked grooves on its own. It can also set your creative wheels in motion, giving you some great ideas to pursue when you may be feeling less than inspired. Propellerhead's ReBirth and ReCycle are useful programs, establishing grooves and processing loops by matching tempos to keep everything in sync.

The only real downfall to composing in this manner is that you can occasionally hear bits and pieces of different games using the exact same loop. To remedy this, try using loop libraries as "audio seasoning" to add some texture and interest to your tracks, i.e., make sure you don't always use the preset key and tempo values of the program. Go out of your way to ensure uniqueness. For instance, I'll use a drum track or pre-built groove as the basic track and then add to it with my own blend of sound.

2.2.10 Sound Modules/Keyboards

Computer? Check.

MIDI and audio interface? Check.

Software? Check.

How about instruments? Yeah, that's probably something you'll need. If you have only a single instrument, I suggest a decent keyboard with a good variety of sounds, including percussion and a MIDI port on the backside. That's really all you need. Later, when we get into the actual composing process, it will make more sense, but know it is completely possible to do it all from one good keyboard. You only use a few patches per song, maybe ten or so at the most, and a keyboard with 256 patches will have plenty of sounds at your disposal. As a basic set-up, this will work nicely.

Do I recommend having only one keyboard? Most certainly not! Have enough sound modules, samplers, keyboards, and electronic noise-making devices to keep yourself inspired and your music fresh. By having an infinite amount of sounds at your beck and call, you'll be more versatile and have a better chance of finding the perfect ones for each project — thus increasing your chances of different types of jobs. The only limiting factor will be your creativity, not your sounds.

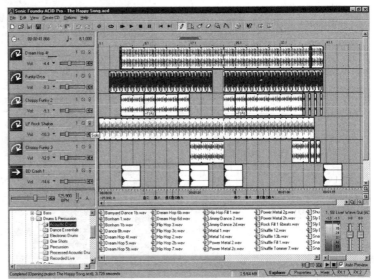

Figure 2.8 Sonic Foundry's loop-based production tool, ACID Pro™.

I once received some very good advice from TV theme great Mike Post. After listening to a tape of mine, I asked him what I could do to make my music better. He said the most immediate, positive effect I could have was to increase the number of sounds available to me. By doing so, I could remain in love with the composing process, always having a new, exciting, aural experience awaiting me with a push of a button. He likened it to the feeling you have when you bring home a new sound module or keyboard and first turn it on, and the creative rush that lasts until you look at the clock again ten hours later. You can be proficient at composing, but the inspiration and emotion that filters through is the key to really standing out. I totally agree. By making your new purchases slowly and wisely, this can be a feeling that lasts for years.

I recommend a good keyboard which you can use as a master controller for the various sound modules and samplers you'll eventually be buying. Try something with a full 88-key compliment so you have plenty of room to split sounds and have the full range available from top to bottom.

Once you have a good keyboard, you can save money by acquiring rack-mountable modules which are usually cheaper versions of an existing keyboard. Make sure these modules are expandable and have plenty of room to grow with additional sounds and memory. You want to buy the most sounds for the least amount of cash — a relatively simple concept in theory, of course.

2.2.11 Other Instruments

Just because we are creating for computer games, it isn't necessary to *only* use computer and electronic devices. In addition to your keyboards, sound modules, and computer, good old fashion analog musical instruments (which can be played live with your MIDI-controlled virtual tracks) are a superb supplement. They can add an entirely new dimension to your music and also keep it from sounding mechanical and boring. Guitars, drums, vocals, various percus-

Figure 2.9 A well-equipped keyboard station is essential when composing for video games.

sions, brass, and so on are all perfect to add that extra flair. Even though we are creating music to play behind a game, it doesn't mean it can't be good music. By using all the tools available to you, the listener will always be surprised by new sounds they hear, thus enhancing their overall gaming experience.

If you don't play another instrument, take some time to learn the basics or have musicians in your talent pool for those projects needing extra zing. By doing so, you will have increased your musical options and kept yourself competitive in the market.

Remember: most game composers are multi-instrumentalists (or can fake it really well).

2.2.12 Remote Recording

Other nice-to-have equipment will serve your sound designing career and add some extra spice to your musical creations. During various sound design gigs, you may be tasked with either FOLEY work or creating sound effects which are truly original. Prerecorded sound effects libraries are easy to reach for, but say you're looking for a fresh sound which hasn't been heard in the last wave of games. You can drag items into your studio to record with, but after you've made a mess a few times, you'll think twice. A better option is to have a portable DAT or MiniDisc recorder and a good microphone which you can haul out in the field in search of unique sounds. Why be restricted to what you can drag into your studio or by the length of your microphone cable? A decent portable rig will open up your world of sound effects immensely and give you a nice competitive edge in the process.

The Tascam DA-P1, Sony TCD-D7, or TCD-D8 are solid, transportable units with great sound and features. Mini disc units like Sony MZ-R70 Silver, MZ-R90, and MZ-R91, and Panasonics SJ-MR100 are nice for the price and size, but the MD format is not known for its stunning sound quality. Use it if you've got it, but if you have a choice, the DAT format is the way to go. Music stores, music catalogs, and online retailers have good selections available.

2.2.13 Sound Effects Libraries

What good sound designer doesn't have an extensive sound effects library? Practically none. Most game sound designers who have been around for a few years either own or have use of practically every sound effects library ever made. Why? In their quest to maintain freshness and added creativity to their sounds, they have scoured the modern world for these pre-recorded, easy-to-use, time-saving, audio wonders. Television and film have used these resources since their beginnings, it's only logical the billion dollar game industry does the same. Cinema quality and extra bang for the buck keeps the game-buying public happy.

Initially, it is possible to do sound design work without a sound effects library. I got away with it for several years, creating effects either from scratch or by manipulating sounds collected with my microphone over the years. It was a great learning experience — delving into the sonic world, learning how sounds are perceived by the human ear, and how to create sounds from practically nothing. It probably would have been much easier to take classes on the fundamentals of sound *and* taken less time. But by discovering concepts yourself, their lessons tend to remain with you longer.

As you mature in the business, projects will require more than what you can create from scratch. Unless you've got friends in the Marines who let you record streaking low-level jets, firing weapons, and explosions, you need an alternate method.

The next step would be to comb the Internet and its offerings. There are many sound hobbyists who post recording on their websites for public use. This approach can get you out of a jam but can also get you into one. Unless you know for sure, there is no telling where these sounds originated and possible copyright violations could arise. A developer is usually not too happy being party to a lawsuit for sounds you don't own or have licensed to you. Most contracts have a paragraph which clears them of any wrong-doing and puts all of the responsibility on the sound contractor to not violate any such copyright laws. It could end up being very expensive for you. Does it ever happen? Rarely, but I wouldn't want to be the one out of a thousand who ends up in court.

The solution: sound effects libraries. They are abundant and cover sounds from almost everything which makes noise on the globe. By purchasing these libraries, while not actually obtaining "ownership" of the sounds, you are granted a license to use them in your work. It doesn't get much better than that.

I've included a list of popular sound effects libraries and where to get them. I recommend asking for their demo CDs to get an idea of their sound quality and the types of effects available and to have the research done when you decide to buy. The Hollywood Edge will even send you a demo CD of "samples" which they allow you unlimited use of. They've saved me a couple of times. Others are available; try searching for "sound effects" on the internet.

There are also on-line dealers which allow direct download and individual licensing for single sounds. This is great when you need just one or two sounds and don't want to buy an entire series of effects CDs.

Sound Ideas
105 West Beaver Creek Rd., Suite 4
Richmond Hill, Ontario, Canada L4B 1C6
800-387-3030 USA
800-886-6800 Canada
info@sound-ideas.com
www.sound-ideas.com

The Hollywood Edge
7080 Hollywood Blvd., Suite 519
Hollywood, CA 90028
800-292-3577
info@hollywoodedge.com
www.hollywoodedge.com

Network Music, Inc.
15150 Avenue of Science
San Diego, CA 92128
800-854-2075
858-451-6409
feedback@networkmusic.com

Sound Dogs	www.sounddogs.com
Sounds On Line	www.soundsonline.com
Sound America	www.soundamerica.com
Serafine SFX Collection	www.frankserafine.com
PowerFX	www.powerfx.com
Sonomic	www.sonomic.com

2.2.14 Development Systems

At the end of our list of essential tools for the discriminating game composer and sound designer is the game console development system. This is specialized equipment that allows you to deliver the final work in the proper format when working on Nintendo 64, PlayStation, Sega Dreamcast, and Game Boy projects. These systems must be licensed to you, at a fairly hefty price, I might add, but are a necessary evil if you intend to work on these particular consoles. It is possible to outsource this conversion work to others who are already licensed and trained, and while it may save you time having to learn the development system, it will more than likely cost the same as buying one yourself.

Now, at this point in time, you happen to be quite lucky. With the introduction of the new generation game consoles — Sony PlayStation 2, Nintendo GameCube, and the Microsoft Xbox — the expensive, stand-alone development system is almost a thing of the past. To create audio content these days, you almost don't need anything beyond what you may already have in your arsenal. There are platform-specific tools you can use, mainly software programs, which will increase your options such as the MusyX tool for GameCube and DirectMusic Producer for the Xbox. These are available through the respective manufacturers — some as free downloads.

Chapter 11 will discuss specifics about each new console and their respective audio production and implementation needs. It is another personal choice whether to add these tools to your line-up. They will require extra time to learn and understand, but you can still work and do well without them.

2.3 Preparing your Studio for Surround Sound

3D audio is quickly becoming mainstream in video games. With the advent of DVD players and home theaters in more and more households, surround sound is creeping up as the new audio standard. That means more people expect to hear it in more things. Whether you do surround for games, your own music projects, or for other media, you will eventually need to have the set-up to make it happen. This section will explain what equipment you need and provide you the basics to set it up for a variety of studio configurations.

TOOLS OF THE TRADE

Stephen Rippy,
Music and Sound Lead,
Ensemble Studios

Stephen Rippy worked on his first game, The Age of Empires, between college classes. It has now sold over a million copies. In 1998, he moved to Dallas to make a go at it full-time and has since worked on every subsequent Ensemble Studio release: The Rise of Rome, Age of Empires II: The Age of Kings, Conquerors Expansion, and The Age of Empires Collector's Edition. His current project is Age of Mythology.

Computer: Pentium III 850 MHz, 256 MB RAM, dual 21" monitors

Software: Cakewalk Pro Audio 9, Sonic Foundry Sound Forge 4.5, ACID™ 2.0

Multi-track: Echo's Layla box

Mixing board: Main Studio: Mackie 32-8. Studio 2: Alesis Studio 24

Monitors: Event 20/20 bas

Mixdown deck: Sony PCM-R300 DAT

Outboard gear: Lexicon PCM 91 and MPX 100 reverbs, Alesis Midiverb 4, dbx 166A compressor/limiters, Ashley 3102 EQ

Keyboards, etc: Alesis QS8, Emu ESI-4000, Boss Dr. Synth

Other instruments: Electric and acoustic guitars, basses, drums, a ton of assorted percussion

Remote recording: Sony PCM-M1 DAT, Audio-Technica shotgun mic

Sound libraries: In-House Ensemble Studios Library, Lucasfilm, 20th Century Fox, and Hanna-Barbara libraries

2.3.1 Equipment and Placement

The first thing you will require are the proper tools for this whole grand application. Software-based studio set-ups can make use of internal surround encoding and decoding script — most of the time as a plug-in to whatever multi-track program you are using. For those who don't have the ability to do it in software or have a tape and mixing-console-based system, separate devices are necessary.

Dolby Labs manufactures specific equipment for just this purpose: the Model SEU4 Surround Encoding Unit and the Model SDU4 Surround Decoding Unit. While it isn't entirely necessary to have the decoding unit, Dolby recommends that playback is heard through it while mixing in order to hear any subtle changes the surround matrix may create. The SEU4 Encoder receives four input signals (left, right, center, and surround) from the audio console and matrix encodes them into two output signals: the Left Total (Lt) and Right Total (Rt) signals. These signals are treated as any stereo signal would be for transmission and recording. The SDU4 Decoder then decodes this two-channel signal into four output signals using Dolby Surround Pro Logic decoding technology. The unit also provides switchable stereo and monophonic monitoring modes for evaluating mix compatibility. A ganged master fader allows all four monitor output channels to be varied together — supporting variations in listening level while maintaining playback balance and calibration.

Consumer Dolby Surround Pro Logic decoders — as found in various stereo and home theater receivers — operate identically to the SDU4 and could be used in a pinch or temporarily instead purchasing the professional unit. However, these consumer decks include circuitry to auto balance and correct left and right channel errors and may pose a problem when mixing because this feature hides the very problem you might be looking for.

Dolby Digital 5.1 is also another option which runs congruent to the Pro Logic surround arrangement. This technology uses five discrete channels of audio and a Low Frequency Enhancement (LFE) channel (the .1) for greater separation. While not used in gaming at the moment, it will only be a matter of time. The encoding and decoding process requires different hardware, two channel rear surround playback, an LFE device, and a bass management system. The Dolby DP569 Encoding and DP562 Decoding units are appropriate hardware for this application. Bass management systems are manufactured by various other companies and are available separately. Bass management redirects bass frequencies intended for the five main speakers and routes it to the subwoofer — recommended because most speakers do not extend to extremely low frequencies. All consumer Dolby Digital receivers have bass management and it is highly recommended for studios as well.

A speaker system — to include a left, right, center, two surrounds, and sub woofer — is necessary for proper playback in a studio environment. Most everyone already has a left and right pair of speakers, so an addition of four would be required.

A center speaker can be added to your existing pair, but be sure the addition matches the acoustic characteristics of the other two for consistency. Or you can install three identical near-field monitors designed just for this purpose. It isn't necessary that all speakers be the same size.

Large left and right speakers and a smaller center speaker from the same line are acceptable. If possible, the center speaker should have the same high- and mid-frequency drivers as the left and right speakers. When placing the front line of speakers, all of them should be equidistant from the mixing position and the left and right speakers should be as far apart as the engineer's head is from the center speaker. This will provide optimum coverage and keep the listener in the sweet spot.

The two surround speakers can be smaller bookshelf-type speakers. The actual frequency response of the surround channel is 100Hz to 7kHz so larger speakers for bass reproduction and extended range tweeters for ultra-high-frequencies are not necessary. It is important to choose surround speakers that sound similar to the front speakers throughout this range. A smaller speaker from the same product line usually works best. The surround speakers should be placed on the side walls approximately two feet behind and at least two feet above the engineer's seated position. They should point to a spot two feet above the engineer's head for maximum effect. It is not recommended that surround speakers be pointed directly at or below the listener's seated position. For a Dolby Digital set-up, the rear speakers should be placed 110 degrees from center.

If all three speakers in the front are identical, the power amps for each should also be rated equally. If the center speaker is smaller and center channel bass is being redirected to the left and right channels, the power rating of the center amp should be at least 75% of the left and right amps. The total power provided for the surround channel should not be less than that of either the left or right channels. The preferred method is for each surround speaker to have a separate amp at least 50% of the power of the left and right amps. If one amp is used for the surrounds, it should be rated the same as the left and right. There are also many active monitor systems available which have amplifiers built into the speaker cabinet which would serve this purpose well.

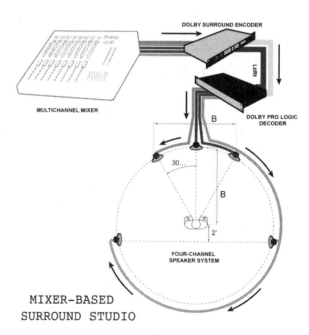

Figure 2.10 A mixer-based Dolby *Pro Logic* Surround studio set-up.

Your current audio console's flexibility will greatly affect its surround mixing capabilities. While it is possible to create a surround mix on a console with as little as a stereo bus and one auxiliary send, the ability to do complex mix moves will be nonexistent. A console, or software, with film-style panning allows the greatest flexibility for desired sound placement. The particular need for an application will depend on the complexity of the mix. When deciding to purchase new equipment, think about future needs and not just what's in store for a current project.

2.3.2 Studio Set-up

We all know there are as many methods of audio creation as there are creators, which supports the idea that the studio set-ups of each will also be different. Budget, location, and accessibility of equipment dictates that no two set-ups will be alike. Integrating surround equipment into them can sometimes prove to be a challenge. New mixing consoles provide the luxury of discrete surround channels, designed for this new day and age. Older model consoles can still perform the task but require a little finesse to make it happen.

On all consoles, left and right outputs are standard, and these will connect to the surround encoders left and right channels exclusively. Older consoles can utilize either the auxiliary send buses or another left and right channel output in order to connect the center and surround channels to the mix. Using the auxiliary bus will be most limiting when panning a signal, but it will work fine for simple music mixes. Using another left and right output source would be the better option if available — though still not as flexible as a film-style set-up with individual outputs dedicated specifically to the four channels.

Once the issue of console channel outputs has been resolved, these discrete signals will be routed to the encoding unit. From there, the encoder's Lt and Rt outputs can be recorded as a two channel encoded mix. Playback and monitoring is accomplished when the two encoded channels are returned to the decoding unit's Lt and Rt inputs and further routed to the surround speaker system as four separate signals.

Computer-based multi-track recording systems can also produce and record surround material with minimal requirements. Starting with digital audio software with multi-channel capability, the signals will flow to a multi-channel output soundcard. From there, the four channels would move to the encoding unit, to the decoding unit, and out to the speakers. For programs which utilize software surround encoding and decoding, the output from the multi-channel sound card will go directly to the speaker system. Computer-based recording using Dolby Digital technology would also require a bass management system to be connected between the sound card and speaker set-up.

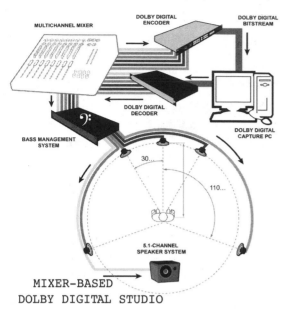

MIXER–BASED
DOLBY DIGITAL STUDIO

Figure 2.11 A mixer-based Dolby *Digital* **studio set-up.**

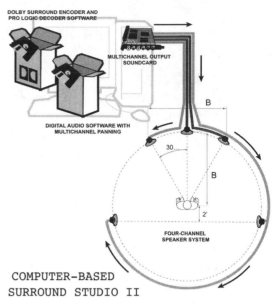

COMPUTER–BASED
SURROUND STUDIO II

Figure 2.13 A computer-based Dolby Pro Logic Surround studio set-up utilizing internal encoding and decoding software.

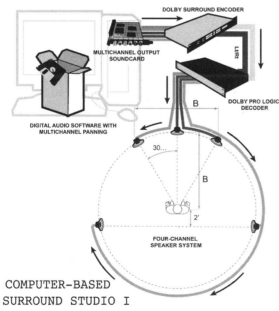

COMPUTER–BASED
SURROUND STUDIO I

Figure 2.12   A computer-based Dolby Pro Logic Surround studio set-up utilizing outboard encoding and decoding units.

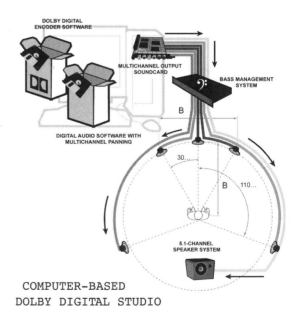

COMPUTER–BASED
DOLBY DIGITAL STUDIO

Figure 2.14 A computer-based Dolby Digital studio set-up utilizing internal encoding and decoding software and an external bass management unit.

2.3.3 Surround Tips

Dolby Pro Logic decoding relies on amplitude and phase differences between the two channels of a Lt/Rt signal to extract the four channels. As a result, there are certain things to keep in mind when mixing in Dolby Surround.

1. Only one signal can be steered at a time by a Pro Logic decoder and this must be the dominant signal. The rest of the mix is distributed equally among the remaining speakers.
2. The surround channel rolls off at frequencies above 7 kHz, so you may notice this limited high-end frequency response of the surround channel in certain situations.

When mixing with four channels, there are some general guidelines recommended to obtain good results.

1. If you want to hear *exactly* what your audience will hear, it is best to monitor and playback through a decoder.
2. Track and pan the sound of all important objects continually as they move.
3. Although the dominant signal is the only sound being steered by the decoder at any one time, it is still OK to pan multiple signals in different directions. When a signal is no longer dominant, the decoder finds the next dominant one to steer. Therefore, it's important that all signals are positioned properly even when they are not dominant.
4. Unless there is a specific reason not to do so, include the center channel when panning from left to right.
5. There should be no essential information in the LFE channel. This should be only be used for bass enhancement.

The best way to understand how Dolby Surround works is to use it. Practice creating different kinds of mixes. Listen to games and movies in Dolby Surround to gain a greater sense of the possibilities of the medium. You can learn many tricks from careful listening.

2.3.4 Dolby Support

Dolby Laboratories has been very active in gaming in recent years; so much, in fact, they established a "game development relations" branch to support game developers and audio content providers. They have extended their hand to the community and are available for questions and advice at games@dolby.com. Just be sure to let them know I sent you.

CHAPTER 3
Getting Organized and Ready for Business

3.1 Understanding the Business of Game Composing

It's getting close to decision time. You have the music and sound design aptitude, a great attitude, and the willingness to make this a successful venture. But, do you really want to? Is the games industry the right place to sell your music? Do you even want to work that hard?

Truthfully, not everyone can do the job. You might be able to compose some fantastic music, but your business ability or lack thereof will stand in the way. Historically, musicians are not well respected by the establishment as businessmen. Management types do not fully understand "creative" people and tend to stereotype them into neat categories which suit their purposes. We, on the other hand, know better. Just because we may come across sometimes as "free-spirited," it doesn't mean we don't have our act together and are capable of comprehending the complexities of the business world. Regardless of the trade you are in, your "product" is almost worthless unless you can sell it. Keep that in the back of your mind.

To do this type of work, you must be creative and be able to craft an original "mood" to enhance the game you are writing for. You must remain detached and objective when asked to rewrite passages or redo any work. You must have a great attitude and always come across in a positive and professional manner despite any instinctive urges to thin the obnoxious producer gene pool. And to be successful, you must have it in your mind you are in this for the long haul. By dedicating your efforts and focusing on your personal and professional goals, you will outlast anyone who thought they could get their music on a major game title within a month of opening their doors for business. It can be frustrating at first, but rewards come to those whose calculated patience remains intact.

3.1.1 Expectations

A lot is expected from a game composer. Because the audio provider is often an aloof character seldom understood by a producer, they usually end up working alone, providing one third of the game experience literally by themselves. Because we can work off-site and at odd hours, the mystery of our creations are nervously awaited for examination — usually in their entirety near the deadline with little chance for reworks. No pressure there.

I spent about five days working tediously on a piece of music for a medieval-themed game project. The artwork presented was dark, ominous, with evil dripping from every scene. The producer let me take it all in, I mentioned the previous adjectives, heads nodded, and it felt like we were all on the same page. Five days later, I submitted completed music, excited by what I felt was a direct hit. Later in the day, I got a call. "Hey, we got your music. Great stuff. But, ah, we all talked about it and decided it was too dark and too ominous for our purposes. We decided we want to try something more whimsical and cartoon-ish instead." Aaaggghh!! So, with two days until the deadline, it was back to the drawing board and music for a whimsical, medieval cartoon emerged instead.

Crazy? Yes, but you occasionally have to change gears and run off in an entirely new direction. As a game's personality slowly matures and the producer's vision takes shape, original ideas for music may not fit when played within the context of the game. If your first submission doesn't fit, carefully crafted after digestion of all the right adjectives describing the game, the content provider is still expected to magically throw another masterpiece together to match the new ideas. That's what we do. We pull sound from thin air and make glorious music out of it. It's a puzzle to most people how we do it. Producers tend to forget that each one of these little tunes we just "threw together" is actually a child we gave birth to, nurtured, watched grow, and then sent on its way out into the cold world. But for those children who do come back, we can put them on our demo reel or save them for the next dark, ominous, and evil game.

3.1.2 Reasonable Costs

Something else to chew on before diving head first into this venture is the costs involved and the return on your investment. Professional music equipment is expensive. It is built to be rugged and hold up under constant use — more so than occasional use of consumer gear. Manufacturers know you are willing to pay a bit more for pro equipment and increase profit margins accordingly. Because this gear costs a little bit more, your income will need to be able to meet the demand.

Initially, you probably won't be making fistfuls of dollars and you will have to weigh the expenses of doing business with the potential of income to be generated, and then decide what works best for you. I'm guessing if you bought this book, you have already made a sizeable initial investment in your equipment and are looking to capitalize on it now, so you probably aren't planning on acquiring much more expensive gear in the near future. If you are making payments or are using this as a sole source of income, it might add some extra impact to my next statement:

Never give away any of your music or sound effects for free.

In the beginning, it is very tempting to do just that, in order to add a project to your resume. But what it does instead is let a game developer take advantage of you and cheapen our profession. At the very least, make sure your expenses are covered. While the rush of creating music for your first game can adrenalize your system, it will be short-lived when you have to sell some of your equipment to pay the rent. It's not worth doing it for free. Your talent adds value to a product they will sell and make a lot of money from. Ensure you receive your fair share as part of the product team.

We'll cover how to determine your pricing structure to be in line with the game industry later in the chapter. Right now, you should be formulating your considerations — how to make a reasonable profit against the cost of doing business within your plans, and if the income you make will be enough to reach these goals. By analyzing beforehand, you can see the numbers in black and white and decide whether it is even worth going into business prior to wasting a lot of time, money, and effort. I'm not trying to talk you out of pursuing this type of career, don't get me wrong; I'm giving you a cold dose of reality to make sure this is a balanced presentation. The reality of business is that sometimes it makes better financial sense to not go into business. Perhaps composing and sound designing as a part-time gig to supplement other income makes better sense.

Whatever you do at this point though, be sure to read the rest of the book for the full story before coming to any conclusions. This would just be one of the many factors in any final decision. While it did cost money in the beginning, my passion for music and many other enticements the gaming industry has to offer was enough to see me through.

3.1.3 Flavor of the Month

While we are on the subject of reality, let's get another dose. Your music will not be perfect for every job. Even if you are well versed in various techniques and can compose jazz, acid rock, and classical expertly, your music will not be perfect for every job. *Even* if a game cries out for your strongest style and there is no doubt that you could nail it, your music will not be perfect for every job. Instead of getting into a one-sided philosophical discussion about this phenomena, let's just agree on this, OK?

We call it "flavor of the month." Even after you've composed for 100 games, your "flavor" may not be what they are looking for and you won't get the job because they like someone else's "flavor" better that month. It's similar in nature to "fads," the unexplainable force which shifts the focus onto someone else for awhile. Your "flavor" is made up of your personal composing and recording style, like a recording artist who maintains their "sound" from album to album. They have their own sound regardless of what they do because of who they are. Not much you can do about that.

The rest of the "flavor" comes from your instruments, your mixing board and recording equipment, your sample and loop libraries, and from the room you record in. They all contribute to the particular sound which people will associate with you. You can change that though. Keep your sounds fresh, trade in your old gear regularly, try different recording techniques — anything to be different than before. Then again, maybe it's your "sound" which makes you money. A paradox only you can solve.

3.2 Composing vs. Sound Design

As you prepare for business, you want to set yourself up to be successful. In our case, we sell our "sounds," whether it's music or sound effects. About now, you should be deciding on what you have to offer the gaming world, what "products" you have to sell, and whether you can sustain your enterprise with what you have. If you've decided to deal strictly with music, then so be it. Get your music together and get out there and sell it. Make your success. If you've decided sound design is more your bag, then get your sounds together and go for it. Take your product and hit the market running.

The main question you should be asking yourself is, "can I make the kind of money I need *and* stay busy in the games industry with the product I am offering?" If you are only selling one product, chances are you are not going to stay as busy as you'd probably like. Well, not at first anyway. With that in mind, you can initially plan to supplement another source of income with this venture until business picks up and you've reached a livable income level.

I mentioned in Chapter 2 that using your audio talents and recording equipment in another form of audio work will increase your income and chances of success. There is plenty of work for composers who go out and search in other arenas, but for those of you who like what you see in the games industry, you should keep within the perimeter and reach into every facet of it. Like I've said, the advantages of making your audio house the only source for a game developer are endless. And as your reputation grows within this tight-knit group, more work will follow naturally so you can spend more time creating and less time pounding the pavement. This means being composer, musician, sound designer, voice talent, engineer, producer, and all-around audio pro.

It can be done selling a single product. You can be successful and meet your personal and professional goals. There are many who have and more that will. But you need to sit down, take a hard look at what you want to accomplish, and then make the decision.

3.3 In-house Audio vs. Independent Contractor

You've decided to indeed compose music, create sound effects, or both for video games. Your next choice is to determine the method you will use to accomplish the task, either as an in-house sound person, working directly for a game developer as an employee on their premises, or as an independent contractor. Both have distinct advantages and also carry their own baggage. There are no particular rules governing the decision; you can bounce around and do it whatever way suits you, gaining experience and exposure from various projects and the many ways of doing business.

Initially, you may face a roadblock or two chasing either avenue. A game developer may not even consider you for an in-house position unless you have certain experience in the industry and perhaps a game or two under your belt. In a case like this, maybe you can get your foot in the door by applying for another position, say, game tester or as an assistant to the audio department. Do a good job and keep your eyes open for composing and sound design opportunities. Once the company knows you, trusts you, and sees how valuable you can be as an audio resource, you may naturally migrate into the job you were eyeing.

Tommy Tallarico started out as a play tester at Virgin Interactive and ended up as their audio director until branching out on his own. Joey Kuras started play testing, then designing game levels, some composing, and is now the sound designer at Tommy Tallarico Studios. Brian Tuey of Thunder Soundscapes, having already done music for a couple games as an independent, was hired on at Gigawatt as a game tester to learn more about the inner workings of video games. They've already started to ask for his assistance in a few audio matters and it looks like it's only a matter of time before he ends up doing it full time.

GAME COMPOSERS AT WORK

Jamey Scott of Presto Studios

When do you tend to be most musically creative? Pretty much anytime for me. I'm most creative when I just force myself to get out of the muck. Once I get going, the creativity just comes, every time. Sometimes I just don't feel like doing it, so I have to force myself into it. I stop setting up the coffee pot, getting everything perfect, turn off the email, and just dig in. I'm a little lethargic in the mornings sometimes but once I get going, I'm OK. Once I get in the 'zone,' nobody better interrupt me or call because I'll bite their head off. When my wife calls, the first thing she'll ask is if I'm in the 'zone' or not. If I say yes, then she just hangs up without saying goodbye and tries again later. I'm kind of quirky like that."

Describe your thought process when scoring a project. Most of the music I write is ambient music; I'm setting up a mood. For that, I just write something, I don't even know where it comes from. If I ever get totally stumped, I'll listen to soundtracks I like from my favorite movie composers to get in the mood. Every once in a while, I'll hear a passage that might spark me into a whole other thing. Most of the time, I'll just come up with something and take it. There is always some minute spark that will set me off. I try not to imitate or steal from other composers as my personal goal is to maintain a unique writing style. Although

I'm inspired by certain composers, I never try to copy them. I prefer to ask myself, 'Now how would I have scored that?'.

One thing that motivates me a lot when I'm writing is that I'm always looking for ways to stray from the diatonicism of a piece. If I'm writing something melodic, the first few bars will establish the tonality then I will instantly shift. I rarely write constant, diatonic music for underscore. With themes, I have stayed diatonic for sections, but I usually stray in B sections or what have you. This is just one of those aspects that establishes me as a stylistic writer rather than a chameleon composer.

When I score to animation, I never score to storyboards. I'll look at them to see what's coming down the pike, but when I sit down to do it, the movie has to be complete. I hate scoring to the beat of the scene editing and then having it changed after I've already done the music. If that happens, I have to start from scratch practically, so I insist the work be finished. When I score, I don't just lay a bed of music; I reinforce the editing and the dramatization. One of the scenes I did this morning, some guys where climbing down a rope, real mysterious. So I started with some high violins, a subtle tremolo viola, and then as they get closer to the ground, the bass starts to fill out. I bring in the bassoons and French horns crescendo as they reach the bottom — that kind of dramatic pacing. As the camera pulls back, you see that they were being watched the whole time. The volume slowly intensifies, then suddenly drops out. This is how I pace a scene and dictate the emotional impact with music. It's important to know what types of musical devices evoke certain emotions like fear, mystery, gloom, etc., and then be able to incorporate those devices into your compositional style. Obviously, a lot of people don't do that. A lot of 'composers' can get away with laying down a two minute synth string chord and that suffices for all of the emotions therein. However, I like to take on a lot more responsibility and really dig into scenes and make an impact rather than just get by.

The more I write, the more dynamic I become. The stuff I'm doing now is more effective, I think, than ever before. I'm definitely on a journey."

What advice can you give to current and future game composers? "The most important thing is to develop a voice as a composer. A lot of people don't have the capability to have their minds open enough to study the masters and other types of music in order to learn the skills. The thing that will separate you from everybody else and make you marketable, is the sound of your music. It's very important. Why do John Williams, Danny Elfman, Hans Zimmer, and James Horner all work consistently while there are a thousand other guys who only work here and there? These top echelon people not only have their politics intact, but they have their specific voice as a commodity.

A lot of the up-and-coming need to get things together. They also need to diversify. Have the composing down, the sound design skills together, be able to program. The farther you can go down the line, the better off you are going to be. If a game company doesn't have to hire three different people and they can hire one instead, that is appealing to them.

If you are interested in working on an assembly line, doing sound work, you can do that. But if you are interested in becoming cutting edge, somebody that will stay in the field and become sort of an icon, then you really need to get it together. And that's my opinion."

(See page 106 of Chapter 5 for Jamey's gear list.)

3.3.1 In-house Composing

Working in-house as a composer or sound designer is not a bad way to make a living. Jamey Scott at Presto Studios wouldn't have it any other way. Tim Larkin at Cyan enjoys the innovative environment working with the company's other creative minds — constantly energized by the surrounding forces. Greg Rahn (formerly at Broderbund, The Learning Company, and Mattel) is partial to the security, health benefits, and the steady income.

Working directly for a game developer gives you more time to concentrate on the job at hand — enabling you to give it your best on a daily basis. You receive a steady paycheck, always confident of how much and when it will arrive. This security goes a long way in keeping the support of your family — relieving the pressure they may have put on you for previously "wasting your time." Additional benefits, such as health coverage and paid vacations can be other carrots dangling in front of you.

Relentlessly looking for work can drain the hardiest of souls. By working in-house, all of your creative efforts can be focused on your music and sound creations. Often, while working as an independent in the middle of one project, you will be spending your prime time looking for the next. Your mind can be more relaxed and focused on music writing without the added headache of searching for more work. As the in-house employee, the company will take care of it for you. Many in-house composers can attest to the positive affects this has had on their music. This is especially true for artists who don't care too much for the business side of the industry.

If you enjoy working in an extremely creative and nurturing atmosphere as an integral member of a team then an in-house position is definitely for you. There is just something about being among other imaginative types, living within the game you are creating, watching it grow, and receiving instant feedback on your role. Communication between other project members is critical and physically being there keeps the lines open, whether you overhear someone talking in the hall or if they come to you directly. There always seems to be a bit of a barrier between a game developer and an independent contractor — even a slight level of mistrust. You feel immersed in the process instead of feeling like an outsider.

Working around other artists, craftsmen, and tunesmiths helps create a mysterious aura, an unexplainable atmosphere which primes the juices and keeps you at your best. If you find you are not capable of self-motivation or sometimes need that an extra kick in the pants, an in-house gig will give you the charge to produce some truly inspired music which might have been difficult when working in isolation. My best work always comes from being around and working with other creative forces directly. There's just something about keeping trusted associates nearby to keep your audio mission on track.

Equipment

Game companies have various policies regarding equipment purchases. Knowing your previous experience with audio has more than likely brought with it a gear list to match, some leave it up to the composer to equip their studios with their own funds. The company's advantage: they don't have the expense of endless equipment purchases. Your advantage: you can take it all with you if you leave and you have complete control over what is bought. They know music and recording gear is expensive — far more so than, say, a computer and a graphics card they'd need to buy for an artist or programmer. Most of the time they will supply a computer without hesitation. The rest is up to you.

TOOLS OF THE TRADE

Greg Rahn, Composer/Sound Designer, Sound Mindz

Greg's a serious player in the Bay area with a respectable number of game projects under his belt: Riven, Warbreeds, Prince of Persia 3D, Where in the World is Carmen San Diego?, Dr. Suess Preschool and Kindergarten, Kid Pix Deluxe. Formerly the in-house composer and sound designer at Broderbund, The Learning Company, and Mattel, he now freelances with the best of them.

Computer/Software: PowerMac G4-Dual Processor 533, MOTU Digital Performer, Digidesign Pro Tools, Peak, plus lots of plug-ins and other little sound apps

Mixing board: Mackie 24 × 8 mixer, Mackie 16 × 2 submixer

Mixdown decks: Panasonic DAT, Sony DAT

Keyboards: K2500S with lots o' libraries, Yamaha VL1m Physical Modeling synth ("I'm a big fan of breath control"), Roland JV1080, Roland JV 880, EPS 16 Plus Sampler, Korg EX 8000, Korg T3, Roland MKS 20, Roland JP 8000, Motion Sound R3 147, Stegler Grand Piano

Other instruments: Cedar flute

Microphones: Various mics but especially fond of my new AT 4050 CM5

"Lately I've been tracking live instruments in various rooms of my home — necessitated by my lay-off from Mattel/The Learning Co/Broderbund. I'm discovering the benefits of a large living room with high ceilings and getting a better sound than I was getting in our $100K studio at Mattel.

I recently did some new cues for KTVU's Mornings on 2 show here in the Bay area. I did the demos using the VL1m for soprano sax and flute, and Hans Zimmer guitars on the K2500. (The creative director thought it was the final version). For the final, I tracked percussion, acoustic guitar, vocals, flute, and soprano sax all separately in my living room. I used the money I would have normally spent at another studio for a new mic. After six years as a staff composer with access to pro studios, I am now pushing the envelope on my home project studio. The gray line keeps getting grayer."

Large game companies may have another view. If the number of games in production warrants it, they'd rather equip their own studio to match their quality and compatibility requirements. Electronic Arts is a prime example. They have a large, state-of-the-art studio complex in-house to use exclusively for their myriad of game projects. By equipping their studios with high-end gear, their sound is completely under their control. The company's advantage: they own all the equipment which stays as people move on. Your advantage: you get to play with top notch gear you didn't pay for and gain some valuable experience you normally couldn't have afforded.

There are also game companies which fall in the middle of the previous extremes. Occasionally, developers may require their audio department to have specialized equipment for which they foot the bill. In other instances, they may have specific sound libraries in mind for a project, either sound effects or samples, and unless you want to buy them for your own collection, they will pay. Generosity is dependant upon budgets, but an occasional bonus in the form of an extra piece of gear is not entirely unheard of. Your relationship with the developer will determine the amount of money thrown your way for purchases in this environment.

Expect the unexpected when working in-house. If it makes noise in a game, you will do it. The purpose of having an audio department is to keep the company from outsourcing any of its work. The last thing they want to do is pay a contractor to do voice-overs or sound effects when they are already paying you to occupy space. Larger game companies may have several working in audio, all with particular specialties. It may not be as critical for a composer to also do sound design. But for other game companies — where the audio department is made up of a single entity — they will more than likely have to be a jack of all trades. For those of you who are self-sufficient, or like to work alone, this is a job where you can thrive. Others, with expertise in one area, may find getting an in-house audio job difficult.

You may also be expected to know or learn how to implement sound in a game as well as writing actual programming code to make your sounds work. You may have to port to other game platforms and be familiar and licensed with any proprietary development systems. A lot of technical work may await you, so it's important to know what you might be getting into when shopping for a company. If you have this kind of wisdom, you will be extremely marketable. If you learn, it can contribute to your job security.

One serious disadvantage to working in-house is that your position and/or the company could disappear at any moment. This is not to say every game company is inherently unstable, but there are many who struggle to make monthly payroll. Instead of paying an in-house composer

$60,000 a year to work on scattered projects, it might be beneficial for them to hire contractors at a lower rate as each project warrants.

In this volatile industry of take-overs and buyouts, your game team runs the chance of being disbanded by new owners — especially if they already have duplicate positions staffed. Most of the time, company acquisitions are a chance to buy the rights to game engines, licenses, AI (artificial intelligence), game titles, development tools, and so on and to make the previous owners some money. Their concern is not really the employees. Every so often, a successful team may survive intact, but it is indeed a rarity.

3.3.2 Independent Contractors

For those of you who enjoy the open road, life as an independent contractor is for you. There is so much more to this business than just composing music or designing sound effects. Little triumphs and exciting moments along the way make you feel like the king of the world — winning that first big contract, negotiating a sweet deal, having developers call you on a project instead of you calling them, having your peers accept you and to invite you in on a project

Figure 3.1 Ensemble Studios **in-house sound room.**

all contribute to the personal triumph you'll feel. It's not always about the music you create; there is that little something extra which motivates us as well.

The advantages are many for those who opt to give up the security of an in-house job. The freedom of running your own business your way and calling all the shots is a serious enticement. How about picking and choosing which projects you work on? Or unlimited income potential? Hey, hey! Now we are talking!

Working in-house is strictly a "work for hire" arrangement. The game developer pays you a salary and in turn, everything you produce as partial or finished work belongs to them. They own all the rights and are free to do whatever they want with your creations. It's painful sometimes watching your work used in a movie or commercial knowing you'll never see another dime from it. As an independent, you are free to negotiate whatever kind of deal makes you happy. You can license the music to them to use for their project, but save the rights to everything else. Music soundtrack releases, use in movies, licenses for other game platforms — they all add up to some substantial income for you. Consider having several projects with the same type of deal simultaneously. Your income becomes almost boundless. There are also game royalty deals or bonuses you can negotiate. If a game becomes a hit, you are also rewarded for your hard work and vital contributions to the project with regular payment. Not such a bad arrangement.

Independents have the freedom to work if and when the mood strikes. But if you do not have self-discipline, you'll end up taking a long, self-inflicted vacation instead. And it is certainly much easier to schedule in time with the family or other obligations. It's nice to have that sort of independence.

It's also sweet to have the liberty to pick and choose which contracts to pursue. In-house composers work on whatever is thrown their way. Occasionally, there may be a project presented to you beyond your abilities or you may not feel comfortable with the company — sensing you'll end up working hard for a game which will never be released. Companies that don't quite have their act together will end up driving you crazy, asking for the impossible, and cost you time and money. Initially, you'll want to take every job that comes your way, but sooner or later, your guts will tell you when it's time to pass this headache off on someone else and let your competitor pull their hair out over it. You can also consider exposure, money, or the good old "fun factor" when choosing games to work on.

Figure 3.2 Jon Holland often uses his location for inspiration when creating epic scores.

In-house composers, as the name implies, work on the game developer's premises. They get up in the morning and fight traffic to get to their windowless studio which was formerly a broom closet. If they are lucky enough to have a window, it usually overlooks a parking lot full of cars or the nearby freeway. So, another big plus for the independent is working where ever you want — letting issues such a convenience and the view guide your productivity and inspiration. Chance Thomas has a stunning location near Yosemite National Forest which serves as his place of business. His studio has two large glass walls; one overlooking a two-story glass atrium, the other opening to the surrounding forested acreage and five huge windows offering inspiring views of nearby Thornberry Ridge and Deadwood Mountain. There is a hand-crafted spiral oak staircase leading up to the studio entrance and a walk-out redwood deck just outside the control room. The studio is decorated with Haitian art, pictures of St. John and St. Bart, photos of his family, and a handful of awards, plaques, and little golden statuettes. Jon Holland also enjoys his personal Yosemite view overlooking forests of 100-year-old pines. These guys are making great use of what inspires them.

Most composers tend to work at home in their project studios — foregoing regular office hours and the commute, preferring to work where they are comfortable and close to the other important things in life. Some have nearby studios and composing space which allow them to get away from any distractions, close the doors, and come out when they are through. An office building isn't always the best place for your finest work.

"All work and no play makes Jack a dull boy." If Jack played music constantly and never took a break from it, Jack would become boring and his music lifeless. As an independent contractor, this can never happen to you. Your business forces you to do other things that help keep your musical perspective fresh. I usually find that after a week or two of working the phones, negotiating deals, and being caught up in the administrative chores, when it's time to do music, I'm chomping at the bit, ready to roll. I'm excited about the music and go into it with a better attitude than say, walking into the studio for the fifth straight week to rework the same "piece from hell" that I can't seem to get right. In a case like that, I end up walking away from it for a week anyway and nailing it by the second day back. The change of pace running your own business is a healthy side effect. The time away for the music will only make it better.

The only serious disadvantage to being out on your own is the eternal question: where will my next project come from? There is uncertainty in this business. A lot, as a matter of fact, for the independent contractor. One day you'll have several contracts lined up, your production schedule overflowing for the next couple of months, then suddenly, you'll be scratching your head wondering where the next check is going to come from. Everyone has experienced it at some point in their careers; it's an inevitability. Make sure you plan accordingly and budget your income for any dry spells.

There are other ways around the empty bank account syndrome. Look for on-going contracts, i.e., open-ended agreements that carry with them several yearly projects. Always consider negotiating royalty agreements where payments are made on a quarterly basis, spreading out your receivables to compensate during downtime. At first, consider composing as a side job and relying on a full-time job for living expenses. The extra income can be put in the bank to support yourself when you make the big break. Stay one step ahead and you'll be fine.

3.4 Audio Demo Reel

Unless you are an established game music composer or sound designer in the industry, chances are, you will need a professional representation of your audio skills to get your name out there and to win the job. Your previous work or current audio samples can be neatly packaged into a *demo reel* and sent directly to the powers that be — giving them a chance to listen to your breathtaking work.

Demos come in all shapes and sizes and everyone seems to have their own philosophy as to what makes them effective. However, in all of those varied opinions, no one will argue the need for one. They are truly valuable tools in the quest for the perfect audio for a project. After talking with several game and multimedia producers, developers, and other sound artists, many points seemed to continually stand out. Consider the mystery revealed.

3.4.1 Putting Your Demo Together; The First Step

The highest priority when considering your demo is quality. Without a doubt, the first thing a producer will notice is how it *sounds*. Cut corners where you have to. Trim out the fancy labeling, stationary, packaging, and the full-color brochures, but never, ever, skimp when it comes to the caliber of your sound. Use high-grade instrumentation, studio equipment, and recording medium. Think quality all the way down the line. Do what you have to; just make your audio sound great. Remember, if it doesn't sound "professional" in a demo that you've had months to work on, how will they believe that you'll sound good when dealing with a rushed, two-week project deadline?

Your mix should contain that pro quality on a variety of playback systems. There is no way of telling what system your demo will be listened to on. If you are extremely lucky, their audio department will play it on studio equipment similar to yours, but the majority of the time, it will be listened to either in the car or on a PC. If you have ensured, through a careful mix-down process, that your music sounds equally good on your studio monitors as it does on your Walk-man, then you've covered all of the bases. Before I am completely satisfied with a final mix, I will critically listen in my car, on my home stereo, on my Walkman, and on my child's boom box. It passes the test only after then.

3.4.2 Demo Content

There are very few rules I actually subscribe to, but this is one.

Put your best work in the first two minutes. Always.

Media buyers are busy people and usually wade through piles and piles of demo reels. Chances are they won't have the time to listen past the first couple of tracks. Always lead with your strongest piece and style. A great song that takes too long to get to the point has no place here. Feature your personal flavor. Show your originality, versatility, and compositional and sound design skills.

Ensure each track has impact and gives a continued strong impression. If you lead with shorter pieces, be sure to include longer tracks to show consistency and to let them know you can hold a listener's attention throughout. If one style is your specialty, that is certainly OK, but keep in mind that it may also limit your clients. Show plenty of versatility on your reel.

Here is some advice gleaned through "pet peeves" producers have willingly shared:

1. Do not repeat works to make your reel longer.
2. Do not place work in chronological order from the beginning of your efforts. They urge you to get right to the point and show what you can do with little wasted time.

3.4.3 How Long is Yours?

Did you know that 40% of media buyers only spend between two and five minutes listening to a demo? Another 40% only spend six to 10 minutes. The average preferred length of a reel is only seven minutes. That is not much time to present all the work you've done over the years, but it is more than enough to interest a producer. By leaving them wanting more, it builds interest, and gives you another chance to present more music and have your name in front of a prospective client one more time. Keep the length of your demo in check. An hour of music is probably a bit much.

3.4.4 Demo Chic — Types of Demos

There are as many ways to present your work as there are composers and sound designers. Your creativity can be let loose to make your creations stand out. There are no hard and fast rules; again, just make it sound great.

I've heard demos which use music, sound effects, and narration — like a radio commercial — to present an audio product. Most producers I spoke with, however, agreed that it distracted them from getting to hear the music or effects and the quality of the tracks. They prefer to hear music either presented as a montage or as numerous, short (1:00 to 1:30) selections in rapid succession. Five full-length pieces of various styles are also acceptable.

The demo montage makes the strongest impact. Five to seven minutes worth of music, fading from one selection to the next, blended together to almost sound like one song of different styles will definitely keep them listening. Include only the best sections of your work, taking them on a musical expedition full of surprising twists and turns. It's unbeatable. I normally include two montages; one with a harder edge, full of intensity, and a softer, more emotional montage. Because the montage does not show your musical thought process or prove you can hold a listener's attention with a single song idea, I also include a few longer tracks, i.e., songs done in their entirety, just in case they are curious and wish to put me to that test.

Minute to minute-and-a-half selections are another sure fire way of presenting your pieces. With only seven minutes on stage, you have to make it fast and this is a great way to show off your musical dexterity. The one thing I've noticed when listening to these types of demos is my urge to hear more! And because I can't immediately hear more of a track, I end up playing the whole tape/CD over again! It's a trick that has been used in pop music for many years. By keeping a song short, it is requested again and again in order to satisfy the hungry radio listener, invariably making it the number one requested song of the week. Chart-toppers are usually just good songs marketed wisely. If your demo is of this style, be sure to include a few longer pieces too.

A demo with five complete selections of music also works well. Pick the current popular game music styles such as:

- alternative/rock jam,
- orchestral,
- ambient,
- sports, and
- playful/quirky.

A spread like this will cover the bases nicely. Make sure each selection is 100% perfect — something you would be proud to put your name on. This is no place for half finished pieces or excuses. They should all be polished and ready.

A sound effects demo can equally stand out. I don't recommend just playing a sound effect, then playing another. It's boring and shows a lack of imagination. Remember, you want to impress the producer and make it impossible for them to look anywhere else.

If you choose to put sound effects tracks on your tape or CD, may I suggest creating a "scene." Forge an action-packed audio journey using your original effects and Foley sounds to create the excitement. It doesn't have to be long or totally outrageous, it only needs to favorably show your sound design and production skills. Producers are most concerned that you have the knowledge and ability to do good sound effects before they hire you. Check out the companion CD for some audio examples from myself and others in the biz. You'll see what I mean.

Another way to present your sound design achievements could be on video tape or as a computer movie file (.avi, .mpg, .mov, and so on). If you've done audio for any multimedia presentations or game intro sequences, for example, these would be a great stage to show your efforts. Nothing quite has the force as project-specific sounds created for moving picture.

Narrations are another breed. If you want to advertise your ability to record superb voice-overs, consider adding a track of narration — on its own or between audio tracks. I don't recommend sticking a microphone in front of your face and talking about whatever comes to mind. Experienced vocal talent, and perhaps even yourself, should perform from a well-crafted script. You can talk about the music and sound effects included on your demo either adding an intimate touch or raising the excitement level. Or, you can include examples of a previous narrative project. Make sure you've added some subtle sound effects or musical bed behind the speaker to give it continuity and keep it interesting.

3.4.5 The Presentation

Demo reels are very personal things — a part of ourselves and a part of our professional image. We want to look qualified but stand out at the same time and draw attention. From the look of the packaging to the impact of the tracks, it all fuses together to convince our prospects we are the best person for the job. First impressions can go a long way.

Think ahead of time about the impression you are trying to make and then make it a good one. Because this is not retail sales, graphics and expensive packaging are not mandatory. Make the demo sound fantastic and look pro. From the moment the package arrives on a producer's desk, you are making an impression. Bright packaging will certainly get you noticed but then again, it may backfire. While musicians are expected to be a little outlandish, a company seeking outside media will more than likely be playing conservatively.

Decide what market you are trying to make it in and customize the tracks on your demo reel appropriately. I try to decipher what sort of music or sound effects a client may be looking for, then I search my existing material for something similar. A producer looking for music to a game marketed to the eight- to twelve-year-old girl is probably not interested in hearing heavy metal, and I don't send it. A custom demo reel for each prospect can help you zero in on their target.

Include your contact information on everything — from the demo to all of the other envelope stuffers. Materials get separated and you'd hate for someone to discover the perfect piece of music for their project without any idea who sent it. Affix your copyright information to the tape or CD also. Other items to consider including in a demo package:

- A cue sheet. Name each track and explain what they are listening to as well as whether the piece has appeared in a previous body of work, what it was used for, and any production notes used to explain your motivation for composing the piece.

- A resume of any past work.

- Promotional materials, brochures, and press clippings.

- Business card.

3.4.6 What Format is Best?

CDs are definitely at the top of the demo reel heap. Whether you burn them individually on your CD writer or have your demo duplicated professionally, they proclaim your musical mastery. They have the best sound quality plus allow a listener to quickly scan through material — saving them valuable time. The disadvantage to you, of course, is they might use that feature and miss the best parts of your music. Another potential problem, they may not have a CD player in their car. I actually want them to listen in their car so I have a captive audience with nothing to distract them. Besides, music just sounds better when the scenery is moving. I will always ask what type of demo they prefer to hopefully alleviate this problem. For the do-it-yourself-ers, there are several CD labeler kits out there that are better looking than a smeared Sharpie pen any day.

Cassette tapes are a very close second. They are equally as convenient as CDs and most people have several players plus the one in the car. Because cassettes are not as easy to skip tracks on, they tend to make people listen longer. This is a great argument for putting your best work up front. Always use quality tape and be sure to label it appropriately with your contact information. When I send a tape, it is normally a 15-minute cassette which allows me to put a seven minute montage on Side A and two complete tracks on Side B. As part of the image thing, I use labels I can run through my printer instead of anything handwritten.

MP3 is slowly sneaking up on the competition. This format still has a few kinks to work out and until MP3 players are as common as Walkmans, it just isn't quite there. It does, however, work very well as a downloadable file from a website. Its file size and good sound quality are an excellent way to strike as the prospective client is browsing your wares. They must be interested or they wouldn't be there, right? This could provide immediate feedback and possibly close the sale for you. This format would also work well if a client asks you to send a demo as an email attachment. You are already making points by giving them what they want.

Sound files — such as .wav or .aiff files — are also generally accepted either as an email attachment or a download from a website. They are quick and allow a prospect to hear your music almost immediately. You will have to find a happy medium, though. The higher the sample rate and the better the sound quality, the larger your file size and longer download times. You must choose wisely. I use these for sound effect "scenes" and music only if requested.

TOOLS OF THE TRADE

Tim Rideout (aka Unkhakook), Independent Composer/Sound Designer, FibiiSonic Studios, Montreal, Canada

This 30-year-old Maritime fisherboy turned composer came to Montreal in 1988 to study music at Montreal's McGill University. Upon completion of his Bachelor of Music degree, he travelled the world over, playing drums and percussion from the Yucatan Peninsula to Alaska, Paris, and the American Southwest. After establishing Montreal as "home for now," the native Frederictonian went on to record albums with Sudbury's Brasse Camarade, Montreal's Chiwawa, Larry Riley, and has recently won a New Mexico Music Award with The Gagan Bros Band. He has recently completed his debut solo album "Reaching for the KAM," an audition for flamenco artist Ottmar Liebert, orchestration for Eyal Bitton's original musical "Freedom," the score for a theatre adaptation of Kathy Reich's new book "Death du Jour," and music for three plays by Geordie Theatre.

Tim's current projects include the music for the new fall show "RDI Junior" on Le Réseau des Informations; music for the CBC Television's "MC: Le Magazine Culturel"; several film scores, including works by Martin Lemieux and Silence! On Tourne; digital editing and mastering for Québec artists Jean-Francois Tremblay, Ila Potvin, and John McGale; performing drums and percussion for the new Larry Riley release; as well as diverse forays into the world of multimedia and the Internet (including writing for Ubisoft-owned "Beatz 4 Geekz" and a CD-ROM and internet video for Chateauguay folk artist Glenna McConnell). Tim's wide range of musical styles varies from the Internet's MP3 underbelly of urban D+B and electronica to classical, ambient, jazz, latin, and folk. Tim also shares his own brand of prose on game audio subjects at Beatz 4 Geekz.

Computer: AMD 800 processor, 32 GB on 3 hard drives, ATI All-in-Wonder video capture card, 19" Viewsonic monitor, Sound Blaster Live!, Yamaha 6416 CDR, MOTU 2408mkII

Software: Cubase VST, ACID, Sonic Foundry Sound Forge, Gigasampler, Probe, Rubberduck, ReBirth, Tassman, Plus many other nifty smaller proggies & plug-ins

Multi-track: MOTU 2408mkII & SB Live! thru Cubase VST or ACID onto Quantum (IDE) or Seagate (SCSI) hard drives

Board & monitoring: Input: Mackie 1202 into the MOTU. Mix: all internal DSP. Monitors: JBL, Laser Phase, RFT and 2 different pairs of headphones

Mixdown deck: Direct to Red Book Audio via Yamaha 6416 burner

Outboard gear: Ensoniq ASRX-Pro sampler with 62 MB memory, Roland R-5, Roland MIDI keyboard controller, Technics turntable, AKG and SHURE microphones, and "11 awesomely crappy VEGA pre-amps I found in a back alley."

Instruments: Ludwig Vistalite drumset, Pearl Masters Birch drumset, hand percussion, including djembes, darbuka, Taos drum, insecticide drum, talking drum, $40 trombone from Texan fleamarket, voice

Sound libraries: XX Large, LA Riot, Transfusion, Distorted Reality, Global Instruments, etc.

3.4.7 Delivery

So, now you've created a demo reel to be proud of. Staring adoringly at it on your desk, though, won't get you very far. You have to get it to your prospect and in one piece. The best way is to hand deliver it and perhaps introduce yourself to some key players at the same time. Sadly, most of us can't afford a road trip every time a request comes in so we have to rely on someone else to make the delivery for us. Here are a few general tips to make it less painful:

- Always ship your tape or CD in its original protective case and use padded envelopes or specialty shipping boxes. Too many demos have arrived smashed and unplayable. The media buyer probably won't have the time to call you to request another and instead will listen to the ones they've received from other potential composers.

- Don't waste your money sending your demo UPS, FedEx, certified, or anything more expensive than first class mail unless specifically asked to do so. While you may feel urgency to send out your reel, believe me, there is none on the receiving end. Save yourself the money.

- Never (and let me repeat this again because, believe it or not, it has been done before), never send your master or your only copy! Enough said.

3.4.8 Follow-ups

You've sent out your demo reel, now what? You start pestering the producer, right? Wrong. The last thing a busy producer wants to do is be hounded. If they got in contact with you for your reel, they know it is coming and they probably already have time set aside time in their schedules to review all submissions. And until that time, you probably won't hear a peep. It's taken months before I've gotten any word back sometimes. Just be patient. It is OK for you to check in with them after a couple weeks to ensure they received the package in one piece. This shows your professionalism and concern for delivering the product to them. But, do not badger them as to whether or not they have listened to it yet. Believe me, if they are interested, they will call. Occasionally, some will send a "no thank you" letter and even return your material. Don't be offended if your hard work comes back. They know sending demos can be costly and they are giving you the chance to reuse it again. I think it's a fine gesture.

I have developed a simple tracking method that I use religiously. I log the date and the company I sent the demo to. After 10 days, I proceed with my follow-up — either a phone call or email. I now know they received my package and I relax. If they call me, I check another box. If they hire me, I check another box. But I never, ever ask them if they've listened to it. I've only done it once and now it seems to be the running joke. Every time I call, he takes mine from the bottom of the pile and puts it right on the top. (I've even been there once to see him do this.) It is soon buried under other arriving packages and sits there until I call a month later and we repeat the process. One of these days he'll actually have the time to listen to it and I know I'll get the gig.

3.4.9 Some Final Demo Reel Thoughts

Never make apologies for your demo. If you feel the need to apologize for the lack of quality or the lack of substance, you are not ready to send it out. No one wants to hire someone who appears insecure. Insecurity means inexperienced which in turn, tells the producer he will be spending a lot of time holding your hand throughout the project. Be confident about what you can accomplish. They are more willing to educate you in the ways of the gaming industry if your self-assuredness shines through and they know you can indeed create fantastic sound.

Keep your demo reel up-to-date. As you add clients, you will have new music to add. If you don't like the customizing idea, be sure to at least produce a new demo every year. Keep it fresh and exciting. Send it to all of your previous clients and prospects.

Sending unsolicited demos has got to be one of the hotter topics in the industry and there still is no definitive answer. If you have the money and the time, you can beat the odds by shot-gunning demos to every game company and multimedia house on the planet. You are bound to pick up a job or two that way. But what good is it to send it to someone who didn't want it, didn't ask you for it, and lets it sit unopened in a box with hundreds of other packages? I would much rather have the extra momentum of having it requested from someone who is sincerely interested.

In my opinion,
your time and money are better spent being selective rather than chasing probability.

Like everything else in business and the game industry, timing is everything and sometimes it's *who* you know, not *what* you know. But by having a professional-looking and professional-sounding demo reel in your possession, you are equipping yourself for success and ready to beat the odds. Someday, who knows, with many successful titles under your belt and a name recognized by millions, you won't even need to look for work. It will find you. Imagine that!

3.5 Determining Your Costs

The final stop before we fling open our doors is to work out our fees for services rendered. However, we can't do that until we've determined what it costs for us to operate. It's an on-going process once you're working but starting out, you need a point of reference. Unfortunately, it's not as simple as finding out what everyone else is charging and doing the same. Until you've been around long enough to demand the higher fees, consider determining what you need to live on and what your business operating costs will be and go from there. Pad in a decent profit and you are in business.

How does the musician/sound designer compute his operating costs to make a competitive bid? It is not as simple as saying, "Hey, I want to make $500 an hour!" Initially, decide on your needs for the project, whether it is purely for recognition sake, a resume project, or just to cover the cost of overhead. We then calculate in many different factors to cover the expense of creation and consider each of them accordingly. For the final numbers, the fees will generally be lumped together. Separate fees are developed for cases when this is not feasible.

3.5.1 Types of Fees

First off, we need to determine what our cost is to do business. In our line of work, several different billable talents are present, which all have value. Until you resolve what the actual costs are, you may be losing money without ever knowing it. This is an important step.

Creative Fees

Creative fees are for the actual creation, composing, recording, and arranging of the music and sound effects. It is based on the time it takes to create a minute of music or a single sound effect and whether or not the work will be licensed for single use or will be bought-out. For most games, the buy-out option is standard, but sounds or music used on websites or in Java applications may be licensed for exclusive use for a period of time. The licensing option is often cheaper, the creator retains the ownership rights, and the sound can be used again after the contract period has expired.

This fee is the hardest to uncover and is generally based upon what the market will bear. It can be added to your total fee structure or can be substituted with your hourly wage. As your name grows, you will be able to charge more, your creative fee increasing exponentially. If you are John Williams, your creative fees might start at $250,000 and move up from there. Johnny Game Composer might be able to command $10,000. The value of your stock is entirely dependant on how valuable or in demand you are for a game project. If they just "gotta have" you, they are willing to pay more for the privilege.

Figure 3.3 Chance Thomas, shown here overlooking Half Dome in Yosemite, can command a higher price than most for an original game score.

The best part about this fee is that there are no costs involved, nothing to buy, and no expenses to cover! Consider it everything you've done in the past — the culmination of your hard work, studying, and music lessons all rolled up into one. It's the investment you've already made that determines your talent's worth. All of this will factor in the negotiations and how much you can make. Think about how it will impact your price and whether or not the product will be sold outright or only licensed for use within one particular application.

If all the rights to your music are sold,
the price should be at least 10 times more than licensed work.

Studio Fees

Renting an outside studio can be expensive, especially when a full orchestra or live band is involved. Studio fees cover that. It is also intended for the composer/sound designer to be able to cover the actual costs, maintenance, and general operation of their personal studio. Equipment payments, insurance, utilities, and general maintenance requirements are factored together to arrive at an hourly rate. Most sound creators, however, work out of their homes and are able to keep the cost down.

This fee is the actual costs to use an outside studio or what you would charge someone to use your project studio if you were to rent it out. It's easy to determine when dealing with another studio, but how would you figure out the value of your facility?

- Are you making payments on any equipment?
- Does your electricity bill go up noticeably whenever you power up?
- How much do you spend to have equipment serviced or repaired?
- Are you paying extra for another phone line, insurance, or internet access?

Add that up and divide by the number of hours in a standard work month (160) and you'll have a rough estimate of what you need to cover your costs. Figure in an appropriate profit margin of 25% to 30% and there you go. Check prices at other local studios for their hourly rates to see how you compare. The advantage you have is that your overhead is far lower than a professional recording studio and that savings can be passed on to your client.

Figure 3.4 This studio, owned by the San Diego-based band Swerve, occasionally rents their room for live sessions to game composers. Because I can't do 'live' drums at my home-based studio, this fee is written into the studio fee to cover the expense.

Here's an example of a typical cost analysis for a basic project studio set-up:

Monthly equipment payments:	$1000
Electricity:	$40
Maintenance:	$50
Phone:	$30
Internet:	$60
Insurance:	$30
Total:	$1210 per month

Divide this total by the number of billable hours per month. This is based on a standard 40-hour work week, although you can work 16 hours a day very easily.

$1210 divided by 160 hours =	$7.56 an hour
Or another way to think about it:	$60.48 per day

If you were working 40 hours a week, five days a week, making money on billable contracts, this would be what you need to charge just to cover your studio costs. Not everyone works that many hours on projects so it will vary, obviously, for less studio time. I just want you to start thinking along those lines.

As you determine the fees to charge for your studio usage, be aware of this. By working out of your house, using your own project studio, you can substantially effect the costs of studio time by keeping it lower than any professional studio. Because your overhead is lower, you can price your services competitively and pass along the savings to your clients. As you start out, an enticement to the smaller game developers will be your lower costs — their hope to get some pretty decent music for much lower than the big boys. A perfect place to start as you build your resume.

Consider a price range between $15–30 an hour for studio time — our example working both one week and two weeks out of the month. We want to play conservatively and make sure we recoup our costs. If you work one week out of the month on an audio contract starting out, you are doing pretty good. Add 30% as your profit margin and the figures change to $20–40 an hour.

Talent Fees

The actual performances by musicians and voice talent are included in talent fees. Some music composers may charge to play instruments on the tracks, others will include their part in the creative fee. Figures will vary based on the caliber of talent requested and outside talent, therefore virtuosos or famous players will increase this price accordingly.

As you build your local talent pool, establish what their per hour or per session fees are and do the appropriate math. It will vary by area, as major cities and music hubs demand higher rates than those in out-of-the-way places. A reasonable per session rate would be between $250–500 for mid-level performers in major cities where talent is in demand. Less prevalent talent can charge between $50–200 per session.

If you choose to charge for your own musicianship or voice talents, select an appropriate figure which will keep you competitive. Again, because you are the creative entity and a one-man-show, you can get away with smaller fees to get the business. Many times, I've been told I was hired because the big guys were just too expensive. Find your niche and price accordingly.

Media and Material Costs

Tapes, floppy discs, recordable CDs, shipping, and any other costs incurred while recording and delivering the final product are covered in this fee.

Any material you use in the creation process needs to be discoverd to figure your out of pocket expenses. Everything from your recording medium to the stamps you put on the envelope. If you had to buy it for use on the project, you need to know the cost and ensure it is covered in the fees. Leaving this out will chip away at your profit margin. A 100% markup is not uncommon for tape and CDs when figuring it into a bid package.

Hourly Wages

The hourly wage is a unique formula calculated using the sound creator's salary requirements based on the available billing hours for the year, the cost of healthcare and other benefits, vacations, holidays, and retirement. Because we don't work for a regular "company," this fee is our actual wage.

After vacations (you'd like to take), sick time, and the hours of administrative duties running your business are factored, roughly 1,000 hours per year are available to bill for your creative work. If you want to make $30,000 a year, you'll need to charge roughly $30 an hour. After taxes and company benefits such as healthcare, you'll charge 30% more or roughly $40 an hour to clear that same amount. This is a fairly close example of what you may find others charging. Insert your own figures to see what you should charge.

The Kicker

Also known as the "fudge factor" or "margin of error," this is an additional fee to cover any unexpected problems or minor adjustments to the project. Because the game development process is a continuously evolving one, additions are common place and this fee allows them to be included without having to renegotiate the entire project. Reactions to the kicker are varied, but time saved from having to renegotiate a contract is priceless and it is always more palatable to charge less rather than to charge more. If the project happens to expand far outside of the original borders, renegotiations will be necessary. 15% is generally a good figure to use.

3.5.2 Rate Calculation

An established composer can charge $1500 upward to $2000+ per finished minute of music. Established sound designers can charge between $150–200 per sound effect or hourly at a rate of $175–250 an hour. While they may be making more money than when they first started out, and deservedly so, their cost of doing business and overhead have also increased. As you gain experience, you'll find that more expensive recording gear will help push your music another step further. As you leave behind the $3000 analog mixing console for a $10,000 digital one, your payments increase to match. There really is no ceiling.

To calculate our rate, we need to have a good idea of the length of time it takes to do what we do. While you are putting together your demo reel, keep track of how long it takes to compose, record, and mixdown one minute of music. Average this out over the course of the production and you have a good idea. Experienced composers, working from scratch, can do two to three minutes a day. Those using loops and programs such as Sonic Foundry's ACID can do considerably more. When I started in radio and TV commercials, my general rule of thumb was that 30 seconds of music took four hours, start to finish. Today, I'm up to around one minute in a four hour period.

Sound designers need to do the same. While working on various original sound effects, keep track of the time it takes to do one sound effect. My working model is an average of two hours per original sound effect. That doesn't mean that it takes that long to get one sound recorded. After many attempts and ideas for a sound are created, the final incarnation of the effect will have taken roughly two hours. Sometimes sound effects happen immediately and you are done. Other times, it's like pulling teeth with two days passing before one materializes. We're looking for the *average* of the process to determine what our costs are.

Using our previous examples, we can finally conclude what our rates should be. I will be using the four hour per finished minute of music and two hours per sound effect models in the calculation with no outside musicians or voice talent.

Hourly wage and/or creative fee:	$30.00
Studio fee:	$7.56
Total cost:	$37.56 per hour

Then multiply by the number of hours to complete using your working model:

1 finished minute of music:	4 × $37.56 =	$150.24
1 sound effect:	2 × $37.56 =	$75.12

Figure in the 15% fudge factor:

1 minute of music:	$150.24 × 15% =	$172.78
1 sound effect:	$75.12 × 15% =	$86.39

Add in the material fee for the project:

1 minute of music:	$172.78 + $15 =	$187.78
1 sound effect:	$86.39 + $5 =	$91.39

In this example, recouping our costs and covering our minimum salary requirements, we've determined the cost of one finished minute of music to be $187.78. If we lowered our salary or were able to complete more music in less time, the price would go down further — what you make on a job being your bargaining room. First out, you will probably only be able to charge $250–300 per finished minute of music, which coincidentally is a 30% profit margin added to our cost. It's a fair price for someone with average musical and no game experience. And when you factor in the number of minutes in a game, say 45 minutes to an hour, that would be $11,250 to $15,000 for a project using your own instrumentation and no outside talent. Not a bad start considering this doesn't even include royalties, bonuses, and any soundtrack album releases which you might negotiate.

Sound design is another animal. If you are offering it as another service of your business, it takes your time away from doing other creative activities so your costs will be the same as above. If you are only doing sound design, your overhead will be much less; the only equipment needed being a computer, sound library, and remote recording gear at most. Looking at the previous example and offering this as another benefit of our business, our cost on a single sound effect is $91.39. Adding a 30% profit margin, $118.81 would be our fee.

Can you get that much in the games industry? Not at first. Sound-effects-only projects tend to be paid on a lower scale — the games market not tolerating the same pricing structure as music. The big boys can command around $15,000 per game project doing sound effects only but this is after a few years under their belts. New sound designers in the games business can expect a rate of $25 per hour or even $25 per sound effect. It varies greatly with the deals you work out.

I have yet to make the same amount on any project — sometimes it's at an hourly rate, other times it's per sound effect. When I started doing sound design several years ago, I started at $25 per sound effect. As my skills increased, I changed to $25 an hour. Later, it changed to $50 per sound effect, then $50 an hour. Nowadays, I charge either $75–100 per sound effect or $75–100 an hour, depending on the situation.

Producers have many different ways of choosing sound effects and some will have you tweak and redo sounds to death to get them just right. My train of thought is usually this: say a small project requires five specific sound effects. If I send 15 sound effects to a producer I have crafted using their specifications and he chooses to use five of those, I charge per sound effect. They trusted my talent, were happy with my judgment, and accepted my first pass. If that same producer would have chosen five sounds but had me rework them several times or wanted different sounds, I would charge by the hour. Obviously, we weren't communicating or I would have gotten them right the first time. They can be extremely picky and have the tendency to micro-manage every aspect of a project, and that's OK too. It's *their* vision for the production, I can respect that and will give them exactly what they want. But, because my time has value, for projects which work this way, an hourly rate is more appropriate — keeping me from losing money and wasting time.

3.6 Organization is Key

At this point, we should be fairly well organized. We know what we plan to do and how we plan to do it, either as in-house or as an independent contractor. We have examples of our work on a great sounding demo reel and know how to send them out. We've also figured out what we want to charge for our services and have the basis to judge our initial income potential. Time to reel in the business!

TOOLS OF THE TRADE

David Whittaker, Sound Designer, Electronic Arts

Computer: Mac: PowerMac 9600-300 PowerPC, 160 MB RAM, 4 GB HD, OS 8.6, CD, Zip, Floppy, Sony 200GS 17" monitor, APS 12×4×32 external CD-RW drive, Rorke removable HD chassis, with 1 × 9 GB drive (Fergie), 1 × 4 GB drive (Diana)
PC: P166, 32MB RAM, 2 gig HD

Software: ProTools v5, Waves ProTools Plug-ins v2.3 (various) – TDM & Audiosuite, Amp Farm

Mixing board and monitors: Mackie CR1604 mixer, Hafler 300 watt amplifier, Tannoy un-powered speakers

Mixdown deck: Panasonic SV-3700 DAT machine

TOOLS OF THE TRADE

Electronic Arts — Studio A

Computer: PowerMac 9600 with NewerTech G3 card, Gefen ADB/Monitor extenders, Rorke Data hard drive receivers and carriers, Bit 3 PCI expansion chassis, DigiDesign d24 Mix DSP cards, Proxima LCD projector, MicroPerf screen

Multi-track: DigiDesign ProTools 5

Plug-ins: Gallery's Turbo Morph, Waves, WaveMechanics — UltraTools T.C. Electronics-MasterX, EQ Sat., etc.

Mixing board and monitors: SSL Avant 96 Channel Digital Console, Genelec 1038, Genelec 1032 speakers, Genelec 1094 subs, Hafler Power Amp, and AuraTone speakers

Outboard gear: Aphex Dominator, Aphex Compellor, Aphex Expressor, T.C. Electronics Finalizer Plus, Eventide H 3500, Lexicon MPX-1, Lexicon LXP-15, DigiTech Effects, Sony PCM 800, MOTU Digital Timepiece, Dolby SDU4/SEU4

Mixdown decks: Sony 7030 DAT, Panasonic 4100 DAT

Electronic Arts — Mixdown Room 2

Computer: PowerMac 9600 that has been upgraded with a NewerTech G3/400 processor card and 256 MB of RAM, Viewsonic P810 21" Monitor, Apple 15" LCD Flat Screen Studio Monitor, Rorke removable hard drives, Gefen Systems Extendit Monitor and Keyboard extenders, Transoft FibreNet Fibre Channel network connected to 360 GB of storage containing our SFX library

Multi-track: ProTools 5.0.1

Plug-ins: ChannelStrip, SpectraFooTDM, A3D Pro 1.0, Amp Farm, Broadband Noise Reduction-AS, Broadband Noise Reduction-TDM, D-FX Chorus, D-FX D-Verb, D-FX Flanger, D-FX Multi-Tap Delay, D-FX Ping-Pong Delay, D-Verb, D-Verb-A/S, DirectConnect, DPP-1, Dynamics, Dynamics II, EQ, EQ II, Focusrite d2, Focusrite d3, Game Mode, Hum Removal, Invert/Duplicate, LoFi, Mod Delay, Normalize/Gain Change, PitchBlender 1.0.6, PitchDoctor 2.5.9, Procrastinator, PurePitch 2.5.9, RectiFi, SciFi, Speed 1.0, Surround Decoder, Surround Encoder, TC|Chorus 3.0, TC|EQsat 3.0, TC|MasterX 1.5, TC|MegaReverb 3.0, TC|REVERB, Time Comp-Exp/Pitch Shift, TimeAdjuster TimeBlender 1.0.6, VariFi, C1 2.8.1, DeEsser 2.8.1, L1 2.8.1, MaxxBass 2.8.1, MetaFlanger 2.8.1, MondoMod 2.8.1, PAZ 2.8.1, Q10 2.8.1, S1 2.8.1, SuperTap 2.8.1, TrueVerb 2.8.1, UltraPitch 2.8.1

Mixing board and monitors: Mackie 32-8 Mixer; Front speakers: 3 Genelec 1037B, Rear speakers: 2 Genelec 1032B

Outboard gear: Digitech TSR-24 Effects Processor, Lexicon MPX 1 Effects Processor, Aphex Dominator II Model 720, Aphex Compellor Model 320A, Aphex Expressor, Drawmer DL241, Symetrix SX201 EQ/Preamp, Tech 21 SansAmp, Ensoniq DP/4, Behringer Denoiser, Peavey TGRaxx Guitar Preamp

Mixdown decks: Panasonic SV-4100 DAT recorder

Keyboards: Kurzweil K2000RS, Kurzweil K2000S Keyboard, Korg Wavestation SR, Korg 01/Wfd Keyboard

Additional hardware: Bit3 13-slot PCI expansion chassis, four Digidesign DSP Farms and one Mix Farm, two Digidesign 888/24 interfaces, Digidesign Universal Slave Driver, Doremi V1 disk-based video deck, Opcode Studio 4 MIDI Interface, Dolby SEU4 and SDU4 Surround Encoder/Decoder

Additional software: BIAS Peak TDM 2.10 plus various custom audio tools written in-house

Electronic Arts — Remote Recording Gear

THE "CUBE": Sony PCM 800 8-track digital recorder, Soundcraft Spirit Pro Tracker 8 Channel Mixer, Symetrix 488 Dyna-squeeze 8-channel limiter, Custom Patchbay by Signal Transport

Other recorders: Two HHB PDR 1000 Porta Dat (one w/TCP 1000 timecode processor), AIWA HHB 1 Pro DAT Recorder, Sony TCD D-100 DAT Recorder (w/modified mic pre-amp), Sony TCD D-7 DAT Recorder

Microphones: Sennheiser MKH60 Shotgun condenser, Sennheiser MKH40 Cardioids condenser, Sennheiser MKH30 Figure8 condenser, Sennheiser MKE-PP4 Stereo condenser, Sennheiser MD-421 Dynamic (2), Earthworks SR77 Matched pair cardioid condensers, Earthworks TC30K Matched pair omni condensers, Sony ECM-55 Lavalier condenser (2), AKG 460 condenser (2), AKG 414B-ULS condenser (2), AKG C391B condenser, AUDIX ST-2 stereo condenser, Beyer Dynamic MCE 86N Shotgun condenser, Crown SASS-P MKII Stereo PZM microphone (2), Shure SM57 Dynamic (2), DSM S6 dimensional stereo microphone

Accessories: Batteries by Eco Charge, bags and straps by Porta Brace

CHAPTER 4
Finding and Getting the Jobs

It's official. You are ready to tackle some challenges and make some money. Unlock the front door, put out your "open for business" shingle, turn on the lights, and prepare yourself for the onslaught of customers who have been patiently waiting for this moment. The phone starts ringing off the hook. Life is good. Not! Unfortunately, you're going to have to be a bit more proactive than that and get a little dirt under your fingernails first.

4.1 Marketing

Drumming up business and getting the customers through your doors with wads of cash in hand will take some considerable effort. For most of us, playing the role of marketing director and salesman is as unnatural as brushing your teeth with your other hand. The best part, though, is after a bit of practice and patience, it can be yet another act we do without even being cognizant of it. After awhile, you'll be throwing a dash of "marketing" in with everything you do. It's not difficult really. Don't let the fact that there are college degrees in marketing, huge companies which do nothing but marketing, and individuals who spend their every waking hour as marketing experts intimidate you one bit. We can use some of their tricks and hard won secrets to our advantage.

4.1.1 Tell Everyone

The very first thing you need take care of is to tell everyone what you do. I mean *everyone*! Don't be shy and play coy little games. Don't consider it bragging or showing off, and while it might feel like it, it's actually "marketing." Tell your mother, father, brothers, sisters, grandparents, uncles, aunts, cousins, friends, coworkers, and neighbors as a start and see what happens. Whether you know it now or not, somewhere within that small group, somebody knows someone who has a friend whose brother's cousin's girlfriend went to school with a guy who is a programmer at a game company.

That guy can be your foot in the door! But, you'll never meet him unless everyone knows you are trying to do audio for video games — so tell everyone! I'm not kidding about the kind of connections you can make by being open about your new endeavor. Let me share a couple of my marketing success stories:

Tale #1

After about six months into my business venture, I decided to take a couple weeks off and serve my country as I do from time to time as a military reservist. I received a phone call from an individual who was gathering information about doing the same. During the course of our conversation, I asked him what he did for a living.

"Oh, I'm the President of a software development company here in town."

"No kidding!" I said, "Do you ever do any games?"

"Yeah, we do contract work for other game companies, mostly programming, but we are gearing up for one of our own game projects."

"Sounds like fun. Do you foresee needing any music for your game?" I queried.

"As a matter of fact, we just let our sound guy go; he just wasn't working out."

"What a shame. Well, you know, I do music. I just happen to run a music production company, maybe we ought to get together."

As it turned out, we lived two blocks from each other and met the next day at my studio. After playing some cuts from my demo reel, I was shaking hands with the President and Vice President of this company, signing on for their first game. Not bad considering that all I did was tell him what I do. It turned out to be my first game project and lead the way to many more.

Tale #2

One evening I received a phone call at the house. My wife handed over the telephone and said it was someone named Mike Post. I chuckled and proceeded to give my friend a hard time. He always calls up as someone "famous" and I smiled at his originality at this one. Well, it turned out it wasn't the friend that I thought and the voice was Mike Post after all! Surprise, surprise. He'd always been sort of a TV theme composer idol of mine, my favorites being *Quantum Leap*, *Magnum PI*, and the *A Team*. It was quite a treat. After my adrenaline rush returned to a more controllable level, I asked him what prompted the call. After all, it isn't every day I get phone calls out of the blue from real life famous people.

The story: a guy I'd met at the local airport asked me to send a demo. He really enjoyed music, shared the passion, and wanted to hear what I was up to. In his garage at home, he was listening to my tape when a friend walked in. Liking what he heard, he borrowed the tape to let another friend of his give a listen. He mailed it to a golfing buddy of his who "plays music in Hollywood." Turns out this golfing buddy was Mike Post! So now, Mike was telling me that he never listens to demos sent to him because if he never hears them, he can't be sued for stealing ideas (or something similar). But at his friend's insistence, he listened to mine and was calling to talk about my future. (This story did not land me a game audio job per se, but shows what can happen when you tell everyone what you do!) Get the word out and see what happens.

GAME COMPOSERS AT WORK

Darryl Duncan of GameBeat, Inc.

Describe your thought process for scoring.   "This is actually one of the exciting parts of scoring for a video game. Unfortunately, there is often no playable game demo available to us. We usually only get storyboards or graphic files to work with. In John Madden, we received pencil-sketched storyboards, which was great. On the recent Ultima Online: Third Dawn game, we were supplied with 3D renderings of several of the new creatures in the game. Fortunately, this was all we needed to put ourselves in the mindset to create the intense period music for this game. We printed out color versions of the creatures and taped them to the walls of the studio. This, although simple, helped us get into the mood of the music. Tarrance, one of our composers, actually went as far as to cut out each of the creatures and glue them to cardboard backs so that they could stand and he placed them all around his workstation. It looked like a little war was going on right at his desk! But the music reflected this level of immersion and Origin loved what we supplied. So although we laughed at the time, those things were necessary to place us in the mood."

How does the scoring process usually start for you?   "For me, the scoring process usually starts with my little digital hand-held tape recorder I call my 'Lick Saver.' Most of my inspiration comes when I am nowhere near my gear, so I need to be prepared to capture a melody or rhythm that suddenly pops into my head. I get my musical ideas different from most I am told. When I write a piece of music, I hear the entire piece in my head fully orchestrated. I hear the melody, strings, drums, guitar — I hear it all before it ever even exists. So nine times out of ten, it is just a matter of me translating what is in my head. It's pretty weird. Most people might go around humming their favorite tune they just heard on the radio; this is how I hum things that I didn't even create yet. For me, the piece is pretty much 98% composed before I even touch the keyboard."

When do you find that you are most creative? What times are set aside for recording/composing?   "I am definitely most creative in my sleep or just before I fall asleep. Why? I don't know, but it seems that most of my inspiration comes when my mind is most relaxed and that always seems to be right before I drift to sleep. On my bedside are my digital recorder, a pen, and a pad. So ideas can hit me at anytime, and I know that if I don't try to capture them right away, they could be gone forever. Then when I get to the studio, I'm able to hash out those ideas pretty quickly and sometimes even be mixing in a few hours."

Are there any particular secrets to your creativity?   "No, no real secrets other than when I am creating with just my 'Lick Saver' or humming something when I'm driving. If I hear anything else musical, it completely disrupts my flow. Strangely, I don't listen to music, the radio, or buy records. It is important to me not to be influenced by anything or anyone, not even subconsciously. So I like to keep talk radio on in the car when I drive."

Do you have any advice for current and future game composers/sound designers? "I often get demos and inquiries from aspiring game music composers and the mistake that most of them make is that they prepare their demo primarily in the style of music they personally like only. I tell them to attract attention in this industry, you need to show extreme versatility in the styles of music you create. I don't know too many developers/publishers that only develop one type of game. One must learn to be proficient and convincing even in styles that they may not like. It is this versatility that will catch the ears of the decision-makers.

Also, and as with every industry, be persistent and do not give up even after multiple rejections. Just continue to perfect your skill and you will ultimately get the attention you are after. Lastly, and I tell this to all aspiring composers, knowing how to compose good game music is one thing, but if you want to truly step into this with the potential for a six-figure salary, learn programming also. It will greatly increase your worth in this industry and quadruple the amount of opportunities available to you."

4.1.2 Look Professional

While we are out there beating the bushes, things are going to start happening fast and furious. Bid requests, information requests, demo requests, and our pricing structures are going to be sent out to prospective customers as fast as they hit your desk. What

Figure 4.1 GameBeat, Incorporated's eye-catching logo.

you send out and how it looks is going to have a big impact on whether you get called for the next step. I am a firm believer in first impressions. What you put inside that envelope can make all the difference. If you handwrite a bid on a scrap piece of paper, you're telling them you are an amateur, that your music product will probably be amateur as well, and that you don't care about little details. On the other hand, if you send an information packet in an expensive binder with high gloss paper, color laser printing, and gilded edging, you're telling them you are way out of their league and they probably couldn't afford you. You want to give an impression that you can do the job within their budget in a professional, reliable manner.

The key is to look professional in every respect. You don't need to spend a lot of money and go overboard. You just want to make your prospective clients feel confident you have your act together, know what you are doing, and won't waste their time or money.

Design a Cool Logo

Work a logo up yourself or find a graphic artist or student if you don't have the ability. I'm sure a graphic arts student would love a "real world" project to put in their portfolio and would work cheap. The idea is to have something eye-catching and something professional. Put it on your web site, business cards, stationery, and envelopes. Put it on your demo reel and make bumper stickers, hats, and T-shirts if you like. Have a recognizable symbol that everyone will associate with you and your quality work. Later, we'll talk about negotiating deals where your logo can appear on the game box cover and splash screen during the opening sequence of a game. You'll definitely need something to show the world by then.

Figure 4.2 Keith Arem's company, PCB Productions, and its simple, yet effective logo.

TOOLS OF THE TRADE

Keith Arem, Composer/Sound Designer, PCB Productions

Nothing speaks louder on a resume than a infinite list of game projects. Keith has either composed, created sound effects and voice-overs, or acted as audio director on a list over a mile long. Guess this guy is doing something right!

Tony Hawk Pro Skater 2, 2X, and 3; Ridge Racer 64; Spiderman 2; X-Men 2; X-Files On-line; Alien vs. Predator; Battle Realms; Shaun Palmer Pro Boarder; Disney's Emperor's New Groove; Legion: The Legend of Excalibur; Pearl Harbor; Draconus; Thrill Kill; Rock 'em Sock 'em Robots Arena; Metal Fatigue; Disney's Lion King; Oni; Exhibition of Speed; Max Steel; Nox; Land Before Time; Wizards and Warriors; Tyco R/C: Assault with a Battery; Hercules 64; Thousand Arms (U.S.); Blues Brothers 2000; Wu-tang Clan: Shaolin Style; Recoil; Sportscar Supreme GT; Sportscar GT; Lands of Lore III: Guardians of Destiny; Command & Conquer: Red Alert Annihilation; Toonstruck; Subspace; Tail Concerto (U.S.); Demolition Man; Rhapsody (U.S.); Persona 2 (U.S.); Creature Shock; Golden Nugget N64; Spot Goes to Hollywood; Disney's Jungle Book; Zone Raiders; Agile Warrior; Neohunter;

Forced Alliance; Grand Slam 97; Saber Ace; Golden Nugget Casino; Cliffhanger; Battletech; and on and on and on…

Computer: PowerMac G4, 500 MHz, 256 MB RAM; PowerMac G3, 400 MHz, 256 MB RAM.
PCs: 500 MHz, 256 MB RAM; Windows NT 4.0 PC, 450 MHz, 256 MB RAM, Win 98, etc.

Software: Cubase Audio VST/24 4.0, Sonic Foundry Sound Forge 5.0, Alchemy, ACID™, Vegas® Audio, etc.

Multi-track system: ProTools 5.1, TASCAM DA-88

Mixing Board/monitor system: Mackie D8B 56 channel Digital Mixing Console, Genelec 1031A Reference Monitors, 1092A Subwoofer, Audix 3A Reference Monitors, Genelec 1030A (rears)

Mixdown deck: Panasonic 4100 DAT, Plextor 8/20 CD-R

Outboard gear: Eventide DSP4000, Roland Vocoder SVC-350, DBX 165A, DBX 166, Digitech GSP2101, Millenia HV-3B Pre-Amp, Dolby DP 569 5.1 Encoder, etc.

Keyboards, samplers, and sound modules: Emu E4XT Ultra, Roland JV2080, Roland JV1080, Kurzweil K2000, Roland JD800, Roland JP8000, Emu Proteus 2000, Roland Juno 106, Roland R8-M, etc.

Remote recording: TASCAM DA-P1, Sony PM-M1 (M2 MOD), Sennheiser 461, Sennheiser 421, DSM 6H

Development systems: N64, PSX, X-BOX, AGB

Business Supplies

Stationery, envelopes, mailing labels, business cards, and CD or cassette labels should all be acquired. You can have them designed by a print shop for fairly reasonable prices. If not, try spending a little time at your computer formatting various templates which include your logo and contact information. The only thing I don't recommend skimping on is business cards. Pay the $25–30 and have 500 cards printed. You'll be passing many of these out and they will be the first impression people get of your company. Cards with perforated edges and dot matrix printing convey a sense that this person won't be around for long.

Web Sites

Potential clients are out there waiting, but they may be a little shy. They have your card, but don't feel like getting into a long, drawn-out conversation to find out what they need to know. Instead, they may turn to your web site. Web sites are easy to set up and maintain and the minor server space cost per month makes them a great marketing tool. So, set one up and pack it full of information.

Make it look professional. This is another great place for that new logo of yours. Explain what you do, how you do it, previous projects, maybe a biography about how you got where you are, any press clippings, some downloadable music and sound effects samples, and contact information. Don't go overboard with the audio samples — just a few short pieces to build their interest and get them to request your demo reel. MP3 or Real Audio formats work well for small file sizes. Your reel will still sound the best, so ensure you have an email available for their orders.

Be sure to keep your web site updated. As you finish projects, get them on there. Be proud, and show prospects that others found you suitable for their projects and that they will too.

A note on embedded audio

Don't use embedded audio on your web site. If you use it within the context of a flash presentation, that's different and perfectly acceptable. The audio I'm talking about is the MIDI music or .wav/.aif files which play in the background while someone browses your site.

First off, not everyone has the plug-ins on their browser which play back the type of audio you embed. Secondly, even if they did, there is no guarantee of the quality which spits out the other end. I know, we do audio. We want people to hear it and why not have it on our web sites? I'd much rather have nothing than have something that could lock up someone's browser or just sound horrible. MIDI music is very prone to sounding like garbage. It sounds great on the computer it was composed on, but the various sound cards out there almost guarantee it won't sound the same on someone else's. Don't use embedded audio and save yourself some embarrassment and some business.

4.1.3 Industry Presence

If you plan on working in the video game industry for very long, you'll need to develop a presence. Some call it a "buzz" or "hype." Whatever you call it, it will build momentum toward your goal as a musician and will keep your name on everyone's lips. The day I got an email from one of the industry's top game composers asking me who I was and "how come I've never heard of you before?", I knew I was doing something right.

Tommy Tallarico has a solid industry presence. His unbridled excitement about video games has gotten his name on over 150 game titles, brought him a regular guest speaker gig at industry functions on all things audio, has gotten his face on weekly television as the host of "Electric Playground," and has him as a consultant to many companies including DTS. Practically everyone knows Tommy Tallarico. This skilled showman made it his quest to become recognized; to have a presence.

Another example of presence is George Sanger, aka The Fatman. He's done over a 100 games, but most people know him as the guy who runs around in glittery, "nudie" cowboy outfits. That's his 'shtick' and it works very well for him. He also acts as a consultant to many companies and goes one step further by awarding his "Fat Labs Certified" seal to game hardware which meets his demanding standards of audio excellence. Now that's presence.

There are many other lesser-known game composers and sound designers who have a presence, albeit at a lower, more subtle volume. Look through any computer music or recording magazine for their interviews. Look at advertisements with their endorsements. Look for their by-lines. They are everywhere,

Figure 4.3 The author's music production company logo.

carving out their particular niche in the industry. There are plenty more to fill. The idea is to have your name out there, seen by your peers and prospective clients. They will definitely think you are doing something right if you are getting all this exposure, even if you are the one creating it all. It's nice having someone recognize your name even if they can't remember why. It gets your foot another step inside that door.

4.1.4 Basic Marketing Tools

How you develop your presence is completely up to you. There are no rules to follow; creativity your winning bet. Nothing beats your music on a hit game though, followed up with a lot of industry press. You can ride the wave into several more games and keep the momentum. Most of us, though, aren't going to have the fortune of a blockbuster project first time out. It's going to take some creative magic of our own to turn on the hype machine. But there are some basic marketing tools to add to your regimen to help make things happen.

Direct Marketing

Build a list of developer and publisher addresses and points of contact. Addresses can be found on the backs of game boxes and from their web sites. Important connections are producers and creative directors, but at a minimum, have the human resources departments dialed in. Put together an information package — an introduction to you and your services — and start sending them out. Unless those in the industry know you exist, you are not going to get the gig. Tell them who you are, what you do, and how your services will make their lives easier.

Some say that sending out *anything* to a human resources department is a grand waste of time. I agree to a point, but I've gotten calls from companies who say they received my name from their HR office and want me to submit a bid. Most of them keep your information on file from six months to a year and forward it to producers when requested. Hey, you have to start somewhere.

Telephone Marketing

Pick up the phone and start calling around. Ask for the audio department or the person in the company in charge of buying outside content. The smaller the company, the better. Large companies tend to have roadblocks in place which can rarely be negotiated. The switchboard operators and receptionists are highly skilled at sensing salespeople and are usually under strict orders to stop them cold. If you run into this situation, explain that you are a game composer or sound designer

Figure 4.4 Tommy Tallarico Studios logo says it all. It capitalizes on his name recognition and his music services.

and you wanted to let them know of your availability. Knowing you're not an office supply guy with extra reams of paper or toner to unload helps break the ice. Unless you are the 20th composer to call that morning, you might get forwarded to a contact within the company. At worst, they'll patch you through to the dreaded Human Resources Department.

Another trick is to ask the name of the person who buys audio, say thank you, and call back a couple days later asking specifically for them. If you get through, great! If not, ask for voice mail and speak your introduction. You can also ask for the person's email and try an introduction that way. Don't be surprised if you don't hear from anyone right away, if at all. They may not need you for their current project, but might keep your name handy to bid on the next. Play the odds. Do this enough times and you'll succeed. Again, at worst, you've made your introductions, they know you exist, and all you have to worry about is following up every few months to keep your name fresh.

This method can be a little costly, especially if you end up making long distance calls. There is nothing written that says you have to call everyone the first week. Spread it out over several months — breaking up the cost into more manageable chunks.

Internet and E-mail Marketing (Pronounced "Spam")

This is by far the most bang for your buck and the easiest way to scope in on the people who make decisions. Case in point: For every 100 letters I mailed the old-fashioned way, I got roughly 10 responses. Seven were, "We'll keep your information on file" letters and three were requests for a demo. If I was lucky, I'd have one bid request out of that whole effort, but it was a lot of work for little reward mostly. Rarely did it lead to a job.

Then I tried emailing my introductions and the most astonishing thing happened. Out of 100 emails I sent, 25 responded. Twelve to 15 of those requested a demo. Three to five of those requested a bid submission or speculative demo for a project. And out of 100 emails sent out, I ended up getting at least one if not two jobs. It was the exact same letter I had snail-mailed, but my targeting strategy was much more focused. Ah, success!

This particular method is fairly time consuming, but indeed a gift from the gods. Start building your email address book with every contact you make. Visit developer web sites and dig around for the right person. Send them an introduction. Personalize it as much as possible. You could save a lot of time by adding everyone to the same "to:" line, but this will come across as impersonal when the recipients see they were just part of another mass email. Try sending to one person at a time (or using a program which does this), put their name at the top of your letter, and their company name somewhere in the text. Even if they are smart enough to see through your ploy, they will still appreciate the extra effort and perhaps you'll score a point. Make your letter succinct, to the point, and leave the impression you mean business. Always invite them to follow up, request a demo, or call just to say hi.

Print Advertisements

Print advertisements can include a classified ad, a corner spot in a company newsletter, or a full-blown page ad in a national publication. It's undoubtedly the most expensive part of a marketing plan and not something to take lightly. A well-designed ad, strategically placed, can build your name recognition and get you a project or two. It will tell prospects you must be doing well to afford such exposure and will make them curious. Obviously, you must be successful to pay for such an attractive ad.

On the other hand, if your ad doesn't look professional or is buried deep within pages of other ads, you might as well just walk over to the toilet, throw in your money, and flush. I've had a few composers tell me they tried print ads and all were disappointed with the results. They also only ran their ad once. To gain exposure through print advertisement, you must continually bombard your target audience using multiple shots across their bow. Try running an ad every other month, several places in the same magazine, or in multiple magazines in the same month. It will eventually bring some business in your door. Even those cheesy late night commercials on TV run more than once. You'll usually see the same one over and over for a couple of weeks before it sticks in your mind. The same principle can be applied to print.

I don't recommend television or radio ads. They cost serious cash and don't necessarily focus on the business you cater to. Unless you could buy some time on a closed circuit company broadcast, you are better off spending your money elsewhere. This type of broadcast media is ineffective for our purposes. I don't know of anyone who has ever used it.

Press Coverage

One medium I know everyone uses is the press. Nothing like having them do a little work for us for a change. Press coverage equals free advertising. You can issue a press release to your local newspapers and television stations highlighting a recent milestone or to give them ideas for a special interest piece — "Local composer signed to score Myst VIII," "Area music production house to offer sound design," "Local musician creates music for video games." For your local market, it will give you a much needed push to help establish yourself. And, if you plan it correctly, you can either saturate for some serious immediate coverage or draw it out over a period of time for continued, lower-key publicity.

Large city newspapers are very effective as is mention in a game development magazine or web site. It gives solid exposure within your immediate market and continues with our motto: *tell everyone what you do*. Small "news bites," mentions or quotes supporting related industry articles, and interviews are great ways to get your name to the point of recognition with your potential clientele. You can build alliances with journalists, giving them leads on interesting stories, and making yourself available as an expert when they need to verify facts. It's all part of the well-oiled marketing machine. Consider using it.

Write Relevant Industry Articles and Books

Are you technically astute and have a way with words? Like to write? Consider sharing your knowledge and expertise with the rest of the gaming

Figure 4.5 The Game Developers Conference takes place yearly in San Jose, California.

industry in the form of magazine or "webzine" articles or a book as another form of marketing. Your by-line is a powerful way to garnish some industry attention and start building a name for yourself. If you luck into a regular writing gig, you'll find folks start to look at you as an expert. It lends much credibility to your resume and keeps your name alive in a world where you are only as good as your last project.

Presence at Industry Events

It's a great idea to be seen at industry events and trade shows. Everyone will see how seriously you take the game industry and that you are very much a part of it. With a high concentration of the *actual people* who make games, chances are very good that you will make valuable contacts which will last for many years. It's an opportunity for everyone to put a face with a name and will make you stand out when they start thinking of audio for their next project. While your music and sound effects in a game is your #1 marketing tool, your personal attention and commitment in showing interest and being amongst your fellow game creationists at these functions runs a very close second. Get out there, press the flesh. Be seen.

Industry events worthy of your attendance:

Electronic Entertainment Expo (E3)	This yearly game industry extravaganza is the chance for game companies and publishers to show off their wares. Truly an experience.	www.e3expo.com	May
Game Developers Conference (GDC)	An industry insiders' event and gathering of game developers from around the world — showcasing the latest game development tools and hundreds of educational forums and discussion groups.	www.gdconf.com	March
Special Interest Group on Computer Graphics (SIGGRAPH)	Their annual international conference and exhibition focuses on computer graphics, animation, and other interactive techniques. A gathering of artists from around the globe. A very interesting look at how they do what they do.	www.siggraph.org	July

Word of Mouth

Another effective marketing tool is word of mouth. By amassing an army to spread the word on your behalf, you've affected a marketing machine which only gets bigger and more effective over time. Beginning efforts with your family and friends will stir up some interest. But, the best way to do this is through previous clients.

People and companies you've done business with in the past carry tremendous weight. If you've worked around the industry for awhile, your reputation will usually precede you no matter what you do to the contrary. Game developers talk. If you were hard to work with, overpriced, produced lousy music, or never delivered on time, that information will spread throughout your market faster than you could ever comprehend. You might as well pack up and move out. It is extremely important to work hard, be honest, deliver superior goods on time, and always go above and beyond what is asked of you. Always. If you do a good job at a fair price, people will remember. When producers get together, you never know when the subject of audio will come up. If I work with someone, I want them telling all their peers what a great job I did.

Use every meeting with potential clients as a chance to market yourself and your wares. Leave them with a positive impression and encourage them to pass on your name to others. Timing is often the key. If they can't use you now, maybe they know of someone who does or will remember you for later.

4.1.5 Other Resources for Marketing Success

There are many titles on bookstore shelves which cover the issues of marketing. None are geared specifically toward the game industry but they are relevant just the same. Business is business and products are products no matter what line of work you are in. The following books will help you get your audio "product" in the face of the games business:

Money Making Marketing: Finding the People Who Need What You're Selling and Making Sure They Buy It	Dr. Jeffery Lant
Guerrilla Marketing, Guerrilla Marketing Attack, Guerilla Marketing Weapons, Guerilla Marketing Excellence, and others	Jay Conrad Levinson
Finding Your Niche: Marketing Your Professional Services	Bart Brodsky and Janet Geis.
No More Cold Calls: the Complete Guide to Generating — and Closing — All the Prospects You Need to Become a Multimillionaire by Selling your Service	Dr. Jeffery Lant
Musicians Survival Manual — Essential Tips, Tricks, Tactics, Advice, and More to Help You Make Money in the Music Business	Jeffery P. Fischer
Cashtracks: How to Make Money Scoring Soundtracks and Jingles	Jeffery P. Fischer

4.2 Where to Look for Clients

If you were a game company, where would you be? That's the question you need to ask yourself when you set out to gather information on prospective clients. And, actually, it's not as hard as you might imagine! Game developers are a fairly visible lot if you poke your nose in the right places. They are all over the planet and every game needs someone to do the music and sound effects. The trick is matching your services to their needs. You need to establish "who" they are and "what" their needs are first.

4.2.1 Internet

The web is the ultimate source for information on computer games and the developers who make them. It is a veritable gold mine which can, literally, make you rich. Practically every game developer and game publisher has a presence on the web and it's a great place to start. You can either search for every game company yourself or use game development resource sites which have pages of game company listings, links to their web sites, and contact information. Many game developers also post job openings on their sites which can lead to solid contacts.

At the time of publication, the following web sites cater to game developers and either include job openings or game developer listings for further exploration. Many also serve as a general forum for development topics and the latest news.

Game Developer Web Sites

Gamasutra	www.gamasutra.com
Happy Puppy	www.happypuppy.com/biz
Game Development Search Engine	www.developer.dungeon-crawl.com
Black Sheep Journal	members.aol.com/blaksheepj/index.html
Music 4 Games	www.music4games.net/directory.html
Gamespot	www.gamespot.com
GameDev.Net	www.gamedev.net
GameSlice	www.gameslice.com
Games Link Central	www.geocities.com/SiliconValley/Park/2745/glc-select.html

4.2.2 Industry Magazines and Books

Hit your local newsstands for these monthly publications which cover a wide spectrum — from technical issues, to the big business side of things, to strategy and gameplay. Every one of these magazines is packed with game companies, either in the form of "help wanted" ads or Internet addresses. These will help define who the developers are and give you an idea of the type of games they produce, rounding out your research files. It is important to determine which companies license game engines, create graphics, or contract out programming services. These are specialized companies who, more than likely, won't require audio and thus you won't need to waste time with them. Concentrate your efforts on the companies who make the end product.

A Short List of Available Publications:

Technical

Game Developer Magazine	www.gdmag.com (free to industry professionals)
The Cursor	www.thecursor.com

Business

Games Business	www.gamesbusiness.com (free to industry professionals)

Gameplay/Hype

PC Gamer
Computer Games Magazine
Computer Gaming World
PC Games

Industry Source Books

Game Developers Marketplace — The Definitive Guide to Making It Big in the Interactive Game Industry	Ben Sawyer, Tor Berg, and Alex Dunne

4.2.3 Telephone Books

Don't overlook the obvious. If your market is a good-sized metropolis, the odds are decent that a game or software company is close by. Pick up the yellow pages or the business section of the white pages and look! Look under Computer Software Publishers and Developers, Computer Multimedia, Software, etc., for some leads, then pick up the phone. If they don't use audio in their work, perhaps they know of someone who does. Be sure to ask. Make every call count — letting people know your availability or intiating a lead to someone else. Get names, numbers, and email addresses of the decision makers, and follow-up with information packages and demos. A phone call may be all it takes to get the ball rolling.

4.2.4 Store Shelves

Take a trip to the local software retailer with pen and paper in hand. Pick up game boxes, look on the back, and find the names of the developers and publishers who are making them. It may seem painfully apparent, but it's a great way to add names to the list when starting from scratch. After awhile, you'll start to notice the trends and the leaders — a particular publisher who has their hands in many games and the ones who seem to dominate the market.

This is valuable information which will keep you up-to-date on the latest types of games out there and what types of music they might be looking for. An abundance of racing games equals high-energy techno or rock music. Medieval games use heavily orchestrated music. The trip to the store can be an important fact-finding tour. It's something you'll do on a regular basis even after you've been composing for a while to remain current on things.

Keep in mind, when browsing through the retail aisles, that it is usually the major game companies that can command shelf space. Retailers are only interested in moving product and aren't interested in having an obscure game take up space for the one or two individuals who might buy it. High volume games are the money makers. Take a look in several different retail outlets and smaller software and "game-only" stores for a broader offering.

4.2.5 Game Developer Headhunters

While hot in pursuit of clients or an in-house job, you might also consider contacting companies who have made a living out of filling vacancies at software and game development firms. These people are extremely connected to the business, earning wages by matching talent to the job, and usually having all the latest gossip about what might be happening inside the compnaies' walls. They normally cater to programming and graphic artist positions but may keep an eye out on your behalf if you ask nicely. They literally live and die by the effectiveness of their networks and are always anxious for any leads. I once offered a small upstart game company to a headhunter (I asked permission first, of course), mentioning they were looking for an artist. In turn, I was rewarded with several names and numbers of local game producers. They understood my needs and were able to share solid contacts. Because you are out there everyday looking for your prize, circulating some of that golden information with the right people could open some doors. Of course, always ask permission from the company before you unleash a headhunter on them and never share privileged information or articles covered by a non-disclosure agreement. You can find these companies after a brief Internet search or in a phone book under Employment Services or Recruitment.

4.2.6 Networking

Starting from day one, every person you come across has the potential to lead to a paying contract, whether they are a programmer, play tester, artist, producer, receptionist, or even the janitor. Other game composers and sound designers, although considered as competition also, can be part of your network and lead to some work as well. By cultivating continued friendly relationships you'll be privy to information on jobs and companies those on the "outside" do not have. Word of a game developer adding bodies could mean they are staffing a new project, hearing that a developer and a sound contractor are at odds, or knowing that an in-house composer is preparing to make a leap into film scoring can all put you in the perfect, opportune place. There is even the possibility for some subcontracting or overflow work being tossed your way from other composers. We all have to take vacations some time and are in a perfect spot to cover for our peers on short-term projects. Keep your eyes and ears open and make yourself available. The last place I ever expected to get a job from was my competition, but it's happened enough now that I'll believe anything.

Next Door Neighbors

It may seem like scraping the bottom of the barrel, but I'm guessing, unless you live far from civilization, that within a block of your humble domicile, you can find some audio work. There are so many jobs which deal with computers, software, and games out there that several of your neighbors might work in the industry or have close connections to those who do.

In my own little block of suburbia, I've

- scored and designed sound effects for one CD-ROM game,
- created sound effects for two web sites and music for one Flash presentation,
- edited music for several ice skating competitions,
- engineered the final mixdown on three CD projects,
- mastered and duplicated an album for a band from Mexico City, and
- recorded and edited narration for a massive multimedia presentation

— all through contact with just my neighbors! Imagine what I could accomplish if I went out two blocks!

Word spreads quickly when people know there is a recording studio in the neighborhood. You'll be their first stop, since the sense of community will make your services that much more attractive. You live in their neighborhood, so you must be OK. You might get the occasional off-the-wall request from time to time; a housewife wanting to sing and record her favorite song for her anniversary, a teenager wanting to get a recording of his guitar prowess as a demo, or some music "without the vocals" for the elementary school talent show. But that's what makes it fun. Perhaps the money comes after the husband hears the tape and wants to hire you for a corporate training video he's in charge of filming or when the teenager gets hired by a well-funded band and they want you to produce their next blockbuster album. Or when a parent in the audience at the talent show happens to be producing a video game and wants you to do the score! You just never know. Never discount the contacts you can make in your neighborhood.

4.3 Finding Your Niche

Creating music and sound effects for video games is like any other business practice. Much time is spent studying the layout, determining client needs, and developing a strategy to get your product in their door. If you have grand intentions, the focus will only be on the largest game publishers and the big money-making game titles. If you are being more realistic, smaller developers, upstarts, and multimedia companies would be the better place to start. Either way, the direction your business is geared towards has to fit in with and deliver the product no one else could do previously. In other words, you need to find your place in life: your niche.

Looking back, it took four years to find mine. Original plans for local TV and radio support gave way to a couple small game developers. Those led to a couple upstart companies who were keeping an eye on their cash outlay. Since I already had another full-time job paying the bills, I could keep my costs low and appeal to their budget. For about two years, most of the projects I did were for small, upstart companies. That was my niche. As my experience grew, my efforts leaned towards the medium-sized companies. Lately, as the medium-sized developers are getting larger or swallowed up by the big fish, I've stumbled upon good fortune and a new niche. My low fees used to be where I drew the most attraction. Now it seems to be my "style" and work ethics. I'm still in search of the "highest paid game composer" niche though. Hope to see you there someday.

4.3.1 Stay Educated

Information is the key to finding your place in the game industry. Games are a multi-billion dollar a year affair and there is tons of data available to those who want it. Keep your eyes and ears open. Read, investigate, research, talk to other industry players, stay educated. The more you know about what is going on around this business, the better. It may seem a bit like what investors continually do, that is, following the trends or trying to stay one step ahead of them. You are out to do the same thing, investing your talent and time instead. It can pay off equally as well. By following the ebb and tide of the gaming industry, your niche will be whatever you make it to be.

Example: gaming platforms come and go. Suppose you decide it's time to become licensed for the Nintendo 64 game system. You go through the process, pay your money, and add it to your company's services. You're all set. Funny thing though, Nintendo's *new* platform is released and developers stop producing N64 titles and begin work on the new GameCube titles. Now where does that put you? That's what I'm talking about when I say, "stay informed."

4.3.2 Start Small

For the composers and sound designers who are ready to cut their teeth and learn something about the industry, my advice: Start small and work up. Unless you happen to luck into a hit game out of the chute, no one from the larger game companies will ever consider you unless your experience can guarantee them a trouble-free production cycle. It helps to have a project or two on the resume.

As mentioned previously, your initial focus should be on small game developers, small web design firms, and small software companies. Look for production teams which consist of 1–5 members only; the smaller the better. Look for the guy working out of his spare bedroom trying to be the programmer, artist, designer, producer, et al. He's the one who is so overwhelmed, he'd be happy to place some of the burden on you and would tolerate your inexperience for the relief it brings. He may be able to teach you more than you could learn on your own — proving invaluable in your career to come. Obviously, the small developer will be working to keep costs down and you should be able to offer savings for the chance to put a project on your resume. Don't work for free, of course, but work out an amicable agreement where you take less on the front side out of the production budget and more on the backside out of the product's returns.

The initial niche you can fill is lower costs. What you lack in experience, you more than make up for with savings to them. Their willingness to spend more time holding your hand through the process indicates their need to save some cash. If you were to charge full price for your services upfront, the likelihood that the game would ever see the light of day is slim. And, as your first game project, you may have some income but won't have a product on the market to show for it, leaving you basically right where you started. The key is to use this as a stepping stone to the next level which will naturally bring in more income as you progress.

GAME COMPOSERS AT WORK

Tim Larkin of Cyan

Do you have any favorite game scores? "Grim Fandango stands out. The music implementation and composition really complement each other. Chance Thomas' score for Quest For Glory V is also one of my favorites. He did a great job. The music Greg Rahn did for Warbreeds was really good too, but the game didn't do very well and as a result, he didn't get as much acclaim as he should have from that effort."

When do you find that you are most creative? "The majority of my musical ideas

Tim Larkin, Audio Director, Cyan

come to me in the middle of the night. I think it's because I'm usually processing all the information about an area or for an idea during the day, and then when I finally let it go at night, the idea breaks through. Then I usually lay awake for a few hours unable to think of anything else. I do have a set-up at home I will use on those occasions to put down some rough ideas, so I can go back to sleep."

Are there any other secrets to your creativity besides insomnia? "I wish I had some secret formula or something. Sometimes it's like pulling teeth; other times I can't stop it. I know there are quite a few composers out there that have much more control over their creativity. I'm not one. It can truly be a struggle at times, but it has always worked out in the end."

Do you at least have a special thought process for scoring? "Usually it's based on the feel I get for an area. I usually get some graphics in my possession, or a pretty good idea of what the story is about at the particular spot, and begin formulating ideas from there."

What advice would you give to current and future game composers and sound designers? "Tough one. I'd say for the newbies, experience. Get as much experience as possible in as many situations as possible. There's always a curve coming your way and experience seems to be the best way around it. For current composers and designers, I still seek their advice whenever I can. There is a great group of peers that have been through the growing stages with me and I think we all have learned a ton from each other over the years. Stay connected. There's so much valuable information from the other people you work with. They might be sitting next to you right now."

(See page 120 of Chapter 6 for Tim's gear list.)

Therefore, use this first game with the small developer as a learning experience. Learn your craft, make mistakes when it isn't as critical. These small developers will tolerate your learning curve for the chance to make their game a reality. It makes better sense to have someone concentrate on making the audio content perfect rather than of an overworked programmer adding in bland stock sound effects between naps.

After you've had experience with a couple of smaller projects like these, you'll be ready to start approaching the medium-sized developers. It's an extremely fluid venture — moving from one role to the next, defining your place amongst the other developers of games.

4.3.3 Start Locally

By now, your list of prospective clients is sure to include several companies which are fairly local. These need to be your first targets so get out there and show your face. If you do it right, every local game and multimedia house will know you are available to help on their projects. Eventually, you'll be expanding your scope until global coverage is attained. Most of the time it is not necessary to meet with clients face to face, nor is it cost effective. Game producers understand that while they may be in San Francisco, their perfect person for the audio job could live in Florida or Italy or New Zealand. With the advent of broadband internet connections and overnight package delivery, audio delivery is not a concern. But your experience level is. Until you've put your name on a couple of game projects, expect a developer to keep a tight rein. And they cannot do that unless you are local. So, for the first couple of projects, expect a bit more face time with the producers until they know you can handle the job. With experience, expand out of your local area.

4.3.4 Getting the Break

The first question any developer or publisher will ask is: "What games have you worked on?". Your answer will determine what happens next. Whatever you do, don't succumb to the urge to fib, thinking you'll get away with it. The first time you do, your credibility will be shot full of holes. Everyone knows everyone in the game industry. While it is actually quite large, enough people move from company to company that at some point, everyone used to work together. A quick phone call to the producer who did the game you claim you worked on will not corroborate your story.

So what do you say? Before I got my first game gig, I didn't have a clue either. It actually took a couple months to figure it out. When someone asks what games you've worked on, and assuming you actually have none to your credit, your answer will be, "None." Then when they've cast you aside and looked away, hit them over the head with: "But I've been composing music for the last 10 years, play keys, guitar, bass, and drums. I've also engineered and produced three local band CD releases — one of which is the band I actively play in. I've done local radio and television spots and just recently completed a five minute public service announcement which won a regional award for the score." Etcetera, etcetera. "While I've never actually worked on a video game, I am expert on all things musical and can, without a doubt, compose the perfect music for your game. Here is my demo reel which highlights the various styles I am proficient in, including one which I think will suit this game quite well. If you'd just give me a shot, I will give this project my full attention and strive to exceed your expectations. So, what do you think?"

See where I'm going with this? No, you haven't worked on a video game, but yes, you are an experienced composer and can do the job. What you are looking for is that first break. Once you get it, you must, at all costs, give them your complete and undivided attention. Kiss their butts, if you will.

You want to ensure they never find a moment to regret hiring you. Make the music great, beat their deadlines, go all out to make the audio shine, and above all, exceed their expectations. Always do more than asked.

Your work on the first game will set the tone for the next and give you a reference who will enjoy bragging about how great you are. There's no better advertisement than that!

4.4 Networking Basics

As I've discussed earlier, the ability to network goes hand-in-hand with your marketing crusade — to connect with others in your profession whom you can trade favors, gossip, rumors, hunches, and maybe a job lead or two. You can trade techniques, equipment recommendations, stories, studio time, or just friendly advice with someone who has been out there making it happen and eager and excited to share their wealth of knowledge. I'm not talking about going out and making a nuisance of yourself, pestering hardworking individuals with a barrage of questions that could take a book to answer. Come to think of it, that's pretty much how I started on this project, but I digress. The point is, your goal is to become a respected member of the industry whom your peers can associate with in a friendly, professional manner. This is no place for a star-struck fan to stalk their favorite game composer.

Your network should have value. For the games business, the obvious choices are producers, artists, programmers, composers, and sound designers. But, also consider contacts further out on the fringe. Try contract lawyers, accountants, other businessmen, and entrepreneurs. Other working musicians, engineers, and producers in the music industry are equally important as are sound designers and composers who work in television and film. You can learn a lot from others who specialize in these fields and additionally, as part of your network, they can answer any question you may have, any problem that arises, with a quick phone call or email. Alliances with journalists, TV reporters, and editors will also expand your public relations possibilities. Networks can be practically endless. It will take a few years to build, but before you know it, you'll be a part of other's networks as well.

The ultimate goal of your network is to make it yet another way to stay connected to your livelihood. Networking goes hand-in-hand with our marketing efforts and will pay off in the end, with income or lifelong friendships.

4.4.1 Industry Functions

Not only will your appearances at E3, GDC, and SIGGRAPH keep your face in front of past and future clients, it is also another way to stay in touch with your networking buddies. I've witnessed several happy reunions that result from people literally bumping into each other on the crowded expo floor. In our busy lives, we can sometimes let correspondence go, but these shows are a perfect way to stay in touch. Everyone is out of their studios and offices with an open agenda. It's a great time to catch a few uninterrupted minutes, say hi, and see how everything is going.

4.4.2 Make Yourself Available. Make Yourself Known.

Building a solid network is almost as complicated as marketing yourself to prospective clients but the same basic principles apply. Review the basic marketing steps posed earlier in the chapter but insert "composer" and "sound designer" everywhere you see "prospective client." Same idea but with a different purpose. Obviously, others need to know you exist and accept you as a peer. Beyond that, you need to make sure you are available to meet with them on their turf as the opportunities present themselves. I'm always curious how other game audio folks do what they do and anxious to see their set-ups in person. It's easy to get submerged in other tasks, but I always try to schedule time to spend an afternoon with peers. You will learn a lot just seeing how the other half lives, what their working spaces look like, and listening to their ideas and visions. You have to make time. It's that important.

As your network gains in stature, consider hosting get-togethers with as many people as you can cram into your domicile at one time. Nothing fancy — just pick a convenient time and start inviting. The idea is to get people together of like minds and interests and watch what happens. I've been to a few, dropping whatever I was up to at the time for the chance to mingle with some

Figure 4.6 Game developers, producers, programmers, artists, and audio folks out of their caves and into the light at the yearly Game Developers Conference.

really neat people. Most others will do the same, thanking you several times for the chance to socialize and exchange ideas with their peers. Don't forget to invite me.

CHAPTER 5
The Bidding Process

5.1 How Much Do You Charge?

Game sound designers and music composers are constantly bombarded by this question. Our first instinct is to answer back, "How much do you have?" or my personal favorite, "For projects I know nothing about, my standard fee is one million dollars." Though we never actually say it out loud, underneath our happy-go-lucky artistic exterior, the businessman inside is thinking it. A list of questions and pertinent details immediately comes to mind to make a competitive quote.

So we estimate a figure. Based on what? We're not sure, but the question was asked and we aim to please. Then one of two things happens. We get the contract or we don't. And if you're just throwing around price quotes with no idea of what you are bidding on, it's usually the latter. The producer or media buyer is asking a sensible question — doing their best to obtain the finest media for the project and keep it within budget, but it is not always an easy task. Unfortunately, leaving out the particulars will cost them more time, more money, and many more headaches. You should take it upon yourself to solve this potential predicament.

Effective communication between producers and sound artists from the earliest stages can bring invaluable teamwork and the exchange of ideas. Producers who have a solid idea of the information needed by sound creators, our thought process, and the guidelines we follow to deliver the perfect quote are effective asset managers who cultivate success. Sound artists utilizing standardized guidelines to determine their fees, options for payment, and winning bid procedures would bring it home.

5.2 Let's Play 20 Questions

- "We are constructing a large multi-player, strategy game and in need of soundtrack help. I can't say much beyond that. What are your prices?"

- "Take a look at the game on our website — we are rethinking the sound effects. Quote us a price and remember, we don't have a money tree, more like a money weed."

- "Can you duplicate sounds? We have copyrighted sound that we need changed slightly, but not much. Let us know a cost."

- "Can you give me an idea of the costs of SFX?"

- "Please send a demo and tell us how much you charge."

These are *actual* quotes from inquiries I've received in the last several months. The questions are well-founded, just slightly vague on pertinent details. So nebulous in fact that I have to fire off a barrage of questions in return, such as:

- "Orchestra or simple MIDI?"

- "Star Wars quality sound effects or humble everyday sounds?"

- "Red Book or .wav files?"

Suddenly the fog begins to clear. The sound guy isn't making this stuff up and actually has some solid points.

5.2.1 Details, Details, Details

From the beginning, the more information provided, the better. Having all the details up front can streamline the process and cut costs for the developer instead of going back and forth with questions and answers. Not only can we anticipate potential problems, but solve them well before they get out of control. If the project calls for a score, sound effects, and narration, it's a great idea the sound creator knows about it! As a full-service production facility with experience directing various musical and voice talents, you could handle the project for less than three different audio contractors. Then again, maybe not. My preference is to have these out in the open first.

I am also fond of the "6 P's" (Prior Planning Prevents Piss Poor Performance) when running my production company. Deadlines are manageable when you plan ahead. An established set of reasonable milestones is a must. Just as the developer has planned ahead, so must the sound artist. We map out our production schedule based on theirs and budget our logistics accordingly. The game developer has a hard time getting artists and programmers together on a project, so likewise they need to understand our plight of getting a bunch of musicians to show up on time and ready to play. We need time to plan and time for the unforeseen. Fickle musicians and their unpredictable gear doth not a successful project make! For the busier sound folks, we may also have other concurrent projects and need to determine if there is time in our production schedules to take on another.

5.3 Asking the Right Questions

Exactly what does the organized musician or sound designer need to determine if they can perform the service and produce a competitive bid? The following list of questions should be answered prior to the final submission.

1) What platform is the project intended for?

Game platforms each have their own idiosyncrasies and ways they manage sound programming and reproduction. Different equipment may be needed to produce these sounds such as a development system. You may have to rent or buy additional equipment or hire a subcontractor because of your lack of expertise in a certain area and this will factor into the projected costs. If you cannot develop for a particular platform, be ready to hire additional help to convert formats. Check with the developer too. They may know of someone who specializes in this type of work and save you some time. Remember, this is a team effort.

2) Are you bidding the project or just one song or sound effect?

Composers and sound designers normally charge less for working the entire project than for creating individual music tracks and sound effects. It makes sense that once the factory is tooled and the "sound palette" is chosen, creating music and effects in the same vein takes less set-up and production time. There are also those times when only a musical piece or sound effect or two are needed and we should have pricing structures available for those instances.

3) How much music is needed? Number of tracks? Lengths? Styles? Format?

Obviously, the more music needed, the more it will cost. A song's length also determines the fee. Because most composers normally charge per "finished minute," it only makes sense that a three minute song would cost more than a one minute one. To plan production time, use your working model.

Four hours to compose from scratch, record tracks, and mixdown for each 30 seconds of music is pretty typical.

Composing and recording in several *different* styles could change the price too. Some composers are capable of many styles; some are only great at one. If a developer only has one genre of music in mind, it should work out well. But if country, jazz, rock, and classical are all needed for the same project, it should cost a little more. Calling in other musicians to lend their talents costs money and should be written into the bid.

The format of the tangible medium — such as Digital Audio Tape [DAT], CD, or cassette tape — should be revealed here to ensure the you have the required equipment. For digital files, the sample rate in kHz, 16- or 8-bit, and stereo vs. mono are all extremely important to know about in advance. I once found out my old computer's processor could not handle recording files using the 44.1 kHz sample rate and forced an upgrade. Not that I mind upgrading, I just *really* hate surprises! Plan on recording everything in the highest possible sample rate regardless of the final format requirements and converting down — your only limitations being your storage medium and processing power.

4) Are sound effects needed? How many? What specific sounds? Recognizable or original creations? Actions to accompany? Critical timing points for avi's or character movement? Type of device used for playback? Format?

If you get the call for music, find out if they also need sound effects for the project and offer your services. The probability is high that you are also equipped to handle effects, right? The equipment used in a recording studio and methods used to record sound are the same for both specialties. The minor difference is the programs you may use. Combining these tasks with one content provider is less expensive for the developer in the long run, plus it is one less person for them to meet with.

Attention to detail regarding sound effects at the outset can help the process considerably. It shows the developer has looked at their sound needs and assessed requirements early in the project. Although the precise sounds may not be planned, ideas for weapons, environmental and administrative functions, and so forth may have formed and an idea of the number should be passed on to the sound designer. Using a personal working model, the designer can calculate how long their production cycle would be.

A general rule is one original sound effect requires two hours of time to create.

The more sounds, the more it will cost, but complexity can also raise the price. Standard or recognizable sounds from natural or man-made occurrences are usually "no-brainers." While effects libraries already in existence can provide some sounds, they may need manipulation to match up to character movement or an action. Other processing may be needed to adjust volume, equalization, or length. But, generally, these are considered elementary.

The sounds which will be the most valued are the "Star Wars" quality, original creations — fresh, wildly fantastic sounds which take your breath away. Completely original, highly creative effects cost more. For the developer, finding the right person with the patience, know-how, and the shared vision may take a little digging, but I don't know of too many sound designers who won't at least give it a shot. We do, afterall, crave a good challenge.

I never thought the type of playback device mattered until a company approached me to do some sound effects. I received a list of effects and the format to save them in, pretty cut and dry. I proceeded to create some really killer sounds, smitten with myself and convinced I had indeed pulled off an impossible feat, ready to shatter the most powerful subwoofer in existence. Turns out, they would never even see a speaker system; they were sounds intended to be burned onto a chip for playback on a T-shirt! Gasp! So now, as you can imagine, I *always* ask what the playback device will be. That way, I can design them specifically for the audio characteristics of the device. Lesson learned.

5) Any narratives needed? Do you need to hire voice talent? Will there be background sounds to accompany narrations? Do you have rewrite authority of scripts?

Narratives fit into the sound recording category and generally, anyone capable of music recording can also record narration. That's how a developer looks at it. As with sound effects and music, packaging this task together will normally yield a lower cost from the sound contractor while also making it one-stop shopping. If they already have narratives recorded, you can usually provide the service of transferring them to digital files, maximizing the sound, cutting them to length, and adding any additional background or Foley sounds.

If narratives are to be recorded, you will need to know if you will be providing the voice talent and budget accordingly. Many sound guys have access to local talent or use talent agencies to find just the right personality. Auditions are usually free, paying only when the talent has performed the work, which surprisingly enough, averages between $250–350 for a day of reading. Well worth the price for professional voice talent. A developer may ask if you have any experience directing narrative sessions. A good question. After dealing with musicians, though, you are probably fairly adept at coaxing great performances from practically anyone.

Rewrite authority for a script is a big plus and can be a money saver when the clock is ticking. Knowing this will determine how large the "fudge factor" will be. I once had voice talent who could not say, "…live to tell their tales." No matter how many times we tried, this tongue twister never came close to resembling the script. A quick rewrite got us back on track instantly. Had we been required to track down the producer for permission, it may have taken longer or worse, the talent may have had to return later, costing me the price of another session.

6) Timeframe needed?

If they need it tomorrow, it will cost more. If they need a half-hour of music in a week, it will also cost more. The more projects put on hold and any severe lack of sleep, the price jumps up accordingly. But, if we have been able to plan ahead and are afforded the time to schedule around other commitments, standard rates will apply. Rush jobs in any industry can be costly.

7) Delivery method?

The beauty of the Internet is the immediate mass distribution of digital data. Attaching a sound file to an email is the method of choice and assuming we have access, it is also the cheapest. Costs begin to rise as the delivery method changes. If the developer requires shipment on removable media such as floppy discs or CDs, there will be a cost involved. Preference of a DAT master increases the price. If they just have to have the original two-inch, 24-track tape reel you used to record with, it changes again. Internet, floppies, and CDs are common; DATs only slightly less so. Those big, bulky tape reels, you can forget.

8) Is a speculative demo needed?

An established development company typically draws upon many musical/sound design resources at once — having them create specific music and sounds for a project from their guidelines and then choosing the best one. If the developer lets you know ahead of time that they require a speculative demo, it will save a lot of frustration for everyone allowing you to schedule it in with your other projects. But normally, a composer's suitability can be easily determined from a previously-submitted demo reel. But be ready, just in case.

9) What is the production budget?

The production budget can be a touchy subject. If they already have numbers in mind for the sound budget, request at least a ballpark estimate. This will disclose the budget to be met and how serious the project is. i.e., whether it is a veteran development team or newcomer to the industry operating on a shoestring budget. For the small developer, you can offer budget solutions dependant upon the information and ask for payment up front, at milestones, royalties, lease or even barter agreements. We are part of the development team and do not want to doom a project before it even has a chance. Flexibility is a practice of many sound professionals. As long as the compensation is worthy of your efforts, there is nothing to lose.

10) Who will publish? What method of distribution?

This question is especially reasonable if the possibility of royalty payments surface in the negotiations. A game which will be self-published by a new, inexperienced developer and distributed by word of mouth does not exactly scream success. A well-established, veteran development team, on the other hand, who is using a giant publishing and distribution company and an onslaught of marketing ultimately has a better chance. Everything is negotiable and it pays to have all the facts in the beginning to help make an informed decision.

11) Payment method?

If a developer already has a standard method of payment, find out and determine if it is acceptable for your needs. No one has a problem dealing with cash; some up front, some after acceptance of the first pass, and the rest upon final approval. It is the standard for most companies.

But if there are other methods in mind, royalties on the backside, or a salary or hourly wage for example, some discussion may be warranted. Would you want to shoulder the risk? You might consider the gamble, if you are willing to help keep your production costs down on the front side for a much larger piece of the pie on the end. It might be well worth your time. You never know when that game will become a smash hit.

12) Target market?

Who do they expect to buy the game? A classically-trained pianist may not have the ability to write music for a game targeted to the teenage male. A heavy metal guitarist may not be exactly right for the three- to eight-year-old female market. As the composer, it is our responsibility to let them know if we can in fact handle the scope of the job and providing this little detail up front can save a lot of time.

13) Who has final authority to accept your work?

This is an important point which needs to be nailed down early; the answer will factor heavily into your bid submission. A producer may stand up and proclaim, "It is I who has final authority!" That would be a perfect scenario and you wouldn't need to worry about all those other little fingers in the pie as much. You could charge on a "per project" or "per sound effect" basis and feel confident you wouldn't lose money. But, if the answer is the entire team, well, you've got your work cut out

Figure 5.1 Knowing a game's prospective audience will allow you to honestly access whether you are able to do the job.

and my guess is you'll be spending some considerable time doing reworks. Achieving consensus would be nearly impossible. An hourly wage might be more appropriate to ensure all that extra time is accounted for and you have something to show for your efforts. Or, you could add 5–10% more into your margin of error to cover what looks to be a severe headache in the making.

This will eventually need to be worked out anyway — no later than the contract negotiations to be safe, and will serve as the last step before any milestone or final payments. When the designated individual accepts your work, ensure a check in your name is being processed. Occasionally, some will try to wait until the game is finished or released before parting with their funds. By having it in the contract, they can be held to their side of the bargain.

5.4 Pre-Production Made Simple

With the previous list in mind, the producer or media buyer can easily increase the chances of a trouble-free bidding process by answering as many of the questions as possible. Make sure you've got them answered to your liking before making your final calculations. Any surprises could change the parameters of the bid causing a devaluation of services.

Even before the project is put out for bid, the media buyer can do their homework. Investigating various sound production companies beforehand is a good idea to help stay ahead of the game. Web search engines, developer resource websites, and the numerous unsolicited emails, inquiries, and resumes can be (finally) taken advantage of. They should request your current demo reel, references, and past work examples. Do your part to encourage them. They'll be thankful when the time comes.

Developers should plan as far ahead of the bidding process as possible, gathering any preliminary work; design documents, artwork, character biographies, storyboards, and lists of other comparable games on the market and have them handy to show the sound artist. I always appreciate getting these extra details at the bidding process. It is a classy gesture — one which will strengthen the new relationship immediately. The more you know, the more likely you will get your part right the first time.

Good developers keep the sound guy informed. Details and ideas change fast and furiously during the development of any title and the timeframe while waiting to receive bid replies is no different. Any major specification changes should be immediately forwarded to the prospective audio providers to ensure accuracy on your part. Platform changes, surround sound, or interactive music scores come to mind as important examples. Timely feedback on rejections, accepted submissions, and words of encouragement are always nice too. Be on the lookout for any information between the lines. Sometimes a developer may swear they gave out certain information, but in reality, it was never said directly. ESP is a good thing if you've got it. Asking lots of questions is your next best bet.

TOOLS OF THE TRADE

Jamey Scott, in-house composer/sound designer, Presto Studios

As *the* in-house audio personality at Presto Studios in San Diego, California, Jamey Scott is indeed the proverbial one-man show. His well-schooled compositional and musical forté, highly adept sound design skills, and programming abilities have made him an indispensable part of an extremely successful team. He's put on quite a show thus far with titles such as Compton's Interactive Encyclopedia, Compton/Softkey's Interactive Children's Bible stories, MGM Babes in Toyland Interactive CD, Presto's Gundam 0079, The Journeyman Project III: Legacy of Time, and Myst III.

His studio is a small, but comfortable space located within the walls of Presto Studios, just large enough to hold his equipment and adjoining sound booth firmly within his creative grasp. It's not uncommon, though, to see him in the courtyard or parking lot with microphone and tape deck in hand bouncing unlikely objects off each other.

Computers: PowerMac G3, 350 MHz, 256 MB of RAM, two 18 GB U2W LVD drives. Two PCs: Pentium III, 600 MHz, 512 MB of RAM, and 28 GB Seagate hard drives

Software: Mac: ProTools 5.0, Digital Performer v2.7, Cakewalk Metro 5.0 sequencer, Bias Peak sound editing software, Quicktime. PC: Gigasampler and Sonic Foundry Sound Forge

Multi-track: ProTools mix+ for all multi-track needs. TDM still has the best plug-ins available

Mixing board and monitor system: Mackie Digital 8 monitored in surround using 5 Mackie HR824s and a Genelec subwoofer

Mixdown deck: None. Mixes are to computer as .wav files

Keyboards, samplers, sound modules, and other instruments: "I use four main controllers. My keyboard, a Roland JV-35, is a cheap velocity sensitive keyboard used for sequencing piano and general melodic ideas.

For melodies, I'm using a Yamaha WX5 wind controller with a VL70m module. It's the best way to get very expressive, realistic melodies of sequenced music.

For percussion, I've got a small set-up of a few drum pads controlling an Alesis DM5 drum module. Most of those sounds never really make it to my final mixes because they sound synthetic, but it's a good way to sequence rhythm tracks.

Finally, I use a Roland GR-09 guitar synthesizer for laying down improvised melodic material. Most of my composition style is heavily pre-composed but every now and then I'll need some improvised melodic material to fill up space. Since I'm a better guitar player than anything else, it's nice to just whip something out using the guitar synthesizer.

As for sounds, I use mostly custom-sampled acoustic instruments, but I do use some commercial sounds. I haven't sampled a full orchestra but have done brass sections and some woodwinds, so I try to retain some individuality from the samples I use. Since every composer has the same boxes and samples, the only thing that gives a composer a unique identity is by the samples that he/she uses. That's why I try to sample everything myself rather than just buy what everyone else is using.

For sample playback, I use two GigaStudio PCs and one Emu E4XT."

Remote recording: TASCAM DA-P1 battery powered DAT deck and an AKG SE300B microphone for field recording and sound effects gathering.

Sound effects libraries: General 6000 series from Sound Ideas, Hollywood Edge's Larger than Life collection, and some other obscure libraries. "However, I only use these libraries as departure points. I never use stock sound effects. There's always something you can do to a sound to make it unique."

Development systems: "I work a lot with Miles sound system."

5.5 Contract Payment Options

During negotiations, the single most recurrent trend is the payment option. Cash flow is important to both parties. You, the contractor,endeavor to receive payment in your favor while the developer strives to keep their money as long as possible. It is a standard practice throughout the business world and not confined to the gaming industry but frustrating nonetheless. There are a few options to ease the pain on both sides of the fence and to help make the bid more attractive. Consider offering some of these options to ease the financial pinch a developer may be feeling. Remember, you're the problem solver and there is no reason you can't take that beyond just doing music and sound.

Salary or hourly wage. The easiest scenario, by far, is to be brought in as part of the development team and accept either a salary or hourly wage as consistent work is produced. No squabbling or haggling as terms of the contract are changed and giving the sound creator a sense of project ownership are highlights of this option. This situation is best for larger or well-funded developers but totally unrealistic if no development money is available.

Payment according to milestones. Given a hard list of required audio content, set milestones and have the developer schedule payments according to them. The downside is that this will force them to plan ahead and have exact specifications nailed down. The plus is that it motivates you, the sound artist, to meet them. (I'm always more focused when I have a deadline to work towards.) If they don't wish to be tied, payment terms of 1/2 up front, the other 1/2 upon completion, or variations in between, are also feasible.

Good faith, barter arrangement, and small royalties. This example has wide-open possibilities. By starting with a small "good faith" payment, the developer is showing commitment to the project and to the sound artist. Because cash may be a problem, barter arrangements of some type are workable depending on each other's needs and offerings. Trades of computer equipment, web space hosting or site design, or graphics such as logos are all practical. A royalties option on the backside would round out the final payment for services. This option is great for the newer, cash-starved developer and for the sound creator who is part-time or has other income.

Straight royalties. By not taking *any* payment during the development process, the sound artist would be entitled to a larger portion on the backside. A generous royalties schedule would be established to pay the content provider after the title is released. While this is indeed the best case scenario for a developer, because the sound creator is assuming the risk, it can be the worst for you. Newer composers and sound designers may elect this option as a way to become established and for the steady cash flow as they work on other titles. Wiser ones will consider it if the game has hit potential.

Variations of the above.   In the free marketplace of our society, creativity is not always confined to art. Utilizing any or all of the previous examples, an agreeable compensation schedule can be established meeting the needs of both parties. All one has to do is ask.

5.6 Speculative Demos

We touched upon speculative demos in Chapter 3, but it's a subject which is important enough to warrant its own discussion. A *speculative demo* is a submission of music done by a prospective composer created specifically for a certain project. It is a way for the developer to see how close you can come to their ideas without actually committing themselves to hiring you. Usually, after deciding upon a few composers, a developer may request this type of demo to help narrow the field.

They should be as specific as possible regarding the type and style of music they seek — giving examples of works in other games or musical groups which feed the right mood. If at all possible, it is best if they have only one person (i.e., the producer) give their input at this point. A favorite spec demo request of mine included this description, "…mid tempo with breakbeats, dark, abstract hip-hop, not too fast or too slow, gritty and industrial but not jarring or abrasive." It was fairly obvious the *entire* development team contributed their ideas to the cause! It's a difficult task to please everyone.

So, it is extremely important to receive a concise description for mood of the game. You only have one shot to get it right. Occasionally, and if I have the time, I include at least two similar musical directions for the "judges" to choose between on a spec demo — doubling my chances.

GAME COMPOSERS AT WORK

Brian Tuey of GigaWatt Studios

What necessary skills should a future game musician have?   "Well, I think the #1 skill that future game musicians need is patience. An old friend of mine told me that eon's ago (not mentioning any names, Aaron). Other than patience, vast musical backgrounds are helpful — whether that is listening to a wide variety of music or participating in different types of bands. The reason for this is pretty simple: as a game musician, you'll need to be able to create fast-paced techno or grunge, then turn around and write a jazzy piano piece. Being able to discern what makes a specific genre what it is, is the #1 key to being able to write a vast amount of different music. Game musicians are normally the 'jack-of-all-trades' of music genres, and not necessarily a master of any of them."

When are you most musically creative?   "As far as when I'm most creative, I'd have to respond with 'when I need to be.' The bottom line is that there are deadlines that have to be met, so you can't really mess around with writer's block. If I'm having a problem with this, then I'll usually try to find a movie that is similar to what I'm working on. For instance, if I have to write the music for an alien landscape, and I'm having trouble figuring out what

I need for the scene, I'll take a break, and maybe watch Pitch Black — just to see what the other musician did. This actually can inspire a completely different type of music than was originally imagined."

How do you normally approach a new project? "Scoring a project is a new beast each time you go to tackle it. Sometimes the client has such a specific sound they are looking for that the musician doesn't have nearly the creative freedom that he might wish for. These are the toughest cases because the musician might be asked to 'duplicate' another artist's sound. In the situations where I have more creative control, I get as much information as possible on the specific scene, screenshots, whatever. I'll even look at the design doc if they'll let me, just so I can get a sense of place, what the characters are doing, and what point in the story the specific location is. After that, I try to live the scene in my mind and just listen to what comes. Then I write it."

5.6.1 Covering Your Expenses

It is a fair business practice to be covered for the very basic production costs for the speculative demo. As incentive, you can also agree to deduct this fee from your contract after being hired. But, unfortunately, this isn't always the case. Developers want to keep their expenditures down to a minimum and may feel that if you want the job bad enough, you'll do it for free. My argument is: if they've heard my demo, they know my production values and should be able to determine whether I am suitable for the job. While I'm not opposed to doing a speculative demo, I believe my time can be better spent working on *real* projects which pay the full fee.

Normally, you won't be able to charge full price for your spec demo. Any charge should cover "reasonable" production costs — basically your time, any outside talent, and material fees. Your standard creative fee is generally waived. For a one minute piece normally sold for $1000 to $1500, consider $300–400 as the most you can expect for the effort.

The ownership issue can blur the fee structure. If a developer asks for a speculative demo and agrees to cover production fees only, you maintain all rights to the music. Assuming, of course, that you aren't hired for the job, it still leaves you with music to sell to other projects in the future and something to add to your demo reel.

Now, let's say you didn't get the gig, but they want to keep the music. What you do here is completely up to you. It's my guess they liked it enough to want to use it in something and I'd be careful. I would charge my full fee, give them all the rights, and call it even. They may counter with "if you give it to us for the spec price, we'll keep you in mind for the next project." Again, it's totally up to you what you agree to, but there are no guarantees and they probably won't call despite what they say. If they like the composer they hired for this project, that person will more than likely get the next one as well. It's definitely a gamble — trying to look like the nice guy — but the odds are not in your favor and rarely will they call again. Put on your business hat when negotiating points like this and make sure you aren't taken advantage of.

5.6.2 Words of Caution

Music created with the project specifications in mind will give the development team a good idea what audio life to give the project and enables them to adopt the best one. They are basically taking advantage of you — looking for free musical ideas for their project. Developers have been known to contact several composers for ideas even though they've already chosen one in advance. It may turn out to be effort in futility. Stay alert.

While asking for a speculative demo is a "win win" situation from the developer's standpoint, it can be a waste of time for you. Newer sound folks are usually more than happy to spend a week or two sweating and bleeding over a speculative demo, investing their time and money only to find out they have wasted it. Established composers don't need to expend this effort — having a proven track record to fall back on instead.

You have a clear choice when faced with this request. If they've heard your demo reel, you can sell them on what you've already done. Point out a piece on the demo which may be similar in nature to what you are thinking musically and play up the value of your production quality. If your argument doesn't sell them and they insist, it's time to decide. At first, your temptation will be to jump on every request. If you have nothing else going on at the time, work out the spec fee and go for it. Income is good regardless of where it comes from. But, keep in mind, this will take your efforts away from larger money-making endeavors such as reeling in the big fish. There is nothing wrong with turning down this type of request, choosing instead to stick with your business plan. Why should you risk wasting your time when there is no guarantee anything will come of it? While it may be a calculated risk, sure things feel a whole lot better.

5.7 The Bid Submission

We have come back full circle to the question, "how much do you charge?". Except this time, we are armed with powerful knowledge, motivation, and a list for success. All the parameters for the game have been laid out and it's time to determine your fee. Obviously, the amount you charge is a big factor in determining whether you get the call or not, so don't take the subject lightly.

After you've set a figure, mull over your interactions with the developer to decide whether they are giving you free artistic rein or will be non-stop thorns in your side and then let that gut feeling be your guide. Let that intuition be the basis for the bid you submit. It's not an exact science, but it will effect your motivation and ultimately the quality of the job you do.

**A wise man once said,
if you grumble through an entire project, you are not charging enough.**

More than likely, there will be other composers bidding on the project as well. If you can find out who they are, great. It will give you an indication of the price range they warrant and you can strategize over how to win the bid. Don't immediately go for the "cheapest composer angle" — under-bidding just to get the project. By doing so, developers will expect all composers to work cheaply and devalue our efforts. You'll end up working on their next project for this cut-rate fee, unable to earn more for your efforts — setting a bad precedent which will take you years to recover from. I'm not saying this because other composers (or myself) are afraid to lose a contract to the lowest bidder. I'm throwing it out in hopes you will understand that once you are known as the "cheapest composer in town," that's the only type of projects you'll get.

5.7.1 The Bid

For the final bid submission, there is no magical format to follow which will land the contract. Most bids are submitted via email these days — plain, old, boring text explaining how much you would charge for the project and what would be accomplished for the price. Occasional submissions are requested through a more formal letter, but either way, what counts is the facts: your professionalism and their gut feelings.

When you make your submission, ensure the recipient actually received it and find out if there are any questions which need answering before their final selection. A phone call is the best way to follow up, especially if you've never met or spoken before. It will add a personal touch and humanize the dry, impersonal bid. If the chance presents itself, request a visit to offer your bid in person and meet everyone face-to-face. Although it is highly improbable you'll be able to afford jetting off to meet all prospective clients, there still is something to be said for that kind of commitment and dedication. But remember, it still won't guarantee you the job.

For a little extra insight into the bidding process, here is an illustration of a bid request you may encounter and an example response.

Example Bid Request

Dear Game Composer,

We are currently requesting bids for an upcoming game release for PC. We will be requiring a number of different types of music for the project. The game takes place in space and is in the "combat/strategy" genre. In making our decision, we will first consider quality, second cost, and third timeline.

For now, if you could furnish us with the following, we will be able to consider your bid:

- Resume of past game work.

- Sample track or part of a track, either done for this proposal or from your archives, which matches one of the descriptions below.

- Cost per track, with any discounts if we request over a certain number of tracks.

- Completion timeline. The project does not require the final soundtrack for 4 months, although we would like to have it much sooner if possible.

- The music tracks will play throughout the game. All voice and sound effects will be heard over the tracks. There will be a bit of silence after a track is complete before the next one begins (done similarly in Command and Conquer).

Here are a few track descriptions. Pick which ever type you want for your bid sample:

- An action piece in a classical genre (Star Wars, Raiders, etc.) — could be a synth mix.

- Rockin' thrash, industrial-esque perhaps.

- Militaristic Techno — hard, driving beat and a cool sci-fi tune. Nine Inch Nails minus the ear-splitting cacophony or Eurythmics "1984," John Carpenters "The Thing."

We want to avoid recognizable lyrics, although voice can be cool as an instrument and stay away from "happy, Disney-action themes." I will be going through the bids in two weeks. Please call or email me if you have any questions. You can obtain information about our company from our website. Thank you.

Sincerely,

Producer X

Example Response

Dear Producer X,

Thank you for the opportunity to be considered for your new space game project. Enclosed is the demo reel and bio you requested. I've included several tracks from my archives in a brief musical montage similar to the styles you described. After I've had a chance to speak with you directly, to get a better feel for the game, I'll be able to hit your target dead center.

Although I do not have any published game titles yet, I am currently under contract with two separate software companies scoring music and designing sound effects. Company A has me contracted for two games, Space Game 1 and another game yet to be named. One project is expected to be released in two months and another by next spring. Company B has contracted me for one title by summer and an option to continue my contract indefinitely. I'm quickly adding projects to my resume, so please don't be alarmed by my lack of published software titles. I have much experience composing and recording music having done many local TV and radio commercials, PSA's, and am involved with several album projects. I can do what you hire me for without question.

My rates depend on many of your requirements but $3,495 would include buy-out fees for five, three-minute songs/themes and five, one-minute pieces — 20 minutes of music in all, using the instrumentation heard on the demo. Additional music is $149 per minute. I can offer 60 minutes for $7500. Individual tracks, per finished minute, would start at $449. The quality and value of my services are guaranteed; if you are not happy with the music I compose for you, you pay nothing.

The timeline is fairly straightforward once approval for the styles and lengths of music are granted. The first piece would take two weeks for composition and recording, each piece after that (1–3 minutes in length) would require no more than one week. Once the factory is tooled, so to speak, and my sound palette is chosen, the music comes fast and furious. A week would also be needed for reworks, if there are any. I say a week to be conservative; five days is usually the norm.

Rest assured, I can get the job done on time and within budget. My musical/produc-tion/computer experience dates back many years and my local area network is always available to draw upon. My reliability is unquestioned and if you'd like to speak with some of my clients, they would be happy to share their experiences. I believe in the utmost quality of each production and strive for perfection. My in-house digital studio is fully equipped to reach these goals and to allow my creativity and inspiration to get quickly to tape. I have been composing for many years, played guitar and drums in various bands, play piano, and have been actively engineering and producing. I have the knowledge and the chops to provide quality music — on time and most certainly within budget.

Please feel free to call if you have further questions or need clarification. Again, thank you for your consideration and I hope to speak with you soon.

Sincerely,

Game Composer

(Note: this illustration is geared towards the new composer. There is discussion about the lack of resume titles and you'll note the price quote is much lower than what an established game composer might charge. The quote was based on a very low overhead for the composer and that the developer was small and fairly new.)

An aspect to note in the example. The entire point of this process is for a developer to survey various sound contractors, find a fee which will fit their budget, and get great audio. They are searching for the most bang for their buck, period. We aren't anywhere close to negotiating royalties, bonuses, and other contract items so don't use this as a forum for that. You'll note the example didn't even breach those subjects. Once you win the contract and they have rallied around, heralding you as their new audio sage, then contract issues will be considered. If you were to walk in with a long list of contract demands, they would definitely consider the path of least resistance, i.e., your competitor, and leave you standing there with your mouth agape.

5.8 There is Still More

After the bids are submitted and the nail-biting begins, there is still more we can do. Maintain an open line of communication, build rapport, ask questions, grow to understand each other's needs. The process is by no means over. There are times I have even been asked to re-bid based on new parameters only discovered during our conversations. When it comes down to two bids, developers should talk to both composers. A gut feeling will let them know who is right for the job. After all, you will be working closely together for some time and it is reasonable to assume you should be able to communicate ideas and get along. Don't be afraid to pick up the phone and do a little digging on your behalf.

The bid is, without a doubt, the least favorite part of the game development process but inevitable. Knowing and sharing the ingredients of a sound bid will make this experience better — setting the mood for the project and establishing a cohesive team that breeds success.

CHAPTER 6
Making the Deals

Dear Game Composer,

Congratulations! You have been chosen among five competing composers and sound designers to score music and create sound effects for Company X's next mega-block-buster smash game! Because you stand well above your peers, the choice was not a difficult one. Your vision is clear, your dedication is evident, and we look forward to working with you on what proves to be a very exciting project. We'll be in touch very shortly to discuss all the pertinent details.

Before we can proceed, however, we will require you to agree to and sign some standard paperwork: a Non-Disclosure Agreement (NDA) and Professional Services Agreement (PSA). You will find these documents enclosed. Please fill them out in their entirety, sign and date in the appropriate places, and return them to us within the next five working days. After we have them in our possession, we can get down to the business at hand.

Again, it is a pleasure to have you on board as part of our team. Should you have any questions, feel free to contact me.

Yours in gaming,

Producer X

Wow! You've hit the big time. Your adrenaline is flowing, your hands are shaking. This is a significant moment — one you've worked hard for. Except, when you sit down to examine the pages of "legalese" they need you to sign, the weight of the situation pulls you unwillingly back down to earth, a touch of fear rising from your stomach. What are you going to do?

Your first instinct may be to just sign and initial everywhere, send it back, and get it over with. You want to make music! Wrong! You have to realize this contract is skewed heavily in their favor; their interests fully addressed. That would be the *worst* thing you could do at this point.

Find a decent contract lawyer — preferably one who is familiar with the idiosyncrasies of the games industry. Consult with them before signing any contract and discuss ways to include your interests in it as well. If you absolutely cannot afford the $200, find a trusted advisor you can rely on — someone who is familiar with business contracts and could recommend an appropriate course of action. Consider, at a minimum, talking with a game producer or another composer who has dealt with these types of situations for advice. By doing so, it will protect your interests, give you an insight into the process from day one, and will let the game developer know you are not just a great composer but also a savvy business person.

Dealing with agreements, contracts, and all the other legal paperwork can be enough to try anyone's patience and make them think twice about this line of work. These basic "formalities," necessary evils which most people take rather nonchalantly, are enforceable and binding agreements between two parties which can be used for or against you in a court of law. In the previous example, Company X, whether knowingly or not, is gently forcing you into their agreement without appropriate time for you to consult your experts and consider each point. If you ever find yourself in this type of position, ask for more time to review the contract and offer any counter-proposals if you come across something unreasonable.

Don't get suckered into signing something you haven't read and fully understood. I've found myself sitting in a boardroom full of company executives staring at me, all seemingly waiting for my pen to touch the paper. While the pressure to look like a "team player" was tremendous, I asked for some time to review the documents first. Another time, a producer kept reminding me my first payment was on his desk and would be sent out as soon as I signed the contract — that is, dangling the carrot. In another instance, a substantial payment was withheld from a previous contract after the company had been bought out, insisting I sign their *new* agreement first. You will meet with many similar situations in your travels.

Never sign any legal document unless you understand and agree to it 100%.
Your livelihood and sanity are at stake.

6.1 Understanding Industry Contracts and Terminology

Before you can make the deals that bring success, you must understand and become familiar with the legal contracts you'll see along the way. Some can be extremely simple statements which proclaim, "Upon receipt of payment in full, Company X owns all rights to the following audio files." Other contracts are pages of undecipherable legalese which can take days to read. Regardless of what you may encounter, common sense and a little knowledge will go a long way. Let's take a look at some of the more common terms and "standard" agreements.

6.1.1 Non-Disclosure Agreements (NDAs)

Before most companies even let you *see* their operation, they require your signature on a Non-Disclosure Agreement. Basically, it is a document that says anything you see and hear is top-secret and cannot be shared with anyone outside the company. It's a fairly simple concept which takes three pages to say, unfortunately.

The following example is a non-disclosure statement in its simplest form. You will often see these as additions to contracts, instead of a stand-alone document.

It is understood by the below signed individual that all information obtained while providing service will remain confidential and that he/she will not directly or indirectly disclose to any third party or use for its own benefit, or use for any purpose other than the above mentioned project.

By signing an NDA, you are sworn not to divulge any information about the company's projects. This legal document will make you think twice about talking. The last thing you need is a lawyer standing up in court waving an NDA with your signature on it. Game companies take this very seriously and I recommend keeping a tight lip for your own sake. Everyone working in the industry has signed one of these, so when conversation turns uncomfortably towards the specifics of your new project, it is always safe to say, "I'm under non-disclosure," and they will understand.

An in-house composer will sign an NDA when first taking a job, but after a few months working with the company, their loyalty would never be questioned. As a contractor, game companies have more of a reason to hold you to such agreements. Because you don't "belong" to them and it's hard to keep a close eye on you, they are a bit more paranoid. You have contact with many other game companies who are all competing in the same marketplace and a slip of the tongue could end up costing a company their entire project. With millions at stake, this type of industrial espionage, whether accidental or not, is highly frowned upon. They would not hesitate to drag your butt into court to recoup their losses.

Consider this example: Say you worked on a project with Company Y and might have overheard some information about their next ultra-secret game title. Over at Company Z, where you are talking to a producer about doing their next game, what you heard over at the other company casually comes up in conversation. It turns out they have a similar game in the making and based on the information you just provided, they move their timetable up in order to beat them to market. The game is released with great fanfare and is acclaimed as an innovative and trend-setting game. Company Z's stock shoots up and orders for millions of copies of the game flood in from around the globe. Two months later, Company Y releases their game with mediocre reception. It's proclaimed a copy cat and dies a miserable death on the store shelves. Company Y can't understand why they failed horribly. Then one of the producers casually mentions to the CEO that you had done the audio on Company Z's game and he remembers how angry you were not winning the contract for this game. Suddenly, their legal team springs into action and decides you had to have been the one who leaked information about their secret project. Whether you were the one or not, they may have a case against you if you signed their non-disclosure agreement.

I don't mention this to raise fear. I want you to understand that video gaming is a serious business and discretion on your part is necessary. What you learn about a company in the course of conversations should *always* be held in confidence — regardless of whether an NDA was signed or not. If you get the reputation of being a blabber mouth, companies will stop talking to you. You wouldn't want competitors learning your secrets, especially if you've discovered a niche where you've cornered the market, so be respectful to the game developers whose lifeblood is the success of their product.

TOOLS OF THE TRADE

Tim Larkin,
Audio Director, Cyan

What does a guy who has worked with greatness like Ella Fitzgerald, Mel Torme, James Brown, Tony Bennett, Lou Rawls, and Huey Lewis do in the game industry? Why, anything he wants, of course. All it took was a phone call to the first game company on his list and Tim Larkin's adventure with Broderbund (and his game career) was off in high gear. As composer, sound designer, and player, he is credited currently with over 15 games including many in the Carmen San Diego series, Dr. Suess, Arthur, Rugrats, Quest for Glory V, Prince of Persia III, JR Tolkien's Middle Earth, and Riven: The Sequel to Myst. He's composed and played for numerous television, film, and live performances and even has a solo jazz album under his belt highlighting his horn playing prowess. His current billing is as audio director at Cyan — hard at work on the "next big thing."

When asked about his gear list and how he acquired it, he gave me some valuable words of wisdom to share: Get someone else to pay for your gear!

Computers: Mac: PowerMac G3, 333 MHz, 256 MB RAM, system 8.6.1. Two 17" monitors, Glyph 9 GB UltraWide with Adaptec SCSI accelerator card, External 1 and 2 GB Jaz Drives, Yamaha 400a CD-R.
PC: Pentium III, 500 MHz, 256 MB RAM, 21" Sony Trinitron dual input monitor with Voodoo 2 3D video acceleration ("I use this for my email!"), and 3D StudioMax

Software: ProTools 5 with plug-ins too numerous to mention, Peak 1.6, Digital Performer 2.7, StudioVision Pro, MetaSynth, SonicWorx Artist, SoundEdit 16, Waveconvert Pro, 3D StudioMax

Multi-track: ProTools Mix with 888/24 I/O

Mixing board and monitor system: Mackie 8 bus and a Trident Series 65. Genelec 1030a stereo monitor speakers

Mixdown deck: "I mixdown right to disk, so no decks are involved, although I do have several Panasonic and TASCAM DAT's hanging around."

Outboard gear: Lexicon PCM 91 and PCM 81, TC Electronics Fireworx and Eventide H3000S. Numerous compressors "that I don't use much anymore due to software plug-ins."

Keyboards and modules: Two Roland JV1080's, JD 990, 2 K2000's and many sample libraries for the Kurzweil

SFX libraries: Digiffects complete; Sound Ideas, 2000, 4000, 6000, 7000 and 9000; Hollywood Edge; Network Sound Effects; The Works; International SFX; BBC; Animal Trax; Warner; Hanna Barbera; and singles from various other libraries

Microphones: "I own many mics, but most commonly use my Neumann U-87."

Development systems: In-house proprietary stuff

6.1.2 Work for Hire Agreements

When a song or sound effect is created, these audio entities are owned entirely and exclusively by the creator unless that creator happens to be working under a Work for Hire Agreement. This type of contract states, in various manners, that any work created for a specific project is owned by the company that hired you. There's little doubt who owns the work in question. In-house composers and sound designers are always under this type of agreement. They work directly for a game developer, the developer pays them a salary to be on their staff, and thus, the company has the rights to everything created on their premises.

There are varying agreements which allow in-house personnel to retain rights to their creations if they are not done for a specific project, but to keep this concept simple, assume if you work in-house, the company owns all your work. It can be negotiated to use the studio for your *own* projects after hours or to do other freelance work during down time which you keep all rights to. Some companies are OK with this; others strictly forbid composers to do any outside projects. Be sure to ask if you apply for an in-house position and intend to continue doing outside contracting work.

For the third-party contractor, this type of agreement is left a bit more open to interpretation and negotiation. It is entirely possible, by signing an agreement in the developer's favor, for them to own everything you do for a specific project. That means every scratch music track you produce during the composing and recording process and every sound used to produce the sound effects could potentially belong to them.

For example, I did a sound effect of an old prospector and his mule walking up to a gold mine where the character says, "Well, looky there Betsy, it's the Lucky Nugget!" The sound is a compilation of the character's voice, a mule braying, pots and pans clanging, and a crow squawking. It was created under a Work for Hire Agreement. The original agreement stated the developer would own all of the sounds used to create the effect — including the voice characterization done by hired voice talent. I negotiated, instead, that the sound they would own would be the work in its final form and *not* the pieces used to construct it. My argument was simple. Everything up until the point of completion was an "idea" and it would create problems trying to control ownership of sound that I don't own the rights to in the first place. Some sounds were taken from licensed sound libraries and some I recorded myself. If they had insisted, I would have explained while it could be done and that I would be willing to sell specific sounds I had recorded, it would severely limit my creativity having to rely solely on my own remote recording abilities and then being able to use the sound only once. Because of the time involved, they could not afford paying me to go out into the field to record donkeys and crows every time I needed one. Having my own library and other licensed sound libraries at my disposal saves an incredible amount of time and money.

The Work for Hire Agreement is not a bad way to proceed if you pay attention to the points of the contract. They are negotiable and it behooves you to ensure your interests are covered. The developer will have to own *something* — there is no getting around that, unless limited licenses are involved whereas you grant them the full use of music and sounds in the one game on the one platform. Then, licensing issues will come into play if they want use it on other platforms or sequels to the game. It gets even more complicated, so hang on.

6.1.3 Copyrights

Copyright issues could easily make for an entire book but instead, I will attempt a few highlights in a couple of paragraphs. Copyrights can be complicated and as clear as mud — needing an entire staff of lawyers to understand completely.

In a nutshell, whomever owns the copyright to a piece of work, being either music or a sound effect, owns the work in its entirety and is free to use and/or license the work for whatever and to whomever they choose.

For our purposes in the gaming world, the developer or publisher will almost always demand to own the music and sound outright leaving little room for discussion. By doing so, they can now reuse your music and sound effects in every sequel to the game, on every platform, in every television commercial, in every movie, even release a soundtrack album — all without you ever seeing another dime.

Now, to sidetrack for a moment, if you end up licensing the audio for every instance mentioned previously, you are set to do very well without lifting another finger. The work is already done; the game companies are just paying you more to use it in the other instances. If they insist on owning the copyrights, it becomes another matter and in order for you *not* to lose future monies for your efforts, you must charge them a much higher fee for a complete buy-out. With development budgets first on their minds, you can offer the same work for less money in a licensing arrangement. If they insist on owning all rights, then they will have to understand it will cost them more for you to leave your work and walk away.

An argument, using the previous story about the old prospector, could also relate to copyright issues. Who owns the voice characterization? In this case, the voice talent does. The only portion the game company owns is the line he spoke embedded in the complete sound effect. This "sound" is just another one of the layers of sounds which make up the entire effect in its final form. They don't own the character. Now, if they were making a CD-ROM game called "The Zany Adventures of Mr. Prospector and his Mule, Betsy," then the vocal characterization rights could be transferred to the game company. When a character is created for a large project, such as Duke Nukem, the game company will purchase the rights for that voice characterization to ensure that other games don't hit the market using their specific character. They will pay quite a bit more to retain ownership and the rights to exclusively use the character.

6.1.4 Licenses

Licensing is when the owner of a copyrighted piece of work grants exclusive or non-exclusive use of the work for a negotiated fee. When a song is composed and recorded onto a particular medium, the composition is protected under copyright laws. If you file an application with the US Copyright Office for the piece of work, you own the copyright in a more official and legal sense. As we mentioned before, if you sell that song to a game company to use in their game, you've transferred the copyright to them and they are free to use it in every game, every commercial, and every soundtrack they produce until the copyright expires and the music enters the public domain. Licensing comes into play when you let another entity, such as a game company, borrow your song for their project, but you retain all rights to it.

Smaller developers would be more likely to seek out licenses to use your work in their game because it is more affordable for them. Because they are not buying the rights to the work, they will instead pay a smaller fee for the privilege of using it. You will grant them limited use of the work to be used *only* in their game and nowhere else. Depending on the agreement, they may negotiate that you cannot not sell the music to another game company for a reasonable amount time, so that they may retain some semblance of originality. It doesn't mean you can't turn around and sell the music to a film or TV project; you can indeed if it's part of the agreement.

Music and sound effect libraries use this concept in their daily business practices. Audio is usually released in CD format; some offered as downloads from the internet. When a purchase is made, it may be implied mistakenly that the buyer owns the music and sound effects. You've got a physical piece of matter in your hand which was paid for, it can be naturally assumed it belongs to you. In the case of library titles, this is a wrong assumption. The company is only granting the license to use the included materials as stated in their purchase agreement. You don't have an exclusive right to the sounds. Any other party who pays the users fee can use it in their projects too.

Licensing is possible in the gaming world although developers usually strive to own the original compositions in their projects outright. But a cost-conscious one might consider the option of licensing instead.

6.1.5 Platforms

Game platforms are considered to be any console, computer system, or game system that a computer or video game can be played on. The PC, Mac, Nintendo, Dreamcast, Playstation, Game-Boy, Xbox, and video arcade consoles are all examples of separate game platforms. You will often hear a developer say a game will be "ported" to another platform, meaning that conversions will be made to the game in order to work on another game platform. Your ears should perk up a little when you hear that word because it could mean some extra income for you. I'll give more details in the section "Negotiable Contract Points" on page 127.

6.1.6 SKUs

A SKU (pronounced "skew"), or Stock Keeping Unit, is another way of saying "game release" or "game platform." It's actually a unique code assigned to merchandise for inventory purposes. When making video games and porting them from one platform to another, a new SKU will be generated for the new version of the game to be sold to the public. These numbers can be found in the product's bar code enabling stores with computerized inventory and point-of-sale systems to keep track of merchandise. Practically every item you find for sale in a store will have its own unique SKU — whether it's the grocery store or the record store.

For us in gaming, it can mean additional income to the savvy content provider who has foresight. Not only could a game be released on a different platform as another SKU, but say the same PC game is translated to another language for sale overseas. The game could be identical in every respect except for the language and this SKU could earn you income if your music and sound effects are used in it. While technically it won't be issued a distinctive code for sale in the US, it's considered a different product and could earn you additional monies.

6.1.7 Ancillary Rights

Ancillary rights pertain to the usage of content outside the project it was originally intended. Music and sound effects for games occasionally stray into other domains such as television, film, and CD soundtrack releases — far from the original purpose of their creation. When working under an agreement to compose music or create sound effects, the intention is to conceive these original pieces for the video game only. This is as far as they ever go most of time. But the billion dollar video game industry is far reaching and there will be instances when music you've composed or sounds you've designed will appear outside the boundaries of the game.

"Earthworm Jim" is an example of a video game character turned Saturday morning cartoon star. Tommy Tallarico had done the music for the game series and because of his negotiation prowess, he was also paid when the music was used in the cartoon series. The game company owned the music rights in the game, but Tommy had included an ancillary rights clause to split any net profits earned by his music outside of that game. Bobby Prince of DOOM fame had also negotiated ancillary rights to his audio work in the game and was compensated after a few sound effects appeared in several movies. This type of agreement allows the composer and sound designer to continue to reap the benefits and rewards of their efforts when their work appears outside of the games realm. While it isn't quite the standard in the industry, enough game composers and sound designers are including it in their agreements that it is becoming more and more commonplace.

6.1.8 Bonuses and Royalties

Being part of a blockbuster game project is like winning the lottery. It's never anything we plan on. After months of putting our blood and sweat into the music and sound obligation, we normally part with a nice paycheck and thanks for our efforts. Occasionally, a game does so well that it breaks sales records around the world. In cases like this, it isn't enough to just be part of the winning team; it has to be in your contract for you to receive a bonus or royalty payments.

Bonuses are usually more palatable for a game company. For example, if their break-even point on a game is 60,000 units, a bonus after 100,000 units sold is a comfortable margin and the game company shouldn't have a problem with sending additional money your way. They can be set up in various stages, say a $10,000 bonus after 100,000 units, a $25,000 bonus after 250,000 units, and so on. It's completely up to you and the company during contract negotiations. Bonuses are easy to calculate and audit because they are based solely on the number of units sold.

Royalties are payments of a percentage of sales, usually made in quarterly installments. Unlike the music industry, the games industry usually turns its nose up at this type of arrangement. Calculating payments demands too much book-keeping and time. It's not unheard of, just not a pleasant experience for the game company. If they scoff at the idea, consider the next option.

A more "planned" form of royalties, similar to bonuses, are straight percentages. These payments are calculated from net profit, after the game company has recouped its costs and has had a reasonable return on the investment. Like bonuses, payments can also be structured in stages based on the number of units sold or amount of money earned in increasing levels. The percentage could also be established at a comfortable number past their break-even point. An acceptable figure in the industry for established game composers is 1–1.5% of the net profits.

Normally, bonuses and royalties are negotiated by game composers who do music or both music and sound for a project. It is less common for a sound designer to negotiate bonuses and royalties for sound effects only, but not far fetched. I, as a sound designer, wouldn't consider asking for a bonus on smaller games where I only do a couple dozen sounds. For major game releases and hundreds of effects, that would be a different story. It is entirely dependent on the situation. But, it never hurts to ask. The worst that could happen is they say "no."

Deals with publishers will be more lucrative — they've got the bigger pie. That pie, in turn, gets divvied up amongst the developer and everyone else associated with the project. If you were to make the deal directly with a developer, unless they are self-publishing the title, you would be negotiating for a piece of their smaller slice of pie. Most of the time, the developer has to consult with the publisher when royalties and bonuses are brought to the table anyway, so why not just deal with them directly on the matter?

6.1.9 Property Rights

To further complicate matters, we can sell music to a game company but keep the property rights to release the music on a soundtrack CD. It is similar in theory to negotiating ancillary rights, but this endeavor won't be split with the game company. "How can that be?" you ask. A game company is not a record company; they aren't set up that way and they don't understand the intricacies associated with it. They sell games. They distribute games. They do not sell music. There are record companies set up to duplicate, market, distribute, and sell game music and its success can be attributed to their years of experience. If I was to release music I'd worked hard on and was proud to share apart from the game experience, then I would want to go with the outlet with the most potential.

Still, the music will be associated with the game it was created for and having the game company's support will make the experience much easier for both parties. While they may be reluctant at first, once they see the excitement your efforts bring to their product, they should be thrilled. You will shoulder the risks entirely — covering all the costs of the soundtrack release, handling all the details, and never involving their time or resources in the process. They take no risk whatsoever and reap the advertising benefits and hype your efforts create. They'd be blind to miss the potential rewards of this type of plan.

6.1.10 Talent Releases

Whenever guest musicians and voice-over talent are involved on a project, it is always a good idea to have them sign a talent release. This legal document releases all the interests and legal rights of their performances to you, the contractor, and/or the game company. By doing so, the developer can be assured their interests are protected and that someone who may have played a small role in the overall production doesn't come back years later, after the game is a hit, and sue for more money. In most cases, these documents are a requirement and will be a part of your contract to ensure no one else has any interest in a piece of work but you.

These documents also serve as a mini contract for your guest talent, outlining the services required of them, how much they will be paid, and any other specific points unique to the project. Professionals expect to sign such paperwork and understand the need. Others, not as accustomed to the particulars, might not be as willing to part with their signature and may need some gentle persuasion. Be careful to not get into a situation where your hired talent doesn't sign the release. If you use it in the project, it could lead to more trouble than you are willing to deal with when the developer comes looking for you down the road. Make the agreement plain and simple; either they sign the release or they don't get paid. Period.

Be sure to check out the sample agreements and contracts beginning on page 143
of this chapter, and on the companion CD-ROM.

6.2 Negotiable Contract Points

When negotiating contracts, the sky can be the limit. The process generally hinges directly on the personalities involved on the two sides, what their interests are, and how creative they want to be when solving issues. Simple and reasonable requests can be taken care of easily, but difficult issues can take weeks before reaching some kind of consensus, leaving behind tension and ill will.

During contract negotiations, your general concerns will be how much work you need to do, how much time you have to do it in, and when and how much you get paid for doing it. In most simple gaming projects, there won't be much more than that. We are gearing up for the larger projects — where you work hard, get paid well, and can receive additional rewards for your efforts. There is much at stake for game companies and for you, which is why we need to be smart when dealing with these types of situations.

Part of being "smart" is knowing and understanding what contract points are acceptable in this particular business. The items discussed next are by no means all inclusive. We will cover some serious ground, but in order to get it all, I'd need to write another book. For those of us who are imaginative with contract negotiations, there will be many "one time" opportunities that present themselves and it will be up to you to take advantage of them. It will simply become another natural part of doing business.

1. Money

The primary negotiable contract point is money — mainly how much will you get paid and by what method. Much time can be spent dancing diplomatically around this particular issue. You know your costs and what you would want to make on the project. This is the leeway you have to play with during negotiations. Assuming the game company had you bid on the project first, they also have a good starting number with which to work from too. You heard right: "starting" point. Don't feel compelled to stay with your original figure to avoid looking greedy. The parameters of the project might have change several times since your original bid submission. You will need to adjust your price accordingly. They need to understand that it is due to their changes, not yours. Be ready for it.

Once a game company brings you in as part of the team, they tend to begin coming to you for everything; advice, favors, or other trivial audio matters. They may think it would be cool to have audio for their company logo. They may need a sound effect for another project and will ask you to do it. They will call on you for almost everything and while it's certainly OK to do these kind of favors, you need to be aware it will be taking time away from other valuable money-making endeavors. Keep this in the back of your mind during negotiations and bring it to the table to justify your request for more money if they challenge your figure. Remember, they are a business attempting to keep as much money in their pockets as possible and since their bottom line is the most visible to management and investors, their need to justify expenditures is tremendous. These "favors" can tip the scale to your favor.

If the amount of money you request for the project becomes an excuse for them to find someone else, concede this "deal ender" and consider making up losses in other areas. If the amount of initial cash outlay is the problem, change the amounts of milestone payments to their liking with the later payments being the highest. Or negotiate your payments, bonuses, or royalties from their incoming receipts instead of from their operating capital. Or negotiate equivocal services; perhaps artwork for your website, programming a simple interactive demo for your promotion package, web site hosting, or maybe even a trade for some computer or recording gear they have laying around. If there is a problem, work together to solve it instead of facing each other unblinking from opposing ends of the table. By being flexible, you will gain points to use during other issues of the negotiation.

2. Licensing

As mentioned earlier, most game companies insist on owning the music and sound effects created for their project. Under a Work for Hire Agreement, this is clearly stipulated and it will give you the impression there is nothing left to negotiate. Again, we could not be further from the truth. Everything is still completely negotiable! There are many types of licenses in this type of work — more than we could ever cover sufficiently. Whatever you do, during discussions about licensing, be sure to keep your options open and ready for anything.

If a game company complains your prices are too high for the buy-out option, suggest they license your music and sound at a lower cost instead. You'll recall that by licensing your music, they don't have ownership; just a license to use it in their work. You would still retain full copyrights and could sell or re-license the work to others at your discretion. Smaller game companies who end up licensing work will negotiate an *exclusivity agreement* that states that the music won't appear in any other video game application or does so only after a pre-determined amount of time has expired (usually a year or two, depending on the life expectancy of the product). You can be very creative here.

Another licensing issue could be your right to self promotion, that is, to use works you created for demonstration purposes. If a company opts for the full buy-out, they own the copyrights, leaving you begging permission to use your own music. Seems silly, I know, but that's the way it is in the big world. Under normal circumstances, they have no qualms letting you promote your work and will license the music back to you for this purpose. They will never volunteer it though. It will be something you have to ask for because it is serving your interests and not theirs. Here's an example of wording you might use for this application:

> Right to Self-Promotion. Contractor has the right to self promotion and is allowed to use, as creator of said works, any works created under this contract, to demonstrate the capabilities of contractor either in demo reel or computer file format at any time after acceptance of the work as final, without any further permissions required from Company.

3. Platforms

You sold your sonic masterpiece to a game company for a CD-ROM project and you assume that is that. Wrong again. What if they port it to PlayStation or Nintendo or GameBoy or make an arcade game out of the darn thing? Would you get compensated for your music and sound effects ported to these new versions? Unless you had it in the contract, the answer is a heartbreaking "No!".

Did you know there are people whose sole job in life is to take another composer's music, reperform, re-record, and convert it to a format compatible with another gaming platform? Why are they paying someone else to do it when they could be paying you instead? Why wouldn't they want the original composer to redo his own music in all its glory? Who knows. In order to protect this future income, have it as a contract point, stating you will do any conversions needed to port the music to any other game platform they request for an agreed upon sum. Assuming the music was great in the first place, you are assuring them that the same quality and feel will be accomplished in the new format, maintaining the high standards originally set forth. Another person's interpretation of your music is an unknown; you risk ruining the entire audio mood of the game. What would game developers rather have: the original composer recreating his heartfelt masterpiece or someone else coldly regurgitating musical notes for a paycheck? Remind them of your value and get it in the contract.

4. SKUs

Almost hand-in-hand with the platform issue is the SKU. Don't walk away knowing they plan to release the project on other game platforms and in other languages to be sold internationally. Are you crazy? The company intends to make fists fulls of cash by releasing the game in several different versions using artwork, programming, and sound already paid for. Except for the cost to port and re-package, their profit margin is huge. What do the original creators receive for their hard work and dedication? Nothing, unless they negotiated this point in the contract. Get it in your contract too!

SKUs, next to royalties and bonuses, allow the greatest income potential you can realize.

In order to take advantage of this potential money-maker, you will have to negotiate that the music and sound effects you create and sell to them are for the *primary SKU only*. If they use it in another, they have to pay you for that right. Big games, with average budgets of $1.5 million dollars, will cost a publisher roughly $200,000 to port to another platform. After much market research, they know this SKU will make a hefty profit for them or they wouldn't have wasted their time doing it in the first place. Do you think they would really care if you asked them for an additional $10,000 for every SKU your audio appeared in? With large budgets, this is just a drop in the bucket and won't affect their bottom line whatsoever. But they will probably resist — saying they've paid you for the audio, it's their property, and they can use it however they like. Until you sign the contract, it's not their music, so you would really be arguing about nothing. If they intend to make other versions of a game, using your audio, and making a handsome profit for themselves, why couldn't they reward the hard-working creators who made it happen for them with a measly ten thousand bucks? As an enticement, you can offer to make any necessary conversions for that fee, saving them the cost of having someone else do it. It then becomes an "extra service" you perform and they can justify it to the bean counters. If $10,000 is still too steep, after you've exhausted every argument, consider dropping it a couple thousand but don't ever give it away for free.

5. Ancillary Rights

Occasionally, other money-making opportunities present themselves outside of gaming. If the popularity of the game spawns a TV show, cartoon, or movie, chances are, your music and sound will be licensed as part of this new undertaking as well. Who gets paid for it? It depends on what's in the contract.

As mentioned previously, ancillary rights are not standard in the industry, yet. For the big composers, however, it is more so and the practice will trickle down the scale as time goes on. One of the ways to achieve this is to make it a standard request for each contract. Eventually, when a game company pulls out their contract for signature, this clause will already be there. After every composer they've dealt with brings it to the table, they'll catch on, and save some time by just doing it upfront. That will be a nice change.

For those who regularly negotiate this point, the usual agreement is to split the net profits derived from the reuse of your music and sounds 50/50. Because they will be spending money to make these new endeavors a reality (hiring lawyers, additional marketing and administrative chores), it is appropriate to split the money *after* they've recouped their costs, i.e., the net — not gross income. Divvy up the profits more in their favor if need be; say 60/40. If you are open to some give and take in the process, you can still walk away with a tidy sum. Or you could hold fast and lose the deal completely. It's a fine art indeed.

The same goes if they decide to release your music on a soundtrack CD. You can either negotiate to split the profits from this type of product or try another tactic: negotiating the property rights to release the music on your own, which we'll talk about shortly. The direction and the mood of the proceedings depend on the personalities at the bargaining table, which points they hold fast to, and what your needs are to secure fair compensation for your work. If they don't like splitting their profits with you for a soundtrack release, consider doubling your fee to make up for the lost income potential. An example: If the CD of your music sells 100,000 copies, your potential income could be $250,000! Doubling your rate from $50,000 to $100,000 for complete buy-out on the project might seem like a lot to them, but it won't come close to the possibilities of what your hit game soundtrack could do in Japan or Europe. Consider what world-wide sales of your music could bring to the publisher and it seems ludicrous not to share in the fortune.

6. Bonuses and Royalties

There are many different ways to proceed when dealing with these types of contract points. Generally, the easier you can make it for them, the more willing they will be to agree to your terms. They shouldn't have a problem spreading the wealth to the people who helped make the game a success, and as a composer and sound designer, you are responsible for 1/3 of the total game experience. Good businesses appreciate the contributions from the creative team and will reward them accordingly. Others, more concerned with squeezing every bit of profit they can from a game, will be less likely. If you have the misfortune of running across the latter type, you will have to work much harder to convince them you are deserving of more compensation. If it becomes a heated contest, then consider walking away from the deal, because at this point, it has all the signs of a rocky relationship and no money in the world would be worth it.

Royalties are not common so the path of least resistance would be to request structured bonus payments as the alternative. Instead of a requesting a percentage of their income from the game, which becomes complicated back in their accounting department, suggest bonuses based on the number of units sold. All you have to keep track of is how many of the darn games they've sold and if it has passed one of your negotiated milestones. Simple enough. And because this money is from incoming receipts and purely based on sales figures, they are assuming no risk and will lose nothing if a game doesn't sell well.

To establish your bonus structure, you need to know their break-even point and then set your first installment at a comfortable level above it, say 75% to 100% more. As an example, if a game's break-even point is 60,000 units, it would be acceptable to ask for a $10,000 bonus after 100,000 units sold, $20,000 after 200,000 units, and so on.

Because these negotiations are happening prior to any work being done, this incentive can have a direct impact on how well you do your job. If they've set a generous payment schedule in front of you and correlate your creative efforts with the success of the game, you will be highly motivated to do the best work you've ever done. With that kind of backing and trust, you will naturally step up to the plate and hit a homerun! Psychologically, it is an incredible boost to your creative powers and you will strive to make this game a hit. Remind them of this, as part of your presentation. Let them know what you can do if properly stimulated. Or, explain what the opposite effect will have. While you are a professional and can provide high quality music and sound effects regardless, the lack of inspiration and the sense that the company is just a sweatshop will have a dramatic, negative effect.

7. Property Rights for Soundtrack Release

As a composer, it is essential for our success and business well-being that a music soundtrack CD is released. It is the type of national exposure and money-making potential that may have enticed you into the music business in the first place, except that we are accomplishing it now in the games industry. If the sales potential exists, you or the publisher will want to do it. Either way, your music has to be able to reach the masses and this is the perfect method. If acquiring the ancillary rights and splitting the gross profits for the soundtrack doesn't appeal to the game company in question, perhaps they would be willing to let you try your hand at releasing one instead. It won't cost them a cent and they will take absolutely none of the risk while gaining the marketing and exposure advantages. Unless they have plans to release a soundtrack in the works already, there is absolutely no reason they couldn't let you give it a try.

8. Name Credits, Logos, and Splash Screens

Naturally, after all of this effort, money is not the only thing you want to negotiate. There are many other points to take advantage of which will increase your business and name recognition. There is no better advertising for your services than the music and sound effects you've proudly created presented within a game. For vanity's sake, millions of people living the experience your audio creates is an uplifting event. For marketing sake, having other game developers researching and playing these games, hearing your efforts, is the best "demo" you can offer. When game companies decide to do a project, they generally examine every other game in the genre. Wouldn't it be great to have them discover the perfect composer for their new production in one of these games? Of course it would!

Now, in order for future clients and fans to know who did the brilliant audio, it has to be seen somewhere. Don't take this point for granted — thinking they will automatically give you space on their credits page. Most companies do attempt to give credit where credit is due, but just to make sure, have it in your contract that they will, at a minimum, include your name in any printed or on-screen credit sections. Take it a step further and have them include your contact information or web address too.

You can also request to have your name and logo on the box cover and as one of the opening splash screens while the game is loading. You can't beat the value of your audience anxiously awaiting the game to start and seeing an entire screen with your name on it, something like: "Music and Sound Effects by award winning composer …". It also builds excitement just before the curtain is opened. Psychologically, it will even make their perception of the sound better because, obviously, this sound guy must be good if they have his logo everywhere! TV and film always give a full screen to the key players so the public is accustomed to this method of presentation. For the rest of the game, the player will be listening a little bit closer to see who this notable personality is. That's what you want, to be noticed!

At this point in time, there are not many composers and sound designers requesting their name or logo on the box cover or on the splash screen. And, to tell you the truth, I believe it's just because they haven't thought of it yet. Here's a chance to get a leg up in the marketing department if you're in the mood. Game companies don't mind flashing a small picture file or sparing some pixels for your name on a splash screen, but logos on box covers may be another story. PC game boxes have generous real estate to accommodate 1/4" × 1/4" logos. They are seldom denied. PlayStation and Nintendo boxes, CDs, and game cartridges are much smaller and it's usually not possible to squeeze them on even if they wanted to. What little space there is they keep and it will be fought over ferociously in-house between their marketing, art, and sales departments. In cases like this, push a little harder for that splash screen because it will probably be all can you get.

9. Final Authority

It is extremely important to have the person who has final approval of your work identified and that person's name put in the contract. Why, you say? Because you want to get paid, that's why. Otherwise, decisions will be put off, waiting for someone else's opinion, and it will go around and around in the company until the game is published. No one wants to take sole responsibility. There are many creative people with varied opinions involved during development and it is impossible to please everyone. Have one named individual who can give "thumbs up" to your submissions, going on their own gut instinct or after taking a poll, allowing you to meet milestones and get paid according to the schedule in the contract.

Another war story for you. I've had a couple of companies whom I've done sound for call me up in a bind and need some sounds done within a couple of days. I jump on it, fire them off, and then never hear a thing back. After a couple of weeks, I start to wonder and grab the phone to find out they are beta testing or waiting for the company president or something else to happen before they make the decision on which sounds they will keep. Weeks turn into a couple of months and still nothing. Finally, after about three months, now that the game has been released, I find out what I need to know and send an invoice. A lot of work to be paid for a dozen sound effects and by the time the check arrives, I've forgotten what project it was for. If we'd agreed upon the final authority at the beginning and in this case, changed my billing method from "per sound effect" to an hourly rate and billed them immediately, we both could have saved the extra effort.

I work best knowing who it is I'm trying to please. Ultimately, it is the game player, of course, but in this business, it will normally be the Executive Producer or Creative Director or someone high up on the project's design team. You'll have to work closely with this individual and it will be important to know their thought processes, what they need to make the decisions, and how best to keep them happy. There is a bit of "schmoozing" involved, but the definitive test will be the quality of sounds you submit. If they get the sense you are working hard, they'll feel they are getting their money's worth and are more apt to use sounds and music you've submitted instead of having you redo them.

6.3 Navigating Negotiations

Musicians and sound designers are not taken to be serious businessmen. The free and easy life-styles we supposedly live makes us a little too "wild" for the business world and we are quickly pigeon-holed into this category. One of the unique traits that set game composers apart from the rest of the musician world is that we do have a fairly good nose for business — we have to be in order to run a successful company. But the stereotype is so well entrenched, you'll have to try much harder to prove yourself.

The demo package is the game company's first look into what we are about. The bidding process is their first chance to see whether we have some brains to go along with our creative genius. The contract negotiations will set the tone of your business relationship, whether you are the whiny, prima donna artiste they originally feared or a professional service provider with a good sense for business and honest concern about the product's success.

Normal contract negotiations start by the person who brought you on board (usually the game producer) faxing or emailing you their contract. You spend a few days looking it over, talking with your legal advisor, adding your points, countering with your version, or simply signing. If you did have something to add, they'll mull it over, talk to their legal people, hem and haw amongst themselves, and will counter with their new version. At this point, you will find it much easier to just pick up the phone and talk directly to the producer. Emails can cloud the process, becoming too time consuming or harmless comments can be taken out of context, unintentionally offending someone. You can safely discuss the points which are most important, reach some sort of agreement, then wait for their legal department to give the final OK. Once they've finalized the contract, you'll sign it and then get down to what you've been hungry for: making music and sounds. Simple enough.

The more complicated negotiations may require you to fly to their office with your team and meet face-to-face with a boardroom full of their people. It doesn't actually happen as much as you'd think, though, so don't get nervous. Be prepared for this possibility only when you start dealing with large companies with large budgets and large global interests.

6.3.1 A Real World Negotiation

Out of the dozen contracts I've negotiated, there was only one which didn't go very well. Most of the time, it's a simple business affair with the two parties calmly and professionally discussing the needs of both companies. We resolved them amicably and moved on with our lives. This particular example was definitely a case of big egos on their part and concrete stubbornness on my part and in the end, we both walked away — them without sound for their game and me without a contract. I mention it here as a real world case of what can happen when the two sides can't see eye-to-eye. Maybe we can both learn something.

I was called to a game developer's office to discuss a work for hire contract with the company's president and executive producer. The game was funded by a big name in Hollywood and, on the outside, looked to be a promising title. It was to be released for the PC and Playstation simultaneously with later plans for a Nintendo version. We were still one year away from the expected release and it appeared I could accommodate the project in my schedule. It looked like the kind of game I wanted to be associated with and I was anxious to get to work.

The speculative demo I had submitted was good enough to beat out three other composers and I was excited to be their man. I showed up 10 minutes early and was ushered into the board-room to wait until the company's key players could attend. After a half an hour sitting alone, the president walked in, apologized for the delay, said it would be just a couple more minutes and disappeared. Forty-five minutes later, three of them walked in, apologized, and we settled in. At this point, I'm forcing a smile. I'm on their home turf, outnumbered, my butt is getting sore, and I have the sudden urge to use the restroom. Instead of giving them the chance to disappear and get involved with something else, I shuffle in my seat and decide to hold it instead. We've got work to do and I have another commitment to attend to later that day.

"Aaron, thanks for coming. We're looking forward to having you on board as an integral part of the team and can't wait to get things rolling. We've got high hopes for the game and we'll probably be working you hard," the president said, firmly in charge of the meeting. I nodded my head, smiled, and continued to listen. They moved into the history of the company, how the game came to be, and mentioned Mr. Hollywood's name about a dozen times. I continued to nod and smile, trying to hold in my excitement as things were building towards a good offer. I was waiting for someone to slide a copy of a contract in front of me, but soon realized they didn't have one. Instead, they verbally covered the high points, all the standard contract stuff, non-disclosures, ownership of the rights, my duties, blah, blah, blah. I kept copious notes during the process, noting that they required that I be on-site three days out of the week. I put a star by it; I'd have to find out what they mean by that. I feverishly continued, trying to digest what they were saying and preparing my rebuttal speech, the opportunity which I knew had to be coming soon.

"All right, Aaron. That's it. Thanks for coming."

"Uh, but I've got a few questions and a couple of items I'd like to discuss." I stuttered, slightly stunned by the speed of my dismissal.

"Sorry. We're out of time," he said looking at his watch. "We've got something pressing to attend to. We'll fax you the contract shortly, just sign it and fax it back. In the meantime, you can start working on some other ideas, and if you could have them to us by the end of next week, that would be great. Thanks again," and they were gone.

I sat alone in silence for a moment wondering what the hell just happened. Did I say something wrong? No, couldn't have been that, I never got to open my mouth. Oh well. These guys are obviously busy, I shouldn't worry. I'll give them a call tomorrow instead.

On the trip home, I couldn't avoid the uneasy feeling I was getting about this job. I couldn't put my finger on it, but something wasn't quite right here. Different game companies have different styles but these guys were downright odd. Why did they keep name-dropping? Why did they call me all the way to their office for that? Why do I need to be on-site? A lot of questions, much to answer. Maybe I shouldn't start any work on this until we have a signed contract.

The next day, I called Mr. President, he was in, seemed to be in a good mood, and more receptive to two-way conversation. He talked a lot about the project, what kind of audio feel they wanted, sticking to a safe subject. I heard him mention they would be doing their own "sound design" in-house, using one of their programmers. They had just bought a sound library they would be using exclusively. "Do you think we bought a good sound library? By the way, what's a good audio editing program? Do you think I can get a good one under a hundred bucks?" he asked. I reminded him I was also a sound designer and could take care of the sound effects instead of leaving it to their guy who would surely be busy doing other duties. I also explained that the sound library he bought had been available for many years and the sounds were already overused. I could make fresh, original sounds for the game, giving it its own audio identity, so to speak. Without even talking price or considering my idea, he said "no," and that was that. I attempted to shift the conversation towards the contract and was suddenly placed on hold. He had another call. Two minutes later he was back on, saying I should be there tomorrow morning at 10 AM to discuss the contract. OK, I'll be there. Here we go again.

Ten AM, I'm steered into the president's office. He's on the phone. I get a nod to be seated and take up position directly across from him. He's not smiling. The phone conversation ends and, without as much as a hello, he rolls in right where we left off two days ago.

"Here's the deal. We need 60 to 75 minutes of music for the game and would like it completed within 60 days," he opened.

"What kind of budget are you proposing?" I asked trying to get a feel for the overall picture.

"The entire audio budget is $10,000 — sound effects and music," he countered.

As I scrape my jaw up off the floor, trying not to look offended by the apparent slap in the face, I do a quick calculation in my head. Hmmm, my usual fee is $1000 per finished minute, that would be $60–75,000. I could discount the entire project to roughly $700 a minute, that would be $42–52,500, and maybe go as low as an even $40,000. But he was proposing 60 to 75 minutes at $10,000. I would have to drop my price to $166.67 or $133.34 per finished minute.

"How much is left for the music if you guys are doing the sound effects in-house?" I ask.

"About $9,000," he says. Then seeing a sign that I'm having some trouble with that particular figure (which I thought was hidden behind my poker face), he continues. "Just think of the exposure you'd have as a composer on this game. This game is going to be big. We've already run the numbers and between the three platforms, we expect at least a quarter million units to be sold. This would be great for you. Just think of it. You could write your own ticket in the industry."

I silently doubt it and continue to grind the appropriate gears in my head. "$9,000 would be for one platform only?"

"Nope, for all three. We need to have full ownership of the music and $10,000 is a firm number."

"If I do the music for that price, would you consider a bonus, say after 100,000 units or perhaps royalties on each unit sold?"

"Nope."

"How about if I keep the rights to release the soundtrack on my own?"

"No can do. We require full ownership."

"Well, since I'd be practically giving away the music, what if I just sold you the rights for the video game? But if the music ever appeared in a TV show or movie or if you released a soundtrack, I could expect some income from that?"

"Aaron, I don't think you quite understand. We are offering you an opportunity to be a part of a very big project. Mr. Hollywood is backing us all the way and we know this will be big. With your name on this project, think of the other games that will practically fall into your lap. To have your name on a huge project is the best advertising you can get. I don't know what industry you are working in, but frankly, your rates are a little high. $10,000 is a very generous offer and we think you would be stupid to pass up this opportunity."

At this point, a hundred comebacks are running through my head, none of which I could actually say out loud. I know what rates are standard in the industry and I'm on the lower end of that. I know having my name on a big project will have a positive impact on my career. I know he makes a good case, but I'd be losing money and spending a lot of time on this. I have to make a living somehow. "You mentioned earlier that you required me to be on site three days a week. What is that about specifically?"

"Ah, yes. We will need your help to implement the sound effects and the music for the cinematics and gameplay. We'd need you here two, maybe three days a week for that. That isn't a problem, is it?"

"Will you pay my hourly wage for those days?"

"No, we were hoping you would include that in your fee," he said.

"Well, if I'm going to be spending time here, I won't be able to work on any other projects and I'd need to make something for my time," I countered.

"We'd like to, but it's not in our budget. We just can't do it. Sorry."

At this point, I think we'd hit rock bottom. They were asking me to score roughly 60 minutes of music plus they wanted me on-site to help implement (translation: help the programmer put the sounds in the game) three days a week for I don't know how long and pay me $10,000 for my efforts. No bonuses, no royalties, no soundtrack, no ancillary rights, no chance to make another dime off this project. I may have considered it for $50–60,000 and negotiated it down to one day every couple of weeks to be on-site, after all, I had to actually be in my studio to do the composing. I could tell this was going to be the veritable project from hell, and these guys were unbending. If it was such a big game with the backing of Mr. Hollywood, why wasn't there money to match? There were too many unanswered questions and I was still a little steamed at his comment asking me what industry I was working in. Somewhere in there I think he called me stupid too.

I didn't know what to do. We'd reached a sort of impasse and my spider senses were all tingly. It's hard to walk away from what could lead to fame and fortune, but I wasn't about to be a prostitute either, grumbling everyday about working for this obviously uncaring company who placed no value on the creative people. It was pretty clear the only ones who would benefit from this "big" game was the management and Mr. Hollywood. I wouldn't be able to convince them of their arrogance without making a scene so I had nothing else to say.

"Well, I appreciate your consideration for this project, it looks like it would be fun, but I'm going to have to pass on it," I said at last.

"What? Are you sure? You're giving up quite an opportunity here. Sure you won't reconsider? Why don't you think about it and call me in a couple days?"

"No, it's pretty clear. I can't do it. I would lose too much money doing this project. You aren't offering me any other chances to break even and I can't take the risk the game will be as big as you say. Unless you could bend on some of the points I mentioned, I just couldn't do it."

"No, unfortunately, we can't. We have everything laid out, budget wise, and it just couldn't be done on our end."

I sat there, unthinking, staring out the window behind his head.

"Well, Aaron, good luck to you then. Sorry we couldn't work together." He said, gesturing towards the door as he got up from behind his desk.

We shook hands and I departed. After a couple of months, I finally let it go. Yeah, I blew a perfectly legitimate chance to score a "big" game title, but what I ultimately saved on headache and lost revenue is what convinced me, without a doubt, I'd done the right thing. There will be other fish to fry, I'm certain of that. But, it's funny how things work out. If this deal had been offered to me just a couple of years ago, I would have jumped at it with both feet and learned many valuable lessons the hard way.

You don't have to live it to learn the lesson. Make sure you never get yourself in a losing position. Always look at your bottom line and the interests of your "company." The unscrupulous developers won't — they know creative people are a dime a dozen and if they dig down far enough, they'll eventually find someone who would beg to pay them to do the project. We don't want to cheapen the industry, so fight the good fight and get paid what you are worth. Sleep with one eye open if you have to.

6.3.2 Negotiation Pointers

The contract and negotiation process is most people's least favorite. The creative process is held up until the contract is complete and signed, and most people are just not prepared for this type of confrontation and find it hard to separate business from personal feelings. You'll find that a lot of people take every issue you present very personally and never quite get passed it. The rest of your working relationship suffers because you turned out to be a different person than what they may have originally perceived. It's not your fault, they just become mad at themselves for not being prepared for the business issues and your professional, business charm. They are like you, creative people who just want to make video games and hate ever having to deal with contracts and legal documents. That's why the big companies have legal departments, they handle the details, and the producer gets to make the games.

When you are presented with a contract and begin the process, keep it strictly business. Stay away from getting personal or taking things personally. When two companies get together to negotiate a contract for service, with teams of professionals sitting on opposite sides of a boardroom table, there is no doubt what they are accomplishing is business. Just because negotiations seem more intimate when it is just you and a producer, it is exactly the same.

TOOLS OF THE TRADE

Aaron Marks,
Independent
Composer/
Sound Designer,
On Your Mark
Music Productions

I consider myself a mid-level game composer and sound designer, having found my niche with mid-sized developers and on-line companies. Always open to catching the big fish, I gear my mindset and equipment list towards that goal. Previously, I had a collection of gadgets — impressive to studio visitors but basically just taking up rack space. I eventually streamlined to inventory only in constant use. If it hadn't been used in a year, out it went.

Computers: Two homebuilt PCs: a) Pentium III, 1 gHz, 512 MB RAM, 90 GB RAID array (two piggy-backed, 45 GB hard drives), CD-R, SoundBlaster LIVE Platinum 5.1 sound card, MidiMan USB 2 × 2 MIDI adapter, cable modem, dual head video card with 19" and 17" monitors. b) AMD-K6, 300 MHz, 64 MB RAM, 20 GB hard drive, CD-R, SoundBlaster LIVE gold sound card, MidiMan 2 × 2 MIDI card, cable modem. And a Pentium II, 500 MHz laptop with USB MIDI adapter

Software: Sonic Foundry Sound Forge, Vegas Pro, Cakewalk Sonar, ACID Pro, CD Architect, Cool Edit, Goldwave, numerous plug-ins

Multi-track: Two ADATs synced to PC, Nuendo, Cakewalk Sonar, Vegas Pro

Mixing board and monitor system: Tascam M2600 24 × 8 × 2, Alesis Monitor One, Alesis M1 active monitors, and Event PS8 active monitors

Mixdown deck: Sony DAT, Sony CD-R, PC hard drive

Outboard: Numerous effects processors and compressors

Keyboards and sound modules: Alesis QS8 with various Q-cards, Akai S5000 sampler and sample library, Roland Juno 106, Kawai K-1, Kurzweil MicroPiano, Akai AX-80

Instruments: Electric and acoustic guitars, bass guitar, Roland TDK-7E electronic drum set, standard acoustic drum set, numerous hand percussions, coronet, saxophone, flute, kazoo

Remote recording: A really long microphone cord

Sound effects libraries: Sound Ideas, BBC, my own collection

Don't be intimidated if you are outnumbered at the meeting. Think of it as a summit between all the team members, working together to solve certain issues. This mindset will keep you away from looking at it as an adversarial confrontation and let you work together towards the common good of both parties. There will be occasions when a developer may try using this intimidation factor — to keep you from asking for too much and digging into their bottom line. You'll have the upper hand instead with this way of thinking.

There will be times when carrots are dangled before you, certain enticements designed to get you to sign the contract without adding your points to it. Be on the look-out for these and never feel like you were pushed into "buying something" from an overly aggressive salesman type. If you feel pushed, back off with the ball in your court and slow the process down to a more comfortable level. One thing I will *not* do is sign something I haven't been able to fully review. I once had a game developer's lawyer fax me a contract with the instructions to "Sign this and return to me ASAP." The red flag went up, I told him I needed a few days to review it with my legal department and we ended up arguing about his take on copyright laws. Turns out, he knew nothing about copyrights and was a real estate lawyer who was helping out the developer and he wanted me to sign a document which would give his company full ownership of sounds I had licensed from a sound effects library! He didn't understand the concept that I could use licensed sounds as part of my work and sell the final product to them. Don't be forced into something you aren't totally comfortable with. While it may be a big company, with huge financial backing, your company is your life's blood and everything you agree to has a direct effect on its well being.

Here is another thought. Let's say I felt strongly about earning a bonus after the game sells 250,000 units and it was the only point I brought to the table. When they say "no" that one time, there will be no psychological effect you could use to springboard on to another point. The negotiations are over. If I brought *several* points to the table, it is nearly impossible for a decent human being to say "no" to every single one of them. Even if they tried, after a while, they would realize they were beginning to sound like parents, saying "no" without good reason.

Experienced salesmen use this trick everyday. They know you will say "no" at least five times before you start to waiver and eventually begin to say "yes." That's when they swoop in for the kill and make the deal. There have been studies done on this very phenomenon and I have experienced it firsthand myself at car dealerships and in other high-pressure sales situations. Our "trick" is to turn this around and use it in our favor.

If you bring every contract point mentioned earlier to the table, I guarantee you,
you'll walk away with one, if not several.

There is no need to be "high pressure" in this instance, but this subtle technique can definitely win you some bonus points.

Now, I don't recommend trying this at your first contract negotiation with a small developer. Save it for the big boys and you'll have good results; the smaller fish may get intimidated and assume you are too high caliber for their needs. Strike a delicate balance between what you ask for and what you know is a reasonable request. I wouldn't fight and claw my way into having a small developer, who is self-publishing a title, give me a $10,000 bonus after the game sells 100,000 copies. An instance such as that would be lucky to sell 20,000 — plus a $10,000 bonus seems like a lot of money to developers on shoe-string budgets. I would rather get my logo on the box and a splash screen in the game. I know they could do that.

Only you know what your business needs to survive, income-wise and marketing-wise. That's what a game project ultimately represents. You alone will have to look out for those interests. Even if the developer works for the most benevolent organization out there, they won't know your needs unless you express them.

You may be sitting there thinking, "man, this guy is a greedy son-of-a-gun." I wouldn't say it that way. I just know what the industry will tolerate and I ask for it. I became a musician for many reasons and being able to actually make a decent living doing it is a dream I am finally living. Business is not a place for timidness. Greatness cannot be achieved without taking care of your survival needs first and then being able to have the equipment to make grand music. It costs money and lots of it. I'm telling you, this is a great way to make it all happen. Make lots of money. Buy your gear. Make awe-inspiring music. Rise to greatness on your talents and achieve the type of recognition you deserve. Ask for the bonuses, royalties, ancillary rights, and property rights and be successful. If you just sign their contract to make a fast $10,000 and nothing else, you've made the quick buck but you've missed the point. You'll always struggle and will eventually be unable to continue in your pursuits. You have to take care of yourself by taking care of business first. That's what the negotiation process is really about.

6.4 Change Orders and Reworks

A *change order* happens when a developer decides the creative route they are taking is wrong and makes the decision to try another direction instead. These moments happen in every business, around the world, but the first time it happens to you, it will literally crush you. How would you feel after spending a couple of months living and breathing a project, composing a magnificent score, putting your heart and soul into it, days away from recording it with a full orchestra, and then having a producer tell you they've decided on a techno score instead?! Or how about actually completing a sound effects project and getting the word at the last minute they need to be redone for a different "period in time"? Your first instinct will be to throw your hands in the air. Your second thought will be: how are these contingencies covered in the contract?

Change orders happen. They are a way of life in the winds of creativity and big business. Expect them, prepare for them, plan for them. But, unfortunately, there is no correct formula to apply when putting it in writing. Just make sure you are not caught in a position where you are taken advantage of and start losing money on the deal.

In a case where you may be working towards milestones, have it put in the contract that if any major creative changes are requested, you will keep the payments already received and a new milestone schedule will be worked out. If you are working for a flat fee, make sure something is in the contract or a separate agreement which covers any added expense and time on your part. Spoken agreements are easily forgotten.

Reworks are a close cousin of change orders and also something to watch for. While change orders are basically starting over, *reworks* are taking the same piece and redoing it until it is right. For music, it might mean replacing certain instrumentation that sonically interferes with something else or changing the length of the piece. Maybe that music needs a gradual fade in and fade out; maybe it needs to be louder. The same for sound effects. Many times the length of the sound corresponds with a character action and has to be matched exactly, or perhaps a certain part of the sound is very grating if heard repeatedly. Maybe it's too loud. Whatever the requirement, you will redo the audio until it works perfectly.

I personally don't have a problem with reworks. They are a completely acceptable part of the job. What does bother me, and most other audio folks as well, is taking it to the extreme where it becomes a change order in disguise. The problems begin after receiving guidance from the producer for the music and sound effects, sharing the work while it's in progress, getting the appropriate nod that you are heading in the right direction, and then having to spend an unacceptable amount of time redoing everything. Communication must be the number one priority and if you are having trouble with it, you are bound to spend much time with reworks as a consequence.

Therefore, there has to be an agreement regarding reworks. When guidelines are established at the beginning of the relationship, a plan will be clear and no one will be taken advantage of. The developer won't have to settle for audio they aren't happy with and the contractor doesn't have to waste time redoing things. With open communication amongst the players, it should be fairly obvious when the contractor has reworked something to death and is starting to lose all feelings for the piece. At that point, whatever contingency was established should come into play. The bottom line is: you should never lose money on a contract, ever. You may feel slightly taken advantage of at times, and it's always a good business practice to go the extra mile for the client without complaint, but there is a limit. To protect your interests, it needs to be spelled out in the contract.

6.5 Sample Agreements and Contracts

The first time I saw a game contract, I nearly fell over backwards. Now, after dealing with them enough, I'm fairly comfortable with them, and more importantly, I am able to pick up on the portions that affect my interests directly. The more you see, the better you will understand —

such as how they are worded and what others are using in the business. One of the goals of this book is to get you primed and ready for these very things. This section includes actual examples to examine closely and as an added bonus, they are included in the companion CD-ROM for your use as well.

Contracts and agreements can come in many forms, from simple to the ridiculously complicated. It is entirely up to you which ones you use. I recommend, however, when dealing with smaller companies, to keep it as simple as possible and not to scare them away by presenting a demanding 10 page contract. They are more than likely in the same boat as you when it comes to experience in these matters and will appreciate your conscious efforts to not cloud the already complicated game production process. As you work up to the big companies, longer contracts with many points will be accepted as the norm.

6.5.1 Sample Non-Disclosure Agreement

The following example is a complete Non-Disclosure Agreement — the type of document you will normally be signing prior to obtaining any detailed information on a project. It has been written by a contract lawyer to cover every detail. This is a standard form in the industry. You will sign many in your career. Most are primarily concerned with guarding company secrets, but occasionally you may find wording which requires you to destroy or return materials used to create a project when the relationship is terminated. Use care when dealing with those types of contracts. Make sure, if they deal with your work product directly, it does not override any other prior agreements and ensure the project contract specifically states it overrides the pertinent paragraphs in the NDA regarding your interests. You don't want to be faced with contractual conflictions like this in court where a good lawyer could distort facts to say you were the one breaching the agreements.

Non-Disclosure Agreement

THIS AGREEMENT is by and between Company X, Inc., a California corporation ("Company X") and the party or business signing below ("Receiving Party").

WHEREAS, Company X wishes to discuss and evaluate a potential business relationship with Receiving Party relating to video game hardware and software (hereinafter "Subject Matter"); and

WHEREAS, the progression of the aforesaid discussions will necessitate the passing of confidential information from Company X to Receiving Party.

NOW, THEREFORE, in consideration of these premises and the mutual covenants herein, the parties, in order to safeguard the disclosed confidential information, agree as follows:

---

1. "Confidential Information" for the purposes of this Agreement shall mean any and all information (1) disclosed in written materials, or (2) obtained visually by viewing premises, equipment or facilities, or (3) disclosed by oral communication relating to the Subject Matter. Confidential Information shall include, but not be limited to, future market and product plans, marketing and financial data, engineering information, know-how, trade secrets, ideas, service and manufacturing processes, product designs, software data and information, and other information of a technical or economic nature related to the Subject Matter. Confidential Information submitted in a written or graphic form shall be clearly marked as "Confidential".

Any information that is transmitted orally or visually, in order to be Confidential Information subject to this Agreement, shall be identified as such at the time of disclosure and identified in writing to the Receiving Party as Confidential Information within thirty (30) days after such oral or visual disclosure. Confidential Information shall reference this Agreement.

2. Company X shall disclose such Confidential Information as it deems necessary for it to fully evaluate its interest in establishing a business relationship relating to the Subject Matter.

3. The Receiving Party agrees to (1) receive and maintain the Company X Confidential Information in strict confidence, (2) use the disclosed Confidential Information solely for the purpose of evaluating the business proposals under discussion, and (3) prevent unauthorized use or reproduction of the Confidential Information, including by limiting access to Confidential Information to employees, agents or affiliates who are necessary to perform or facilitate the purposes of this Agreement and who are bound to hold such Confidential Information in confidence pursuant to the terms of this Agreement. (As used herein, the term "Affiliate" shall mean a corporation or business entity that, directly or indirectly, is controlled by, controls or is under common control with the Receiving Party). This obligation of confidentiality and limited use shall not apply to (a) Confidential Information that at the time of the disclosure is in the public domain; or (b) Confidential Information that, after disclosure, becomes part of the public domain by publication or otherwise, except by breach of this Agreement by the Receiving Party, the public domain by publication or otherwise, except by breach of this Agreement by the Receiving Party, or (c) Confidential Information that the Receiving Party can establish by reasonable proof was in its possession at the time of disclosure by Company X or is subsequently developed by that Receiving Party's employees who have no knowledge of or access to the Company X Confidential Information; or Company X Confidential Information that a Receiving Party receives from a third party, who has a right to disclose it to that Receiving Party.

4. Either party may terminate the discussions without prior notice, for any reason, at any time, and without liability or restriction, other than the obligations of confidentiality and nonuse and the obligation to return the disclosed Confidential Information as provided for herein.

5. Upon conclusion of the discussions contemplated hereunder, unless otherwise agreed by the parties in writing, all written or graphic Confidential Information together with all copies thereof shall be returned to Company X, provided, however, that one copy may be retained in the Receiving Party's legal counsel files for archival purposes as a means of determining any continuing obligation under this Agreement.

6. The Effective Date of this Agreement is defined to be the latest date below written. The obligations of confidentiality and nonuse under this Agreement shall expire five (5) years from the Effective Date.

7. Nothing contained in this Agreement shall be construed, by implication or otherwise, as an obligation for any party hereto to enter into any further agreement with the other, or as a grant of a license by Company X hereto to Receiving Party to use any Confidential Information disclosed other than for discussions or evaluations relevant to the purposes of this Agreement.

8. This written Agreement embodies the entire understanding between the parties and supersedes and replaces any and all prior understandings, arrangements, and/or agreements, whether written or oral, relating to the Subject Matter.

9. This Agreement shall be construed in accordance with the laws of the State of CA.

10. This Agreement is divisible and separable so that if any provision or provisions hereof shall be held to be invalid, such holding shall not impair the remaining provisions hereof. If any provision hereof is held to be too broad to be enforced, such provision shall be construed to create an obligation to the full extent allowable by law.

11. Each party represents and warrants to the other that it has the right to enter into this Agreement without breaching or violating any fiduciary, contractual, or statutory obligations owed to another.

IN WITNESS WHEREOF, the parties hereto caused this Agreement to be duly executed by their duly authorized representatives.

COMPANY X , INC.Receiving Party

By:By:

Title: Title:

Date: Date:

Distribution of Originals

One (1) to Company X Inc.

One (1) to Receiving Party

6.5.2 Sample Talent Release

This example of a talent release is about as simple as they get and as complicated as they need to be. Because the purpose is for you to obtain the rights to their performance, there isn't much more to discuss or negotiate. You may run across professional voice talent who have been around the industry long enough to see the potential of their contribution — say in film or other non-game releases — and might persuade you to pay him or her more. They may even attempt to secure ancillary rights for the same reason. I would never deny someone running their business and negotiating use of their "product" this way, but as the sound recordist, in this case, I am not in the position to negotiate this type of request. When games use high caliber or name-brand voice talent for a lead character in the story, it is usually the game company who will handle the deal making with the individual. All you may need to do is just record them, edit their narration, and convert it for the company. In cases where you've hired voice talent on your own, for a smaller contribution such as in a sound effect, it would be easier to hire and pay for their performance outright. If it goes beyond that, you'll spend more time than you could imagine being the intermediary between the game company and the talent, the unwilling go-between. My advice: Find someone who will perform their part, sign the release, and except a lump payment as a fair trade.

Authorization of Release

For value received in the sum of _____, I, the undersigned, give and grant Composer/Sound Designer/Company X, its affiliates, successors, and assigns the unqualified right, privilege, and permission to reproduce in every manner or form, publish and circulate video games, compact discs, videotapes, audiocassettes or films of recordings of my voice and/or my musical contribution arising from the production titled _____ and hereby grant, assign, and transfer all my rights and interest therein.

I specifically authorize and empower Composer/ Sound Designer/Company X to cause any such video games, compact discs, videotapes, audiocassettes, films and recordings of my voice and/or musical performance, to be copyrighted or in any other manner to be legally registered in the name of Composer/Sound Designer X.

My contribution to this work shall be considered a work made for hire, and as such, I, my heirs, executors, administrators, and assigns, hereby remise, release and discharge Composer/Sound Designer/Company X for and from any and all claims to any kind whatsoever on account of the use of such recordings, including, but not limited to any and all claims for damages for libel, slander, and invasion of the right of privacy.

Nondisclosure

It is understood by the below signed individual that all information obtained while providing service will remain confidential and that he/she will not directly or indirectly disclose to any third party or use for its own benefit, or use for any purpose other than the above mentioned project.

I am of lawful age and sound mind, and have read and understand this Authorization of Release.

Signed this _____ day of _____, 20____.

_____ (Signature)

_____ (Print name)

6.5.3 Sample Contracts

Contracts can be particularly difficult to comprehend and their impact, dramatic. What you agree to by signing on the dotted line may return as a surprise, having not fully understood the convoluted legalese. To understand these potential nightmares, learn to read them, become familiar with them, and spend some time with them prior to having to negotiate your first one.

Contract A

Our first contract example is simple by contract standards but just as legally binding. It is designed with new or small developers in mind — the idea being to keep it simple for them as well and not to scare them off by making it more complicated than it has to be. New game companies are learning right along with you. Many have never dealt with sound contractors before. If you present them with a contract like the last one in this section, they'll end up thinking they can't afford you and will go find someone else. Later, after you've done several games and start approaching the big fish, they'll end up scaring you with their contracts and lawyers instead.

Work Made For Hire Agreement

This Work For Hire Agreement (the "Agreement") is effective as of _____, 2000 ("Effective Date") by and between Company X, Inc. (hereinafter referred to as the "Company"), a California corporation located at _____, and Composer Y (hereinafter referred to as "Contractor"), an individual residing at _____ _____.

In consideration of the mutual covenants herein contained, the parties hereby agree as follows:

---

1. Services

    (a) Contractor shall create audio content as determined by Company from time to time in a manner consistent with the outlines, explanations, and designs established by the Company (hereinafter "Services").

    (b) The Contractor agrees that any work he submits to Company under this contract, when accepted and payment is honored, becomes the property of Company and Contractor further agrees and acknowledges he has no proprietary interest in any of these works. Ownership rights to any work not paid for shall be returned to the Contractor immediately.

2. Term and Termination. This Agreement shall continue until terminated by either party upon 10 days' written notice, provided that termination by Contractor shall not be effective until completion of any work requested by the Company.

3. Payment For Services. The Company shall pay Contractor in a manner mutually agreed upon by each party for each project contemplated. ("Payment") for Services.

4. Independent Contractor. It is understood and agreed that Contractor shall perform the Services as an independent contractor. Contractor shall not be deemed to be an employee of the Company. Contractor shall not be entitled to any benefits provided by the Company to its employees, and the Company will make no deductions from any of the payments due to Contractor hereunder for state or federal tax purposes. Contractor agrees that he shall be personally responsible for any and all taxes and other payments due on payments received by him from the Company hereunder.

5. Warranties

    (a) Original Development. Contractor represents and warrants that all work performed by him for or on behalf of the Company, and all work products produced thereby, will not knowingly infringe upon or violate any patent, copyright, trade secret, or other property right of any former employer, client, or other third party.

    (b) Warranty of Expertise. Contractor represents and warrants that he is highly skilled and experienced in providing the Services required. Contractor acknowledges that the Company is relying on his skill and expertise in the foregoing for the performance of this Agreement, and agrees to notify the Company whenever he does not have the necessary skill and experience to fully perform hereunder.

    (c) Other Agreements. Contractor represents and warrants that his signing of this Agreement and the performance of his consulting Services hereunder is not and will not be in violation of any other contract, agreement or understanding to which he is a party.

6. Indemnification. Contractor shall indemnify the Company from all claims, losses and damages that may arise from the breach of any of his obligations under this Agreement.

7. Protection of Confidential Information

(a) Confidential Information. For purposes of this Agreement, the term "Confidential Information" means all information that is not generally known and that: (i) is obtained by Contractor from The Company, or that is learned, discovered, developed, conceived, originated, or prepared by Contractor during the process of providing Services to the Company, and (ii) relates directly to the business or assets of the Company. The term "Confidential Information" shall include, but shall not be limited to: inventions, discoveries, trade secrets, and know-how; computer software code, designs, routines, algorithms, and structures; product information; research and development information; lists of clients and other information relating thereto; financial data and information; business plans and processes; and any other information of the Company that the Company informs Contractor, or that Contractor should know by virtue of his position, is to be kept confidential.

(b) Obligation of Confidentiality. During the term of this Agreement with the Company, and at all times thereafter, Contractor agrees that he will not disclose to others, use for his own benefit or for the benefit of anyone other than the Company, or otherwise appropriate or copy, any Confidential Information, whether or not developed by Contractor, except as required in the lawful performance of his obligations to the Company hereunder. The obligations of Contractor under this paragraph shall not apply to any information that becomes public knowledge through no fault of Contractor.

8. Ownership and Assignment of Rights. All Work Product created by Contractor shall belong exclusively to the Company and shall, to the extent possible, be considered a work made for hire for the Company within the meaning of Title 17 of the United States Code. To the extent the Company does not own such Work Product as a work made for hire, Contractor hereby assigns to the Company all rights to such Work Products, including but not limited to all other patent rights, copyrights, and trade secret rights. Contractor agrees to execute all documents reasonably requested by the Company to further evidence the foregoing assignment and to provide all reasonable assistance to the Company in perfecting or protecting the Company's rights in such Work Product.

9. Duty Upon Termination of Services. Contractor shall immediately deliver to Company all Work Product created under the Agreement. Contractor shall not delete any Work Product for 6 months after expiration or earlier termination of the Agreement unless such deletion is requested by Company.

10. Subcontracting and Assignment. The Agreement and the rights and obligations of Contractor hereunder may not be subcontracted, assigned or transferred by Contractor, in whole or in part, without the written consent of the Company. The Company may at its sole discretion assign or transfer the rights of the Agreement.

11. Governing Law. This contract will be governed by and construed in accordance with the laws of the State of California.

12. Consent to Breach Not Waiver. No term or provision hereof shall be deemed waived and no breach excused, unless such waiver or consent be in writing and signed by the party claimed to have waived or consented. No consent by any party to, or waiver of, a breach by the other party shall constitute consent to, waiver of, or excuse of any other different or subsequent breach.

13. Gender. Whenever the content of this Agreement requires, the masculine gender shall be deemed to include the feminine.

14. Right to Self-Promotion. Contractor has the right to self promotion and allowed to use, as creator of said works, any works created under this contract, to demonstrated the capabilities of contractor either in demo reel or computer file format at any time after acceptance of the work as final, without any further permissions required from Company.

15. Sound Credits. Credit for creation of any sounds produced under this contract will be included in the appropriate "credits" section of any software product and its corresponding print media in which the sounds appear, as created by Composer Y.

16. Entire Agreement. This Agreement constitutes the complete and exclusive statement of the agreement between the parties with regard to the matters set forth herein, and it supersedes all other agreements, proposals, and representations, oral or written, express or implied, with regard thereto.

IN WITNESS WHEREOF, the parties have executed this Agreement as of the Effective Date.

CONTRACTORCOMPANY

By:_____By:_____

Its:_____ Its:_____

Date:_____Date:_____

Contract B

This next contract example is the one our mutual friend, Tommy Tallarico, has been kind enough to share. Skewed rightfully in the game composer's favor, it is full of all the appropriate paragraphs which cover the interests of composers who wish to retain ancillary rights and obtain bonuses or royalties for the success of the game. The majority of the time, large game companies have their own agreements drawn up and seldom entertain a composer's contract, again because they want their interests protected. The workaround is to use like paragraphs and wording when introducing your points to their contract. By all means, present this kind of contract to them first.

It will show your professionalism, business prowess, and the fact that you know what you are doing. They may not make full use of it, but you've at least put them at ease in regards to the job you can do. Conversely, you might raise their guard — introducing points they are not familiar with which will lead them to gather their legal forces. Negotiations are a game of wits and their lawyers give them a sense of security. All the more reason to have your ducks in line and stay one step ahead.

Audio Development Agreement

This Audio Development Agreement (the "Agreement") is made and entered into by _____ ("Composer") and _____("Company").

WHEREAS, Company desires to retain Composer to develop and deliver to Company the audio known as _____musical score (the "Composition") for _____ (the "Game"); and

WHEREAS, Composer desires to develop the Composition on the terms and conditions set forth herein.

NOW THEREFORE, The parties hereto do hereby mutually agree as follows:

1. COMPLETION DATE; DEVELOPMENT: Composer shall develop the Composition according to the schedule attached hereto as Schedule 1. Composer agrees to use diligent good faith efforts to develop the Composition according to the dates specified on Schedule 1. Composer acknowledges that time is of the essence of this Agreement and that Composer's best efforts must be utilized to complete the development of Company's Game. Composer agrees to be readily available for all reasonably requested revisions to the Composition. Composer shall develop the Composition in accordance with the information, materials or other instructions provided by Company. Company acknowledges that Composer can only achieve timely performance of the matters required of Composer if Company timely delivers to Composer appropriate information and guidance. Company shall not attempt to declare Composer to be in default of this Agreement for delays caused by Company's inability to deliver information/guidance to Composer in a timely manner.

2. COMPENSATION: As compensation for the Composition, Company shall pay Composer the fees specified on Schedule 1. Composer acknowledges that this payment by Company represents the complete and entire obligation owed to Composer or any other party, either by Company or any other third party, for the Composition to be provided by Composer under this Agreement. If Composer uses any third parties in providing the Composition not specifically authorized and required by Company, Composer shall be responsible for the additional costs. If this Agreement is terminated without cause by Company, Composer shall be entitled to receive the next unpaid milestone within a reasonable time deemed appropriate by Company not to exceed six (6) months. All milestone payments will be invoiced by Composer and due within thirty (30) days upon completion and acceptance of milestone by Company.

3. RIGHTS: All results and the proceeds of Composer's work hereunder including without limitation, the Composition and any revisions, amendments, modifications, translations, alterations and enhancements and sequels thereto, and derivative works therefrom, whether produced by Composer, or a third party and regardless of form, including without limitation, mechanical, code or written, and all materials produced by Composer in fulfillment of its obligations hereunder, including but not limited to reports, memoranda, drawings, documentation and models, shall be deemed to be a work made for hire for Company within the meaning of the copyright laws of the United States or any similar analogous law or statute of any other jurisdiction and accordingly, Company shall be the owner throughout the world. However, where sounds or "demo" songs are rejected by Company and not made a part of the Composition, such rejected sounds or demo songs shall remain the property of Composer.

Without limiting the foregoing, Composer hereby assigns all right, title and interest in and to the Composition and all of the foregoing furnished to Company hereunder, whether copyrighted or not. Composer shall assist Company and it's nominees in every proper way to secure, maintain and defend for Company's own benefit copyrights, extensions and renewals thereof on any and all such materials. The Composition shall be used in connection with all video game systems including CD-ROM, all personal computer and home multi-player systems and or consoles and all distribution of such games through other entertainment systems or media presently known or unknown, now in existence or hereafter created or developed (collectively the "Uses"). In the event that the Composition is published for purposes other than or not related to the Uses such as cassettes, CD's or albums, TV broadcasts, etc. that are not published in conjunction with the Game as samplers (collectively the "Additional Uses"), fifty percent (50%) (the "Percentage") of the Net Profits ("Net Profits") will be compensated to each party. Net Profits shall be defined as money which is actually received with respect only to its direct sales related to exploitation of the Composition for the Additional Uses less any monies that has been spent or is required to spend with respect to negotiating, developing, producing or in any way preparing the Composition for the Additional Uses.

4. CONFIDENTIALITY: Composer acknowledges and agrees that any information which it may receive from Company, will be proprietary information of Company (the "Proprietary Information"). Composer agrees, both during and after the term of this Agreement, to hold in confidence all Proprietary Information of Company and to prevent the unauthorized copying, use and/or disclosure of Company's Proprietary Information. Composer will place or cause to be placed on the Composition or any portion thereof any intellectual property right notices as requested by Company.

5. CREDIT: Company shall request that Composer receive credits within manual documentation, print ads and on screen, it being understood that the publisher shall have the absolute discretion in such credit determination. The form, style, size, placement and nature of any screen credit provided for herein shall be determined by Company (or its assignee, publisher, or licensee) in its sole discretion. Any unintentional and/or inadvertent failure to give screen credit as above provided, whether because of lack of broadcast time or otherwise, shall not be a breach of this agreement.

6. NAME AND LIKENESS: Subject to Composers approval, which will not be unreasonably withheld, Company shall have the right and may grant to others the right to use, disseminate, reproduce, print and publish Composer's name, likeness, voice and biographical material concerning Composer as news or informative matter and in connection with advertising and for purposes of trade in connection with any motion picture or television program in which the Composition is used, and/or in connection with any other uses of the Composition.

Composer hereby pre-approves the use of his name, likeness, voice and biographical material in and on packaging for the Game and within the body of the Game, as well as in printed materials concerning the Game. The rights granted herein shall not include the right to use or to grant to others the right to use Composer's name, voice, likeness and biographical material in any direct endorsement of any product or service without Composer's written consent.

7. TRAVEL: In the event Company requests Composer to travel on behalf of Company, Company shall reimburse Composer for business class airfare, lodging in a first-class hotel, meals and local transportation, both to and from the airport and at the place at which Composer is required to travel on behalf of Company. All reimbursements shall be made only after Company receives itemized bills for all expenses incurred by Composer pursuant to this paragraph and on a form approved by Company.

8. AWARDS: Company shall retain all awards won by the Composition. Company will use its best efforts to obtain a duplicate of any award won by the Composition to furnish the Composer.

9. COMPOSER'S WARRANTIES AND INDEMNIFICATIONS:

(a) Composer represents and warrants to Company that:

(i) Composer possesses full power and authority to enter into this Agreement and to carry out its obligations hereunder;

(ii) with respect to the Composition which Composer will deliver to Company in performance of this Agreement, Composer warrants that it has the right to make and disclose thereof without liability to any third party;

(iii) Composer has not sold, assigned, leased, licensed or in any other way disposed of or encumbered the Composition in whole or in part to any party other than Company;

(iv) the Composition is new and original and capable of copyright:

(v) neither the Composition, nor any portion thereof, shall infringe upon or violate any right of privacy or publicity or any patent, copyright, trademark, trade secret, or other proprietary right of any third party;

(vi) the performance of the terms of this Agreement and the performance of Composer's duties hereunder will not breach any separate agreement by which Composer is bound, or violate or infringe any rights of any third party, and so long as this Agreement remains in effect, Composer shall not commit any act or enter into any agreement or understanding with any third party which is inconsistent or in conflict with this Agreement;

(vii) there are no, and there will not be, any liens, claims or encumbrances against the Composition which would derogate from or be inconsistent with any of Company's proprietary rights with respect thereto;

(viii) Composer represents and warrants that it is, and at all times during the term of this Agreement will be the holder of all consents necessary for it to perform its obligations hereunder; and

(ix) there is presently no litigation or other claim, pending or threatening, nor a fact which may be the basis of any claim against the Composition, and Composer has not taken any action or failed to take any action which would interfere with the rights of Company under this Agreement.

(b) The representations, warranties and indemnification rights set forth in the Agreement shall survive execution of this Agreement, the performance of the obligation of Composer hereunder, and cancellation or termination of this Agreement.

10. TERMINATION: Company shall have the right to terminate Composer for cause, provided Company compensates Composer in full for all Compositions completed and accepted as of the date of termination. Composer shall have the right to terminate this Agreement for cause. For purposes of this Agreement, cause shall mean a material misrepresentation or a material breach of this Agreement.

11. ATTORNEY'S FEES: Should any arbitration, litigation or other proceedings (including proceedings in bankruptcy) be commenced arising out of, concerning or related to any provision of this Agreement, or the rights and duties of any person or entity hereunder, the prevailing party (solely as between Company and Composer) in such litigation or proceeding will be entitled, in addition to such other relief as may be granted, to recover its reasonable attorney's fees and expenses incurred by reason of such proceedings.

12. GENERAL:

(a) This Agreement shall be governed and interpreted in accordance with the substantive laws of the State of California.

(b) Composer shall be deemed to have the status of an independent contractor, and nothing in this Agreement shall be deemed to place the parties in the relationship of employer-employee, principal-agent, partners or joint venturers. Composer shall be responsible for any withholding taxes, payroll taxes, disability insurance payments, unemployment taxes, and other similar taxes or charges on the payments received by Composer hereunder. Company shall have no responsibility or liability of any kind to any subcontractors providing services to or for the benefit of Composer.

(c) This Agreement and the rights it creates may be assigned by Company, but not by Composer, except that, with the prior written consent of Company, Composer may assign this Agreement, in whole or in part, and the rights it creates to Composer or any corporation in which Composer is the sole shareholder. This agreement shall be binding on the parties and their respective successors and assignees, and all subsequent owners or licensees of the corporation.

(d) Should any provision of this Agreement be held to be void, invalid or inoperative, the remaining provisions hereof shall not be affected and shall continue in effect as though such unenforceable provisions have been deleted herefrom.

(e) This Agreement, including the Exhibits hereto, sets forth the entire agreement between the parties with respect to the subject matter hereof and supersedes all prior negotiations, understandings and agreements between the parties hereto concerning the subject matter hereof.

(f) This Agreement may be executed in counterparts, but shall not be binding upon the parties until it has been signed by both parties.

IN WITNESS WHEREOF, each of the undersigned has executed this Agreement as of the date set forth below.

"COMPOSER"

By:_____Dated as of _____

Title:_____

"COMPANY"

By:_____Dated as of _____

Title:_____

SCHEDULE 1

Milestone 1:	Upon signing of Agreement	Date	$15,000
Milestone 2:	Complete audio for levels 1–3	Date	$10,000
Milestone 3:	Complete audio for levels 4–6	Date	$10,000
Milestone 4:	Complete audio for levels 7–9	Date	$10,000
Milestone 5:	Upon completion & approval of composition	Date	$25,000
TOTAL:			$70,000

Any additional new music needed by Company from Composer will be charged at $1,000 per minute per Company's approval.

Royalty or bonus terminology goes here. For example:

Provided that Company actually incorporates the Music, or a substantial portion thereof, into the Game, if sales of the Game, not including promotional or complimentary copies, exceed Two Hundred Thousand (200,000) copies, Composer shall be entitled to receive an additional Twenty-Five Thousand Dollars ($25,000).

or

In addition to the above payment, Company will also compensate Composer five (.05) cents for every unit & SKU sold throughout the world.

or

In addition to the above Milestones, Composer shall receive a ten (10) cent royalty on each SKU sold after 125,000 units.

or

Composer shall receive a profit participation of One Percent (1%) of Net Receipts from any product for which Composer is entitled to receive any compensation hereunder after Company has sold 125,000 units of such product. For purposes of this Agreement the term Net Receipts shall be defined as all monies actually received by Publisher from the sale of a product in excess of 125,000 units less deductions for the direct cost of manufacturing the product, royalties payable to third party hardware manufacturers such as Nintendo and Sony, returns or refunds, and all forms of taxes.

Contract C

The final contract example is from one of the big boys in the game development and publishing arena. Being much larger and much wiser than us common folks, they've assembled an army of officials and lawyers to cover every possibility and have used more big words than I've ever had the pleasure of seeing at once. This is the kind you will want to spend much time with, understanding each sentence, and what impact it will have on your interests *before* you ever put your pen to the paper. It will be blatantly missing any points referencing SKUs, ancillary rights, soundtrack rights, logos, splash screens, and credits. This should be no surprise. Knowing this in advance, you can look to adapting it to make it agreeable to your interests. Keep your eyes open.

Professional Services Agreement

Beginning on the ___ day of _____20__, _____, a _____ ("Contractor"), agrees to perform services for Company X, Inc., and its direct and indirect subsidiaries ("COMPANY X") pursuant to the following terms and conditions:

1. Acting as an independent contractor, Contractor will render the services as stated in Exhibit A ("Services"). Contractor will take direction from and report to Producer X or Creative Director X. Contractor acknowledges that time is of the essence regarding its performance of the Services.

2. In consideration for performance of the Services and upon Company X' acceptance of completion of same, Contractor will receive from Company X a fee which is payable in accordance with Exhibit A.

3. Contractor understands that he/she is not authorized to incur any expenses on behalf of Company X without prior written consent, and all statements for the Services and expenses shall be in the form prescribed by Company X and shall be approved by _____, or his/her supervisor.

4. Company X has the right, in its sole discretion, to terminate this Agreement for any reason with seven (7) days prior written notice. In the event of such a termination, Company X's sole obligation will be to pay Contractor, pro rata, for the fees with respect to all milestones achieved or Services performed, as applicable, which shall have been accepted as of that date by Company X. Company X will have no further obligation, whether financial or otherwise, to Contractor after such cancellation. Company X may terminate this Agreement immediately upon Contractor's refusal or inability to perform under, or Contractor's breach of, any provision of this Agreement.

5. Contractor will not, either during or subsequent to the term of this Agreement, directly or indirectly disclose any information designated as confidential by Company X, including but not limited to proposed products, product plans, product features, specifications, and human-readable source code; nor will Contractor disclose to anyone other than a Company X employee or use in any way other than in the course of the performance of this Agreement any information regarding Company X, including but not limited to Company X' product, market, financial or other plans, product designs and any other information not known to the general public whether acquired or developed by Contractor during performance of this Agreement or obtained from Company X employees; nor will Contractor, either during or subsequent to the term of this Agreement, directly or indirectly disclose or publish any such information without prior written authorization from Company X to do so. Unless otherwise specifically agreed to in writing, all information about and relating to projects under development by Company X and/or parties doing work under contract to Company X including the Services rendered hereunder by Contractor shall be considered confidential information. Contractor acknowledges and agrees that all of the foregoing information is proprietary to Company X, that such information is a valuable and unique asset of Company X, and that disclosure of such information to third parties or unauthorized use of such information would cause substantial and irreparable injury to Company X' ongoing business for which there would be no adequate remedy at law.

Accordingly, in the event of any breach or attempted or threatened breach of any of the terms of this Paragraph 5, Contractor agrees that Company X shall be entitled to seek injunctive and other equitable relief, without limiting the applicability of any other remedies.

6. Contractor will return to Company X any Company X property that has come into his/her possession during the term of this Agreement, when and as requested to do so by Company X and in all events upon termination of Contractor's engagement hereunder, unless Contractor receives written authorization from Company X to keep such property. Contractor will not remove any Company X property from Company X premises without written authorization from Company X.

7. As part of this Agreement, and without additional compensation, Contractor acknowledges and agrees that any and all tangible and intangible property and work products, ideas, inventions, discoveries and improvements, whether or not patentable, which are conceived/developed/created/obtained or first reduced to practice by Contractor for Company X in connection with the performance of the Services (collectively referred to as the "Work Product"), including, without limitation, all technical notes, schematics, software source and object code, prototypes, breadboards, computer models, artwork, sketches, designs, drawings, paintings, illustrations, computer generated artwork, animations, video, film, artistic materials, photographs and any film from which the photographs were made, literature, methods, processes, voice recordings, vocal performances, narrations, spoken word recordings and unique character voices, shall be considered "works made for hire" and therefore all right, title and interest therein (including, without limitation, patents and copyrights) shall vest exclusively in Company X. To the extent that all or any part of such Work Product does not qualify as a "work made for hire" under applicable law, Contractor without further compensation therefore does hereby irrevocably assign, transfer and convey in perpetuity to Company X and its successors and assigns the entire worldwide right, title, and interest in and to the Work Product including, without limitation, all patent rights, copyrights, mask work rights, trade secret rights and other proprietary rights therein. Such assignment includes the transfer and assignment to Company X and its successors and assigns of any and all moral rights which Contractor may have in the Work Product. Contractor acknowledges and understands that moral rights include the right of an author: to be known as the author of a work; to prevent others from being named as the author of the works; to prevent others from falsely attributing to an author the authorship of a work which he/she has not in fact created; to prevent others from making deforming changes in an author's work; to withdraw a published work from distribution if it no longer represents the views of the author; and to prevent others from using the work or the author's name in such a way as to reflect on his/her professional standing.

8. None of the Work Product is to be used by Contractor on any other project or with any other client except with Company X' written consent. If any part of such Work Product is the work of a subcontractor employed by Contractor, then Contractor will require such subcontractors to execute an assignment document in the form attached hereto as Exhibit B so as to secure for Company X exclusive ownership in such Work Product. In the event Contractor is unable to obtain exclusive ownership from such subcontractors, Exhibit C must be signed to obtain a license for the benefit of Company X. Contractor shall promptly thereafter deliver such originally executed assignment or license documents to Company X.

9. With respect to all subject matter including ideas, processes, designs and methods which Contractor discloses or uses in the performance of the Services: (a) Contractor warrants that Contractor has the right to make disclosure and use thereof without liability or compensation to others; (b) to the extent that Contractor has patent applications, patents, copyrights or other rights in the subject matter which is set forth in writing in Section 5 of Exhibit A, if any, Contractor hereby grants Company X, its parent, subsidiaries, affiliates and assigns, a royalty-free, perpetual, irrevocable, worldwide, non-exclusive license to use, modify, make, have made, sell and disclose and distribute such subject matter in any form now or hereafter known,; and (c) Contractor agrees to defend indemnify and hold Company X harmless from any claims, litigations, actions, damages or fees of any kind (including reasonable attorney's fees) arising from Company X' or Contractor's use or disclosure of subject matter which Contractor knows or reasonably should know others have rights in, except, however, for subject matter and the identity of others having rights therein that Contractor discloses to Company X in writing before Company X uses the subject matter.

10. It is understood and agreed that in performing the Services for Company X hereunder, Contractor shall act in the capacity of an independent contractor and not as an employee or agent of Company X. Contractor agrees that it shall not represent itself as the agent or legal representative of Company X for any purpose whatsoever. When Contractor is working on the premises of Company X, Contractor shall observe the working hours, working rules, and security procedures established by Company X. No right or interest in this Agreement shall be assigned by Contractor without the prior written permission of Company X, and no delegation of the performance of the Services or other obligations owed by Contractor to Company X shall be made without the prior written consent of Company X. This Agreement shall be deemed to have been made and executed in the State of California and any dispute arising hereunder shall be resolved in accordance with the law of California. This Agreement may be amended, altered or modified only by an instrument in writing, specifying such amendment, alteration or modification, executed by both parties. This Agreement constitutes and contains the entire agreement between the parties with respect to the subject matter hereof and supersedes any prior oral or written agreements. Nothing herein contained shall be binding upon the parties until this Agreement has been executed by an officer or agent of each and has been delivered to the parties.

Agreed to and Accepted:

Company X, Inc. Contractor

By: _____Signature _____

Title: _____Social Security #/Fed. ID #

Date: _____Date: _____

Exhibit A

1. Services

The expected completion date is _____.

Date	Milestones	Payments*
__-__20__		$
__-__20__		
__-__20__		
__-__20__		
__-__20__		
__-__20__		
__-__20__		
__-__20__	Final Delivery	

* Payment shall always be contingent upon timely delivery and acceptance of each milestone.

2. Payment

Contractor shall be paid for the Services in increments as set forth above after acceptance at each stage of the work performed. Anything to the contrary notwithstanding, the compensation for the Services performed hereunder shall not exceed $_____ _ without the express, written consent of _____.

3. Expenses

The following authorized expenditures are the maximum that Contractor shall be eligible to receive as a reimbursement. Contractor must produce receipts for all pre-approved expenses for which Company X will reimburse Contractor within thirty (30) business days of receiving such receipts and expense reports. All expenses incurred by Contractor not specifically approved herein shall be the sole responsibility of Contractor.

Amount	Approved Expenses
None	None

4. Payment Schedule

Subject to Company X' prior acceptance of the milestone as provided herein, Company X will remit the fees associated with a delivered milestone to Contractor within thirty (30) business days following Company X' receipt of Contractor's invoice. All invoices must be sent to the designated representative set forth in Section 1 above.

5. Work for Hire Exclusions

The following includes all subject matter that is excluded from the assignment of rights granted in Section 7 and the non-use provisions of Section 8, but which is licensed in accordance with Section 9(b):

1. NONE

Exhibit B

SUBCONTRACTOR COPYRIGHT ASSIGNMENT

For valuable consideration separately and previously agreed to between the undersigned and Company X, Inc., a California corporation, having a principal place of business at _____, the undersigned hereby assigns all rights, title and interest in and to the materials described below, including the copyright thereof, in the United States and throughout the world, together with any rights of action which may have accrued under said copyrights, which are owned by the undersigned, for One Dollar ($1.00) and other good and valuable consideration, the receipt of which is hereby acknowledged, to Company X, Inc.

Work: Materials relate to "_____."

Dated: _____

By: _____

Print Name:_____

Company Name_____

Address:_____

Phone: _____

6.6 Conclusion

Hopefully the information shared in this chapter will help you handle the challenge of deal-making with confidence. There is a huge advantage to being knowledgeable about what goes on in this industry and knowing what types of deals are out there can increase your earnings potential exponentially. I'm certain I've given up a good deal of money in my first couple of years at bat because of my inexperience. But because game composers and sound designers have created their own behind-the-scenes network and support groups and have seen the advantage of sharing their experiences, it has paved the way for the rest of us to profit. We talk to one another and discuss our deals quite openly. Because I know what the next guy is making, I know I can ask for the same and actually get it. Once our way of thinking becomes standard in the industry, we won't have to expend so much of our business energy because everything *we* want will already be in *their* contract. Then we can get on with why we joined the industry in the first place: making music and sound effects.

CHAPTER 7
Setting the Stage

For the most part, this is where the creative process begins for us sound guys and gals. Occasionally, game developers will have you on as part of the team from the beginning, this being the best situation, of course. But more often than not, they'll have a good amount of the work on the game already completed. Before they even call you, the developer will have been at work for many months planning, creating, and methodically carrying out production phases. Entering midstream is more the norm and you can help minimize the anguish by planning ahead and knowing what to do. Getting the information you need, at the right time, and understanding your exact role and what is expected of you can save you enormous grief and creative setbacks. This will be the basic thrust of this chapter.

7.1 Company Liaisons

During the contract process, you will have identified who has final authority over your work. This person will be where the proverbial buck stops — the person who will approve your submissions so you can get paid. But, you will also need to know who your primary point of contact is as well. It may be the same person, and usually is, but at large development conglomerations, there may be several people to work with. Find the main one and get to know them.

Your contact will have a working style all their own and it will behoove you to find the best way to work with that person. Communicate through every step of the process, keep the lines open, and keep them informed. It will take some time to fully understand their creative guidance and to know what they mean by it. Every human being is different, their life experiences making them so. What means one thing to one person could mean something completely different to another, even if the exact same description was given.

For example, if I were to tell you to write a song and the only direction I gave was "Make it red!" — what kind of music would you compose? I envision a searing bright red color, an upbeat, fiery, heavy metal piece with blazing guitar solos and impassioned vocals. But maybe you see a dark, scarlet red, a sexy, slow jazz number, with hot saxophone licks and piano that would tear your heart to pieces. See what I mean? By learning what makes this person tick, you'll have a better chance at knowing what they really mean. Use all of your senses and ensure the translation is pure.

Is your company liaison hands on or hands off? Some will want to be a part of every step of the creative process, which means you'll need to get their OK for everything. You'll create many musical "sketches," letting them choose which ones are closest to their vision. Once they've approved them, you'll flesh them out to their final versions, submitting them again for their OK on instrumentation, arrangement, length, volume, and EQ. You'll rework them until they are perfect. Many versions of sound effects will be offered and they'll pick the ones which are closest and you'll rework those until they are perfect as well. The "hands on" types are usually a little bit high strung, highly passionate individuals who live and breath a project, taking their role very seriously. Some meddle to the point of almost interfering with your creativity; others genuinely care that the project be the best and have their fingers in every aspect of it. Their name is on the product and their future in gaming is the true motivator.

"Hands off" individuals work differently. Because of their need to be in a hundred places at once, they are more comfortable delegating and letting content providers "do their thing" without much interference. They will set the scene for you, give you all the proper adjectives, and then let you create audio using the expertise they are paying you for. These types of individuals understand — either through years of experience or from their lack of it — they are incapable of doing a great job at everything. Instead, they go with their strength in leadership and put faith in you. It puts a lot of pressure on you to perform brilliantly, but don't worry. They will be there every step of the way to help keep you on track. The "hands off" type appears to be laid back, but underneath they are just as passionate about the success of the project as the next guy; they just go about it differently. They will keep the atmosphere fairly relaxed and will let you set your own hours and working methods, as long as milestones are met as promised.

Most of your company contacts will be somewhere in the middle of the previous extremes. Which one is the best to work for? It will depend on your personality type and what you need to prepare an inspired atmosphere. The "hands on" folks keep you on your toes, pushing you to do the best work you've ever done. They demand a lot, but the rewards gained by your astonishing audio will make it worth it. "Hands off" people will give you all the room and support you need to fulfill your vision of the project. They will protect you from the outside world, placing you in a cocoon, enabling you to give 110% and to take advantage of inspiration as it strikes. This person may have let you create on your own, letting you work your brand of miracle untouched, but they are just as responsible for the final masterpiece.

7.1.1 Executive Producers

The Executive Producer is generally the project lead. They have grasped the total creative vision and ensure each department is fulfilling their appropriate missions, on time and within standards. At most game companies, this individual has the final say on everything from artwork, game play, sound effects, music, narrations, cinematics, and so forth. They are normally encumbered with many tasks at once, but have the ability to know what each hand is doing. This ensures the audio you are doing will mesh precisely with audio from any other sources, such as narrations or sound effects, and will fit in perfectly with the game.

Executive Producers may also be in charge of multiple game projects, especially at large developers or active internet game companies. In cases like this, other help is needed in the form of a Producer.

TOOLS OF THE TRADE

Michael L. Henry, In-house Composer/Sound Designer, Atari Games/Midway Games West, Inc.

Michael Henry is the busy in-house composer/sound designer and Audio Group Manager at Atari Games/Midway Games West. With several games to his credit, his most notable projects — San Francisco Rush 2049, Rush 2049: Hot Rod rebels, War: Final Assault — continue to raise the bar of coin-op audio. His many other coin-op, console, and PC projects include music and/or sound effects on: Vapor TRX, Gauntlet Legends, Gauntlet Dark Legacy, Slamscape, Indian in the Cupboard, Joe's Apartment, Beavis and Butthead (Assorted), Intel Groove Machine, Thrasher: Skate and Destroy, Dave Mirra BMX, and Jack's House.

Computer: PowerMac 9600 with 244 MB RAM, 12 GB storage and a Pentium III 333 MHz w/128 MB RAM, 8 GB storage, zip, and SCSI

Software: Mac: ProTools 5.0 with TDM plug-ins: Fusion Vocode; Lo-fi, Recti-Fi, Sci-Fi, Vari-Fi; Waves C1 compressor; Waves L1 Ultramaximizer; MaxxBass; Waves Q10 EQ; Renaissance Compressor and EQ; DaD Valve; Aphex Aural Exciter; GRM Tools; TC Electronics EQ, Chorus, and MegaReverb; Waves TrueVerb; UltraPitch; Sound Designer II 2.8; Peak 2.0; Studio Vision Pro 4.2; Rebirth; Recycle; Retro AS-1; SampleCell; Barbabatch; Csound.
PC: Sonic Foundry Sound Forge 4.5, ACID, Vegas, plus some PC-based proprietary audio tools developed in-house

Multi-track: "Generally speaking, I record to hard disk in ProTools or StudioVision (using the ProTools hardware). I also have an ADAT, which I have used from time to time."

Mixing board/monitor system: Panasonic DA-7 Digital Console, with MAX automation software, which supports 5.1 mixing. 5 Event 20-20 BAS bi-amplified monitors, and Event 20-20 250 watt 15" sub

Mixdown deck: "Often I mix to DAT, a TASCAM DA-30mkII. Either that or I simply mix to disk in ProTools."

Outboard gear: dbx 166A compressor/limiter, Drawmer DL241 dual compressor, Lexicon JamMan, Digitech Studio Quad, Yamaha SPX90, Lexicon PCM80, Lexicon PCM90, Lexicon LXP1, Eventide Harmonizer H3500

Keyboards, samplers, and sound modules: Yamaha EX5 Sampler/Synth, Kurzweil K2500R, Roland JV 2080, Korg Triton, Novation Supernova, SampleCell, and many more

Instruments: french horn, trumpet, theremin, Nyle Steiner custom EVI (electronic valve instrument), guitar

Remote recording: Sony DAT walkman, Sony MiniDisc

Mic: Core sound high-end binaural mics

Sound effects libraries: Sound Ideas 1000, 2000, 4000, 6000, 7000, Sci-Fi; Larger Than Life; Hollywood Edge PE, Signature Series; Hanna Barbera; Cartoon Trax; Lucasfilm; Different Realm; Animal Trax; The Works; Valentino

Development systems: Sony Playstation, both PS1 and PS2; Sega Dreamcast; Nintendo N64

Other equipment: "Legacy and proprietary audio tools going back to the days of Pong and Asteroids, up to San Francisco Rush 2049's proprietary discrete multi-channel audio system."

7.1.2 Producers

Game company structures are designed for the most efficient use of time, money, and personnel. The Producer steps in to fill a more focused role in a game project, either overseeing a single game project in a company producing multiple game titles or managing a single department for one project. Normally, there is not an "audio department" Producer to report to per se; as an in-house composer, you are the audio department. They wouldn't be calling you in as a contractor if they have a true audio department. So, there would be someone else assigned to direct your efforts in this case. There is the occasional, huge game company which does have an in-house audio department with an audio Producer and even as a contractor, you may get a call to assist on projects in rare instances. Don't be too surprised if companies like Lucas Arts or Electronic Arts give you a call. Their guys have to take a vacation sometime.

A Producer's role is essentially the same as the Executive Producer except they are a step down in the chain of command, so to speak, and report directly to the Executive Producer. If the two work well together, there will be little change of direction and what the Producer tells you is the same word passed down from the boss. In situations where the word isn't clear and you feel confliction, ask the Producer before you go over their heads to get clarification. You have to work closely with these people so be conscious of egos and the need to be in control of their assignments.

7.1.3 Creative Directors

The Creative Director is another term for the Producer. Their job is essentially the same, acting as the central contact point for the elements of game production. This job is commonly filled within the on-line gaming communities or multimedia production houses where this fast-paced environment requires a common thread throughout the many simultaneous projects. In expanding companies, you may work with a Creative Director until a Producer is hired to fill the role.

7.2 Meetings with the Game Development Team

It is essential to the success of a project that the many different contractors and in-house employees all work together as a cohesive team. Each player should know a little something about what each other member is doing and how it will all fit together in the final product. The one way to do this is to be present at the many meetings and discussion groups along the way. As a contractor working off-site, this may present more of a problem if there are many miles separating you. Teleconferences are a great alternative or, better yet, have a speaker phone available at a meeting for you to participate. If that isn't possible, have someone attend the meetings who will fill you in on all pertinent details. Either way, make sure you are in the loop and get information in a timely manner. This will save a lot of "didn't I tell you?" and "I thought you knew" comments. If you run into the phenomenon known as "information blackout" and feel the data you are missing is essential — talk to your point of contact, find out why, remind them you are under a non-disclosure agreement, are fully committed as part of the team, and need the facts to make informed, creative decisions. Do what you can to stay "in the know" especially when it can affect your part of the job.

7.2.1 Details to Discuss

If you were hired as the result of a bid competition, you will already have a solid idea about the parameters of the game. Don't be satisfied that all the information has been presented and don't make any creative decisions until you have more data. Now that you are on board as part of the team and have signed the contract, the key players will be more willing to share their thoughts about where things should go sonically. As the outsider coming into a project already in production, you will have to ask many questions to satisfy your requirements prior to starting work. Obtaining a solid, overall view for the entire project will give you exactly what you need. Start with broad questions and work on the finer details as you learn more about the production. The first question will set the tone for the rest of your investigation and for the eventual audio you'll be creating.

1. What is the general theme of the game?

Music and sound effects can make or break the immersive effect a game is designed to have. The most important question you can ask is "What is the theme of the game?" in order to have the style of audio accurate for the genre. Examples of themes are: space, medieval, sports, racing, children's, religious, horror — all of which conjure up specific images and sounds. Even if the developer wants to attempt a new approach with the audio, there will still need to be basic elements of the genre to provide that certain familiarity for the players. If a game company tried to produce a medieval racing game, you can guarantee there will be orchestral instruments playing medieval melodies all backed by a fast-paced rhythm section.

Find out their *interpretation* of the "theme" even if you know what it is. What may look "horror" to you may instead be artwork of a tunnel you'll be driving your Ferrari through or some other small inconsequential scene which has no bearing on the rest of the game. I'd hate to see this "horror" scene, decide it was the "look" of the game, and run full steam off on a tangent. Not only will this false start be costly in wasted time, but it will harm your creativity. Ask lots of questions, see every bit of artwork you can. Have no doubt in your mind what the game is all about.

2. What genre of music will set the mood?

Discuss their interpretation of the music they feel would enhance the game. It may seem rather odd, you being the composer and all, but asking them will only clarify your musical direction. Remember, they've been living with this game for several months and I'm sure the subject has already come up amongst themselves. Listen to what they have to say and don't be judgmental at this point. Any idea is a good idea when brainstorming. What may sound silly might give someone else the winning idea. Better yet, you might be the one with the idea and look like a hero!

Examples of genres of music to consider are many — orchestral, techno, industrial, rock, country, spiritual, and so on, but only a few will fit the bill for a game project. Much is dependent on the targeted age group, the theme of the game, and the taste of its creators. Your job is to blend these elements to remain true to what the game is about and who it will be sold to. Discuss the demographics with them, identify the intended audience, and add that to your growing list of parameters.

3. What examples of pre-recorded music will fit the game?

Remember our earlier "red" example? Even after you've narrowed down the discussions about what kind of music is suitable for the game, it doesn't mean everyone's *perception* of that music is the same. What I believe to be "techno," for example, may not be what the next guy thinks is "techno." That's why you need examples to listen to together. Play tracks from the various suggestions and work on a consensus. Now everyone will be in agreement on the style and know what to expect.

Take this a step further. Find out the elements of this style which appeal to everyone. Is it the beat? Is it the instrumentation? Is there something in particular which stands out that would be perfect for the game? Sometimes you'll find it isn't even the genre of music they like but a specific sound used in a song or by a band. Give them chances to present their ideas clearly and to put their finger on all the sonic tidbits that will give the game its final personality. Your job is to listen.

The idea isn't to have someone else do your job, but to make the game better and help your mental processing. It will be enough of a challenge composing, recording, and mixing the music but having no idea where to start can make it that much more difficult. It's been said, "Good composers borrow, great composers steal!" In this day of highly enforced copyright laws, I don't recommend stealing, of course, but by utilizing key elements of a band or style, you will be more able to hit the nail on the head the first time. There isn't much of a chance you could recreate someone else's work even if you used the exact same instrumentation and sounds, so don't sweat it. You could take five composers, give them the same five loops to use, and I guarantee you'd get five very different musical presentations.

Getting your team to listen to and review pre-recorded music may be the best way to start off on the right foot, but unfortunately, isn't always possible to accomplish. In the beehive of activity within the game developer's lair, time is always of the essence and this step may get left by the wayside in favor of more important developer issues. After all, they hired you as the audio expert and are paying you to do a job, so it may be necessary to use the information you do have and your gut instincts. Try your best to schedule a meeting where you can discuss this particular issue.

4. What are the sound effect needs?

If you are contracted to do the sound effects, you will want to know as much as you can about any preconceived ideas the development crew has been working under. Just like the music, they may already have some ideas about what sounds would work best. The creators of certain characters may have a close, personal relationship with their works and would love to share their ideas of what makes this particular character special. You can translate their thoughts into some fitting sound effects and have an impact just by paying attention and asking the right questions.

If you aren't doing the sound effects portion of the game, it is still a good idea to find out what other audio your music will be competing with. If there are to be heavy background sounds during gameplay, it will have an impact on the complexity of the music you can offer. As the audio expert, you may have to point out to the developer that background sounds, music, and narrative playing simultaneously will cause confusion in the soundscape. Instead of the player having to turn the volume down, suggest the music you create be less dense — enhancing the experience, not highlighting a battle between all the sonic elements.

More often than not, when there is more than one sound contractor on a project, no one knows if all these separate elements will blend together or destroy the audio atmosphere until they are pieced together near the end of the project. To prevent this possible setback, it is extremely important to understand what other sounds might be competing and work on the problem from the beginning. Also consider staying in close contact with the other audio contractors to share information and prevent massive reworks for you both.

5. What are the narration needs?

Are you recording and editing the narratives too? If you are, your tasks are getting more complex and at these initial meetings, it's a great idea to find out so you can schedule your time appropriately. Since the contract negotiations, parameters may have changed — maybe you originally weren't going to have anything to do with the narration but now that your skills are evident and since you're on their team, why not? Be sure to renegotiate in this case and find out the details.

- Are you expected to audition and select the voice talent or have they already taken care of that?
- Do the narratives simply need to be edited or do you need to bring the talent in and record them?
- Are you expected to write the scripts yourself?

Just a couple of thoughts. It will ultimately decide how much extra work you'll have in store and if you are doing the music and sound effects too, you'd best get busy.

If you aren't touching the narratives, character voices, or voice-overs, it is still appropriate to find out what they will consist of. Does the main character have a voice like James Earl Jones, low and intense, or is it something on the other end of the range? Instead of having to turn down the volume of the music as an answer, how about building a hole in the frequency spectrum? What the characters and other voices are saying are more important than the background music and a little pre-planning will save you having to redo that slamming bass line competing with Darth Vader's orders to squash the universe. Normally, the most understandable part of vocal work, especially on tinny multimedia speakers, is in the upper-mid to high frequency ranges. By determining the needs of the game project first, you can ensure the soundscape is equitably managed and every facet is heard.

These first creative meetings are important. The details may seem inconsequential to the game developer, but it is imperative you discover as much of this "trivial" information as possible before you even sit down to compose. You will be very anxious to start creating, like a thoroughbred waiting for the race to begin, but exercising some patience is the way to go. Gather all the pieces of the puzzle, sort them out, build the border frame, and then you can begin.

By sorting out the fine points first, your creative energies will be spent producing music and sound effects which have a better chance of fitting perfectly the first time, instead of dealing with the creativity-sucking frustrations of false starts and redo's. Set the stage for your best work and then blow them all away with it!

7.3 Pre-compositional Considerations

Somewhere within the many initial meetings, someone is going to have to make an important decision: How much physical memory will be allotted to audio? The answer will have a direct impact on you, the final output quality of your audio, and how you will be able to achieve the best balance of file size and sound quality. Each platform hard drive, game disk, and game cartridge will ultimately determine the memory available for all that makes up a game: programming code, engines, drivers, artificial intelligence, artwork, animations, and sound. For example:

CD-ROMs	654 MB
Playstation 2 and Xbox (using DVD)	4.8 GB
GameCube	1.5 GB optical disk

There is a hard limit to the amount of data competing for space in each game.

Sound, fortunately for us, has moved from being the bastard child to an important aspect of gaming. Instead of getting what scraps of memory are left over after the others have their fill, audio is actually getting planned for ahead of time to share the real estate equitably, based on the needs of the game. If a game is touted as a graphical masterpiece, artwork will take up the majority. If surround sound is the big selling point, audio will have the space.

GAME COMPOSERS AT WORK

Kevin McMullan of Ensemble Studios

Do you follow a specific thought process scoring for a project?   Ultimately, game music must support, and not stick out from, the game itself. Therefore, the most important thing to do before jumping in on a project is to learn and understand the design of the game. Once you have achieved this, you work up a concept and design for the music you see applying to the project. Stephen and I start a lot of our musical research at this stage. We try to gather and maintain as much reference material as we can (Books, CDs, Internet articles, etc.) to use throughout a project. Once we actually start completing pieces of music, we just playtest with it a lot, until we are satisfied that we have scored a soundtrack that is appealing and supports the game."

When are you most creative?   "I tend to be the most creative when I just 'let go.' Many times this occurs when I am closing in on a deadline, or working late. I sometimes have a tendency to overanalyze my own work, which can extend the writing process. With a deadline in sight, however, I free myself from this and I tend to be more creative. Working late allows me to look out my window at the night. As corny as it sounds, I find it quite inspiring. Inspiration, wherever it comes from, always produces creativity."

What skills are important to game composers?   "There are the obvious skills such as compositional abilities and knowing how to play at least a few standard instruments. Also, a big plus in this industry is to have some experience scoring game music. Conversely, since everyone has to start somewhere, you shouldn't let any 'lack of experience' sway you from applying for any job. Overall, I think it is most important to be in completely head over heels in love with music. You need to truly appreciate how powerful music is on its own, and as a part of a project."

The Big Trade-off

One must evaluate:

- how much space is available,
- what method of audio playback to use,
- the processor speed which will be doing it,
- how much audio there is, and
- then, what quality of sound for all of this is acceptable.

Cartridge-type games actually don't require much space for sound. Because they use small files that tell the unit's internal sound device what notes to play and when, their actual file size is tiny compared to the rest of the information. Games which utilize "sound fonts" use more cartridge memory because the triggered sounds are actually stored in the cartridge. Most hard drive-, CD-ROM-, or DVD-ROM-based games play recordings stored on the discs. If the game you are working on is one of these latter types, the sample rate, resolution, and whether or not mono, stereo, or surround are required will determine your best methods of creation.

Game developers actually use many different considerations before deciding on the final sound format and parameters. I mentioned physical memory first because it is the easiest concept to grasp — there is only so much space and you can't fill past the limit. The first and foremost factor a developer will consider is "speed." Is the game we are developing going to run smoothly on our target platform? Not only is a game's content competing for physical, read-only memory (ROM), but when the game is in play and all that data is moving through the computer's insides, the pipeline through the processor has to be able to handle all the information.

Complicated AI (artificial intelligence) and graphic-intensive scenery will chew through the available assets in a hurry, leaving little room for anything else. A way for programmers to make it all work is to cut down on the size of the data, including the audio and graphic files. Programming code is basically text files and not much can be done to squeeze the file size any smaller. Graphics and audio are different in the sense that using less "detail" will free up more room while still presenting the visuals or audio in one form or another. You will see the same picture or hear the same sound, only the quality will be less as the file size becomes smaller. You can see why complicated games of the past weren't much to look at or listen to.

A way around overloading the processor in a PC is to use Red Book audio which is played directly off of a disk, bypassing the motherboard altogether via a cable connected from your CD-ROM drive to the sound card. This gives you great sound that never gets near the processor and frees it up to do other chores. Other games use streaming audio and heavy compression to save on both space and processor performance too. As music is needed, it is loaded from the disk a little at a time, decompressed, buffered into Random Access Memory (RAM), and played back.

All of these particular methods of processing and playback will have some impact on your job as the sound person. By discussing these details with the developer at the beginning of the job, you'll be working from the same page, have an understanding of the entire production process, and could possibly present alternative ways to accomplish certain goals if need be. Plus, you'll be able to achieve the greatest possible quality on your end which will make the project sound good. And isn't that what we are all about?

7.3.1 Sound Quality vs. File Size

Table 7.1 Memory storage requirements for one minute of sound.

Type:	Mono	Mono	Stereo	Stereo	Encoded Dolby Surround	Encoded Dolby Surround
Resolution:	8 bit	16 bit	8 bit	16 bit	8 bit	16 bit
Sample Rate						
44.1 kHz	2,646k	5,292k	5,292k	10,584k	5,292k	10,584k
22.05 kHz	1,323k	2,646k	2,646k	5,292k	2,646k	5,292k
11.025 kHz	661.5k	1,323k	1,323k	2,646k	1,323k	2,646k
8 kHz	480k	960k	960k	1,920k	960k	1,920k

Sample Rates

We've all heard the term "CD quality" and equate it to outstanding sounding audio. 44,100 kilohertz (or 44.1 kHz), the magic number associated with CD quality, is actually the number of "snapshots" taken of a sound within one second. Comparing this to standard movie film which uses 24 frames per second, like the eye, your ear perceives 44,100 samples to be lifelike and is fooled into thinking so. Use of sample rates below this value will cause a loss of detail and dynamic range and is something we must consider as game audio providers. What are we willing to give up in quality to have the quantity needed for the game?

In the first chapter, we discussed the future of game audio as leaning towards an audio standard of 44.1 kHz. Eventually, as storage space increases, all audio, music, and sound effects will use this high quality sample rate in games. For now though, samples rates of 22.05 kHz (or just 22 kHz) are the most common and can sound pretty good with good quality control, much like an FM radio broadcast. Sample rates of 8 kHz are widely in use in Java and Flash games. These generally sound horrendous but are designed with small file size and quick loading in mind. All the previous concerns will ultimately determine what sample rate you end up with.

As musicians, you may already be working with sample rates as high as 96 kHz. It is doubtful we will see anything that high in games for quite some time, the argument being the gain of sound quality is imperceptible to the average listener and the space it would consume too valuable. It would also be some years before hardware that could accurately play back this quality of sound would be affordable to the masses. Would the player even be able to listen for all this extra effort on our part while engaged in an all-encompassing gaming experience? When will "good" be "good enough?" Of course, I subscribe to the school of thought that says you can never have too much of a good thing, the more the merrier, the bigger the better — well, you get the idea. It will happen someday, that we do know.

Resolution

Another consideration in computer games which will have a direct impact on sound quality is *resolution* or bit size. CD quality not only uses a sample rate of 44.1 kHz to obtain its high quality, but also a resolution of 16 bits. Professional recording equipment today has resolution of 16, 20, and 24 bits and while higher numbers make the end audio product better, it can confuse the issue when talking about games. Generally games use either 8-bit or 16-bit resolution; smaller web games may use as low as 4 bits.

So what is resolution? You could think of it like you do sample rates. While sample rates refer to the accuracy of which a sound is sampled within a period of time, resolution is the accuracy of which that sound is stored. 8 bits can store 256 different values, while 16 bits can store 65,536. To put that in over-simplified terms, say I have two colors, black and white, that I need to store. If I was able to store only two values of colors, everything would be perfect. I have one box for black and one box for white. But the world is not "black and white." There is a lot of gray and I want to store as many shades of gray as possible. With 8 bit, I can store 254 shades of gray between the two extremes (black would be on one end, white on the other) for a total of 256. Using 16 bit, there would be storage for even more precise values of gray — giving a smoother transition between each shade, not such a noticeable jump as with 8 bit. I could store a better representation of our little world. Does that make sense?

Another way to describe it uses musical metaphors. If I wanted to store a sample of every musical instrument in the world on my keyboard for some grand performance, I would need almost an infinite amount of banks to store them. If I were using 8 bit, I could only store 256 instruments. If I needed an instrument I didn't have stored, I would use one which sounded close to the one I wanted instead. If I were using 16 bit, I would have a better chance of finding the exact one I needed or a close cousin with 65,536 banks to chose from. What this is saying, in a round about sort of way is, 16-bit resolution gives you more precise storage capabilities allowing fairly accurate playback of what was initially recorded. The higher the resolution, the better.

The game's resolution depends on the programming side and the sound driver used. You need to find out what resolution the final audio files will be presented in to plan your quality control accordingly. It is good practice to start your process with the highest sample rate and resolution available to you, knowing the final parameters will help make up your mind about how you may approach certain bits of audio. For example, an 8-bit resolution game will give you a lot of headache with "quiet" sounds or musical passages. A residual effect of converting down to 8 bit is quantization noise, which has a very prevalent hissy, static-like quality if the sound doesn't mask it. You'll end up compensating by making the sound as loud as possible. We'll go over this in greater detail in the following chapter, but I wanted to get you thinking early. Maybe you'll think about staying away from quiet sounds if 8-bit resolution is in the cards. You'll quickly discover, too, that sometimes it is not just about making killer tunes and sound effects; it's also the science that goes into making them sound their best.

Mono, Stereo, or Surround?

Probably the most important aspect of the sound issue is whether or not the end audio product will be in single channel (mono), 2 channel (stereo), or multi-channel 3D audio. The amount of memory available for audio will more than likely be the determining factor. Stereo files take up twice as much space as mono; surround, luckily, is encoded into two channels. Narratives and voice-overs will normally be mono, unless there is some special effect requirement added to give the voice a specific sonic character. There may be audio processing available either through the game engine or through the game's platform which would add some depth to the aural experience and in these cases, most sounds would be in mono.

It is important from an artistic point of view to know ahead of time which kind of audio the music and sound effects will require. On a very basic level, music is always done in stereo; sound effects in mono. That's what we have been trained as consumers to believe and accept. Music on the radio or on CDs is always presented in stereo and as musicians we create music in stereo. Now, would you ever have an occasion to do it in mono? Yes, you would. How about surround? You bet. We need to start thinking outside the norm and be able to adapt our craft acoordingly.

For good sound design, it is important to know how many channels to create for from the start. When I first started officially doing sound design, I approached it from a very flat, one-dimensional perspective. Only after visiting with someone with dozens of games under their belt, watching them create sound effects in Pro Tools, did I realize I'd been missing much of the equation. I watched this master create effects using the full stereo spectrum, swinging sounds from side-to-side, skillfully pulling you into the whole experience. It was like a slap in the face! I ran out the next day and bought a multi-track editor and haven't looked back since.

If you are creating for a game in mono, you'll work hard to get the most out of the sound. If the sounds are done for stereo, you'll have an extra channel to work with and be able to add much more dimension to your work. Even though I create almost every sound effect in stereo, if I know it will be converted to mono later, I don't waste any time having sounds fly around from the left to the right channel. Instead, after I convert to mono, I'll spend a little extra time making the sound interesting — adding some effects processing or creative EQ. The amount of work you put into the task is dependent on how many channels of audio you are creating for.

File Types

What file format will the audio be delivered in and what format will be used in the game? Most of the time these will be the same, but occasionally you'll deliver it in one and find out it will be converted to another later. Knowing the file type, such as .wav or .aiff or .au, is important for final quality considerations. Because each type of file uses its own unique brand of compression and sound quality, there will be different things you can or cannot do.

Generally, the standard formats are .wav for PC and .aiff for the Mac — both regarded as the best way to store sound in the digital domain. The trade-off though is large file sizes. One minute of 44.1 kHz, 16 bit, stereo audio stored as a .wav file will take up 10.6 MB of space. A game using 60 minutes of total audio in this format would leave little for the rest of the game. Solutions to this type of problem include:

- reducing the file size by using a lower sample rate, lower resolution, or less channels, or
- using a different file type.

Previously, developers would keep audio file sizes in check by lowering sound quality, but as new formats are born, they are willing to try them in favor of giving the player decent sound.

MP3 (.mp3 or MPEG Layer III) is the latest audio format to hold promise. Its sound quality is comparable to FM radio, but uses far less space. You'll remember an earlier comparison of a 22 kHz sample rate being equivalent to a radio broadcast. But .mp3 can sound better and take up less physical memory than reducing the sample rate. (See the following chart.)

1 minute of 22 kHz	16 bit, stereo	= 5.3 MB.
1 minute of 44.1 kHz	16 bit, stereo converted to .mp3	= 2.3 MB (and sounds better!)

By this little comparison, you can see it may be better for the game experience to use a different file type to squeeze a slightly better sound quality from the proverbial stone. As the sound expert, recommend this option if it hasn't already been considered. Or simply be ready to make whatever audio format they've chosen sound its best.

As an example, let's compare different file formats with their size and sound quality.

1 minute of 44.1 kHz	16 bit, stereo	.wav (Microsoft Wave PCM),	= 10.34 MB
		.aiff (Macintosh PCM)	= 10.34 MB
		.smp (Sample Vision)	= 10.34 MB
		.voc (Creative Labs VOC)	= 10.34 MB
		.au (Java G.177 u-law)	= 5.17 MB
		.dig (Sound Designer)	= 5.17 MB
		.mp3 file	= 2.3 MB
		.vox (Dialogic VOX ADPSM)	= 1.29 MB
		.ra (Real Audio)	= 113 KB

All of these were converted from the same original file using each formats' standard compression. A different format alone can change the amount of storage space needed in a game.

By looking at format sizes, you may wonder why we don't use Real Audio, a .vox file, or any other similar configuration as standard. The easiest way to understand this is to conduct your own personal experiment. I recommend sitting down at your computer, opening your audio editor of choice, and simply practicing converting file types. Once you've done several, do a side-by-side comparison. I guarantee you will choose the original .wav or .aiff file for the best quality. You'll be better able to share your audio knowledge with developers because you've converted them, heard them, and developed your own opinions. Go ahead; it'll be good for you. Sound quality is a subjective thing, of course, but most who are "in the know" would never consider formats just because of their small size. The programming language initially determines what type of format is used. But occasionally, there are options where other choices can be made.

7.3.2 Setting Up Shop

The final pre-compositional consideration rests squarely on your shoulders. You've soaked up vast amounts of information and now the time has come to finally make some music and prove to the developer that they chose wisely when they called upon your expertise. So, how are you going to hold up your end of the bargain?

Plan ahead. From now through the end of the project cycle, plan your production schedule, write it down, and make sure it looks reasonable. I don't recommend madly composing and recording and hoping you complete everything by each milestone. More often than not, it will never happen and you'll fall short. Plot out how many pieces of music, sound effects, and narrative recordings are needed for each block of the production, decide how much time you'll need for each task, and then map out your schedule. Based on your working model, you can see fairly rapidly if you have a snowball's chance in hell of completing everything on time. If not, approach the developer and let them know you may not have enough time — instead of dropping a bomb on them the day before your work is due.

As part of your production schedule, be sure to set aside time for mental breaks, whether it is a half day, whole day, weekend, whatever — just do it. Living with a piece of music every day can quickly zap a musician of any objectivity. By letting a couple of days pass between listens, you'll be able to pick up on parts which don't work and have other fresh ideas ready to go. Get out of the studio, get out of the house, change your scenery every so often. While it is tempting to immerse yourself in work, and tight project cycles have a way of pushing you to that limit, understand what even a couple of hours can do for your mental well-being and plan for them. Also ensure you get plenty of sleep and eat right. I know I probably sound like your mother, but in the heat of battle, it is easy to forget physical necessities. You can't expect to produce your best work if your basic survival needs aren't met. You may laugh now, but wait until that first contract when you've been in the studio a week straight before even realizing it. You don't want to burn out in this business. Pace yourself for the long haul.

Allot a day or two of prep time. Make sure you have plenty of storage medium, tapes, CD-R's, and any other equipment you'll need for the endeavor. Make sure any maintenance you've been meaning to do is done; all construction and admin projects hanging over your head are either done or out of the way. Try to prevent distractions from arising when you are on a creative roll. A couple of days at the beginning to clear all of this out of the way will help ensure a smooth production.

GAME COMPOSERS AT WORK

Chance Thomas, HUGEsound

When scoring for a project, how do you focus in on the central elements?
"Years ago some of my friends were involved in a recording session for a national commercial jingle. The client was Kraft Foods and the product was Velveeta Shells and Cheese. The session wasn't going very well, and the young producer — desperate to bring the right vibe to the singers' performance — in exasperation finally blurted out, 'BE THE CHEESE!'.

The comment was ridiculous, of course, and we have all laughed about it for years. But the concept is pretty close to the mark when applied to scoring for film, games, and other entertainment media. Get as deeply into a project as possible. Almost like method actors, you really need to lose yourself in the role. To help with this, I like to get lots of concept art sketches, video footage, designer's documents, desktop wall paper, etc., so that I can immerse myself in the world. Read everything about it you can get your hands on. Think it. Dream it. Feel it. Or in the words of our young and exasperated producer friend, 'BE THE PROJECT!'.

Chance Thomas conducting a full orchestra for the video game Quest for Glory V soundtrack.

I like to interview the director, writer, designer, artist, etc., frequently and try to ferret out as much of the psychology and emotion underscoring their creations as possible. After all, that's the job of the composer — to convey the deeper undercurrents of a story, a quest, or a conflict so that the end user feels those things internally.

Think about San Francisco sitting on the surface of the earth. Big trucks rumble along I-80; jumbo jets rise from and fall to the runways of the airport; cars, bicycles, and pedestrians scurry around the town. All of this commotion on the surface is frenetic, but creates relatively little impact on the city structure itself. Now think far beneath the surface to the sub-terrainean tectonic plates upon which the city rests. Movement in these plates (otherwise known as an earthquake) causes a HUGE impact on the city and everything in it.

Like traffic in the city, there are lots of little busy things going on in a film, game, or other media presentation. But all that frenetic energy has little real impact on an audience. Something in that presentation must resonate beneath the surface, must 'rumble' deep in the human heart or psyche if it is to have real impact. Music is a language that speaks to those places when used skillfully. Understanding the emotional sub-context is a foundational step for any composer who hopes to speak in the language of music to the deeper understandings of the audience. BE THE PROJECT!"

When are you most creative?   "Nothing inspires like a deadline and a big paycheck. A tight production schedule and ample compensation are wonderful tools for focusing creativity and heightening motivation."

What skills should composers have to succeed in the games industry?   "A great understanding of the language of music. At the end of the day, great game music is still about great music. I chair the Music and Sound Review Committees for the Academy of Interactive Arts and Sciences. We review the submissions in the Music and Sound categories for the Interactive Academy Awards — narrowing the field from 20 or 30 nominations to four finalists. We play the games, listen to the games, and decide what we feel represents outstanding achievement in our industry. The committee members come from a variety of technically- and/or musically-oriented backgrounds. Guess what? Great music always rises to the top. Implementation can be clever, even brilliant, and that always impresses us. But we all respond most profoundly to the music that moves us. Understand the language of music. It all begins there.

(See page 280 of Chapter 11 for Chance's gear list.)

Get in the Mood

Have the developer send you pictures, artwork, storyboards — anything visual for you to look at and then plaster your creative space with them. If it's a "dark" game, turn off the lights, set out some candles, cover the windows, and be ready to create within the virtual environment you are composing for. Conversely, for a "happy" children's game, open up all the shades and turn on all the lights, let sunshine in, and watch lots of comedy. For adrenaline-packed games, do jumping jacks, run, listen to pumping music at full volume, get the blood flowing every time you sit down to create. Put yourself in the center of the game. Live and breathe every creative moment visualizing the virtual world. By doing so, you will instinctively compose inspiring music and sound effects without having to force it. Prepare your room within the first couple of days and you will reap the dividends throughout the production. Remember to take frequent breaks from your make-believe world to keep the stimuli strong and effective. Working in the same room for weeks on end, staring at the same walls, tends to drive one a little crazy.

High Quality from the Start

From the word "go," make sure every recording, every sound source, every sample, and every piece of audio you use to construct instrumentation, music, and sound effects is of the highest quality you can afford and obtain. "Why on earth would that matter?" you wonder. Take sound effects creation for example. Most of the time, it is a blend of several different sounds pieced together to form a desired effect. By starting with the best quality at the onset, you can build from a strong foundation and make the sound do what you want it to do and not have to be stuck with something you get from a bad source. Normally, sounds will be resampled to a lower sample rate or resolution — not the other way around. Initial sounds taken from 11 kHz, 8 bit mono are going to have a lot of noise and other artifacts present. Trying to produce a quality effect from sounds like these is going to be difficult no matter what you do. It's kind of like recording an AM radio broadcast from 500 miles away in the middle of a thunderstorm then burning it to a CD for playback on your studio equipment. Just because it is on a CD doesn't mean the quality will be good. It is still going to sound like that scratchy, noise-ridden broadcast you originally heard.

When collecting sound libraries — either buying them from professional outlets, borrowing them from your buddy's web page, scavenging them from various sources over the years, or producing them yourself — obtain and keep only the best. Over the years, I had amassed quite a collection of sound effects as a personal hobby. When it became time to create sound effects professionally, I first gave a close listen to the sounds in my inventory. Because most had been created and saved with a low sample rate and resolution to save precious storage space, none were even close to sounding acceptable — full of noise and a definite embarrassment if I ever considered selling them for money. I refused to put my name on anything that didn't pass my quality standards so out they all went. As I look back on the entire affair, I would have saved a great deal of my time had I started from day one collecting only superior sounds.

Initially, you may have some budget studio equipment and instruments in your possession. Because we are talking about quality, ensure you know how to get the best sounds out of them until you can afford better gear. I started out with junk. The little, 4-track cassette deck was noisy, the old spring reverb had its own definitive personality, the drum machine was tired and mechanical but because I'd lived with these things for over 10 years, I actually got some pretty decent recordings from them. If an initial cash outlay is a problem, take what you have and make it shine. Squeeze every thing you can from your gear. There will be small developers who won't know the difference anyway and will hire you despite the equipment you have. As the income starts rolling in, start thinking about what you can replace to make yourself sound better, give you a competitive edge, and make more money. After a few years, you will have accumulated an envious collection of high quality gear that facilitates the superior job you are now known for. In the end though, developers don't really care what you have, as long as your audio sounds good and works with the game.

7.4 'Gotchas' and Other Things to Watch Out For

The art and science of developing video games is over 20 years old now and we are slowly approaching normalcy in an industry involved in continuous change. With this comes a standard, a tried and true method of creating audio for games. Different teams, however, do things just a bit differently to meet that same end result. The road occasionally becomes wrought with unseen perils and unwanted frustrations inhibit our creativity at a time when it needs to flow. These are what you need to be on the lookout for.

7.4.1 Placeholders

Building and piecing together a video game is a huge undertaking and developers take some shortcuts to create their virtual worlds before bringing in the professionals like us. In order to test the audio drivers and spice up the silent game tests, they may put in "placeholder" music tracks and sound effects. They usually borrow something close to what they have in mind from other games or from commercial music. This can be a good thing in some cases. Now all you have to do is replicate something similar and you're all set. Most of the time, though, this can be bad for you and bad for the game.

As the game is produced, tested, and played amongst the development team, these placeholders will be heard hundreds of times. By the time they bring you in, everyone will be used to hearing them and will more than likely be attached to them. Anything you come up with runs the chance of being subpar; new sounds and music of yours not quite living up to the developer's expectations. It can be nerve-wracking to say the least. Instead of the developer letting the audio expert lend their particular brand of artistry to the mix, they will hurt the potential of the game by not giving you the opportunity to try something fresh.

Be cautious when approaching a game using placeholders and be ready to sell your ideas a little harder. It isn't impossible to get your ideas across but, as the new guy on the team, you might not be listened to as closely as you would hope. You do have one advantage in this type of situation though. As the new guy, you are able to take an unbiased look at the game and provide the unclouded perspective of someone who hasn't been living and breathing this thing for the last year. As you see more of the game, you will notice things which everyone else may have missed — from simple word misspellings to artwork of characters missing body parts. Use this to your advantage to quickly build credibility and show your commitment to the project. Once you've shown that you are only looking out for the game's best interests and not your own "personal" inclinations, you've got it licked.

7.4.2 A Developer's Listening Preference

You wouldn't think in the professional video game industry a publisher or developer's personal tastes in music would be a big factor, now would you? Don't be so sure. Imagine trying to present music to someone who hates a particular style. Even if the music is perfect for a project, a decision maker up the line may dislike your submission just because they don't like that genre. There are the occasional few who lose sight of the big picture — failing to understand who the game is designed for and the make-believe world they are trying to immerse the player in. Those are the guys you need to watch out for.

I've never heard of a fishing game using techno; country would definitely be the better choice. The same with a medieval game; rock would never work. But don't think somebody won't try to get you to do it. If they hate country or classical music with enough passion, they may try to influence you and those you deal with. In times like this, you need to remind the Producers that, while you can appreciate their personal tastes in music, the project definitely calls for a particular style. Help steer them back on the path of what is best for the project. Can't get your point across? Then do the style of music they want you to do, but make sure you don't end up redoing the work for free. This brings us to the next point.

7.4.3 Endless Reworks and Change Orders

Reworks and change orders were covered in Chapter 6, but I want to reiterate their potential impact on you. They are definitely something to watch out for in our business and one of the more standard "gotchas." There is an acceptable amount of reworks; the exact number being as many as you can tolerate. When it goes overboard, you need to stand up and say something. Perhaps you have already negotiated something in your contract about reworks and change orders and you've opened the lines of communication for a free-flowing exchange of ideas. You've done all the right things and still you seem to be working hard on several reworks. What gives?

Some good investigative work on your part may be in order. The Producer you are reporting to reports to someone else and maybe they are the ones who are throwing a wrench in the machinery. The Producer is trying to look good too, making you work extra hard in order for him to be able to present several options to his boss. This is fine to a point. But when you are wasting your creative energies taking new approaches, these little moments quietly disguised as "reworks" appear to have become "change orders" instead. You might want to subtly remind the Producer about the particular clause in the contract which requires new milestones for change orders and see what happens. I'm not trying to say you shouldn't work hard to make a game the best it can be sonically, I just don't want you to be taken advantage of without appropriate compensation.

I had a situation once where I seemed to be working harder than normal on sound effects. I couldn't understand why the sounds I'd already sent weren't working and was getting no feedback from the Producer. I just kept getting requests for different approaches to the same effects. My gut feeling was telling me to quit, but my head was saying to go that extra mile for this new client and so I continued to march. A month went by and I'd submitted five separate approaches. Creatively, there was no where else to go and I secretly prayed there wouldn't be anymore requests. When the list of sounds they picked for the game finally arrived in my email, every sound was from the first batch I'd sent! Turns out it wasn't even the Producer making the decisions but his boss who had the final say. I promptly renegotiated an hourly wage for the next project and made a point to include the Executive Producer in my little network the next time.

When working as a new composer and sound designer on your first couple of projects, it is important not to let your inexperience appear obvious. Be easy to work with, but maintain that air of professionalism to ensure you are taken seriously when raising valid points such as the ones mentioned. Most of the time, developers don't know or don't care about the impact they may have on you with what seems to be "simple" requests. They are in the business of getting the game to the marketplace and everyone on the team is expected to work hard toward that goal, including contractors. Don't be afraid to express your concern over events which may interfere with your creative activities. The Producer is managing an entire team and needs to know when nothing is happening on your end. Maybe they can help. The times I've called Producers in this situation, I've ended up getting either an extension of a milestone (to ease the pressure and give me a day or two to regroup), or I've gotten brilliant ideas that pointed me immediately towards a solution. They are a valuable resource and their experience should be used wisely.

7.4.4 Communication Breakdown

From the very first meetings with a developer, do what you have to do to be included in the creative process and to stay there. As discussed previously, creative ideas have a tendency to change rapidly and as a contractor, you'll end up being the last to know about important issues unless you are on the distribution list. Changes that seem "inconsequential" to the developer can have a great impact on your musical perspective and cause grief on your end.

An experience I had with an out-of-state developer illustrates this point clearly. At our initial creative meetings, we had discussed the personality of a particular character and all seemed to be in agreement. I received the scripts for the rather long narratives, hired the voice talent, and spent two days in the studio recording and editing the sequences. I was very happy with our work and sent them off to the developer. I received a phone call after the Producer had heard the recordings saying they had changed this dark, evil character to a more mystical, less intimidating one instead. "I thought you knew," was the chilling statement I received. "Uh, mmm, ah..." was about all I could come up with as a response. We ended up throwing out that version and went back into the studio with new talent for another round. I was lucky the developer was understanding and that the breakdown in communication was not considered my fault. I didn't have to eat the cost of the first voice talent. It could have easily come out of my budget.

Another example: I got the parameters for a slot machine game and it looked cut and dried. I had done over 40 similar games for this developer and lately, they had been giving me carte blanche, that is, accepting my own sonic interpretation of each game. I didn't receive any advanced artwork but was given a link to the game sponsor's web site from which to glean some ideas. Unfortunately, the site was void of any artwork, accept for one little icon in the top corner and didn't provide much help. I fired off an email to the new Producer I was working with, explained my predicament, and got the go ahead for a "fun ship" theme for this ocean liner slot machine game. I spent a few days working up the sound effects, even spending money for a new sample disc, determined to outdo my previous game submissions. I sent off the sound files, feeling pretty good about my efforts, and went on to other business.

I usually got confirmation within a day or two that the sounds were received and which ones they wanted to use for the game. I heard nothing for a week. After two weeks, while conversing with the company's Executive Producer on another matter, I found out the Producer I was working with wanted to chat with me — something about needing different sounds for the game. So I pick up the phone to find out what's up. The artwork came back and the new artist had interpreted their take on the game as the "golden age" of ocean liners instead of "fun ship." Now that there were two ideas in the barrel, the sponsor decided on "golden age" and since then, the Producer was trying to figure out how to tell me. It seems somewhere in there, I got nudged out of the loop and missed out on important creative direction. I went back to work and created some "golden age" sounds, having to push the rest of my schedule back by a couple of days. As a contractor charging per sound effect and not by the hour, I lost money on the deal. Lesson learned: staying in the loop saves both time and money.

7.5 Conclusion

The stage has been properly set for our mesmerizing performance. We've discussed and planned our strategy, opened the lines of communication, and are poised to bravely leap into the fray. There isn't anything left to do but press the little red button and start recording the music and sound effects which will launch our meteoric rise. As long as we jump into this wisely, we will be able to get our best efforts accepted on the first try and save some serious headache. I strongly recommend using the points talked about here — not because I'm cloning an army to take over the gaming world — but because the lessons previous game composers and sound designers have learned will save you tremendous grief and make this entire experience something worthwhile. After all, satisfaction in our chosen career is the reason most often given for staying with it, not the monetary rewards.

CHAPTER 8
Creating Music for Games

Music is a powerful force in the modern world. The right music coupled with the right images is pure magic. Film and television has much to do with our perceptions, as is the music we choose as our own life's soundtrack. When we are emotionally "up" or psyching ourselves to be that way, we listen to music that is upbeat, has a positive rhythm, makes us feel alive. Conversely, when we feel down or making an effort to relax, we feel better listening to slower, less complex music. Music affects us at a purely emotional level. Great composers know how to capitalize on this and, by their design, make you feel how they want you to feel.

Movies are a great way to learn methods of emotional manipulation. These complex screen dramas use music as the force to portray what pure visuals cannot — enhancing them appropriately to express what a character is feeling. There is a problem comparing movies to video games though. Movies are linear. They start, they play, they end. Each scene is perfectly planned and the composer knows exactly what to compose and where to take you emotionally because it is all scripted. Most video games are not presented in linear fashion; each time a game is played, something different happens. It would be extremely difficult to score a game as you would a film, so different methods are used.

The future is leaning towards interactive music — music which follows each twist and turn in the plot, matching your every move. It is possible to create the right atmosphere for what is to come, causing tension or giving a sense that something is about to happen as is popular in film scores. Not all games require this type of adaptive music and rely on music instead to set the mood and provide a certain "pulse" to the accompanying scenery. The two mediums require different skill sets, obviously, and some of us are better suited for one over the other.

Writing music for games is not necessarily a difficult thing. It does require a different mindset to deal with the number of intricacies the games business has to offer. Because you are proficient at composing music for yourself or your band, or for commercials and film, doesn't mean you will automatically enjoy something like this. In games, you wear all hats: the composer, arranger, copyist, engineer, producer, musician, mastering engineer, CD manufacturer, and so on. The pressure and challenge of dealing with all facets can be incredible. One of the objectives of this book is to present you with the details to help you make a decision about this line of work.

8.1 Game Music Varieties

One of the beauties of game music is that you rarely get bored working on a project. Within video games, there are several musical specialties that guarantee to keep the perspective fresh and your skills employed. You'll get to compose scores for cinematics, background gameplay ambience, and in-your-face title themes all for the same project. It's a great testing ground to prove your compositional skills, but it can also tax your creative stamina. It's definitely an exciting prospect — one worthy of the paycheck you receive for your talents.

Let's turn to an overview of the various types of music required in games. This is by no means a complete listing because there are no specific rules for when and where music should be applied. But certain similarities exist where game players expect to hear music and these are the ones we'll discuss.

8.1.1 Intro, Closing, and Credit Sequences

The first piece of music the player will encounter is the opening (or introduction) sequence. This is presented either as a "main title theme" or a score accompanying opening cinematics. The music will help build the momentum and excitement of the game, set the mood, and establish the main storyline. This first moment capitalizes on the player's exhilaration for purchasing the game and reassures them they have spent their money wisely. This music plays an important role establishing the quality of the game — the crucial first impression that will last until other opinions are be formed. If the music sounds cheesy, it cheapens the purchase immediately, regardless of the quality of the graphics. If a compelling orchestral score greets them, the player has a sense that they are in for a first-rate experience.

Closing and credit sequences are normally where the final musical cues occur. This late in the game, they might not enhance the player's opinions, but they still serve an important purpose in the overall scheme. The closing cue will accompany a final cinematic sequence, a slide show, or the credit sequence. It is designed to give the player a sense of closure after the effort of playing the game. Normally, it's a big accomplishment to actually finish a game and this final fanfare will reinforce the moment. The music will set whatever final mood the developer wishes to leave the player with — whether it be triumphant and happy, or calm and serene. Someone has spent $50 and weeks of their time playing your game, and we want to congratulate them and give them every reason to believe all of our games are worth playing.

The credit sequence is the chance for the development team to have their name in the spotlight and get a little public recognition. The slide show or scrolling display is either triggered by the player from a game menu or will automatically play after the objectives of the game are accomplished. If it plays at game's end, the sequence will also serve as the closing sequence. If the sequence is activated at the player's whim, the music accompanying it will generally be designed as background music. Because a player might be exploring the menu features or taking a break from gameplay, the music should still somehow connect with the rest of the game, keeping the pace and remaining on theme. This particular music is sometimes considered "throw away" music. A player will only hear it once or twice in the course of playing the game and is normally considered unimportant to the rest of the project. But you, as the composer, could also look at it in a different light. For pure vanity's sake, or as brilliant marketing, a composer could create their best music cue to attract prospective clients (who also play these games) or to gain some extra name recognition.

8.1.2 Cinematic Sequences

Game cinematics are merely "mini movies." They are used as part of opening sequences, transitions between game levels, advances in the storyline, and a multitude of other functions that require moving pictures. From a scoring point of view, it is exactly like composing for film, that is, a linear presentation that flows from start to finish in a pre-scripted fashion. The music will serve the very same purpose: creating a mood, setting the pace, highlighting plot shifts, and adding tension and excitement to all of the appropriate spots. This type of composing work requires a certain skill level and is often quite difficult to do properly. Those experienced in this type of music composition generally thrive in games that rely heavily on cinematics and can also dabble successfully scoring for film.

This type of animation sequence is often paired with a full and very expensive-sounding orchestral score — usually a multi-layered synthesizer and sampler arrangement. More often though, live orchestras are being used to fill this role for total and complete realism. A lush audio soundscape can put a small screen cinematic sequence on par with a full-scale movie production and smart developers will try to capitalize on this. It's not to say that other types of music won't work; a myriad of musical styles will deliver the same affect. But a good game composer will practice their orchestral proficiency despite their love of rock or techno in order to stay marketable in the industry. It can definitely take your appreciation for music to an entirely new level. Be sure to check out the examples on the companion CD-ROM.

8.1.3 Menu Screen Music

Menu screens come in all shapes and sizes, but all act as the user's interface for gameplay parameter adjustments. The player can push buttons or select various objects to set video, keyboard, audio, and other basic functions to personalize their encounter. Music for these screens can perform an assortment of objectives dependent upon *when* they are experienced in a game.

Initial menus are the "calm before the storm" or where the sense of excitement is built. They may require a more complex tie-in from preceding cinematics or other opening sequences and tend to be busier than a standard menu — generally opting to keep the energy level high. Menus accessed during the game can give a moment of rest from the onslaught of gaming over-stimulation. Both types require music within the theme of the game, but "mid-game" menus are usually less dense than standalone music. The player isn't particularly interested in hearing an "in your face" soundtrack during these moments. They are making needed adjustments that require some concentration. The music here should keep the player immersed in the virtual world, but not annoy them. Because there is no way to predict how long the screen will remain active, music which loops continuously is normally used to maintain a seamless rhythm.

8.1.4 Game Play Music

Music that occurs during gameplay can have various purposes, dependent upon the type of game. The music for driving games, for example, is usually dense, upbeat, and very loud. The player doesn't need to think about much besides where the road is and what obstacles they are trying to miss. These games rely on constant movement in both the screen and audio track to keep the player's adrenaline high. This type of music is very different in contrast to low key background music.

Driving games are a good example of games which use "soundtracks," that is, individual songs that can usually stand up well on their own. They could easily be popped into a CD player to enjoy while out on the "real" open road with the same effect. Other games, such as strategy games that require more brain power and less distraction, use more of a musical score. This music sits subtly in the background creating the mood and remaining unobtrusive. It generally flows smoothly underneath the surface to anchor a player to the virtual world while they interact in a concentrated effort to the task at hand.

Sports titles don't usually make use of background music — opting instead to use background ambient sound effects and random noises to add realism to play. There may be an occasional need to compose music for marching band flurries, drum ditties, or stadium organists.

8.1.5 Plot Advancement Music, Cut Scenes, and Tie-Ins

As a game progresses to the next level or drastically changes direction during play, visual and audio cues assist in the transition. As mentioned previously, small movies are often used and are scored per usual from a musical perspective. These changes are significant — requiring a dramatic score to grab a player's attention and motivate them to make it through the next level to see the next movie. These offerings often serve as a reward to the player, where they are able to watch the on-screen action and inwardly pride themselves for making it happen, translating to satisfaction for the game purchase.

For shifts that don't use cinematics (for example, a character entering a room to meet the level's big bad guy), the music will act as the set-up for the upcoming confrontation, subtly warning the player. The visuals don't typically change until the bad guy actually shows himself. The audio becomes all important in this instance. Without it, the player doesn't have any foreshadowing and won't know to take out their weapon or to get out of the room until it is too late. While this can lead to a learning experience for a player, repeatedly dying and having to start a level over can be frustrating enough to stop playing the game. Audio cues, in this case, will play to their intelligence and allow them to use more senses than just their sight — keeping them in the fight longer and preserving their happiness.

8.1.6 "Win" and "Lose" Finale Cues

We've all heard these types of music cues. Since the dawn of the video game era, this particular musical feature has become a standard. When you win, an optimistic flourish of sound rewards your superior efforts. When you happen to be less successful, the music is either demeaning or mildly encouraging, prodding you to try again. It is almost unnatural to *not* hear something at the end of a game level now. These types of cues provide proper closure to the player's experience.

Musically, these cues will remain within the game's genre and will normally utilize the same sound palette and instrumentation. Winning cues will tend to be upbeat, composed in a major scale, and with a lot of pomp and circumstance. Afterall, the player just won! They deserve a glorious finish and a boost to their ego. It is human nature to want to win and good games will capitalize on the basic need for recognition.

A loss can be presented to the player as a defeat or a minor setback. Some games go all out with the losing cue and really put it to the player — making a spectacle and giving them a good razzing. These will be heavy on the minor scale and occasionally make use of childish musical put-downs to make their point. Other games are more sensitive to the player and choose not to go to that extreme. Losing isn't always a bad thing, especially in children's games. If you were to slam a younger player for their "failure," it would eventually discourage them enough to give up on a game. Leaving them with the sense they were still successful and can do better next time will ultimately prove to be a better approach. Music should set the tone and not be condescending in cases like this. These cues can be difficult — the perfect blend of defeat and encouragement. You can often get by simply using a toned-down win cue, still positive but just not full of the enthusiasm.

8.1.7 Interactive Music

Developers are turning towards interactive music as the next major improvement in gaming. The chances are pretty good you will run across this type of project in your career as the appropriate enhancements are made and its popularity increases. This activity will require a good working knowledge of many musical styles and how they can be implemented into the game. It won't be enough just to know how to compose good music. You will need to know how to ensure compatibility between the many musical pieces which could play at any time.

By design, interactive game music will adapt to the mood of the player and the game setting. Music will be slow and surreal as a player is exploring a new environment. If the game character moves from a walk to a run, the music will also keep pace by increasing in tempo. As danger approaches, the music will shift to increased tension, then to an all out feeling of dread as the bad guy appears out of the shadows. The player chooses a weapon and begins the attack as the music shifts again to a battle-esque theme to fire the player up. As the player gets hacked to pieces by the bad guy, the music will turn dark conveying that the end is near. But, as the hero gets his second wind and begins a determined counterattack, the music will morph into a triumphant flurry as he imposes death and destruction on the villain's head. This is a good example of interactive audio — music which swings with each turn of events and provides an adaptive soundtrack, giving the feel of participating in an interactive movie. If you were to watch a recording of another person playing the game, a good interactive soundtrack would seem as if it was specifically scored to the scene, similar to a linear movie. When it works right, the feeling is indescribable. That's where we step in.

The basic rule to composing interactive game music:
any change in the soundtrack must blend with any other music cue at any time.

Game players are not predictable. We don't know when they will walk, run, hide, enter a new room, meet the bad guy, draw their weapon, or do any of the other hundred possible actions that can happen during a game. But, truly adaptive music is prepared for any possibility. Ensuring the music can transition naturally is what makes it work.

Obviously, the first key to interactive music is to use the same sound bank and same instrumentation. This provides an inherent similarity working in our favor. Another recommendation is to base all of the music around the same key. This provides a solid foundation to make key changes within the same scale and enables the music to return to a familiar root. These changes will have greater impact, while blending perfectly with the rest of the soundtrack. This is used in film scoring and there is no reason it can't be applied here. Fade-in and fade-out music cues work very well and are used liberally to make adaptive audio applications succeed. Music that begins with a sharp attack is also beneficial — especially when the game mood swings quickly from peaceful exploration to combat mode or when the bad guy jumps out of the bushes. A quick, loud beginning to a musical piece has emotional impact and if done right, will take the player's breath away, catching them completely off guard.

8.1.8 Loops

When physical storage space, processor speed, or RAM is a factor, efforts will be made to save space wherever possible. For audio applications, one of the best ways is to achieve this goal is the liberal use of music *loops*. A music loop can quickly load into RAM and play repeatedly without placing further demands on the processing pipeline. Gameplay, menu screens, and finale screens are perfect places for this type of music. Because it is difficult to predict how long a particular screen will be active, music with the capability of continuous repetition works great. Developers may also ask for "loopable" cues as a cost-saving method. Less music equals less money to pay out and cost-conscious businesses are always looking at the bottom line.

As a composer, loopable cues are not difficult. The only real secret is finding the perfect spot after a bar or measure to abruptly cut off the music, enabling it to seamlessly begin again. A little trial and error and quick, imperceptible fades are effective in the audio editing environment. Various loop software programs are also available if you end up doing this type of work often.

Any type of music can be looped, from orchestral to techno, with agreeable results. Longer loops are best, especially during gameplay, where the same 15-second loop would get stale after listening to it for an hour. In these cases, 3–4 minute loops would be preferred; basically full-length songs which can be repeated without a noticeable break point. Menu and finale screens work best with 30–60 second loops; 15–20 second ones for inconsequential, low-level menu screens.

8.1.9 Ambient Tracks

In an effort to battle silence, ambient music can be used to maintain continuous audio activity within the game environment. This type of background music is purposefully designed as light, uncomplicated, mood-setting pieces set to linger almost unnoticed in the soundscape. Of course, if it wasn't there, it would be noticed and other non-game sounds would have a chance to disturb the player.

Ambient music still remains within the style of the main theme, just a less dense version of it. These lighter cues utilize long, sustained notes and occasional percussion to break any monotony. An orchestral score would make use of string sections and the occasional timpani thrown in. Modern music could use various synth pads or simple, ambient keyboard samples. Regardless of the style you are composing in, there is always a unique instrument to be used. Just be sure to keep it simple and the volume low.

Normally, ambient music is perfect in long, gameplay scenarios where a player may need to concentrate. Think of the last time you drove somewhere unfamiliar. While you are on the highway or in familiar territory, the music is usually up pretty loud. But as soon as you turn off the freeway and need to start concentrating, the volume comes down or gets turned off altogether. It's the same in gameplay — except we don't want them to turn it off, instead we make it simpler for them.

More and more these days, I'm noticing ambient music in places I'd never heard it before. Sports games and flight simulators are typically devoid of gameplay music; they tend to let the stadium crowd or the roar of the jet engine provide the realistic effect. But, if you listen closely, you may hear a slight bit of music playing way in the background — subtle proof that developers are continuously working to improve the overall game experience.

8.2 Exercises to Create Fitting Game Music

A question I often hear from prospective game composers is, "What can I do to create music that fits?". It's not enough to write good music; you have to be able to make it work perfectly within the environment. There is a little bit of human psychology involved in game composing whether you believe it or not. You don't want the game player to turn down the volume and it will take some effort on your part so nothing annoys them enough to do it. You will definitely need to get your point across without being obtrusive.

There are game developers out there who don't consider this, who ask for slamming music tracks and put them into the games without contemplating what the player will feel as they play the game. They take music they themselves are absorbed with and expect everyone else to like it too. Turns out, the 6–12-year-old female who would play the game is completely repelled by the sound. The developer just didn't get it and wonders why they aren't around to make another game. Developers: please don't just use any music; make sure it fits the project. Composers: don't compose garbage because the developer tells you to; make sure it will work in the project and if it doesn't, let them know. If the music doesn't fit the game, no one who sees it will ever consider hiring you for their project.

So, how does one get good at composing game music? Let's take a look at what other game composers have done to boost their success in this industry.

GAME COMPOSERS AT WORK

Jon Holland of Xyxu Studios

How do you go about scoring for a project? "I like producers to give me specific examples of music. I need names of songs or pieces of music that are close to the direction they want to go, that way I know where the producer is coming from. If he tells me he wants Vangelis or Hans Zimmer and then he ends up playing me some acid jazz, we might have a problem. I save a lot of time by finding out exactly what piece of music influenced that producer in the first place. If it is a cross between John Tesh and Korn, you may have to nail them down a little more specifically to what it is about John Tesh that turns them on. What is it about Korn? When you start compartmentalizing, it gets you into the zone quicker. Sometimes I may have to redo a demo, but it's rare. Especially if I ask enough questions before I start. Most of the time it just takes the right interrogation methods on my part to pinpoint exactly what they are talking about musically.

It is hard for me to look at storyboards and have somebody explain to me what a game is about. It's better than nothing, definitely, but I like to see animations that are far enough along that I can see what the environments look like. It doesn't have to be completed art by any means. I immediately start getting ideas when I see animations. You can explain to me for three days something that I will see in an animation in 15 seconds."

During the scoring process, when do you seem to be your most creative? "Ironically, stringent deadlines tend to do wonders for the imagination, however, some can be downright ridiculous. After viewing animation loops and reading a few notes, I can get crackin'. Fortunately, 95% of my music themes come to me within the first 120 seconds of composing. Unfortunately, tight deadlines have a way of reducing options and experimentation but in the end, the producers get something that they're happy with. I play it safe with situations like that because there is little if any time for redo's. By the same token, when I have a harsh deadline, I usually get into a groove, working from one piece of music to the next quickly. Detail in my music arrangements is usually where I have to censor myself. Usually, the more time I have, the more intricate the arrangement will be. I've been called a perfectionist, but I really know when there is enough info on a piece to keep the listener interested and when there isn't."

How should other composers go about getting into this business? "Most of my work comes from word of mouth, but there are no rules. To me, music is all about flavor. I have a style that I compose in and fortunately my clients seem to like that flavor. Whether I'm writing drama, racing, or sports music, it will always have my flavor stamped on it. But in reality, it is not going to be the flavor that answers every producer's needs. Maybe a producer will want bluegrass music for their game. Well, that may be your shot because I don't write that kind of stuff and maybe you do."

Jon Holland enjoys creating epic, emotional game scores.

(See page 257 of Chapter 9 for Jon's gear list.)

8.2.1 Watch and Listen

The single most often used technique to gain insight into the craft is simply exercising your ability to listen. Listen to the musical world around you. Listen to music while you drive, to the music in the grocery store, to the background music at a party — whatever music is playing during another activity. Think about what the music does for the happenings around you at the time. Analyze what makes the music work or not work. Is it your mood, how you feel, the action, the drama? What element is present that enhances the experience? For me, driving down Interstate 5 with heavy metal blaring works great! Sitting in a Texas Barbeque eating ribs and listening to old country music is heaven. Hearing a children's lullaby as I put my daughter to bed at night is fitting as well. A romantic dinner with the wife and some light jazz makes for a fine evening. Whatever music enhances the experience I am living at the time works on an incredibly emotional level and is what I strive for when composing. It's a great exercise for you to try. Would speed metal work at my daughter's bedtime? What about opera at a BBQ? Get the picture? This is an easy way to get it straight in your mind before doing it to picture.

Speaking of scoring to picture, you can learn a great deal from our cousins in Hollywood. They've been making music fit to picture for a few years and are getting pretty good at it. Watch a lot of movies. After you've watched the movie, go back again to *listen* to it. Listen to the ebb and flow of the melodies, to the techniques used to increase tension, build suspense, and create an atmosphere unique to the film. Listen for the music that you don't hear as well. This is the music that fits the the visuals so well, it doesn't register in your mind. This is the kind you want to do for games — especially for the background gameplay segments. Learn from the masters. They don't get paid a million dollars per movie for nothing.

Another great way to discover scoring techniques is to analyze movie trailers. These 2–3 minute mini-movies can display the entire range of a movie in a short span of time. Not all trailers are done by the original film composer; most of the time, other composers who specialize in trailers perform the task. Many times, the music in the trailer has nothing to do with the film score. It's focused on building excitement to draw you into the theater. This kind of musical stimulation is perfect for learning the art of cinematic game scoring. Game cinematics are normally 3–5 minutes long with rapid changes of scenes and characters — packing enough information to carry the story to the next level with little wasted motion. Listen and learn how movie trailers get the blood pumping and build the mood for the experience to come.

After analyzing the real world, you can also learn the subtleties of composing for games by actually playing them. Play them and pay close attention to the music, not getting the bad guy. I want you to start forming opinions about the musical soundscape, that is, what music is really good and what music stinks. You can learn valuable lessons from both. Pay close attention to how they match the theme of the game, what instrumentation was used, the density and complexity of the music, and how the score affects the mood of the game. Can you do it better? What other directions would work? What other instruments could be used effectively? I want you to get to the point that you *know* you could have done as good if not better. This confidence will land you jobs and knowing exactly what has worked (or not worked) in the past is experience you can advertise. Being familiar with your craft is a whole lot easier than learning as you go. Dig in now, have a little fun in the process, and reap the rewards later.

8.2.2 Create in Different Styles

This particular idea was touched on in Chapter 3 when I talked about putting together a solid demo reel. Put various musical styles on separate pieces of paper, put them in a bowl, and every day, take one out and compose a one-minute piece in that style. Try rock, country, hip-hop, dance, techno, orchestral, ethnic, bluegrass, R&B — whatever you can think of to hone your skills. You don't need to be elaborate or spend more than an hour on the piece; just do a rough sketch and then decide whether you portrayed the style believably. If you didn't, determine what elements were missing and try again another time. If you nailed it, put this in your "stronger styles" category and push it hard to prospective clients. You can listen and talk theory all day long but it won't make any sense until you actually sit down and do it. Prove to yourself and prospective clients that your capabilities match what comes out of your mouth.

While you are performing this little exercise, take a look at the methods you use to compose each style. Did you try something different each time? Was that method conducive to the creative process? Should you have tried something different? Loop-based production is great for techno and dance, but not so good for orchestral or bluegrass. MIDI- and sampler-based production is perfect for orchestral and ethnic creations. Live recording methods are good for rock. You get the message. The method is just as important as the style you are creating in. Work out all the kinks before clients are putting the pressure on you to deliver the goods and get some great practice in the process.

8.2.3 Try Something New

Keeping compositional chops fresh can be a chore when working on video games. You can get pigeon-holed into the same style very easily, either for a large game project or for a series of them and your other skills will rust. It's not a problem until you get the call for an orchestral score after you've spent two months doing an industrial soundtrack. It will probably take almost a week to get spooled up, get organized, and get comfortable with the style before you even begin to roll tape. When time is money, a week of downtime won't help your bottom line very well. Stay ready and stay practiced to keep life easier.

Keep pushing yourself into new directions. Try styles you dislike, combinations of styles, and made-up ideas such as "Venetian techno" to prod yourself into new territory. Continuously push yourself and your abilities to new levels of competence. Music in entertainment is all about creating a mood while using unique approaches. If you gain the reputation of being "distinctive," it will do a lot to help your career and the money you can demand.

Personally, whenever I spend too much time on a particular cue, the different versions I try all end up sounding

Figure 8.1 Composing with the help of a studio full of talented musicians can also keep your musical perspectives wide open. Even though most game composers work alone, this approach can bring fresh air to our creativity. It can even be fun!

blah. It's not that they won't work. It's more that I'm not happy with them because none break any new ground. A certain stale quality can snowball and every subsequent effort continues downhill. I lose the excitement for the cue and it shows in my work. When this happens, I find taking a step backward and approaching from a different angle yields better results. Try a different rhythm track, different instrumentation, or a different frame of mind. Get out of the studio, watch a movie, go for a jog, listen to some of your favorite music — change your latitude, as they say. But, over time, as I get deeper into the game world, this happens less and less because I have other musical experience to fall back on.

By rounding out your compositional experience, your creativity and production of other styles of music (and even your specialties) will benefit tremendously. Adding elements from other styles into your music brings an entirely new feel to your work, something exclusive, something your own. Game composer Jon Holland has many musical "side projects" to keep him busy. My favorite is his "Orphan Sister" project. This jazz offering is characteristic of the light jazz genre but with a distinctive "electronica" quality to it. The melding of two very independent musical styles has resulted in an interesting sound completely identifiable to Jon. That's the kind of distinction I'm talking about. The way to achieve this is through experimentation and experience.

8.2.4 Practice Makes Perfect

Here is another great exercise: take existing game cinematic scores and replace them with your own music. Do the same with company logo animations, stock film footage, or the mass-emailed video clips everyone keeps sending — whatever you can find. Most CD-ROM games have .mpg, .mov, or .avi video files in them somewhere. Make a copy and get to work. Practicing with real cinematics is a perfect way to learn the art of scoring. You can even use them as examples of your abilities. Just be sure to make it clear you didn't perform the work in its original release; you don't want to misrepresent yourself.

Most of today's audio editing programs have the capability of replacing audio in video files. Find out what yours does and look for those types of files to practice on. It's a relatively simple process. Open the file in the editor. The video will be in one block, the audio in another. Erase the audio and re-save in the video file format. Use the new audio-less video to apply your brand of music. Don't just replace the music with a similar style. Try different ideas, see what works and what doesn't. Practice timing, build and fade as the on-screen actions dictate. Shift the music as new scenes cut in, paying close attention to what each is about and how the music can provide enhancements. Remain true to the overall presentation and ensure all of the music fits together as one cohesive piece. This type of valuable practice will pay off when the time comes to do it for real. Take advantage of any downtime to practice and stay on top of your game.

8.3 Some Technical Considerations

Before sitting down to write a game score, there are a few points that should be defined first. These pre-compositional technical considerations will identify the direction you will take to compose — whether it's a full DVD-ROM, surround, orchestral score or a simple melody for a GameBoy title. As touched upon in sections 7.2 and 7.3 of the previous chapter, knowing all the details in advance, before you even write a note, will help prepare you for the challenge ahead and save any false starts.

I've made many references to the importance of communication, especially when working as a contractor. By asking the right questions, it will be clearer in your mind, you'll be able to hit the mark the first time, and it will make you look that much better in the developer's eyes. After all, you don't want them looking anywhere else for their music and sound needs.

Many of these concerns may already have been addressed through the bidding process and previous discussions with the developer. Don't ever assume all is constant; double-check to make sure that none of the parameters of the game have changed and then keep a close eye out for further modifications as the production continues. I've worked on a game where the final cue was changed from MIDI to audio at the last minute. Not a terrible change, but it would have drastically changed the way I had approached the piece if I'd known about it earlier.

8.3.1 Which Platform Is the Game Being Developed For?

Secrecy is a huge issue in the billion dollar games industry. There have been times when I didn't find out what platform a game was being developed for until the last minute. Developers are weary of outsiders and are rightfully afraid to give any hints of future game releases. Sometimes, even after signing the Non-Disclosure Agreement, they will remain tight-lipped until they feel comfortable releasing information. I guess it just goes with the territory.

It is important that you, the composer, know what system the game will play on as far in advance as possible for many obvious reasons. A Nintendo is not a Playstation is not a CD-ROM game — they are all completely different systems with different constraints and different methods of addressing audio issues. If I was doing a GameBoy title, I wouldn't go out and hire musicians or a full orchestra. That would be insane! I might though for a Playstation 2 or CD-ROM game because the chances of using direct or streaming audio are good. GameBoy and Nintendo 64 don't utilize that particular type of audio and the composing process is far simpler.

8.3.2 What is the Playback and Delivery Format?

You cannot compose a masterful score without knowing the delivery and playback formats. The platform a game is developed for will give a good indication of what type of playback system will be used. Console games will be played through a TV or home entertainment system. CD-ROM or internet games will be played through either a desktop or laptop speaker system. Arcade games will use a customized system.

Developers study their demographics. They like to know in advance if the people who buy their games also own a home theater and surround system, or if their PCs are equipped with upgraded or surround speakers. Find out what their research indicates and cater towards that particular type of playback system. Ultimately you want your mixes to sound great on any system, but you can pull out all the stops for those earth-shattering effects for systems with subwoofers.

Figure 8.2 Ensure you know what type of playback system your audio will eventually be heard through and gear your production towards making it sound great!

For coin-op games, find out what the developer has in mind for their customized game consoles. Larger systems have subwoofers and several different speaker pairs. Some utilize discrete playback channels for narration, music, and sound effects that keep the audio separated and providing for clearer presentation. If you are lucky enough to be creating music for this type of game, you know the music will be receiving the attention it deserves and will take a prominent place in the overall gaming experience. Make it shine.

If a developer requires delivery in MIDI format, you won't waste time with live instrumentation, vocals, or audio loops. Instead, you will break out your keyboard chops and spend extra time tweaking that MIDI guitar solo to perfection. While use of MIDI greatly reduces the actual musicianship of some instruments, it's characteristically small file size will far outweigh this disadvantage. As the composer, you'll have to use a different skill set to make the music dynamic and exciting. It's an entirely different frame of mind from the process of bringing in a live band and composing with traditional methods. But who ever said composing for games had anything to do with tradition? Find out what formats the developer needs as soon as practical.

Delivery and final playback formats can be the same; other times they are far different. Sometimes you will deliver a MIDI score and sound bank and they will convert it using a development system. Sometimes you will make delivery in 44 kHz, 16-bit, stereo .wav format and they will convert it to 8 kHz, 8-bit, mono .au format. Ultimately, you want the music to sound great in its final format, no matter what it may be. If the delivery and final formats are the same, you stand a pretty good chance. If it changes, fate will more than likely take over instead. Perhaps you can work out a deal where you also deliver music in its final format. That way you retain control over the outcome of your hard work. Most game composer will throw the service in for free as a purely selfish way for them to ensure their work sounds good. With their names in the credits, they want to make certain their work is represented accurately. If you don't have a particular platform's development system handy, that may be difficult.

8.3.3 Is a Preset Sound Bank Available?

Some game platforms make use of an internal *sound bank* — either in the system hardware itself or on detachable game cartridges and disks triggered to play by a MIDI file or some other proprietary format. Some sound banks (or sound fonts as they are sometimes called) are preset into the hardware; others are changed as a new game cartridge or disk is placed into the machine. It is important to find out if you will have to compose using a preset sound bank or not. A predetermined set of sounds will greatly limit the tools in a composer's arsenal and may force you into unfamiliar territory. If orchestral music is your specialty, a game platform with only a drum/percussion, piano, bass, and a synth patch will limit your abilities to do a piece the way you want. The same way a sound bank with only strings, brass, and timpani will prevent you from composing anything techno or rock-ish.

Most pre-set sound banks have a decent variety to accommodate several of the most popular styles of music. But, they still force the composer into using sounds which may be uninspiring and ones which weren't chosen specifically for the piece. Look at it this way; this can be a challenge which will only make you better musically. You may have to try a little harder to make this limitation work for you, but I guarantee the results will be worth it. You can't get around a predetermined bank so make the best of it.

Attempt to get a hold of the actual sounds first, either as samples or sound fonts, or at the very least, listen to the sounds and match them with ones you already have. By doing so, you will be able to compose using similar characteristics and dynamics and allow your mix to be close to the final game version. Don't assume that because the developer says they have a piano in the collection that it is what you think it is. Their little "toy" piano will be a surprise if you understood it to be a grand piano instead. That teary grand piano ballad will take on a different meaning when you hear it in the game played on a toy. The tears you'll be crying won't be from joy.

8.3.4 What Memory Parameters Will You Have to Work Within?

All of the music you compose has to fit on the game cartridge, CD, console, ROM, or RAM. Find out ahead of time what physical memory restrictions your audio will face and plan accordingly. If 60 minutes of direct audio has to squeeze into 10 MB, you'll probably have to downsample, adjust the resolution, and save them as mono tracks. This is an ugly example, but it gives an extreme idea of what you should be thinking about.

What instruments will be lost with the lack of high-frequency sounds? As you downsample, the high-frequency range shrinks and instruments like hi-hats, cymbals, and acoustic guitar begin to disappear. What noise floor will you have to stay above? As the resolution is dropped, quieter passages of music won't cover up the quantization noise introduced by lower resolution values. If the music will only play back as mono, there won't be any need to spend time with stereo sounds or effects. Additionally, extra care should be taken to ensure that the final mixes don't have any cancellation when the original stereo tracks are paired.

8.3.5 Technical Wrap-up

The short list of non-musical considerations just discussed will ultimately define the restrictions your compositions must remain within. I choose to have these technical issues clear before I ever begin to compose. Writing music is an intense experience with no place for distractions. Understand the environment and it will almost subliminally guide the process of creating appropriate audio.

8.4 Musical Details to Reconsider

These particular "musical" questions need to be asked, just like the previous "technical" ones, before the composing process begins. Some of them may have been answered during the bidding and contract phases as well, but they may have changed slightly. The answers may not give you the information you need to actually do the music. Previously, you needed to know how much music was needed, what formats, what platform, and so on to determine how you were expected to create and deliver your "product" and to give the developer a dollar figure for your services. The following list is specific for creating the magic which is music, without the business distractions.

What are the specific intentions of the music in the game?   Is the music to serve as the main title theme, subtle background ambience, or other music cues designed to create tension or announce victory — or all of the above? The music's purpose should be clear prior to a first note being composed.

What is the genre of the game?   Is it a sports, horror, children's, strategy, board, puzzle, shooter, racing, flight sim, adventure, role playing, action, or arcade game? Find out, if you don't already know, the overall theme of the game project and your musical choices will narrow themselves automatically. Knowing the era and the locale of the game ahead of time will also help dictate the direction the music will take.

What similar music styles can be used as examples?   If a developer tells you the score should be "industrial, not too gritty, but with an edge," what does that mean to you? They seem to know, so ask them for *specific* examples of music from a band, movie, or commercial. Then, find it and figure out what they are talking about. After listening several times and becoming familiar with the music, ask them specifically what it is about the music they like. Is it the beat, the guitar, or that great synthesizer patch? Is it the reverb tail on the end of each snare hit or is it the swirling effect on the electric guitar? Is it the melody or the rhythm that catches their ear? Have them put their finger on the elements they would like to hear in their game exactly. Discuss it with them until you are positive. But, even then, there are no guarantees.

An example: a developer sent along an audio example with their request for music. I listened to it several times, got a good feel for it, and decided to jump in without discussing it first. I used the same instrumentation, almost the same beat and tempo, and thought I'd matched their idea fairly well. Turns out, it wasn't any of those elements they were looking for. They liked the distortion patch on the electric guitar and wanted me to focus on that! Aaahh!!! Funny, there was absolutely no discussion about it.

Is there a preference for instrumentation?   Here we go again. You're supposed to be the audio expert, why can't you choose the instrumentation? Ultimately, you can and will most of the time. I prefer to throw out this question for ideas on what the developer is thinking — yet another chance for communication to be concise and allow the music to match their vision the first time. Find out if there is anything special they would like to hear. It makes them part of the music creation, lets them in on the decision process and gives you something to fall back on if they try to change their minds late in the game. I'd rather not waste time just because someone forgot to mention they didn't want a crunchy-sounding guitar in that racing game. Find out at the same time which ones they are definitely *against*.

Is the sound bank predetermined or will you be creating it?   The answer to the earlier question will have made it clear whether or not a sound bank will be used. The question here is: will you have to create the sounds yourself or is it preordained? Established sound banks will limit your use of instrumentation and effects, forcing use of sounds chosen by someone else. If the sound bank is left up to you to create, find out some details. How much space is allowed? What format is needed: .wav files, .aiff files, audio? What parameters are required? What sample rate, resolution, and will the sounds be stereo or mono? In a sense, these sounds will be played back as the sounds in a sampler would, so it's up to you to find out what it takes to make them work.

A PlayStation 2 game I recently completed allowed for a sound bank of 2 MB. The final samples were delivered in .wav files, but the parameters were left totally up to me. All I had to do was ensure the sounds were delivered under the 2 MB limit. Using various drums and percussions, piano, bass, organ, and synth samples, in 44.1 kHz, 16-bit stereo, the total size came to over 5 MB for my original sound bank. I composed the music in the highest fidelity possible, mainly as inspiration and because I had to listen to them throughout the entire two month project. When the final delivery was made, I downsampled to 22 kHz, 16-bit mono, did a final remix of the music without a noticeable difference in quality, and made my budget of 2 MB. The best part of the experience was being able to pick and choose sounds which were inspiring to my style of composing and not being stuck with someone else's idea of instrumentation.

What is the length of each cue?   The bidding process may have revealed estimates for the lengths of needed audio. Now that the recording and implementation phases are quickly approaching, ideas may have been amended for various reasons or levels may have disappeared altogether. If it is important to have the final length set in concrete for the pieces you are creating. If you don't and the length changes, you'll be starting over.

Will the music transition, fade, or loop?   Find out what the developers will be doing to your music as it is implemented in the game. What happens to the music when a player clicks out of a menu screen, for example? Will the music end suddenly or will it fade out for a couple of seconds? Then, will the music behind the next screen slowly fade in? Will these transitions overlap or will one fade out completely before the next fades in? What will your music sound like as these two cues cross-fade? This type of situation has the potential to sound like fingernails across a chalk board as the two cues overlap. If you know ahead of time, perhaps it's possible to use the same key for each piece — something to tie them together successfully.

If the music is expected to repeat itself, will it be as a seamless loop or will the cue fade out then fade in from the beginning? Most of game music that repeats continuously is composed as a loop arrangement, but that doesn't mean it can't repeat using fades and a little bit of silence in between as a contrast. Learn what the developer has in mind and be wary of changes as new ideas are implemented.

Cues that will seamlessly loop are generally more difficult to compose. The challenge is to have enough going on — enough layers of audio events to hold the player's interest through several passes. Loops tend to become predictable, especially the shorter ones. Experimenting with different musical structures, where beats fall randomly or where the rhythm is more free-flowing is a good way to hide the fact the player is listening to a loop. If you do it right, it will take several passes before they even realize the music is repeating. Making the loop longer is another great way to fool the player. The less a piece repeats, the better. Of course, the reason loops are used in the first place is to save space and longer ones are not always the answer. But do what you can.

GAME COMPOSERS AT WORK

Keith Arem of PCB Productions

How do you go about scoring for a project?   "Once the style and theme of a project is established, one of the biggest initial challenges is to identify how the music will be implemented into a title. This is not just for creative purposes, but also for technical issues. Most next-generation platforms can deal with streamed digital audio files; however, making this interactive with gameplay can be very challenging. Once the blueprint has been established for how and where

Keith Arem is a serious force in the games industry with over 150 game titles, not to mention several film scores, to his credit.

the music will be placed, I try to schedule my composition time to allow me enough time to work with the files to prepare them for implementation into the game. One of the most important things to remember with music or sound design: even the best score or sound effect can be destroyed, if it is implemented poorly in the game."

When are you usually most creative? "I tend to be most creative at night. Besides the absence of daily distractions, working at night allows me to focus directly on the score at hand. I find that the more music I write, the more ideas develop and I become re-inspired to create more. It's obviously difficult to 'schedule' creativity, but as in most entertainment-based professions, when you're on a deadline, you need to score whenever the inspiration hits you.

What skills do other composers need to get into the games biz? "Besides a strong passion for playing games, fluent computer skills, and knowledge of music, a game composer must have excellent communication skills to be able to articulate requests from a developer or producer. Having a firm understanding of how games work, and having the patience to deal with technical limitations and time restrictions, is just as important as having great musical talent."

(See page 79 of Chapter 4 for Keith's gear list.)

8.5 *Compositional Methods*

Composing and recording music today is a blend of traditional methods using tape recorders and what some consider "old fashioned" studio recording techniques and new, highly-specialized and integrated audio production systems. The good news is you really don't need to buy all of the latest and greatest software to make impressive music. The bad news is you will need it if you plan to get it into the computer and in a format the developer can use. The good news is if you already have the latest and greatest, you don't need the old, traditional ways. The bad news is you'd better learn those complicated programs inside and out if you expect to be able to use them to their full potential.

Music is music, no matter how it is composed or recorded. As long as the final output is of a professional quality in both composition and how it sounds, your audio product will stand along side other authorities in the industry. The key is to develop a process you are comfortable with and that allows maximum output with minimal effort. Never work any harder than you have to. You'll get plenty of sleepless nights — nights where that next cue comes to you at 3:00 AM or when you're far away from your studio. There will be plenty of aggravation that only us creative types are familiar with, so why make the process any more difficult than it already is?

Get your system organized, stay focused, and be ready to turn on that creativity with the flip of a switch. Don't think about that looming deadline, concentrate on the music, and it will literally happen by itself.

8.5.1 Determine Your Best Personal Methods

If you don't know already, find out when you are most creative. You want to love your job and forcing it when you don't have to will quickly turn a lifelong dream sour. Settle on a daily working model where you compose at your creative best and take care of the logistical and business tasks when you are not. This will work wonders on the quality of your creations and the longevity of your career.

If it's a peaceful, ambient piece I'm working on, my mood will match before I begin composing. If it's a hyper, energetic piece, I'll run a mile, drink a case of Mountain Dew, and intake a lot of sugar before the tape starts running. Put yourself in the appropriate mood, and the music will naturally follow. It won't always happen that way, professionals can and do create impressive music without ever reaching that plane. It may drain you physically and emotionally doing it this way, so be sure to compensate with some down time to recover.

8.5.2 Choosing the Best Palette of Sounds

Many years ago, a veteran composer offered me the advice of collecting as many different musical sounds as possible. The idea was to "stockpile" an assortment of samples, keyboard patches, and noise makers and draw upon them to keep my sound fresh. The only problem with having a great quantity of choices is resisting the urge to use all of them in each project. This is where the idea of choosing a "sound palette" comes into play.

Before composing for a new project, sort through the collection of samples and patches. Develop a list of sounds and instruments which initially seem to fit the theme of the game. Slowly narrow this list down to roughly a dozen or so sounds which will serve as your "palette" and begin the composing process. By doing this first, you will make a conscious effort to determine which particular sounds will work well together instead of having to search during a hot streak and ruin your concentration. Other sounds can still be used, nothing is preventing additions to the palette, but the main instrumentation will be set. This, in turn, provides an audio personality to the game leading every piece of music to fit automatically. A neat little trick.

8.5.3 Stay Within the Theme

When the clock is ticking and milestones are waiting to be met, resist any temptation to be distracted or follow other paths. How do you stay on theme? The best way is to surround yourself with it. A couple of years ago, I did a heavy metal score. I like metal but I don't normally listen to it 24 hours a day. During this project, though, it was a completely different story. I played every metal band I could get my hands on. In the car, in the studio, making breakfast, and eating dinner. I did the same thing with an orchestral project recently. By listening to and *living* with the type of music you are composing, you will be able to pick up on the subtle nuances of the style. This focus will help keep things on track and on theme.

When composing for cinematics, another trick is to watch a lot of movies and movie trailers, as was mentioned in section 8.2.1. My least creative time is between 2:00 to 5:00 PM; I'm generally sluggish and unmotivated. Whenever I am doing cinematics or a film-like score, I'll break for lunch and then watch a movie during this "off-peak" moment of my day. By the time it's over, I'm fed, digested, and extremely motivated after watching a multimillion dollar Hollywood production!

8.5.4 Immersion

Many game composers choose to to fully immerse themselves in a game's "virtual" world. I don't mean playing the game for 10 minutes then writing a score for it, I'm talking *full* immersion. Get your hands on as much artwork, storyboards, full-sized cutouts, and other game design paraphernalia as you can from the developer and surround yourself with it. Cover your walls from floor to ceiling with everything related to the game. Study the storyline; live and breath this new environment. Spend some time playing whatever versions of the game you can get a hold of.

As discussed in "Get in the Mood" in section 7.3.2, you'll also want to prepare your writing/composing/recording space. If it's a dark game, compose at night, turn the lights off, light some candles, and be totally consumed by the atmosphere. A happy kid's game will require sunshine and should be worked on during the day — keep the mood light and smile a lot.

Much of what happens when writing inspired music takes place on the subconscious level. Music created while immersing yourself in a game's environment will affect other listeners subliminally. You won't be able to compose like this every time, but important scores will benefit greatly from this approach.

TOOLS OF THE TRADE

Nicola Tomljanovich, Composer, AMC Interactive, Rome, Italy

AMC Interactive comprises a team of young sound artists and musicians endowed with wide artistic backgrounds, brought together by the passion for video games and sound expression. Since 1990, they have experienced formative collaborations in the video  game market — with European developers/distributors such as Team17, Electronics Arts, and Virgin Entertainment — while developing the audio for sport simulations, role-playing adventure, and arcade shoot 'em-ups.

Computers: Four last-generation computers, WIN98-based SCSI system, SoundBlaster Live 4 speaker surround system, Event Gina sound board

Software: Cakewalk Pro Audio for MIDI music sequencing and FMV handling, Cool Edit Pro for audio digital processing and HD recording

Multi-track: Alesis multi-track digital audio recorder for live sampling (live band performance)

Keyboards: Two keyboards Korg Wavestations, sound module Korg Trinity and Roland JV1080

Mixing board: Samson 16 tracks mixer

Mixdown decks: Sony Portable DAT unit for live sampling, and a studio DAT unit for tape mixdown

Other instruments: Guitars: Manne custom, Fender Stratocaster, Ovation Collector 92 acoustic guitar, Yamaha acoustic guitar 12 strings, Yamaha classic guitar, Digitech sound processor + whammy pedal, Mesa Boogie Preamp, Peavey power Amp, Marshall Cabinet, Roland guitar synth

Microphones: Shure SM57

Sound libraries: 12 GB of sound effects libraries and original instrument samples

8.5.5 Compose While Recording

Composing does not necessarily have to be a separate step apart from recording, although it can be. When writing for games with a tight deadline, consider recording while you compose. Typical music creation phases consist of an idea-gathering segment, a writing stage, an incubation period (where the music begins to germinate), and then the recording phase. When working on an everyday music project, say for your band, this method allows for the music to develop into something over time through experimentation. Other ideas have an opportunity to surface. When making music for games, there is usually little time for this particular approach and shortcuts are needed to stay on schedule. That's were recording while composing can be a valuable tool.

A recent project proved to me how beneficial this technique can be. With five days to compose a four minute orchestral score, there wasn't much time to reinvent the wheel. Instead of using the standard songwriting method, the situation dictated a more rapid output of music which wasn't going to happen unless I made critical changes. I made the decision to create the piece with three movements, to prevent it from getting stale, and established the tempo. The music was to accompany gameplay as background music but also as a display piece for the developer to use in previews of the upcoming release. The tempo was consciously set to match the game character's walking pace, since this loveable guy seemed to have a good rhythm. I fired up a sound bank, specifically created for orchestral pieces (no time to design a specialized sound palette on this one), started the sequencing program, and went to work. But, instead of working out ideas first, I chose to go straight into recording and compose as I went.

The piece began with percussions, a little bit of timpani, snare, and bass drums laid the foundation. The opening flourish was the next step and other instrumentation was layered from there until the piece began to sound like something. I wish I could say I had a plan; instead I was relying heavily on instincts and a cliché or two in the process. But, by the end of the third day, the piece had a melody, counter-melody, rhythm, bass, and plenty of percussion. I spent the next day cleaning up the various bits and pieces and fixed flubs and missed notes. At the close of the fourth day, the music was finally tight, cohesive, and ready for the last step. The final day was spent mixing, EQ'ing, adding effects processing, and recording the mix to disk with time to spare.

While I could have spent a couple of days toiling over the perfect note to play where, I opted for the adventure of just letting it happen. As each layer is recorded, your musical mind starts to hear other ideas and those are the leads you go with. It's like writing an essay in a testing situation; start with the first sentence and the rest will follow. When taking the plunge like this, it is important to listen to that little voice and run with it. No time to pine over that approaching deadline, you have music to make.

8.5.6 Using Loops as a Tool

For a one-man band with lots of work and little time to do it in, music loops have got the be the greatest lifesaver ever. Where else can you pop in a CD, load up a pre-recorded and fully mixed beat, bass line, rhythm section, and various other band members in your own mix and lay a melody line over the top? These little gems are perfect for composing, generating other ideas, or as final production elements themselves.

Whenever you happen to be devoid of ideas, need something with an interesting flair or outside of your musical abilities, reach for a loop library and see what happens. I don't know how many times I stared blank-faced at my drums begging them for a good groove. When they don't answer me, out come the loops and usually within a few minutes, new life is injected into the creation process. Purists may argue they aren't original musical creations — that your recordings contain elements anyone can license, or even that you've stolen someone else's work! Music in the games industry is a different animal and nobody really cares unless it detracts from the experience. As long as you've properly licensed any material used in the final work, everything is all nice and legal-like and there isn't anything to fear.

8.5.7 Experimentation

The one thing I love about music is there are no rules except one: If it works, it works! Creating new music day after day will eventually leave you without any new fresh ideas. You'll hit that plateau where frustration grabs hold and your musical future will be in doubt. So, we must fight the phenomenon with experimentation.

For those multi-instrumentalists who have got gadgets and nifty toys strewn about, start mixing and matching. It took many years for me to consider running keyboards through the guitar effects, especially distortion. Wow! What a revelation! How about playing your instruments in unconventional ways? Banging on your electric guitar strings with a drumstick can bring interesting results. How about using effects processing in ways that aren't expected? Most people mix reverb onto drum tracks, but what about using a flange or chorus instead? I'm sure you've got plenty of ideas and have tried many already. When the going gets rough and the music starts to sound lifeless, stand on your head for awhile and look at the musical world in another way. The ideas you glean from experimenting might bring the excitement back into the creation. Don't be shy.

8.6 Recording Methods

Recording music for video games is no different than standard music production. There is no mysterious underground system. There is no top secret recipe you'll be handed after you join the club. Nothing like that. Music recording is music recording no matter how it is done. The only element which differs from audio CD production is the conversion to the final in-game format completed at the end of the cycle.

I'll continue to assume that most, if not all of you, are familiar with getting sound to tape or disk. When it comes time to record your game score, carry on with what works for you. This section will explore alternatives which may or may not have been previously considered. For those of you who are musicians and have never had the pleasure of pressing that big red button, this will give options to pursue as you get settled in. When working on game music, especially as a one-man show, it is essential your engineering and recording chops are solid.

Whether you're an experienced artisan or taking your passion to a new level, it is definitely good to be familiar with other methods. After all, different forms of music are easier to work with using different recording techniques. In a business where several styles could be recorded in a short time, it helps to have something extra in your bag of tricks.

8.6.1 Traditional Recording

Traditional recording methods refer to those that have been around for many years and are the essential foundation for all other techniques of recording. It's a predictable scheme near and dear to many. After the initial composing phase, musicians are brought in and their performances are tracked to tape — whether it's analog or a digital medium. They can be recorded all at once or one at a time, whatever happens to work best for the music. Multi-track tape decks provide for separate controllable layers and the ability to overdub without affecting previously recorded music. The mixdown process follows the completion of the "tracking" phase, where a mixing engineer and producer toil for hours over a mixing board. They adjust volume levels, equalization, and placement of instruments in the stereo field. They add effects processing, compression, and noise gates to control or enhance each track and finally record the multi-track efforts down to 2-channels for a stereo mix. After all of the music for that particular project is completed, each song is "mastered." This step takes each separate tune, adjusts its overall equalization, volume, and "sound," and matches their sonic characteristics. The overall effect is a cohesive assemblage of songs which sound like they belong together.

This type of recording is perfect for the one-man band with a need to record live instrumentation, such as guitars, horns, or vocals. Despite the use of a MIDI rig — which triggers notes from samplers and keyboards — multi-track tape decks can supplement computer playback with a human feel. It also works well for orchestras or music groups who might play off each other during a performance. The number of

Figure 8.3 These Alesis ADATs perform traditional tape-based, multi-track recording.

tracks can be limited by your hardware, but when synchronized with a sequencer, additional "virtual" tracks can be added that are almost unlimited.

8.6.2 Progressive Recording Methods

As technically savvy musicians and engineers pursue the elusive better mousetrap, new and improved ideas begin to take shape alongside traditional music recording. At first, these techniques merely assisted in the process — making certain aspects easier. These new processes evolved as complete and separate entities capable of incredible things. Today we have a solid marriage between ideas and technology and eventually, the traditional methods will fall by the wayside.

As luck would have it, many of these improved processes are perfect for recording music for video games. Gaming has a tendency to influence and drive computer technology. Coincidentally, music production has become almost completely computer-based — from sequencing programs, multi-track recording, audio editing, effects processing, and sound generation. It is completely impossible to produce music for games without one.

MIDI-Based Recording

As the recording scene evolved over the last 20 or so years, one of its greatest contributions was the invention of the Musical Instrument Digital Interface, or MIDI for short. This standard allows for computer-based electronic instruments and effects to interact, to allow one person to perform using multiple electronic instruments at once or to program them all to playback prere-corded routines at the touch of a button.

Initially, dedicated hardware sequencers were designed to record a performance and allow others to be layered on adjoining tracks until a piece was complete. All you had to do was press play and your electronics came to life, each playing a dedicated instrument through its own dis-crete data channel. This allowed for huge productions to be composed and performed by a sin-gle person, something unheard of only a few years earlier. The greatest advantage during final mixdown was the ability to skip a generation of tape and recording the actual performance, instead of a tape recording of one. In the analog domain, this meant one less chance for unwanted noise, the constant quest.

The sequencer then moved inside the computer with loads of added features to assist in the creation. Today we see these types of programs paired with multi-track audio recording capabili-ties, more powerful than anything we've seen before. Composers have the capacity to sequence triggered sound patches and samples and record synchronized live tracks right alongside them with ease.

This production technique has incredible advantages making traditional ways pale by com-parison. Where else can you change instrumentation on a whim? Don't like the bass? Reset the patch until you find the one you like, all without having to rerecord. That darn snare hit was late. No problem, grab your editing tool and move it where it should be, right on the beat. Piece of cake. The one-minute piece is over by two seconds? Adjust the tempo a couple of beats faster, now it's exactly one minute long, just as the client wanted. See what I'm talking about? This MIDI stuff is sweet!

Some developers want their music done as a MIDI file. These files are tiny; simply containing the data telling notes when and how long to play. The developer, in turn, takes that file and pairs it with a sound bank and has instant game music. There is no way to do something like that with the traditional tape-based, music recording process. The format is incompatible.

Multi-Track, Computer-Based Recording

Multi-track still has its place in music production — a fact which will most likely not change for many years. Like any system that works, it has been improved upon and has discarded many of its weaknesses in the process. Gone is magnetic tape; replaced by the reliable hard drive. With affordable drives available with over 100 GB, storage is no longer a problem. Gone is the hard-ware-limited recording channels, now replaced with a virtually unlimited number of tracks. With processor speeds over the 1 gigahertz range and affordable RAM, this far surpasses the need for a room full of mechanical tape decks. Gone is the need for huge mixing consoles and banks of effects processors. All of these are included inside the machine, accessible with the click of a mouse. Can't afford one of those high-priced automated mixing desks? Don't worry, most multi-track programs have their own form of automation which can handle everything from volume and panning adjustments to effects processing.

In addition to the huge operating advantages to computer-based, multi-track systems, recording on a computer allows for easy editing, limitless "undo's," and file sharing previously impossible on tape-based recordings. Computer-based, multi-tracking also allows importing into an audio editor — either one track at a time or to manipulate the final mix-down prior to delivery. And if you are using the .wav format, it is only one step away from becoming red book audio, the music CD standard.

Only a few years ago, the

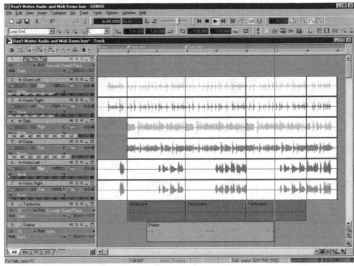

Figure 8.4 Cakewalk's SONAR fulfills the roll of both computer-based, multi-track audio and MIDI production.

weak link in this formula was the sound card. Computers are full of noisy components, generating electronic artifacts that are detrimental to clean recordings. Today, most of those issues have been successfully dealt with and computer-based recording has nearly reached the sonic level of professional recording studio equipment. This allows us all to attain high quality at a reasonable price in the comfort of our homes. With the addition of a stable of high-priced microphones, pre-amps, effects, and other equipment, we just might give the Big Boys a run for their money.

Loop-Based Production

As music production advanced, so did the methods to create truly unique compositions. Instead of instrument samples only being sold to musicians, some smart entrepreneur discovered a market for entire beats, rhythms, and instrument riffs. These performances were organized into tempos and packaged as music "loops" — bars and measures of repeatable patterns — that became an entire musical piece when layered together. Initially, only a small subculture of musicians took to this new form of music but others quickly joined the movement discovering the advantages were too great to miss.

Along with the advent of MIDI, loop-based production has become another great milestone in music. With literally thousands of loop libraries available today, almost every conceivable instrumental combination has been presented, making this an indispensable tool for any game musician.

No matter how good you are at composing, there is no way to think of every musical idea. Loops can be a tremendous conduit for new ideas. With a strong groove played by a professional musician as your backing track, the music you compose on top of it will sound that much better.

Playing with talent, whether they are in the room with you physically or as a recording, has a way of bringing out the best.

Want to add a live drum track to your mix but you're afraid your neighbors may not approve? Piece together a few loops of prerecorded live drums and, voila! Instant drums without all the trouble. Need a smoking guitar solo but are strictly a keyboard player? Grab a loop CD and take your pick. There are hundreds to choose from. What if you need to do a 30-second looping menu cue in a hurry? Loops are already designed to seamlessly repeat; just time them out to 30 seconds, layer the instrumentation over the top, and you've saved the day.

Loop-production and music software has also made great strides in the past few years. Like sequencing programs, loop-based production tools, such as Sonic Foundry's ACID Pro, have integrated live, multi-track recording into their line-up. After building solid backing tracks with loops, it is possible to record your own flavor of live instrumentation right alongside. Do the final mix and export the new stereo tracks to whatever format you need for mastering or conversions. This is an incredibly powerful music production system all on your computer screen.

8.6.3 Other Music Making Methods

New programs and methods of music making are introduced to the masses almost monthly (some good, some not so good). It's up to you whether you pursue new methods as they appear or not. I prefer not to. I take a more "wait and see" approach, letting other people try them out and write reviews in magazines about them first. I'll show an interest after the cream floats to the top. Programs such as Reason, ReBirth, ReCycle, and Reaktor, for example, have introduced new concepts in music production by integrating software synthesis, sample triggering, loop production, and MIDI sequencing into intuitive products.

The trend seems to be leaning towards combining past music production methods into one integrated system. For a game composer, this is a good thing. In order to drive the entertainment value of our audio to the next level, we must be able to stay with the times and consistently push into new areas of music creation. Most game composers use every one of the music production methods discussed previously. It's not a "keep up with the Jones" kind of thing — it's a matter of survival in the highly competitive music trade. Keep your ears open and be ready.

8.6.4 Streamline to the Final Format

If the music will be delivered to the developer in a pre-specified format, it is possible to streamline the recording process and save some time on your end. For example, if MIDI files are requested, why compose an audio score on a multi-track tape deck? Some composers prefer, in order to be enveloped by their creation, to write and record their score as audio to make sure it works first. Then, when they are happy, they transpose manually, note by note, instrument by instrument, to the MIDI format. What a grand waste of time! The music will change as a MIDI file and will sound nothing like the original. So, why not compose in MIDI from the start, always knowing what it will sound like?

Conversely, why compose in MIDI if audio files are the final format? Let's say, you plan to bring in a few musician friends to help record the music. Instead of relaying your ideas to them directly, you decide to let them hear a rough sketch of the intended music. So, you beat out each drum hit, each bass note, each psuedo-guitar part on a keyboard, and record on a sequencer. It takes you a week but, darn it, you want to have something for the boys to listen to first. Well, you're wasting your time. Bring the guys in, sit them down, vocalize your ideas, and let them play. It may take a day at the most to practice and get their parts down and at the most, maybe another day to record. Streamline the process, don't waste time. Go straight to the final format.

Game composers don't often have the luxury of waiting for a muse to strike or to record under perfect conditions. Audio is usually the final content implemented in a game and we can't hold up the Christmas release because we need an extra week. Keep things simple and cut corners in the production, *not* in the quality. Set yourself up to do the 25 games a year and this business will indeed be kind.

8.7 Editing Music

After the music score has been recorded, it will need to be mixed down into a 2-channel, stereo version. The equipment available determines whether you record this mix to DAT, 2 track analog tape, cassette, MiniDisc, CD, or even straight to the hard drive. For me, it also depends on the size of the project and whether I will need a separate back-up in case of computer failure. Larger projects are normally mixed to DAT; smaller ones go straight into the computer. The choice is yours, but always keep a reliable back-up somewhere just in case. DAT is a digital format which can be cleanly recorded onto any hard drive without loss or corruption of the sound. I don't recommend cassette due to the tape noise, nor MiniDisc which isn't known for its superior audio quality. Always mix to the best sounding end result available. Keep it clean and don't introduce unwanted artifacts.

8.7.1 Audio Editing Software

The next step is to import the music mix into an audio editing program for any clean-up and maximizing. If the music was recorded onto a hard drive, make a copy and save it in your normal working format, usually as a .wav or .aiff file. If the recording was on any other medium, record it into the computer using an audio editing program like Sound Forge or Cool Edit. Depending on the sound card, it is possible to input via standard analog (either RCA or 1/8" stereo jacks), digital coaxial, or digital fiber optic (also referred to as Lightpipe or Firewire) inputs. If at all possible, utilize digital inputs and outputs; these provide for the purest audio.

When recording into an audio editor, always record the music at the highest possible sample rate and resolution. I recommend 44 kHz, 16-bit stereo as the absolute minimum. Later, when making any conversions, this will be important. You can always sample down without any grief; sampling up is a problem. Once the computer recordings are made, save the file and prepare for editing.

Sound File Clean-up

From your audio editing program of choice, open the music file to be edited. It's a good idea to save the file you are about to work on under another file name like "music file new" or "music file 2." That way, the original file is left untouched in case something goes horribly wrong and you need to revert to the beginning.

The first plan of attack is the dead air on the front and back of the file. Give it a listen. Do you hear any background noise? If it is prevalent, highlight the space and let your noise reduction plug-in analyze it and process the rest of the file. If you don't have this feature, fear not. If you recorded the sound at a good level, and if it isn't a quiet piece, most of any noise floor should be masked anyway. Trim off the dead space from both ends being careful not to cut any of the sound wave. Use the zoom feature to see exactly where the sound begins and ends if you need to. This process will ensure the file is as small as possible and so the music plays immediately after it is triggered, no silence first. Save the file.

Visual File Inspection

The premiere feature of audio editing software is the ability to "look" at the music. By visually inspecting the file, you are able to actually see noise, peaks, and clipping and get a good idea of the overall quality of the sound. What should you look for specifically?

Is the sound centered on the zero baseline? The line that runs through the middle of each channel is known as the *zero baseline*. If there are electrical mismatches between the sound card and input device, it can cause the entire sample to be centered somewhere above or

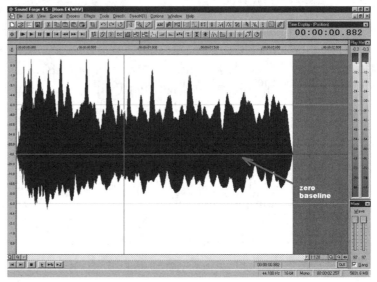

Figure 8.5 This example shows a horn sample which sits slightly above the zero baseline. While this is normal for horns, it illustrates something to be on the lookout for when dealing with other sounds.

below it. This can cause unwanted audible artifacts that you'll need to get rid of. The DC Offset function will analyze the file and re-center it to zero keeping the file as clean as possible.

Does the wave file look "healthy"? Does it fill much of the screen or is it a bunch of puny little lines barely perceptible until you zoom in? It is important that the actual sound is louder than any noise floor in the recording and louder than the noise on any playback system. If the volume is at least medium intensity or thereabouts, you can beef it up by either increasing the overall volume manually or using a normalization function. *Normalization* will scan the file and increase its overall gain, set by you, without clipping. This will maximize the volume proportionally leaving a strong, solid sound.

Does the sound look too intense?

Has the waveform saturated the screen completely? If the sound file shows a solid wall from the zero baseline to infinity, with the edges of the sound cut off, chances are this file will be distorted and totally lack any dynamics. Depending on the effect you are trying for, this may be all right, but the majority of the time, you'll need to give something else a try. First attempt to reduce the overall volume or apply a moderate amount of compression. If the peaks are severed, peak restoration plug-ins are available to repair this type of damage. Listen to the results and decide if it sounds any better or if you just simply reduced the volume and applied "band-aids" to a distorted sound. In that case, re-recording the sound will be your only option — just be sure to do it at a level a couple of notches below the previous attempt.

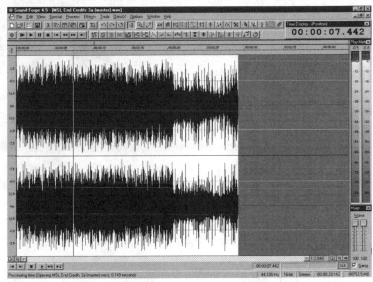

Figure 8.6 This is a normal, healthy looking music file. It's not too weak or too strong and is what most of yours should look like when working in an audio editor.

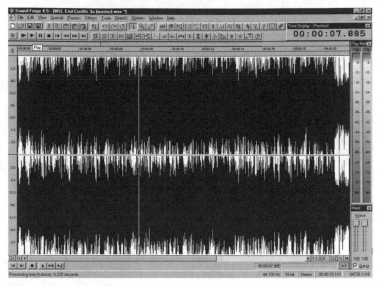

Figure 8.7 If your music looks like this, chances are it will sound like a distorted mess! Keep the overall levels under control for audio the way you intended.

Are there any points in the file where the volume peaks or causes clipping?
Nothing sounds worse than a digital file passing 0 dB on a level meter. These prominent peaks cause unwanted clicking and distorted screeches in sound files and need to be dealt with. One option is to reduce the overall volume of the file enough to bring any peaks below the point of clipping. Another is to apply a slight amount of compression, like a 2:1 ratio, which in effect, will squash the peaks and raise the quieter levels proportionally. My personal favorite is to use a peak limiter set to –0.01 dB which allows for the highest possible levels

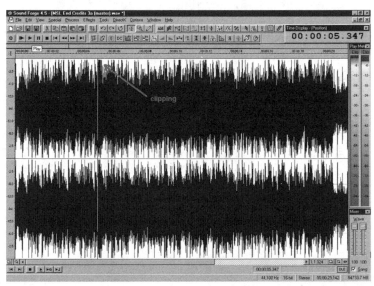

Figure 8.8 Peaks, such as the one noted here, will cause digital distortion and ruin a perfectly good take if not properly controlled.

without reaching 0 dB. Depending on the playback system, you may have to adjust the peak limiter to a lower setting to compensate for poor speakers. Keep an eye on the peak levels, especially after adding EQ or other processing and be prepared to repeat this step if necessary.

The previous items have been addressed by simply looking at the sound file. Audio editing programs are unique in providing visual input to creating sound. But what the file actually sounds like is obviously as important. Give the music a listen. Does it sound good? Is there any distortion or clipping? Is it a good representation of what you where trying to accomplish? Answer these questions truthfully and take care of any repairs prior to the next step.

8.8 *Conversions*

The music file is almost complete and ready for delivery. If the developer requires a 44kHz, 16-bit stereo uncompressed audio file, we're done because that's what we should (at least) be working in. If you happen to be working in anything higher, follow the next steps to accomplish the conversions in the same manner.

The developer in this example requested a 22 kHz, 8-bit mono file so we'll need to do a couple of things. Using a copy of the last saved version of the music file, resample it to 22 kHz using the editor's resample function. Ensure the anti-alias filter setting is used to prevent any of the lost high frequencies from becoming low frequency distortion. This will keep the sound file as pure as possible. Keep in mind the higher frequency ranges are not represented at lower sample rates and the sound will change. Listen to the file again after downsampling and EQ to boost the sounds are necessary. Remember that the higher frequencies will not be available.

The next step is to convert from 16-bit to 8-bit resolution. Selecting this feature on your editor should give choices such as: *truncate, round*, or *dither*. Try each choice and listen to the results. You should be concerned with is the introduction of quantization noise which sounds similar to high frequency static. In this example, you will notice it most where the music loses intensity and any ending fade-out. This is one of the reasons why we maximized the sound earlier either using normalization or volume increase; it masks this particular phenomenon. The noise you hear after the conversion depends on which setting you use, of course. My personal experience dictates I use either the *round* feature or *dither* with a value between 0.5 –1.0 bits. Dithering adds what is known as *Guassian noise* which is designed to mask the more obtrusive quantization noise. Your opinion and the sound effect's application will determine which is best.

The final step is to save the file in the required format. If you happened to be using .aiff or anything else, simply save the file as a .wav, give it one last listen, and you are done. For those who edit in this format anyway, there is nothing left to do but move on to the next project.

CHAPTER 9
Creating Sound Effects for Games

Sound effects are an integral part of any game, equal in importance to artwork, music, and game play. Good sound effects create an impact which rounds out the entire gaming experience; without them, that experience would suffer. They are designed to completely absorb the player into a virtual world, making it believable, entertaining and satisfying. Continuous ambient sounds keep the player from being distracted by the "real" world, ensuring game silence doesn't ruin the immersive effect of a game. Foley sounds assure believability. Action effects provide guttural satisfaction.

In this chapter, I won't pursue the psychological aspects of sound and its effect on the human psyche. For those who are serious about this particular aspect of audio, I recommend pursuing the subject to complete your skill set and increase your design effectiveness. For now, we'll focus on the creation process for games, how particular sounds are chosen, how they are made, and how to make the process less grueling to both development team and sound designer. I've asked fellow sound designers and game producers in the industry to share their experiences, their sound design creation and selection process, and how they came up with particular sounds. We'll also delve into how to create professional sound effects and prepare them to drop into a game.

9.1 The Creative Aspects of Sound Design

Anyone can do sound design. Not everyone can do it well. The difference between the average sound "hobbyist" and the professional sound designer is not just that the professional gets paid, it is an intangible quality running through their veins which allows them to create audio magic out of thin air. If you are a musician, you already know what I mean. We share the same passion for excellence with the expert sound designer — having spent thousands of dollars on our "hobby" just for the sheer joy of making our own brand of genuine noise. Musicians, and anyone who has the desire, can put this same enthusiasm into making great sound effects for games.

Creativity, a microphone, the ability to listen to the world around you, and some way to edit sounds are the basics you need to jump into this occupation. To take it to the next level and beyond, you'll need:

- remote recording gear,
- a collection of sound effects libraries,
- a computer,
- multi-track recording software,
- a high-end audio editing system, and
- experience.

The best part about sound design for the gaming industry is that there are plenty of new developers out there who are willing to let you cut your teeth, gain the experience, and have the cash to propel you to that next level. There are many composers and sound designer today who started out with the bare bones minimum and have amassed quite a collection of studio equipment from their gaming contributions. It may take a couple of years, but it is possible for those who are patient and smart.

Chapter 2 discussed the equipment and software recommended for this type of work. Refer to section 2.2, "Tools of the Trade," to refresh your memory. It's about time we uncover the mysteries of what it's all used for and a quick review might help if this is new to you.

9.2 Types of Sound Design

In Hollywood, the art of making sound for picture is highly specialized and compartmentalized. There are experts who spend years sharpening their skills in this one particular area, a fairly constant profession. Careers as a sound recordist, Foley artist, sound editor, and sound designer can easily consume a lifetime of work. For games, the term "sound designer" encompasses all of these activities into one package. Are you ready to take all of them on? As a musician, you are already a composer, arranger, copyist, engineer, and producer. What's a few more titles to add, especially when they can earn you some extra income and sustain you through the dry, music-less times?

9.2.1 Foley

In film work, *Foley* is the art form which adds believable sound garnishment to on-screen character movements. Imagine a character running on wet pavement, slipping, then tumbling into some metal trashcans. Foley artists would perform this sequence in a sound studio while viewing the dry footage, matching each movement precisely using various props and a team of artisans. Someone would jog in place on a wet, gravelly surface with similar footwear as the on-screen character. Someone else would create a slipping sound by quickly scraping a couple of shoes on a matching surface. Over in another corner, someone would perform a "body fall" by throwing themselves on some appropriate facade and it would all be wrapped up with yet another artist tossing a couple of metal garbage cans full of empty "trash" around in another area. After a few rounds of practice, it's recorded and sent out to be dubbed into the project. It's always entertaining to watch these guys at work — shuffling around, manipulating various objects, and tossing things around in concert. They seem to have a lot of fun themselves.

Doing Foley work for video games is slightly different. The advent of digital audio editing software and synchronizing capabilities make "performances" such as the activity described previously less likely. I can't equivocally state it would never happen (and somebody would do it just to prove me wrong) but the chances of it happening are slight. Doing this kind of sound work for an animation file would utilize the same concept, but with a different delivery method.

If you were to add sound to the same scene from the previous example, most game sound designers would record the sounds separately or grab them from stock sound libraries, then sync them to the actions. With every instance of the character's foot hitting the ground, they would lay an appropriate sound at the same spot, repeating the sequence until the slip. A slipping sound is added followed by a body falling into the garbage cans to complete the scene. In the simplest form, you would only need three sound effects to make it believable: a footfall, slide, and spill sound. To soup it up a bit, you could use: a left and right footfall (because each step in real life never really sounds the same), some hard breathing (because the character is supposed to be running), a sliding sound, a gasp (because the character is surprised), a bodyfall, a mixture of several clanking and spilling sounds which dissipate slowly as objects come to rest and the trashcan lid stops spinning, and punctuate it all with an annoyed cat screech. Seems like a lot of work for this short scene and most of the time, someone watching it will only hear the sounds subconsciously. But, if the sounds were inappropriate, out of sync, or missing all together, they would stick out like a sore thumb.

There are plenty of sound effects libraries with many different versions of the sounds you'd need for our example. You'll eventually have a good supply of them to reach for, but in order to keep the sounds you produce fresh and original, you'll do your own version of Foley. This won't be as complicated as how it's done on the Hollywood scene. There won't be any pressure of performing an entire scene on the fly. Instead you'll produce individual sounds to edit in later.

Continuing with the same example, let's say we have chosen to create the sounds ourselves. You can create off-site using remote recording gear such as a portable DAT recorder and a quality microphone or bring the props into your studio to create in a noise-controlled environment. Let's take a look at the remote method first.

Remote Recording

Noise is always a factor, whether you are recording inside the studio or out in the field. Always be conscious of it and whether it has the potential to destroy your recordings. Loud, obtrusive, off-subject sounds will ruin your efforts every time. Recording between landing jets overhead or cars whizzing by on the street is a must in the worst case scenarios. The only things you can control when doing remote work is when and where it takes place. Either find some place which has negligible background noise or pick a time, such as at night, when the chance of silence has improved.

For times when you absolutely can't prevent extraneous noises, there are still ways to repair or salvage a good take. Background ambience is made up of two types of sounds: continuous and random. In the office building I'm sitting in at the moment, I can hear a ventilation fan (continuous), the hum of my hard drive (continuous), footsteps (random), distant voices (random), a door opening and closing (random), and fingers typing on a keyboard (random although it's beginning to feel like it's continuous). Recording sounds within this atmosphere, I would have a fairly good chance at success, timing my efforts between the random sounds and blocking them out when I could. The only sounds which pose a serious problem are the continuous noises, but they too can be dealt with appropriately.

Noise reduction software and plug-ins these days are fairly good at neutralizing continuous background noise. It is highly recommended at some point that you beef up your arsenal with this type of application. While you can get away with creative use of equalization, it has a way of negatively effecting your sound while eliminating all noise in the respective frequency ranges. If you tried to remove a noise, say in the upper frequency range, like tape hiss, as you pull down the EQ faders, you lose all the other sounds in that range. You get rid of the hiss, but it also makes your sound dull. Noise reduction software analyzes the continuous sounds and totally eradicates them using complex algorithms. To take advantage of this, be sure to record a few seconds of the atmosphere you are recording in, all the background sounds from the mic position where you plan to do your Foley work. The software requires this to examine the sound you wish to remove and then applies what it learned to the rest of the sound file. Of course, the best way is to make sure you get a clean recording.

Another way to rid yourself of the evil background noise is to edit around the sounds you are recording. If I was recording footfalls, I have the choice of making a sound file for each footstep or one of the entire running sequence. Doing it singularly, you would copy the single footfalls to their own individual files ensuring there is no blank space on the front and backside of the sound wave. There may be some background noise in the actual sound, but because it happens so fast, it would barely be noticeable except to the expert ear. EQ adjustments would suffice if needed. Doing it with the entire sequence, you would mute all the space between each footfall, yielding a clean sequence which could be edited in later. Other layers of sound that you add to the soundscape would mask the unnatural sound of a footstep, then silence, then footstep, then silence. Or you could add a touch of reverb to simulate the environment the character is running in. Either way, experiment to see which works best for you and the sequence you are working on.

A good rule of thumb when recording sounds in the field: record at the level you plan to play back in the game.

If you are creating footfalls from the player's perspective, they will be louder than if a bystander was watching them run by. Street ambiance shouldn't be loud, "in your face" sounds unless your character is a mouse scurrying along a gutter. You want to ensure the sound you are capturing is based on the perspective used within the game. You can adjust volume levels to suit, but your quality and realism won't be the same. If you record a garbage can tumbling from 50 feet away, increasing the volume to make it sound like your character is falling into them will also increase the background noise as well. You'll end up with a very noisy effect that sounds very amateur. Always consider the context of the sound before hitting that record button.

TOOLS OF THE TRADE

Charlie Stockley, Sound Designer, Electronic Arts

Computers: PowerMac 9600 with G3 Processor, 224 MB RAM, Adaptec Ultra SCSI Accelerator Card, Rorke Data Hard Drives (40 GB total)

Multi-track: Digidesign ProTools 5.01 with one MIX Farm card, two DSP Farm cards, Bit 3 Expansion Unit, Digidesign 888/24 I/O, Digidesign USD Universal Slave Driver

Plug-ins: Aureal A3D Pro, Digidesign's PDD-1, D-Verb, Focusrite d2&d3, D-Fi, D-Fx, Line 6 Amp Farm, Metric Halo's Spectra Foo, Channel Strip, Steinberg's Declicker, TC Works' MasterX 1.5, Wave Mechanics, Waves TDM Bundle

Mixing board and monitors: Mackie 1604-VLZ Pro Mixer, Genelec 1031A Monitors (Left, Center, Right), Genelec 1030A Monitors (Rear)

Surround: Dolby SEU4 Surround Encoder Unit, Dolby SDU4 Surround Decoder Unit

Mixdown decks: Panasonic 4100 DAT Recorder

Outboard gear: Lexicon PCM 70 Digital Effects Processor

Keyboards: Korg O1/W Music Workstation

In-Studio Recording

Most of the considerations discussed for remote recording apply to your in-studio Foley work as well. While the environment may be a bit more controlled and the potential of unwanted noise less, there are still some things to watch out for. Listen closely to the room or studio where you plan to record. Computer fan noise, fluorescent lighting hum, dogs barking, street noises, and so on can have the same effect as your on-location recordings and unless you have a soundproof room. Using the same techniques for recording and editing will prove successful as well as the potential for higher quality because of your enclosed location.

The best place to record would be in a soundproof studio or perhaps a soundproof booth, that is, if you like those telephone-booth-looking things in your creative space. Imaginative uses of modular sound-absorbing dividers and gobos can help. Even creating a tent made of blankets will work miracles. Close your doors, close the windows, push towels into the cracks, tack blankets up on the walls ,and you've got a pretty good spot to do your Foley work. Stay flexible and creative and be ready to do what it takes. After all, these sounds will have your name on them.

One of the perils of recording in-studio is the mess and destruction of valuable studio components while caught up in the performance. For those who are resourceful enough to have their own separate control rooms apart from their main recording room, the dust and debris might not be too difficult to clean up after a session. Trying it within your control room may prove an expensive endeavor if some flying object manages to smash into your new monitors. Keep mindful of the sounds you are creating and the consequences of the performance. If you plan to smash cement blocks with a sledgehammer for a cool sound, consider dragging a microphone outside via a long cord instead. You laugh, but I'm telling you, it's going to happen and you're going to live with the inevitable, "I told you so!"

Doing Foley sounds in your studio is really no worse than allowing an entire band of musicians and groupies trash your sanctuary. Even though I know the consequences, I still stand back after each session to survey the damage and shake my head. When I'm in the creating mode, I work furiously, maneuvering all sorts of debris and carnage around, focused intently on that one little sound effect I'm giving birth to. When it's complete, I'm routinely surprised at my now cluttered surroundings, left wondering how all this garbage got there. Next time I promise myself to take it outside.

The Acquired Skills of Listening and Manipulating

Developing a good ear for the business takes some time. We are relied upon by the game makers to conceive the perfect sounds to establish the atmosphere and believability of the virtual world they are presenting. We gaze at dry pictures and animations letting our aural imagination take control, hopeful we can translate what we hear in our heads into a sound effect.

Turn on your TV and mute the volume. What do you hear in your head when you watch the picture without sound? An experienced sound designer will have a multitude of sounds firing off, adding their own brand of personality to the picture. This is the first step in doing sound design. If you are staring at the screen and hear nothing in your head, try this instead. Pretend a new client just gave you this cinematic to put sound to and your career depends on hitting the nail on the head. Do you hear anything now?

As another exercise, turn on a movie or something with a lot of action in it. Don't look at the screen, instead listen to what is happening aurally in the scene. Listen to each sound, how it is placed in the soundscape, what effect it has on your perception of what is going on. Pick a few and figure out how they were made. Which ones are Foley sounds? Which ones are actual recordings of the action? Which ones are manufactured from other sounds? Sometimes it's hard to tell.

It is surprising to learn that what you thought were actual sounds are something else altogether, used in a context which makes you believe they are the real sound. Take gunshots, for instance. In the real world, most small caliber firearms are a rather boring "pop." Hollywood sound designers — always looking for something bigger than life — add small explosions notched up in pitch, the crack of a whip, a snare drum, or any sharp sound which makes a huge impact on the audience when the weapon is fired on-screen. Is what you hear the actual sound of a gun firing? Probably not, but your perception makes you believe you are hearing one. So much so that if you ever hear a gunshot for real, you won't be impressed. It will assist you in this line of work if you leave behind the preconceptions built over a lifetime and move from the audience to the artist's perspective.

Listen to the world around you. Every sound you hear is a reality-based phenomena corresponding to an action. Many of these sounds, in a different context, could work for something else. If you were shown an animation sequence of a raging storm, how would you create thunder? You could wait for a storm to blow by and record it, hoping to get some usable thunder, you could reach for a sound library, or you could grab a sheet of metal (like aluminum or copper) and shake it. Foley artists have been doing this for years and you know why? Because it works! What if you needed a crackling fire; are you going to light a fire in your studio? I'm not sure I'd subject a microphone to the heat. Instead, try slowly crushing some dry paper and plastic wrap. By itself, it might sound like paper being crushed, but presented along with a picture of a campfire, it will work great. That same sound could even be used as radio static. Need a hatching egg sound? You could buy a dozen eggs to crush or slowly peel some Velcro apart. That same Velcro sound done right could pass as radio static too. See what I'm getting at? You can creatively use commonplace objects to produce some believable Foley sounds without all the mess or anguish of destroying perfectly good (and expensive) objects.

9.2.2 Sound Libraries

Close cousins to the art of Foley are sound libraries. These initially started in Hollywood years ago as a way to save some time on the Foley stage by recording a vast array of everyday sounds which are then licensed to the user. Instead of running off to have footsteps and background sounds created, a sound editor could just grab one of these and have them instantly. Car door slams to cracks of baseball bats to a crying baby to explosions are all within your reach. They were great then and have only gotten better in quality over time. Now, crisp, clean digital recordings are available from several different sources as all-inclusive CD libraries. Not only can you find everyday sounds, but some sound designers have even licensed their original creations. Larger than life and make-believe sounds are also available to us mere mortals for licensed use. Entire game projects have been done using nothing but library sounds, and while I don't recommend using them exclusively, they can save the day for those last minute changes the night before going gold.

To most sound designers, sound libraries are a good stepping-off point. Everyone I've ever run across uses them, but few use them as is. The one major problem with licensed sound libraries is that anyone can have them and some sounds have a tendency to be overused. Originality is important and when one of those overused sounds breaks the immersive effect of the game, it becomes obvious. The way around this is to creatively manipulate or use small pieces of the original sound to make something new and fresh.

At the very least, a sound designer will take a stock library effect and change its pitch either up or down. It still has the same basic presentation except the tone has changed and while it may be recognizable, it won't be the same old tired sound. Other basic tricks would be to apply some severe EQ, either by dramatically sharpening the sound, making it dull, or utilizing effects processing (like reverb or flange) to give it new character. Manipulation of the sound will breathe some new life into that stock sample.

Using sound libraries for long, background ambiance — like a city street scene behind a skateboarding game — can also benefit from some subtle manipulation. Changing the pitch up or down a couple of notches can provide enough of a change to get away with using the same sound within the same game. You could also cut the scene into several pieces and rearrange the order to keep people guessing.

Sound designers use sound libraries as one of the many tools in their arsenal to piece together good sound effects. By taking bits and pieces of an existing library sound, they can produce the exact sound effect they were after. This saves valuable time by relieving them of starting from scratch or having to run out with a microphone just to grab a simple engine noise.

In a space game I'm working on, the design team discussed ways of making the use of some new gizmos easier for the player to recognize by having them sound like what they are. If it's a power pack, have it sound like one. If it's a type of communications gear, have it sound like one. But because none of us live in space and have never heard these things (and partly because they don't really exist), we decided to base them on earth-bound objects so you recognize them immediately. For instance, one of the vehicles has a massive power plant and one of the options for its sound is to have a mixture of a revving Indy race car and a jet turbine. I can't easily record either of those objects so I turned to a sound library instead. The power pack and shield will have elements of "electrical" sounds in them, the communications gear will have some static and transmission sounds as well as a few computer bleeps. I'll get most of these sounds from an effects library, and edit and layer them to make my new sounds.

9.2.3 Original Development

Our third and final stop in the trilogy of sound design methodology is original development. Game sound designers masterfully use all three techniques to achieve their magic — either grabbing a mic and recording a sound, picking up a sound effects library, or pulling one out of thin air. By using combinations of tone generators, software, synthesizers, and everyday objects in unusual ways, inventive sound effects emerge at the hands of the artisan. The beauty of this approach is there are no rules and no limits except one: the sound effect must enhance the corresponding action by providing the player with suitable aural feedback.

Each sound designer has their own style whether it's "over the top," "bigger than life," "cartoony," or "believable." It is dependent upon their way of thinking and creating, their mindset, their personality, and what motivates them. Secondary factors that also help create a "sound" are sound effects libraries, equipment, recording methods, software, microphones, and even the tape they use.

As mentioned, original creation can come from practically anywhere. Look around you. Everything makes noise if you drop it, hit it, scrape it, or move it around. Pick up objects, smack them with something. Fill them with water and hit them again. Dig through your drawers, the dumpster behind the mall, the junk yard — there are plenty of sounds to be had. While you are on the hunt for individuality, don't be unique for unique's sake; listen to how these sounds can be used for your purposes when brought back to the studio.

Another appealing source for sound is a synthesizer or sampler. Manipulating a preset sound using LFO's, filters, modulation, varied attack, sustain, decay, and so on can create some interesting effects. It can be done either manually or through a sequencing program which allows management of these parameters. Sequencers are great for tweaking your performance prior to recording the final version, especially when multiple sounds are triggered. Some audio editing programs also come with built-in synthesis to create simple tones, FM, and DTMF (Dual Tone Multi Function — the sounds you hear when you push numbers on a touch tone phone). These tones are particularly useful when doing games with either cartoon or computer-type sounds. By manipulating them with linear pitch shifting, they make some neat beep and boop effects. Experiment and see what you can come up with. Try a flange, reverb, and chorus. Try distortion, amplitude modulation, and EQ. Try a vocoder, doppler, or reverse. Try every on-board effects processor you have and listen to what they can do. Understand what each one does and you will be able to skillfully apply them to other, complex sounds.

Original development is definitely a state of mind. As you become immersed in the virtual game world, it will be easier to create within this atmosphere. By placing yourself in the game, you can better imagine what something will sound like than by standing outside, looking in.

9.3 Editing Methods

In section 2.2.5 of Chapter 2, I listed some audio editing and multi-track software programs you could use when doing sound for games. I also discussed editing techniques for music creation in section 8.7 of Chapter 8. I recommend having a good audio editing program like Sound Forge or Cool Edit at the very minimum. Multi-track software like Vegas Audio, Nuendo, or Pro Tools are also fantastic tools you should consider as your resources allow. These tools are key to what sound designers do and are indispensable in their everyday creative activities.

I've learned a lot from other composers and sound designers over the years by watching them in action. I've walked away from every session with another trick in my bag, usually scratching my head at how obvious it was. The tools sound designers use and the way they use them is pure magic, except these magicians are eager to share their secrets. This particular section will communicate techniques and tricks myself and others use in professional game sound

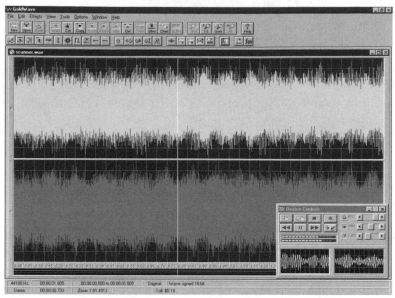

Figure 9.1 GoldWave is an excellent audio editor at an affordable price. It even has some great effects processing included!

design as if you were standing behind us watching it all happen. The intent is to start you with a strong, solid foundation, then let you loose on the gaming world.

Most audio editing and multi-track programs are capable of performing the same types of edits and processing. I won't get into the specifics of the dozens of programs out there, but I can present generalities and features common to them all. Let's take a look at the three most common type of programs and their use in sound design.

9.3.1 Using Audio Editing Software

The cornerstone of game sound design is audio editing software. As you'll recall from section 8.7.1, these versatile programs can record, edit, and convert sound files in a multitude of ways. The best way to explain how they are used is to put you into the action creating a couple of sounds. We'll try something easy and move into a complex sequence.

A Simple Sound Design Example

A developer has asked you for a sound of a kitchen pot clank for a children's game to be delivered in 22 kHz, 8-bit resolution, mono, .wav format. Grab a pot, something to smack it with, a microphone, and some method to record it. For this example, let's assume you'll be recording direct to your hard drive, saving us the step of getting it into the computer from a tape deck.

The first order of business is to open a new file in your editor and determine the parameters of the recording. Always start with the highest sample rate and resolution; in this case, it will be 44.1 kHz and 16-bit resolution. Unless you're using a stereo microphone, we'll record this in mono for simplicity's sake. If for some reason you need this sound in stereo later, it is an easy step to open a new stereo file, paste the mono sound to both sides, and apply a psuedo-stereo effect to it.

Now, set your recording levels as high as possible without clipping and press record. Bang on the pot in different spots at various strengths to provide plenty of takes. Your ear may perceive things differently than the microphone; a take which you thought sounded bad might actually be the one you go with. Each take should be about one second apart, being careful to let the ring completely fade each time.

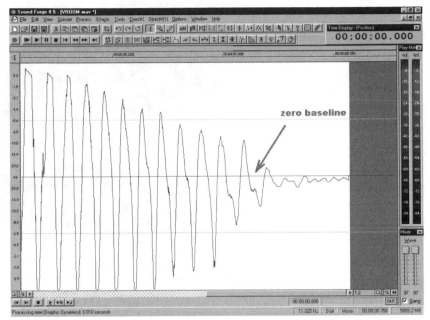

Figure 9.2 The tail of this sound effect is below the zero baseline and could cause unwanted noise in the file.

After six to eight of these, stop recording.

A waveform will appear on your screen. It will have blank space and the obvious waveforms of each clank. Most sound editors have an automatic backup of the file stored in case your computer crashes, but to be on the safe side, store this file and name it something like "pot clank roughs.wav." Before doing any editing, listen to the entire file and choose the best take. As you are listening, it may be helpful to place filemarkers near the ones with potential, saving yourself having to re-listen to the entire file over and just concentrating on your favorites. Once you've found the one you want to go with, highlight the take, leaving a second of blank space on each end if possible, then drag it to the program's desktop or copy it. The programs that allow files to be dragged will automatically open a new file set to the parameters previously specified, ensuring it is set at the same sample rate and resolution as your rough file. For those without that capability, open a new file manually and paste the clank sound into it. Save this new file as "pot clank 1.wav."

You're probably wondering about that dead air on the front and back of the file. Give it a listen. Do you hear any background noise? If it is prevalent, highlight the space and let your noise reduction plug-in analyze it and process the rest of the file. If you don't have this feature, it will still be fine; the pot clank sound is much louder than the background noise anyway and won't be noticeable with such a quick

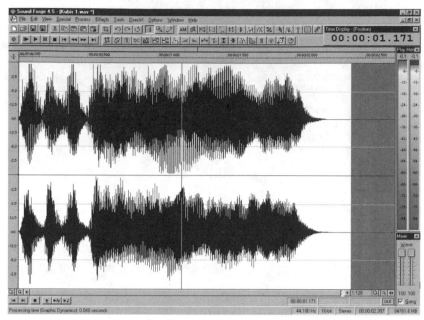

Figure 9.3 This sound effect looks good. It has all the properties of a "healthy" file.

sound. Trim off the dead space from both ends, careful not to cut any of the sound wave. Use the zoom feature to see exactly where the sound begins and ends. This process will ensure the file is as small as possible and so the sound plays immediately after it is triggered, instead of playing silence first. Save the file. This will be the basic file you'll be working from.

By visually inspecting the file, you should be able to tell a couple of things. (If you've read the section "Visual File Inspection" for game music in Chapter 8, the following outline will be déjà vu. Move on to "Making Your Effect Unique" on page 234.)

Is the sound centered on the zero baseline?   The line that runs through the middle of your sample is known as the zero baseline. Occasionally, when there are electrical mismatches between your soundcard and microphone, it can cause the entire sample to be centered somewhere above or below it. This can cause some unwanted audible artifacts that you'll need to get rid of. The DC Offset function will analyze the file and re-center it to zero keeping the file as clean as possible.

Does the wave file look "healthy"?   Does it fill much of the screen or is it a bunch of puny little lines barely perceptible until you zoom in? It is important that the actual sound is louder than any noise floor in the recording and louder than the noise on any playback system. If the volume is at least medium intensity or thereabouts, you can beef it up by either increasing the overall volume manually or using a normalization function. Normalization will scan the file and increase its overall gain, set by you, without clipping. This will maximize the volume proportionally leaving a strong, solid sound.

Does the sound look too intense?

Has the waveform saturated the screen completely? If the sound file shows a solid wall from the zero baseline to infinity, with the edges of the sound cut off, chances are this file will be distorted and totally lack any dynamics. Depending on the effect you are trying for, this may be all right, but the majority of the time, you'll need to give something else a try. First attempt to reduce the overall volume or

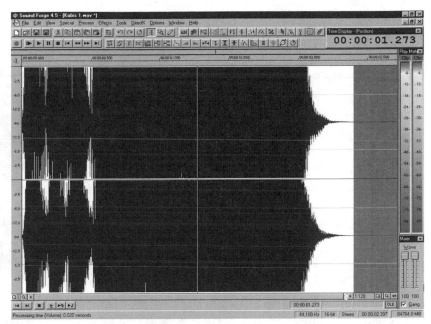

Figure 9.4 This is the same "healthy" sound file example turned up a few notches too many. The meter to the right doesn't begin to describe the pain this sound effect is feeling.

apply a moderate amount of compression. If the peaks are severed, peak restoration plug-ins are available to repair this type of damage. Listen to the results and decide if it sounds any better or if you just simply reduced the volume and applied "band-aids" to a distorted sound. In that case, re-recording the sound will be your only option — just be sure to do it at a level a couple of notches below the previous attempt.

Are there any points in the file where the volume peaks or causes clipping? Nothing sounds worse than a digital file passing 0 dB on a level meter. These prominent peaks cause unwanted clicking and distorted screeches in sound files and need to be dealt with. One option is to reduce the overall volume of the file enough to bring any peaks below the point of clipping. Another is to apply a slight amount of compression, like a 2:1 ratio, which in effect, will squash the peaks and raise the quieter levels proportionally. My personal favorite is to use a peak limiter set to –0.01 dB which allows for the highest possible levels without reaching 0 dB. Depending on the playback system, you may have to adjust the peak limiter to a lower setting to compensate for poor speakers. Keep an eye on the peak levels, especially after adding EQ or other processing and be prepared to repeat this step if necessary.

Making Your Effect Unique

Because the file will be 'downsampled and left as a mono signal, we don't need to spend any time creating a stereo or surround effect. We can apply effects processing such as reverb, chorus, flange, pitch shift, and so on in mono with good results to add "seasoning." The clank is a short sound so the chorus or flange will make it "meatier." The reverb will sustain the ring portion of the sound. Equalization can alter cer-

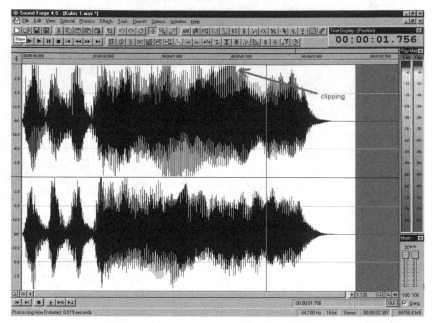

Figure 9.5 These peaks are caused by high levels and can be tamed by simply decreasing the volume, adding compression or applying a peak limiter.

tain frequency ranges adjusting to your taste and the playback device. Depending on the type of microphone (and proximity), it will have its own coloration. Different mics are better at capturing certain frequencies than others. Use your ears and make adjustments accordingly. Save the file.

For our example, I would use a slight touch of reverb, using a bright, small room setting. You'll notice the end of the sound does not decay naturally and is cut off before it fades. We can fix this. Highlighting the tail and using a linear fade out will force the sound to gradually disappear before the end of the file. For our short sound, this will suffice because we never intended for it to echo for very long. But, if for some reason you wanted the sound to appear with a normal sounding fade, add 0.5–1.0 seconds of silence to the end of the file, add your reverb, then delete any remaining dead space after the fade. This will allow more room for the effect to decay naturally, making it more realistic.

After processing the file, you should save it as its own file, keeping the original file untouched in case you decide later you didn't need the adjustments. Using this type of editor, you will be unable to undo additions selectively; the last edit is layered over the previous changes. In order to undo something you did three edits back, it would be necessary to undo the last two as well. Saving your file in various stages will give you something to go back to in case an idea changes or an effect doesn't work out as planned. Be sure to label them accordingly or use the summary or notes to describe the sound. Staying organized is essential when dealing with a large number of files.

The sound effect is almost complete. The developer requested the file format of 22 kHz, 8-bit mono and because we built the file as 44 kHz, 16 bit, we'll need to do a couple more things. Using the final version of the file, resample it to 22 kHz using your editor's resample function. Ensure the anti-alias filter setting is used to prevent any of the lost high frequencies from becoming low frequency distortion. This will keep the sound file as pure as possible. Keep in mind the higher frequency ranges are not represented at lower sample rates and the sound will change. I once recorded brass shell casings landing on cement for a game project. The best part of the sound was the ring they produced which became totally lost when I downsampled to 11 kHz. They ended up sounding like pebbles being dropped and were barely usable. Listen to the file again after downsampling and EQ to boost the sounds are necessary. Remember that the higher frequencies will not be available.

The next step is to convert from 16-bit to 8-bit resolution. Selecting this feature on your editor should give choices such as: *truncate*, *round*, or *dither*, as you'll recall from Chapter 8. I could go on all day about which one is best for each situation, but I will defer to experimentation instead. Try each choice and listen to the results. You are mainly concerned with the introduction of quantization noise which sounds roughly like high-frequency static. In this example, you will notice it most where the sound loses intensity and fades out. This is one of the reasons why we maximized the sound earlier either using normalization or volume increase; it masks this particular phenomenon. The noise you hear after the conversion depends on which setting you use, of course. My personal experience dictates I use either the *round* feature or *dither* with a value between 0.5–1.0 bits. Dithering adds what is known as *Guassian noise* which is designed to mask the more obtrusive quantization noise.

The final step for this simple sound effect is to save it in the required format. I normally work in the .wav format and in this case, no further action is necessary. If the client wanted an .au format, this particular popular Java format creates its own change to the sound and additional EQ may be necessary to compensate for the loss of high frequencies. But, if you were using .aiff or anything else, save the file as a .wav, give it one last listen, and get ready for the next sound effect.

A Complex Sound Design Example

Building a sound effect using an audio editor is normally a simple affair. It gets wildly more complicated when you have to string together or layer other effects in order to compose an involved sound effect such as a full audio sequence for a cinematic or animation. In our next example, the developer has requested a realistic multi-part sound effect of a low-flying aircraft getting shot down by an angry, rifle-toting farmer. The file is to be no more than six seconds in length, delivered as a 44 kHz, 16-bit stereo .wav file. Let's put this together using just our 2 channel audio editor of choice.

This sequence will be made up from several layered sounds to form the final version. The first step is to gather all of the individual sound files and manipulate them accordingly. Using our first example as a guide, record and save the following stereo sound effects:

- an airplane flyby
- a single gunshot
- a short explosion
- small crash with metal fallout

Develop an idea in your mind of the "scene" you plan to create and where the listener will be during this. The farmer's perspective seems like the logical choice so we'll start from there. I picture him miffed watching his cows pestered by the low-flying aircraft and rushing out to the field with his rifle. The aircraft enters from the far left, the farmer takes a potshot at it when it gets to the center, and as it moves to the right side, it explodes and crashes in a burning heap.

Luckily for us, the developer wants this in stereo, so we'll get to show our stuff. Unlike our previous mono example, the manipulations and processing will have an effect on the stereo spectrum. Depending on what sound file you acquired, the aircraft flyby could pose the greatest challenge. Using the panning feature, adjust the effect so the aircraft sound begins in the left channel, moves to the center around 2.5–3.0 seconds, and ends on the right. The explosion effect will happen to our right. Using the panning feature again, adjust the explosion so that 60–75% of the volume of this is to the right side. The crash sound will happen far to the right so manipulate this to 85–90% of sound to the right. You don't want to put 100% of the sound of the crash to the right because in real life, your left ear would pick up a good portion of the sound. This will keep it sounding natural. If you are using the other suggested sounds, also consider them in the stereo spectrum and run them through the pan feature. We plan for the gunshot at center stage so no adjustment is necessary on this file. Save all the new files.

For effective realism, also consider using a *doppler effect*. Apply it to sound effects which are in motion either to or from the listener's point of view. In this example, the explosion and crash could probably stand a touch of this because their sound sources start close to the listener but move away at the speed the aircraft was flying. Be careful not to overdo the effect; a slight touch is all that is needed. If the airplane engine sound you started with was static, you could apply this particular effect to its maximum extent and get a believable flyby.

Now let's piece this baby together. Open a new file as 44 kHz, 16-bit stereo and make it six seconds long or insert six seconds of silence if that feature is unavailable. Starting in a logical order, grab or paste the flyby pan effect to this new file. If it's longer than six seconds, don't worry. At the four second mark, mute the remainder of the sound. Because airplane engines don't make engine sounds after they've exploded, you won't need the rest of that noise. Save the file as version 1. Next add the gunshot file and place the beginning of the file around the 2.5–3.0 second mark. The important part here is to ensure the volume of the gunshot is consistent with the rest of the sequence. It will be louder than the flyby, but not overwhelming the scene. Mix the volume without fades and give the entire sequence a listen. More than likely, the gunshot will have caused the wave to peak and possibly distort somewhat so pay attention to what it sounds like. Apply compression or a peak limiter to control it, and save the file as version 2.

Next, we add the explosion. Find a logical spot after the gunshot where you feel the airplane might explode. It should be somewhere between the 3.5–4.0 second mark — definitely not passed the point where you performed the mute. Unfortunately, six seconds isn't a lot of room to get an explosion and crash to decay naturally, so we have to keep an eye on the rapidly approaching finale. I chose to have the explosion happen quickly after the gunshot in order to save room on the end for the other sounds. Paste the sound over the existing file in the same fashion as the gunshot. The explosion will indeed be a big moment in the scene so make it as loud as you can in the context of the rest of the sequence. Don't sweat having the sound decay passed the six second mark; we'll take care of that when we add the crash sound. Check for distortion and apply the peak limiter or compression if needed. Give the entire sequence another listen. If you like what you hear, save this as version 3. If you don't, undo your edits to the point where it went astray and take it from there.

For the final addition, we'll add the crash element. If the explosion sound took us past our six second max, this is the time to make a decision. For me, it depends on what qualities the crash effect has and how much it will add or detract from the explosion. In this case, I have chosen to cut off the existing explosion sound right at the six second mark and use a linear fade-out for the last second of the explosion. This will fade the explosion sound so it doesn't cut out noticeably and give some room for the metal fallout. Since my crash sound has a nice impact, using it within the explosion sound will add an interesting overall effect. So, as I add the crash sound, I carefully align the sounds so the point of the explosion and crash impact coincide. Adjust the volume and mix them appropriately. Because the explosion and impact sounds are both loud, be careful not to mix so that it becomes overly distorted. Once you've mixed the new sound, listen to the entire sequence again. Adding sounds with high transients guarantees some out-of-control peaks, so you will definitely have to keep them restrained. Pay close attention to the levels and adjust any peaks with a limiter if needed. Also listen to the structure of the sequence. It should flow believably from the left channel to the right without being obvious. Save the file as version 4.

Before we can stick a fork in this and call it done, critically listen to the overall sequence one last time. The sounds should all blend and give the perception they were recorded as the action was played out for a microphone in the farmer's field. A touch of EQ and light reverb might help bring them together if needed. If worse comes to worse, you might need to go back to a specific sound, EQ it, and then start the process over from there. Because we saved several versions along the way, we can go back to any step and not have to redo acceptable work. It takes a bit of work using an audio editor, but it can be done.

If you are satisfied with the sequence at this point, cut off any excess sound past our six second max and fade the last 0.5–1.0 seconds of the file. This will keep the file within specifications and from cutting off unexpectedly. Save the complete sound effect using an obvious file name, like "farmer flyby.wav" and you are done.

I chose the previous two examples to introduce you to concepts you will encounter making sound effects using an audio editing program. With a little patience and practice, you can produce both single sounds or complex layered effects. Once you get the basics down, they become second nature and you'll soon find yourself whizzing through the entire creation process without much trouble. There is much more audio editors can do and I encourage you to become familiar with yours. The tools are available for serious sound manipulation, but it takes a little bit of digging to find out what all your editor can do. Spend time experimenting before you get busy with work. That way your creativity won't have to fight with technology when making professional sound effects.

9.3.2 Using Multi-Track Software for Sound Design

The day I discovered the use of multi-track software for sound design creation was a professional rebirth for me. I remember exactly where I was, who the sound designer was, and the color of the massive brick that struck my thick skull. Ah, the years of headaches I could have prevented! If you plan on making sound design a part of your audio production services, I implore you to acquire a good multi-track audio program. Your creative life will become infinitely easier with this powerful tool at your disposal. If this is the first time you've been introduced to this concept, I guarantee you are five years ahead of where I was.

A good multi-track program, however, cannot stand on its own. Your audio editing software is still required for final sound effects editing so don't make the mistake of only buying a multi-track program. If you have to make a choice, buy the audio editing program first and make upgrades later.

You'll soon discover the extreme joy of creating sound effects in multi-track. If you tried the previous complex sound design example on your standard audio editor, you will immediately realize the simplicity and flexibility you have doing it this new way. Imagine having the ability to add effects and EQ, and control panning and volume in real-time to each individual track, then instantly hear the results. You won't have to save every step nor suffer through numerous undo's and redo's as you mold a sound. It will be great.

Let's take the farmer flyby example and create it here again as a comparison. The delivery parameters shall remain the same: no more than six seconds in length, delivered as a 44 kHz, 16-bit stereo .wav file. Gathering individual sounds will be performed and created the same way using the audio editor. Nothing changes here except there isn't any need to cut to length or add effects processing to prepare for the mix process. Collect your sounds: some cow pasture ambience, an airplane flyby, a mumbling farmer voice, a rifle loading sound, a single gunshot, a sputtering engine, a "mayday" transmission, a short explosion, a scream, and a small crash with metal fallout — let's use them all. We can mix this longer list of sounds without even batting an eye.

Again, before slapping sounds together, start with a picture in your mind of how the scene will play out. This time, though, we will be adding additional sounds plus an ambient track of the cow pasture so the overall soundscape will be a bit more dense. Pay close attention to what sounds are "action" sounds and which ones are purely "window dressing" to add additional realism. This much layering can get busy and may work against us unless we keep a close eye.

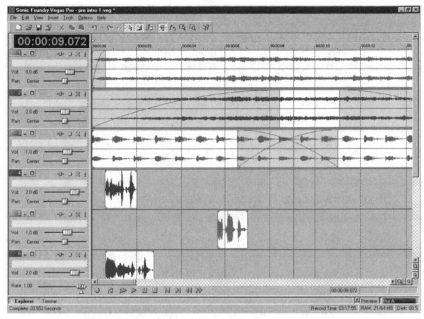

Figure 9.6 Sonic Foundry's Vegas Pro allows for non-destructive, complex audio editing which guarantees to take your sound design to another level.

A good rule of thumb is to keep background sounds in the rear
and those sounds which tell the story in front.

Resist the urge to have mooing cows and chirping birds hogging your scene. Use them sparingly, as a chef does with seasonings.

On your multi-track program of choice, open a new window with at least 10 available tracks. It is possible to create the sequence in one track, using cross-fading and mixing, but since you paid extra for the convenience of multiple tracks, we'll put one sound on each track and use its full potential. If the number of tracks does become an issue for you because of hardware resources, it is possible to place multiple sounds on each track. By placing non-overlapping sounds on the same track, it is still possible to adjust individual volumes, durations, and fades while cutting down on the number of tracks your processor has to deal with. Any effects processing or EQ which is inserted in a track, though, will effect every other sound as well. For our purposes, we'll assume one sound goes on one track and all processing will be done separately.

Track number one will start out with six seconds of cow pasture ambience. If you have a longer piece, shorten it to fit or mute the track after the six second end mark. How you do this depends on the features of your program; some will even allow you to size a file by moving either end to fit. If your ambient file is only three seconds, consider simply repeating it twice or overlapping them with crossfades to allow smooth transitions between the pieces and to keep them from sounding like a loop. Play the track listening for any unnatural sounds like clicks or pops. Don't worry too much if the overall sound isn't 100% perfect because this is the background sound. The volume will be low and other sounds playing will cover up most of the discrepancies. With the background in place, save the file and begin adding the rest of the sounds.

On the next track, let's add the flyby starting at about 0.5 seconds. We want the background ambience to be heard first, this way the listener's subconscious will hear it even though it will be buried. If the airplane noise started simultaneously, the listener would pay attention to the airplane and probably never even hear the cow pasture. Human nature will lead you to key in on the "action" and disregard any background distracters. This form of selective listening can sometimes work against our efforts causing us to compensate appropriately.

Depending on the flyby sample you are using, you may have to shorten it to about four seconds to fit the scene. If it already works well as a stereo effect with the aircraft coming from stage left to the center at about 3.5 seconds, set the volume, and save the file. If you are using a mono sample, exercise the panning feature to get the desired movement. Set your index points for the panning controls to simulate the flyby and ensure the sound moves past center stage about half way through the sequence. Adjust the volume and save the file.

For the rest of the individual sounds, place them on their own track with start points in roughly the order you would expect to hear them. Have the farmer mutter, load his gun, and fire it. Then have the engine sputter, a short "mayday" from the pilot, an explosion, and scream, then cap it off with the fallout ending at six seconds into the sequence. Adjust the pan for the final sounds to have them play further and further to the right to keep a fluidity over the whole scene — from the sputtering engine to the fallout sounds. Adjust any sounds which are longer than the sequence length, fading before six seconds. Once that is complete, save the file then proceed to adjust volume levels.

As in our previous example, make sure the levels all blend together from the listener's perspective (i.e., the farmer). Make the gunshot and explosion the louder of the sounds. You may also want to add compression to these sounds with a sharp attack for an extra boost without suffering from clipping. For sounds that might get buried, such as the muttering farmer and "mayday," consider using a touch of EQ to increase the higher frequencies, just enough to be able to understand what's going on. For the pilot's emergency transmission, EQ out the lower and mid frequencies to give it that tinny, radio quality. You might even have a preset for this very effect. The artist has the discretion to use any other effects processing, some slight reverb perhaps, or a hard flange for the tail end of the explosion just for fun. This example doesn't really require much. Again, save the file. Yeah, I know; I keep harping on this but the first time your system crashes and you lose two hours of hard work, you'll become a believer.

Building a complex sound effect in the multi-track environment is fairly simple. Once the sequence is tweaked to perfection, save the work as a "mixed" file for further processing. This process renders the multi-track sequence into a single sound file which will then be further manipulated. From the audio editor, open this mixed file and run through the checklist we were introduced to in the first sound effect example.

- Is the sound centered on the zero baseline? Utilize the DC Offset function.

- Does the sound file look "healthy"? Increase the volume level or use the normalize function.

- Is it too intense? Apply compression or decrease the volume.

- Are there any major volume peaks or clipping? A peak limiter or slight compression will take care of these.

How does the sequence sound now? There is definitely a lot going on in our soundscape — everything from very subtle sounds to "in your face" explosions. If you can make this sound great, you are on your way to making some professional, high-quality sound effects. Comparing the two processes now, you might feel this method is far superior than the time consuming, almost archaic way of doing business using a straight editing program. Multi-track affords many options to layer complex sounds without having to save and resave multiple files. Non-destructive editing is a godsend and I often beat myself up for waiting so long to incorporate it into my creative practices. If you intend to be in this business for any length of time, this will be an investment that will pay for itself everyday.

9.3.3 Sequencing Software and Samplers

The final stop on our sound design creation tour is the use of samplers and sequencing software as production tools. This method goes back many years to the Hollywood scene — sound designers in film having paved the way for the invention of audio editing software while pioneering this particular technique. This routine is still in use by some as their system of choice using either hardware- or software-based elements. Whether you physically load a hardware sampler full of basic sounds and then manipulate them via keyboard or sequencer, or trigger samples stored on your computer with an internal software sequencing program, the end results are the same.

It is still necessary to have an audio editor in your arsenal even if you use a sampler and sequencer set-up. Editing basic sound elements before loading into a sampler has to be done somewhere, as well as editing and formatting of the final product. It is impossible to create audio for games without one so again, a sampler and sequencer will only supplement the creative process. It all comes down to what works for you, what drives your creativity, what method serves the means.

The simplest form of sampler-based creation is its use as a basic pitch shifter over the chromatic scale. My personal favorite is to record party guests at their uninhibited best, load it into the sampler, and listen to their uproarious laughter accompany the playback. Middle C becomes the unprocessed recording; everything up or down the scale from there becomes cheap party fun. The lower the notes triggered on the keyboard, the lower the pitch of the original recording. Opposite is true for the higher notes. This is an easy way to instantly find out what pitch of sample works best for your application. It can also be used to layer the same samples — adding a note lower or higher to the original to fatten it up or to add some interesting artifacts. This doesn't work the further you stray from the root. As pitch is dropped, the sample playback becomes longer; as the pitch is increased, it becomes shorter making it difficult to seamlessly overlap. If you triggered three notes of the same sample to simultaneously playback, the higher pitched one will finish first, the lowest pitch will be last.

The best creative use for sampler-based rigs is to layer multiple elements for one large effect or sequence in a real-time atmosphere. In this manner, it is perfect for performing to a cinematic (much like a Foley artist would with their props) except all of your "props" are pre-loaded into a sampler. Some artists prefer to perform this task manually, matching keys visually to the actions or sequence, relying on their own timing skills. Others utilize a sequencer to create complex effects, layering triggered sounds using MIDI data synchronized to specific visual cues. Both methods require an understanding of your particular sampling device and how to set up sounds across a keyboard for optimum use.

Our previous sound effects sequence of the farmer flyby can be done using this sampler-based technique, although a couple of extra steps are needed to prepare. Pre-production now includes loading the various sound effect elements into the sampling device and assigning each sample to a key or group of keys.

To make this already complicated process less demanding, let's build the sequence using the four basic sound effects: flyby, gunshot, explosion, and crash samples. You could simply load these four sounds and have each triggered by one key and get away with it, but where would the fun be in that? To illustrate the potential of this set-up, let's load them chromatically so they have an octave "keygroup" from which to be triggered. This way, we can pick and choose which pitch we like and layer multiple explosions and crash effects as the feeling strikes us.

It is possible to perform this sequence while recording to tape, but you'll be bypassing important features of the sequencer. By recording MIDI data to sequencing software, we can take advantage of automated panning and fader controls — not to mention some limited effects processing and the ability to tweak the multiple triggered sounds to perfection.

Open a new file in your sequencer and set-up four tracks to the same MIDI channel, preferably the one which your sampler is also set to accept commands from. Either from a master keyboard controller or by using a mouse on the piano roll screen, trigger the flyby sample to start on track 1 at the 0:00 mark. Save the file. On track 2, trigger the gunshot sample to play at 0:03 seconds. The explosion can start at 0:035 seconds on track 3 and the crash around 0:04–0:045 seconds on track 4. Save the file. This will be the basic sequence.

Start by adjusting the pan of each track. Different software accomplishes this in different manners. Some merely establish what percentage of left, right, and center the track will play for the whole playback sequence. You set a number value and it never changes. More advanced programs will allow linear changes to this feature that serve as a sort of software automation. If your software will only let you "set and forget," pan the flyby sample between full left and center. Since the gunshot, explosion, and crash will fill the soundscape, it will make it hard to distinguish the location of the initial engine noise, totally masking the fact that it isn't moving. Also, by panning the other sounds appropriately, it will give the sequence the desired movement even though we are only using static settings. No adjustments need to be done with the gunshot because it is fired from the center position anyway. The explosion can be set at about the "one o'clock" position, just right of center, and the crash sound almost to full right. This will give the stereo field plenty of action and give a believable feeling of movement. But we can go one step better.

If the program allows for automated panning, movement can happen in real time. Start the flyby sample from the full left position and set the automation to adjust the pan position until the aircraft comes dead center at three seconds. The gunshot can be left where it is in the center because our listening position is with the farmer. The explosion can start at the center and pan further right as the sequence progresses, the crash starting further to the right to also end full right at six seconds. This type of automation will create the desired movement for the sequence on its own — leaving the dirty details to the program instead of having to deal with it manually in an audio editor. Save the file.

We can also set the individual track volume levels in the same manner as was done for the panning process, either "set and forget" or automated. Usually, fixed volume levels will work fine in a short sequence like this, but depending on the original samples, a little manipulation may be in order to make it sound good. It is a good idea to use linear fades on each of the samples — especially the explosion and crashing sounds in order to stay within our six second limit. All sounds should fall to zero by the end; if not, later work within the audio editor will need to be made.

As further tweaks are made to tighten up the sequence, consider adjusting equalization for each track or adding compression or other subtle effects. If the sampler outputs are split to run through a mixing board, use any built-in features on the board and any outboard gear to add that perfect final stroke to the piece. It is also possible to run this into a multi-track program as individual tracks to take advantage of its features as well. If worse comes to worst, record it as a mixed file into an audio editor and make adjustments from there. Keep in mind, though, anything you do will affect the *entire* sound file — not just the one sound you may have been trying to deal with. Regardless of how the piece is mixed and brought together, utilize an audio editor to complete the final checklist in the previous examples and save to the desired file format.

The same sound effect sequence has been built using yet another array of tools, all with a similar result. For quite some time, this last method was considered the only way to do post-production sound design work and still has a place with some of the more established creation teams. The method you use is dependent on the tools you currently have, your personal sound effects "thought process," and, above all, what gives you the best results for the effort. My personal recommendation is to use both multi-track and audio editing software paired together as the ultimate sound effects creation tool. Don't discount the sampler-based set-up entirely. You never know when a developer may call asking for a MIDI-triggered bank of sound effects.

We've spent a considerable amount of time discussing the mechanics of sound design creation. Let's turn our attention back to how this fits in with video game production.

9.4 Sound Design in the Production Cycle

Sound design creation can begin at any point in the development. Experience, however, dictates it not be done too hastily. Initial artistic concepts and storyboards can provide a decent advanced look at the intended genre and what sort of sounds may be needed — whether it be general Foley sounds or imaginative, "far out" sounds. But because early concepts of art and gameplay have a tendency to evolve continuously, actual sound design this early is a waste of time.

Joey Kuras, sound designer for Tommy Tallarico Studios with personal credits of over 60 games, was given a list of effects needed for the James Bond game, Tomorrow Never Dies, very early in the project. He designed and delivered over 200 sounds per the developer's request only to have almost 90% of them discarded as the production matured, redoing them later in the project. On another project, he received a list of unspecific and vague sounds. For instance, a request for a "splash" sound has little meaning. Was it a rock, a 400-pound person, a cannonball, or a building? Is it in a bathtub, a pond, or an ocean? No one could be specific and they ended waiting until later in the project.

This is an an easy lesson for all of us. Sound design at the outset of a project is usually not wise. Producers have the difficult task of determining audio needs of a game early in the development cycle, and if a contracted sound designer is used, the producer must find and negotiate with an individual whose skills and credits match those of the game being developed. When a game company is spending up to $30,000 for sound effects alone, they want to get their money's worth. If the game will have a wide range of settings and characters, trying to imagine and pinpoint a large bank of effects can be tricky.

It's important to bring the development team together to begin thinking conceptually about the game audio as early as possible. Planning is key. If they've decided on a sound designer/s, that person or team should be brought in on discussions and given an opportunity to share their experience. Developers shouldn't wait on the audio implementation details until later. But starting work on the actual creation of game sound effects too early often leads to major headaches down the line.

If money isn't a terrible concern, the developer can choose to add rough sound effects to help inspire the team. Putting in placeholder sounds can give life to soundless artwork and open the floodgates of creativity. As the sound designer, don't do this for free, of course; negotiate fair compensation for your work. And be careful. These "temporary" sounds have a way of becoming final sounds and unless your payment plan is already spelled out ahead of time, you may be out money. As an example, say you get a call to do 10 placeholder sound effects. Your normal rate may be $100 per sound effect, therefore $1,000 in your pocket. But because the developer needs them today, you knock out these rough ideas in eight hours and charge them an hourly fee for your services. As the project progresses, the team gets used to hearing your rough sounds and decides they should stay in the final version. When it comes time for payment, you discover these 10 sounds have been left off the final invoice. The developer reminds you that you have already been paid at an hourly rate for the effects. So, now these 10 sounds bring in only $400 (working at $50 an hour). Don't naively think a developer doesn't have some money-saving tricks up their sleeve. Suddenly working on a "per sound effect" rate makes some sense.

Most of the time, a game is far enough along that characters, movements, and a defined gameplay model are present before a sound designer ever enters the picture. Being able to meet with the development team, view some rough game levels, and perhaps see some animation is crucial to churning out applicable sound ideas.

9.5 Specific Sound Design Questions to Answer

Once the final contract negotiations have taken place and documents are signed, the other details regarding the project are normally released to the sound designer. This is the point where "clear and concise" means the difference between complete audio bliss or a sound disaster. Ask for the specifics in order to make things crystal clear.

What genre of game is this intended to be?   It is important for the music and sound effects to keep within the spirit of the game — whether it's space, driving, fishing, or sports. Get a good, overall "feel" for the game. Find out which current games are similar in tone and investigate them. (This is where buying video games becomes a tax write-off, by the way!) See movies that fall in the genre to look for ideas and set the stage for your creative juices.

Sample rate, resolution, stereo vs. mono?   At some point, the development team will have done all of their homework to determine how much space will be allotted for graphics and sound. This will help decide how high the sound quality can be and what parameters the sounds will be created within. While you should always create sound effects in the highest sample rate and resolution possible, conversion to lower ones will affect sound quality and destroy any subtle nuances you may have added.

Will the sound effects be treated through any software or hardware processors?   Driving games are an example where reverb is used quite frequently. Most of the sounds will have an "echoey" quality as the player drives through a tunnel. This is the kind of information you need to know as the sound designer. Additional processing by a game engine will determine to what extent certain sounds are processed beforehand. You could have a problem if the developer plans on applying reverb to an already processed sound. The developer should decide and communicate as soon as possible if there are plans for this type of processing. That way, you can be sure to not over-process any files on your end.

Are any ambient sounds needed?   Remember, we don't want the player distracted by silence. While this is more of a content-type question, the creation process is complicated and many details fall through the cracks. By asking this question, you may jog memories or present ideas the developer may not have thought about previously. The sound designer wouldn't know if they intend to play music instead unless he or she was also the composer. This alleviates a phone call to you late in the production for forgotten ambient sounds or music. If these types of sounds are required, determine if they need to be loop-able or will playback as random background sounds. Looping sound effects get monotonous and delicate surgery may be necessary to make them less so.

Will certain effects have priority during playback? There can be instances during gameplay — such as when a player unlocks a hidden door, stumbles into a trap, or is attacked by a villain — when one single sound punctuates the moment. These are the ones you want to have the biggest bang for the buck. Because other sounds won't be drowning them out or playing over them, you won't have to make considerations for other effects being heard at the same time. These are the type of sounds you want to take the player's breath away. Have a developer point to them so you'll know which ones to pull out all the stops for.

Will there be any voice-overs or speech commands that need to be heard? As the sound designer, you may be involved with voice recordings and can process them via EQ or volume to ensure they can be heard and understood. This process is similar to having the vocals stand out in a song mix. If you're not involved directly, you can add that particular service to your list and offer it to the developer.

Are any narratives needed?   Background sounds to accompany narration?   Narratives fit into the sound recording category and generally, anyone capable of sound design can also record narration. If narratives are pre-recorded, you can usually provide the service of transferring to digital files, maximizing the sound, cutting them to length, and adding any additional background or Foley sounds. If narratives are to be recorded, you need to know if you will be providing voice talent and budget accordingly. Developers may ask if you have experience directing narrative sessions; if not, the producer may fill that role. Maybe *you* will be the voice talent. If so, make sure there is appropriate compensation for your efforts.

Any special sound considerations?   Is the game intended to be Dolby Surround Sound or DTS, with studio quality speakers or subwoofers? Are they planning to advertise the game's cinema-quality sound? Ensure your longevity in the business and seek out this tidbit of information.

What platform are the sounds being created for?   This will suggest what type of playback system the consumer will use and the confines the final sound effects. I mix to several playback systems, from "el cheapo," grocery store multimedia speakers to high-end studio monitors. The sound effects should work well with them all, but the main focus should be the system the majority will be using.

What type of music, if any, will play as the sounds are triggered?   This will give you an indication of other sonic activity happening during gameplay. If the music is a softer, orchestral score, the sound effects can be geared towards that mood and not sound obtrusive. If a rock soundtrack is to play, then harsher sounds and careful manipulation of effects in the higher and lower frequencies will ensure they stand out. The sounds should all work together to enhance gameplay, not aggressively compete. The last thing we want to do is cause the player to turn the sound off.

Are any sound resources available to the sound designer for licensed materials?   Alien vs. Predator, Star Trek, and South Park games, for example, are based on film or television properties produced under licensing agreements. If the publisher or developer has secured use of the actual sounds from these works, do you have them at your disposal to manipulate for the game or are you expected to recreate them from scratch? While you may not have an actual hand at creating them, you are equipped to convert them to the proper formats and sample rates and need to know if this will be part of your services.

Are any special filenaming conventions required for final delivery of sounds?   If the development team is overly organized or if they waited until late in production to bring you on board, they may already have file names programmed into the code. While renaming files is not a big deal, it may help cut down on confusion when delivery is made if they are already named appropriately. The developer should make this need clear or define an acceptable method. This is also an extra service you can provide.

9.6 Determining Necessary Sounds

The process of determining which sound effects are needed can take on many forms. There are times when the sound designer will be presented with a long, grocery list of sound effects to create; other times the developer will present a pre-release copy of the game and let your experience decide. Either way, it's not a cut and dried process and will require much patience, flexibility, and teamwork.

Tommy Tallarico describes his experience. "I've been in the industry long enough to know you can have a sound effects list, on average of 200–250 sound effects per game which will end up changing at least 400 times. Sound effects are most definitely post-production. The developer will insist they need a series of sounds, let's say, of magic appearing, a loop, the magic sound traveling, and then one sound hitting a person and one hitting a wall. In reality, it's going to be one sound of the magic releasing and one generic hitting sound. So, where they've listed 12 sounds, you'll do two."

Initially, a developer will want a sound effect for every action in the game — from simple button clicks on a menu screen to intricate character movements, weapons, environments, background ambience, and so on. Providing this type of feedback to a player is, in essence, the magic that draws them into the virtual world. They interact with the game and are rewarded with aural and visual cues adding to the feeling of being *inside* the game making things happen. Sound effects play a grand part in this design and, at the onset, the developer will want to cover every possibility. As reality slowly creeps in, they will discover there isn't the need or the want of every sound effect on their list. The soundscape would become grossly overloaded, random access memory and processors would be jammed, and new programming issues would arise from the chaotic use of sound — not to mention the sanity of the game player as their ears are bombarded with too much information. It should become clear which sounds have priority and which ones aren't really needed. Unfortunately for you, this won't happen until late in the game. Try to have it narrowed down as soon as is practical.

9.6.1 Sound Effects Lists

If you stick with game sound design business long enough, you'll end up seeing practically every form of sound effects list imaginable. I sometimes refer to these as "wish lists" because they often never get totally fulfilled. Most will look like the following:

Game: Video Poker

Sound effects needed:	Intro
	Background ambiance
	Card shuffle
	Card turn-over
	Card select
	Button push
	Win 1
	Win 2
	Jackpot

This example of a small video poker game isn't much on detail. It leaves a lot of questions to ask prior to beginning work. Without artwork accompanying this request, it's pretty much open to interpretation. I'd guess it would be a standard Vegas-style video poker machine with all the bells and whistles, a fairly straightforward project. But what if the producer had taken time to fill in some details? A better sound effects list would look like the following.

Game: Jungle Adventure Video Poker

This game will have the look and feel of a jungle with ancient ruins covered in overgrowth. The game screen will consist of an ancient temple with the five cards appearing in the entryway. These cards will be made of old stone tablets with early inhabitants on the face cards. Two large waterfalls will sit on either side of the temple, creating a relaxing cascade of water. This game should have a tranquil atmosphere, with an occasional, tribal drum beat heard far in the background, nothing dangerous sounding, just enough to add to the ambiance.

Sound effects needed:

Intro	Plays as the opening screen appears. This will set the mood for the game. Play heavily on establishing the jungle theme while giving the flavor the player has stumbled across an ancient game.	4 seconds maximum
Background ambiance	Starts after the intro sound effect stops. This looping effect should be of gentle, cascading water to simulate the waterfalls, adding to the relaxed atmosphere.	2–3 seconds maximum
Random, ambient sounds	(4) different effects. These sounds will be triggered at random as background ambiance. Ideas such as bird calls, tribal drums, jungle noises, etc would work well here.	no more than 2 seconds maximum for each one
Card shuffle	This sound will indicate gameplay is ready to begin. Since we are not using conventional cards, some sort of primitive sound — perhaps wood hits or a short drum beat would work well.	3 seconds maximum
Card turn-over	This sound will play as cards are turned over. The sound of a heavy stone being moved or dropped may work nicely.	1.5 seconds in length
Card select	This sound will be heard as the player touches the card to indicate which ones they will hold. This should be a firm, but neutral sort of sound because the player will hear it many times during the course of play.	1 second maximum

Button push	As the player presses any button on the game console, this sound will play. Similar to the card select sound, it should be neutral, but slightly more "fun" in nature.	1 second maximum
Win 1	This sound will be triggered for a small win. It should stay true to the jungle theme, giving positive reinforcement to the accomplishment without going overboard. A mixture of animal noises and jungle sounds might work well as an example.	3 seconds maximum
Win 2	Another notch in intensity up from Win 1. The player will have achieved a substantial win when this sound is triggered. Stay within the theme and make it positive.	3 seconds maximum
Jackpot	This sound will be heard after a Royal Flush. It should be loud, triumphant, and attract a crowd when the player achieves this rare reward. Pull out all the stops and make this one really shine!	5 seconds maximum
Delivery format:	22kHz, 8 bit, mono .wav files	
Delivery date:	1 week from the date of this request	

This is a good example of the kind of sound effects list you would like to receive every time. The developer has put some serious time and thought into the game. Their vision is clear and concise and there is no doubt concerning the atmosphere they are trying to create. They have given you precise ideas yet have left enough room for your interpretation as a sound artist. If artwork is available, now would be the best time to ask for it — the visuals will give you extra ammunition to do your work.

More detailed lists may accompany a developer's request for sound effects, especially when animation and artwork are unavailable. Using the previous example, intricate timing may need to be matched.

Card turn-over	This sound will play as cards are turned over. There should be a 0.5 second delay for the card select sound to fade before this one begins. Once the card is selected, the stone will rise slightly, then proceed to turn for 1.5 seconds before settling back down with a small cloud of dust. Key timing points to hit: 0.5 delay from trigger of sound before the sound plays; at 00:00.5 — the stone rises; at 00:01.0 the tablet begins to turn over (lasting 1.5 seconds); at 00:02.0 the stone settles with a thump and a small cloud of dust appears from the edges.

This one small animation sequence is very intricate and the developer is trying hard to provide you with every detail. But, until the animation is complete, it will be impossible to know for sure if all this planning will pay off. More than likely, you'll have to redo this sound later, after the animation is finalized. The more details, the better when doing sound effects, but, effective sound design is best when completed post-production.

When receiving any type of list, I recommend going over it line-by-line with the

Figure 9.7 A picture of the game describes much more than words alone. This graphic shows us exactly what the game is about.

producer in person or at least over the phone. Get as many details as possible for each item, discuss every possibility, and narrow down the field to a couple of solid ideas. I once had a ridiculously simple request for the sound of a small, stone game piece being placed on a wooden game board. Without even talking to the developer about it, I proceeded to record a marble hitting several types of wood at varied intensities and sent back a dozen sounds. None of them were accepted. I tried again. Another dozen, another rejection. I asked which ones sounded close and received an answer. Another dozen, another rejection. As you can imagine, this was starting to get a little bit frustrating and I picked up the phone. We talked. He performed the correct sound of a stone hitting his personal game board over the phone and within 10 minutes, I had the sound and pitch he wanted. After submitting over 50 sounds, we were finally done. A simple task had become an ordeal because I didn't think it was important to talk to the producer. Now, it is another item on the checklist before I begin any work. Again, there is something to be said for actually communicating with other human beings on the team.

9.6.2 Alpha Game Versions and Other Visuals

In addition to receiving a list of requested sound effects, it is likely the developer will forward a rough version of the game. This isn't possible, obviously, for console or arcade games, but it's a good option for a CD-ROM- or web-based game if one is available. It's a perfect way for you to interact with the game, as a player would, and determine the best use of sound effects. These rough versions will be lacking many of the game options, levels, and artwork but will give a rudimentary idea of what the title is about. While you may be tempted to have a little fun, pay close attention to the details and what you can do to improve upon the visuals. Your job is to enhance the work of the rest of the team — adding the perfect audio touch. If the developer is thinking ahead, they will even have made it easy for you to add in your sound effects and test them in the game during your design phase. By having a separate sound folder under the games root directory, it becomes a simple task of replacing and renaming files. All you have to do is fire up the game to get instant feedback.

For non-CD-ROM games, developers may provide video tapes of various parts of the game, character movements, animations, menu screen shots, and so on. Some even go as far as to tape someone playing, stopping at every menu screen, flipping to each option, meticulously going through every action currently in place. For sports games, I've even received tapes recorded at an actual game — not of the players, but of the crowd reactions and various other happenings on the sidelines which they want recreated. Their research gave me exactly what I needed without having to attend a game myself. Organized development teams will also provide a *track sheet* which specifies times and events to pay close attention to as you watch. If you can't be there on site, this is a great way to share information.

Whether you receive your visuals in the form of a video tape or an alpha version of the game, it is also possible the developer will rely entirely on your ideas and experience to provide sound effects for the project. Basically, they will say, "Here's the game. Make some noise." The perception of free reign doesn't mean the developer won't have anything to say about the sounds, far from it. They will provide specific guidance and will always be close by to share opinions. The company climate may be one where artists are given space to work without overbearing management types constantly peeking over their shoulder. This lack of micro-management will be appreciated and let you create freely.

As you play the rough game, keep meticulous notes. Gather ideas for every place a sound effect should appear and any initial thoughts of what they should sound like. Develop your own comprehensive list. After some quality time, present these ideas to the developer for approval before starting any work. Some selling may be involved, explaining your reasoning for including some sounds and not others. This is basically the same process they would have followed in-house had they developed their own list, except they are choosing to have the expert make the determination.

There are no hard and fast rules governing the choice of sound effects. Understand how a particular sound will impact the game, the player, and the soundscape. A pinball game should have sounds happening almost constantly, even when the ball is at rest. This game is designed as a fast-action, stress-relieving game. An intellectually stimulating game requiring concentration, such as chess, would require fewer sounds, maintaining a serene atmosphere instead. The overall theme of the game, level, or section will guide the final choices. At this point, there is no problem going overboard with suggestions. It will make for some extra work on your part having to create sound effects that may end up getting dumped anyway, but for the sake of the game, it's worth the effort to go all out.

The other school of thought says that because you don't get paid any more or less (depending on the negotiated deal), why should you do more work? There is a fine line between doing enough work to "get by" and going beyond what is expected. Your judgment and experience will ultimately dictate your decisions but, personally, I like to leave a developer feeling I did my best and insist on always working hard and going the extra mile. If that means creating more sound effects than the game will use, then so be it. Working hard will pay off in the longevity of your career.

There will be times when no matter how hard you do work, a developer will never be satisfied. You may think a sound effect is perfect, but they continually request reworks or new sounds altogether. Your best approach may be to pull out your best diplomatic skills and talk to them. Eventually a sound will be good enough. Eventually you'll have a case where any of a couple of dozen different sounds will work just as well. Remember, though, if *none* of your efforts seem to satisfy them, it may be they are just plain difficult to work for. It happens.

9.6.3 Beta Testing

Another important practice of determining sound effects for a game project is the process of *play testing*, also referred to as *beta testing*. Game companies have different methods depending upon their resources. Larger ones have an in-house staff whose job it is to play the game, look for bugs, and suggest improvements or they farm out this type of work to outside firms who provide this service. Small game developers use themselves as the guinea pigs. The end result is the same — a list of needed sound effects from different people and personalities. The variety of opinions gives a good cross-section. Typically, the developer will stick with the majority and put this plan into action.

Play testing is also a good test bed for valuable outside opinions of sounds that may already be in place. If sounds have been created earlier in production, it becomes hard for the developer and sound designer to fairly judge what they've heard every day — their familiarity clouding the ability to gauge a sound's effectiveness. By letting play-testers express their unbiased thoughts, the game can only benefit. They aren't there to bolster anyone's ego, just lend their opinion. This final form of checks and balances will help get it one step closer to the marketplace. Ultimately, the game player will have the final say about your work, but it's too late then for any changes. This process is the next best thing.

9.7 Creating Original Sound Effects That Fit

It's been said that those of us who create sound in the video games industry should take a lesson from Hollywood. Bobby Prince, of DOOM fame, presented a paper in 1996 at the *Game Developers Conference*, "Tricks and Techniques for Effective Sound Design," which listed common attributes of movies that had won Academy Awards for best sound effects. The listed commonalities offered a good jumping-off place when thinking about game sound design. These sounds:

- focused the viewer's attention,
- were bigger than life,
- didn't get in the way of each other,
- placed the listener into another "reality," and
- always had some sort of background ambiance in place as well.

These basic ideas will work just as well in games.

9.7.1 Getting Organized

It's time to start making some noise! You've been hired, your list of questions has been answered, and we are off to a good start. If it hasn't happened already, the developer should assign one or two individuals to act as the liaison to the sound designer. Rather than getting mixed signals from numerous artists, programmers, and so on, the company can assign the producer or creative director the task of communicating the specs and signing off on the work. This ensures clear and effective communications, which I believe is *the* key to obtaining sounds which match the developer's vision

If you are a locally-based contractor, stop by the developer's site, meet the rest of the creation team, and discuss the game's intention. It's a good fact-finding mission; become a mental sponge and absorb everything related to the project. If you are unavailable to visit, be sure to obtain copies of artwork, storyboards, and any story text as has been mentioned. Now is not the time to have secrets. You are part of the team and on their side.

An alpha version of the game can be delivered with placeholder sound effects already in place. Library sounds or effects taken from other games can be inserted as a way to give life to soundless artwork and to show you where new effects are needed. Placeholders can be words instead of sounds. In a game I worked on, the producer inserted words such as "click," "bonk," "explode," or "shot." As I played the game, every time I heard his voice, I created a sound to match the action. This worked out very well for me and the producer maintains the psychological advantage, his booming voice having an interesting effect on my psyche.

9.7.2 Creating a Sound Palette

The first order of business is to choose a sound "palette" and organize your computer or sampler files so they are easily called upon, as was also discussed in section 8.5.2. I generally grab sounds I've developed or recorded within the genre I will be creating, put them into a computer folder, and draw upon them as the work progresses.

Create new directories and start throwing in any sound that might sound like it belongs in the game. If it's a cartoon-type game, grab your "cartoon" sounds. If it is a war game, grab all the gunshots and explosions you have lying around. You won't necessarily be using them all, or any of them. You are establishing a theme and a good starting point. You'll look to this folder for the bits and pieces to form the core of your game sounds.

Why bother with a palette? I too was resistant at first. Why spend extra time preparing to create when I could just jump right in and create? On a couple of larger games I tried just that, but found I was spending administrative time away from the actual design process looking for ideas anyway. By spending a couple days at the beginning, I only had to break my creative spell a few times now that all of the sounds were handy. You would drive yourself crazy choosing from millions of possible sounds. By narrowing the possibilities down,

a) you naturally build an aural theme based upon the 100 or so sounds you've chosen,

b) the game sounds will have similar qualities because most are made from elements from your palette, and

c) you will design better, more original sounds by limiting your choices and forcing yourself to be more creative.

Try it both ways and I guarantee you'll always start the process by forming a sound palette, whether it be computer- or sampler-based.

Jamey Scott, sound designer and composer for Presto Studios (developers of Myst III, The Journeyman Project series, Gundam 0078, and others), believes putting together the initial palette is the most important step; finding sounds that will mix well together. He uses a sampler (Emu Emulator E4) in his sound design process and for each game, develops an entirely new sound palette to keep them original. He finds using a sampler has many advantages over straight computer files and sound editors. "Layering sounds internally in the E4 works very well for me, more so than doing it on a computer. That way, I can save my banks as a palette rather than having sources in various folders all over the computer. They are all looped, EQ'ed, and noise filtered to my specifications. Plus returning to them to make any changes is a simpler task."

9.7.3 Effective Creation

Most sound guys believe video games are on the level of interactive movies and strive to grab the player's attention with their sounds. Nothing is more satisfying that having a player remark that the sounds are cool. Either realistic Foley or "over-the-top" sounds can have that impact and we certainly aim to please.

Most sound designers are never satisfied with stock library sound effects. If they use them, they are manipulated several different ways — either pitch-shifted, filtered, layered, textured, reorganized, reversed, inverted, compressed, expanded, or cut into smaller elements — anything to give them a new life and make them less recognizable. Nothing is more annoying than hearing the same sound effect used on television, radio, and in other games. It happens more frequently than you probably notice. I have a large German Rottwieler who runs excitedly around the backyard barking at the sky whenever he hears a certain hawk screech sound. I have a Hollywood Edge sample disk I used to enjoy playing for the neighbors and friends. We would all laugh at the stupid dog and his antics. The exact sound is in dozens of TV shows, commercials, and video games. The poor dog must run barking into the backyard several times a week without my help. These library sounds can be overused. Our job is to change that.

As an example, let's talk about the creation of a different sound effect, using one from a project I'm currently working on. The game is within the "space strategy" genre where units are maneuvered in formation to battle against other players. It is a PC game with final sounds to be delivered as 22 kHz, 16 bit .wav files. This particular sound is a "shield" sound which activates when the unit is fired upon.

I wanted the shield to have an electric quality to it — a controlled surge of energy that might sound as if it was absorbing or deflecting a shot from a laser weapon. I wanted it to be original so I stayed away from the stock library effects and turned instead toward one of my synthesizers for inspiration.

I ultimately settled on a patch (similar to the keyboard sound in Van Halen's "Jump") and recorded about four seconds of a three-note chord. I saved it into my audio editing program, Sound Forge, as 44.1 kHz, 16-bit stereo. Experimenting with a few different effects processors, I opted for a nice doppler effect in another program, Goldwave. I edited an existing effects patch to give it a quick, one second doppler increase with about three seconds of doppler decrease. Back in Sound Forge, I pulled up a radio static sound file, ran it through a 1hz stereo flange effect and equalized it to increase the high frequency range. I then cut that file to four seconds to match the manipulated keyboard sound and mixed the two sounds, keeping the static barely perceptible. I gave the new mixed file about a one second fade-in and faded out the last two seconds with a linear fade. Now it was beginning to sound like something. I normalized the file to maximize the sound, adjusted for any abnormal level peaks, and finally saved the new file as "shield.wav."

Later, the producer wanted a dull, metallic clank mixed in to give the player some distinction between a shield hit and a hit to the unit's space suit. I pulled up a nice clank sound, EQ'ed out most of the highs, and mixed to the shield file. All is well, producer happy.

To convert down to 22 kHz is a simple task. The resample feature in Sound Forge does the trick. Because some of the higher frequency band gets lost in the conversion, I usually add some EQ to compensate; just a slight amount gives it the right touch. Another check on the levels and now the effect is ready for the game. Total amount of work on this one sound effect: two hours, 15 minutes. Lots of manipulation? You bet! You could do this same edit using a multi-track editor.

9.7.4 Creative Forces

Jon Holland, a former game sound designer turned full-time composer, with many game credits, reflects upon a past project. "Combining unexpected sound sources with recognizable sounds or timbres will yield truly original sound FX's. I remember a few years ago on Vectorman, I combined the sound of detuned dinosaur steps with the crack of a bullwhip. Then I layered that with a regular thunder sound to get a lashing thunderstorm feel. Even though it was a Sega Genesis game, the sound was very effective and had definition that cut right through. You have to be creative and try things even if you can't see an obvious correlation immediately. Experimentation should be paramount if you want sounds that are difficult to duplicate."

TOOLS OF THE TRADE

Jon Holland, Composer/Sound Designer, Xyxu Studio

Jon Holland is a music composer of boundless creative energy. He is in constant motion, whether creating music for game projects like Ms. Pacman or physically en route to another wondrous destination on the globe. Personable, witty, talkative, and outgoing are some previous words used to describe this good-natured character. I'd have to agree. By the way, he also happens to be one of the highest paid composers in the industry.

The music world is where Jon has chosen to be. He loves what he does and couldn't think of being in any other place. Actually, he has a passion for getting lost in the wilderness, but that's another story entirely. With his love for both electronica and orchestral music, he has not only composed scores for such games as Vectorman 1 and 2, Goosebumps: Attack of the Mutant, Assassin 2015, 3Xtreme (original score), Xwomen, and numerous other game projects, but also ESPN, a USAF Thunderbirds documentary (at age 19), and a recent surf film for Reef Brazil Corp. entitled "The Reef @ Todos." In addition, he has been featured on the Powercuts1 and Vectorman Soundtrack CDs for Sega/Polygram.

Computer: PowerMac G4 (1 GB RAM), Medea SCSI Audio Raid, MOTU Midi Time Piece AV

Software: Pro Tools Mix Plus, Emagic Logic Audio, software synthesizers, samplers, and various plug-ins

Multi-track: Pro Tools

Mixer/Monitors: Mackie keyboard mixers; Apogee Stage and Yamaha NS10 Speakers; Sumo, VTL and Crown Amps

Outboard gear: Neve 1272 Stereo Mic Preamp, Drawmer 1960 Stereo Compressor Mic Pre, dbx 160X (Modified), Lexicon Reverbs (Modified), Sony R7 Reverb, Alesis Quadraverb, Yamaha SPX90 (Modified), LA Audio Classic Compressor

Keyboards: Roland JD800, Juno 106, JX10, PC200, JV1080, MPU101 Midi-CV Converter; Minimoog (Lintronics Midi Mod); Arp 2600; Oberheim Analog SEM Modules (12); Sequential Pro One; Alesis D4 Drum Module; Novation Bass Station and Drum Station; Voce Electric Piano Module

Other instruments: Fender Walnut Strat, Ibanez Pat Metheny Archtop, Ovation Deacon, Ovation Legend acoustic, G&L Bass

Jamey Scott has many tricks up his sleeve too. For a previous Presto project, the game had many machines that required their own personality and uniqueness. He normally starts with stock engine or mechanical sounds but runs them through a fast LFO filter, warbling the pitch, and then mixing in what he calls "clunketty-clunk" sounds. For machines that are primitive, he ensures they sound rickety and unpolished on purpose. He will also start completely from scratch on some, preferring to mix low-frequency rumbling sounds, mid-range mechanical noises, and on top, some high-frequency whining. He tends to shoot for a full-frequency spectrum sound, massive and very full.

For odd creature sounds, Jamey creates something like an exaggerated insect noise — a high-pitched screech but with a very low-frequency sound to make it memorable. He's been known to use his own mouth noises, or to grab someone walking by in the hall, as interesting touches. After tweaking and layering, you would never know their origin.

Joey Kuras makes good use of the world around him for his sounds. Sometimes there just isn't a particular sound in any of the libraries he uses, so he ventures out with his portable DAT and microphone. A previous "Beavis and Butthead" game required the sound of large gymnasium bleachers opening. So he went to a local school and had the maintenance crew open them while his tape ran. Instant sound effect.

The boxing game Knockout uses a lot of embellished punching sounds, occasionally punctuated by the sounds of a breaking jawbone. Joey made use of many stalks of celery to add just the right touch of crunching and snapping.

Test Drive 5 and 6 required over-the-top engine and car sounds. His trek led him and his microphone to southern California's Marconi Auto Museum to record some track-ready muscle cars first hand. Play these games and you'll agree, the effort was worth it.

Several games' need for sounds of grenades bouncing led him to a military surplus store for dummy grenades. An quiet afternoon of grenade tossing produced some nice effects.

Assaf Gavron and **Oosh Adar**, sound designers in Israel who worked on EA's flight sim, USAF, relayed this interesting method of effects creation. Oosh describes this particular session, "In flight simulations, there is a lot of mid-frequency activity in the cockpit. Most of those sounds are being processed by filters and a bit of distortion. I had to create a "G" effect (heavy breathing in a "over G" situation) that needed to sound like you were hearing yourself over the headphones — the sound being in the same mid-range area. I didn't want to repeat the same software treatment as in the radio connection because it's a bit different and it's better to avoid a crunchy mid-range overload. I decided to record it live."

"I made a heavy breathing session and listened to it. It sounded oddly like phone sex. Every detail of the breathing was so clear and it was not even sexy; it was dirty, full of "aahhcchhs" and "fifs." There was nobody else around to replace me except my girlfriend and we all know that fighter pilots are males. Staying away from the mic and the other usual tricks didn't work either, it was too dynamic no matter what I tried. So, I closed the mic in the closet to imitate claustrophobic air pressure ambience and I brought a long plastic tube (1 1\2 meters) and connected it to the mic. The plastic tube acts as a natural band pass that creates the illusion of distance. Now, if someone was looking through the window it looked dirty but sounded perfect. The breathing was far away but still close and it sounded filtered but not software generated. The "resample" to 22.5, plus some fine-tuning tricks, made it sound right."

Experimentation, experience, and the willingness to leave the studios once in awhile can lead to some fantastic sound creations. These guys are at the top and only climbing higher. I can't wait to hear what they have coming up next.

9.8 Presenting the Final Work

Now that you've spent a great deal of time creating these fantastical sound effects, it's time to make delivery to the client. It is not just a simple matter of sending a CD or emailing the sounds and saying, "Here they are!". It can be done that way, but usually there is a little more to it. You are making a presentation and selling them to the client.

When presenting finished effects to the producers, I always send more sounds than needed. I work up several effects, letting them in on the process and giving them the chance to choose the ones that match their vision. Some have minor, subtle differences, changes in length, layering, or effects processor settings. Others use completely different angles to get the same point across. Some are "happy accidents" I'll throw in that might work from a completely different angle. These serve two purposes: to give an idea so far out that it might just work or to make the others sound that much more right for the game.

The producer will more likely be happiest with their choice, believing in it enough to sell it to the rest of the team. If you had made the choice for them, it would be like swimming upstream against a strong current. The psychological trick is for them to make the choice, take the responsibility, and do the rest of the legwork. I usually have my favorite, and if I believe in it enough, I'll say so, to help slant the decision. But, most often, it's their choice entirely.

Also occasionally included (if it isn't already obvious by the filenames) is some sort of documentation that describes what each sound effect is for. It will highlight which sounds are for specific actions and which less critical ones could be mixed and matched, such as button presses. This key will save some headache for everyone involved and score points for the organized sound designer.

Other sound designers have their own unique delivery methods that help them stand out from the crowd. Darryl Duncan, of GameBeat, Inc., has a fresh idea which works for him. "Aside from delivering good work, we feel that our package and delivery method must give attention to detail. We find that it truly is the little things that the clients appreciate. A small example of that is this: when we deliver music or sound effects, we create a detailed Excel spreadsheet that allows the client to listen to all of the delivered assets right from the Excel document. They simply click on the music/sfx title and the music or sfx plays right from within that document, as they read a detailed description of the version they are hearing, what it is meant for in the game, etc. We have found that this is one of the simple things that our clients really appreciate and has even led to other projects from word of mouth about this simple service feature we offer."

9.9 Conclusion

Have you ever watched a 'B' movie and actually liked the sound effects? Occasionally, the amateurish production has some charm to it, but for the most part, they are not very good. Would you buy a 'B' video game or even set out to make one? Of course not! With all of the competition for shelf space, we set out from day one to make a product that will be profitable and perhaps even win us a few accolades from our colleagues in the process.

There are no hard and fast rules, no secret formulas, and no prescribed methods for creating the consummate assemblage of sound effects for a game. It takes fluid communication and a firm vision from the development team coupled with a sound designer who shows no bounds to their creativity and patience. The tips and tricks illustrated here should give a solid foundation for you to build upon and thrive in this gratifying industry. Knock 'em dead.

For further reading on game sound design, see:
"Tricks and Techniques for Sound Effects Design," by Bobby Prince,
www.gamasutra.com/features/index_sound_and_music.htm

CHAPTER 10
Blending the Total Soundscape

An assault of unorganized audio is nothing but noise — pure and simple. With an onslaught of narratives, music, and sound effects, a game can quickly become a chaotic nightmare, forcing the player to run away screaming or to simply turn off the racket with a flip of a switch, neither of which are good for the games business. The development team has the difficult task of finding the perfect balance, relying heavily upon the audio content providers. Sometimes this cohesive blend materializes entirely by accident; other times after months of planning and perfecting. I've heard people say they would take luck over skill any day, but in the billion dollar games industry, success rides squarely on abilities, not chance.

How many times have you walked into an arcade and been blasted by sound as the door was opened? The same for the trade show scene where each booth has a noise-making machine determined to attract attention. That is what a really bad game sounds like, the kind of mess where so much is happening at once, you have no idea of what's going on. And, believe it or not, there are games out there where sound overpowers the experience instead of enhancing it. Some games attempt to combat this lack of foresight and experience by giving the player the "power" to adjust all of the audio elements, making them responsible for their own experience. If it doesn't work, the blame can be placed on the consumer, not the developer. Of course, there are some advantages to this feature, but the point is: we can make a difference and can affect the success of the soundscape *ourselves*. By simplifying the game experience and mixing the sound elements ahead of time, the player can spend their time playing and enjoying a game instead of adjusting parameters.

Can music, sound effects, and narratives exist simultaneously in the soundscape without negatively impacting the game experience? Yes, they can, but a certain amount of care needs to be taken to ensure they do. When working on a new piece, a composer's initial mindset should be to create music able to stand on its own. The majority will add several layers of melodies, counter melodies, and percussion tracks to keep the music interesting and alive. Afterall, this is what musicians and composers do. There are times when this type of music actually works in games: intro sequences, cinematics, menu screens, and other stand-alone cues where no real thought from the player is required. Music intended as background music, though, has to be just that — in the background. Layers tend to interfere with other audio in this type of situation. I know you want to make some great music to showcase your talent and sell lots of soundtrack albums, but busy, complex scores do nothing for the overall soundscape of the game. If music is the only audio playing at a particular time, you are home free; knock yourself out, make the best music you can. But if your music will be sharing real estate with other sounds, lay back a little and make some room for the rest of the audio. Save your elaborate performances for the soundtrack remix release and let your professionalism shine through for the sake of the product.

Sound effects require a bit of finesse. During gameplay, they must take priority over the music in order to ensure the player receives the needed feedback. A driving game may be the exception, where music creates the pulse and rhythm. For something as simple as a menu screen, a jamming techno cue could be playing, pumping up the player for the experience they are about to receive. The player clicks on a button, and except for the visual cue of seeing the button depress and the screen changing, gets no other feedback. There may have been a sound effect associated with the button depress but it was either too low in volume or lost in the music. Some choices need to be made. Do you turn down the volume of the music? Do you increase the volume of the sound effect? Do you dump the sound effect? Another alternative, and probably a better solution, is to create a sound which will actually stand out from the music or to create a hole in the frequency spectrum of the music. Either way, this will enable the sound effect, whether subtle or not, to be heard. By utilizing opposing frequencies, or ones that are not overloaded by other audio, the game can be experienced as the developer intended, not sacrificed to chance.

As an example, a bass-heavy rock track will definitely not leave room for any other low-frequency activity in the soundscape. Sound effects, such as hits or explosions, may barely be heard or overload an audio playback system causing distortion. Instead, consider keeping those sound effects in the mid to upper ranges or remix the music with less bass. Look for the hole in the frequency spectrum and jump into it. Music with a lot of high-frequency, percussive activity won't leave much room for small effects that go "click." Consider making them "thumps" instead. By maintaining awareness of other audio in the game, you can create practical sound effects which work the first time.

Voice-overs, narratives, and speech require the same considerations as the other sonic activity. Rules that apply to FM radio jocks won't work in this business. They get away with full-bodied vocalizations that saturate the entire frequency spectrum because they can. They want you to pay attention — they want that booming voice to grab hold or else they would be looking for another line of work. If other audio is present when they speak, a technique called *ducking* is used to decrease its volume and keep the voice on top. This type of speech unrealistically becomes what producers expect of their narrative recordings as well. They want them full, with lots of low and high end, making them bigger than life. But they do not realize the impact it can have on the rest of the audio. When an overly full narrative is mixed with music and sound effects, it becomes mud. By narrowing the spectrum the voice uses and developing a good mix with EQ, the words will be easily heard and understood, and the rest of the audio can be heard clearly too.

A common mistake inexperienced musicians and music producers make when doing final mixes of a song is to solo each instrument and individually tweak them to perfection. When all of the instruments are brought together later, the resulting competition for space creates a mix which is generally muddy and blurred. Another few hours of adjustments will follow to persuade them all to sound good together. Most of the time, if you were to solo one of the instruments, like a piano or guitar, it will sound thin and unimpressive, nothing like what you would expect it to. But what ultimately matters, for the good of the song's overall production and when doing *any* audio for video games, is that everything blends. By allowing each instrument to work within a narrowed spectrum of the frequency band, they can all be heard clearly and as intended in the compilation. The misconception that all of the elements must sound perfect on their own needs to be overcome and us sound guys and gals must ensure that developers understand this concept and stick to it.

Consider a wailing sax, hammering piano, or guitar riff competing with a narrative as an example. All of these elements have primary occupation in the middle range of human hearing. If they just happen to all be playing at once, you wouldn't be able to understand a word a character is saying. To put it more musically, you never hear a vocalist singing during an instrument solo, right? Same idea. Saturated soundscapes mean degraded effectiveness, with the only options being to turn it down or turn it off. We can prevent either from ever happening.

10.1 Maintaining Consistency in Production with Audio Elements

Fitting together audio elements like puzzle pieces is just one of the many tricks to effectively master game sound. Maintaining consistency is another issue an audio content provider must apply. All audio requires the same character; that is, the element which cements it to this, and only this, particular game experience. Having an effect distract the player during gameplay because it sounds out of place or like it's from another game breaks the magic. Even that one, innocent, little sound effect thrown in the game as an afterthought has the ability to screw up an entire production.

The easiest way for a developer to ensure consistency is to use the same composer, the same sound designer and the same voice actors for every aspect of the game. This will provide the same basic flavor by using the same recipe ingredients, thus providing overall uniformity. Each artist has their own style and equipment which contribute to their 'sound' and by utilizing the same providers, this will keep a game's audio sounding cohesive.

In the event where last minute audio is needed and the original content provider isn't available, extreme care should be taken by the developer. Ensure the stand-in audio provider has other music or sound effects from the game to measure their new offerings against. If possible, find out what settings and effects processing were used during the production to at least increase the chance of similarities or maybe even get the audio folks in touch with each other so they can talk about it and share ideas. It's no secret that if I ran all of my sound effects through some acoustic processor to add ambiance, you can hear it. The setting I used is the unknown and, unless it's a company secret, I shouldn't have a problem sharing it with someone else involved in the project. All they have to do is ask.

Another way for an audio content provider to ensure consistency is to devote time to only one game for the duration of the project. If a developer is particularly concerned about this, they will more than likely ask prospective composers and sound designers up front whether they can commit solely to one project at a time. Often, this focus alone will obtain the desired consistency.

Another good rule of thumb is to not separate working sessions with considerable gaps of time. For instance, Joey Kuras had to revisit sounds he created for Tomorrow Never Dies many months after he had completed the initial sound list. After designing new sounds, the old ones didn't quite sound like they belonged. He ended up spending extra time EQ'ing and adjusting the volume of the previous sounds to bring them up to speed. Although he used the same equipment as the first time around, his mixing board and equipment settings had changed enough in the interim to make the new effects sound different. By making adjustments during the same timeframe, the chance of this level of edit is remote, and better consistency results.

10.1.1 Consistency in Music

There are some specific steps we can take when composing, recording, and implementing a game score to help maintain its uniformity. Recording artists in the mainstream music scene work hard to ensure their CD releases measure up to other music on the market and that all of the songs on that CD sound like they belong together. We can take a lesson from this.

I recently worked on a project that could have benefited from this type of consideration. By the time I became involved in the project, the opening title sequence and main title screen music had already been done. These had been licensed from the mother company and were done by two different composers. They had similar qualities, with similar style, but were obviously recorded in different studios with different musicians and instruments. They sounded very different. The plan was to implement these into the game as direct audio. I was tasked to write several cues, one as direct audio and the rest as MIDI files to trigger a small sound bank, chosen with the guidance of the audio director. So, now we had three different direct audio tunes composed by three different composers, recorded in three different studios by different musicians and instrumentation *and* several other pieces of music done in a completely different format and style using a sound bank with only average quality samples. Yikes!

Musically, the game didn't show any consistency and sounded uneven, but somehow most of it worked. The intro sequence was designed to tie the game into its real-life counterpart that used the same theme song and because it would probably only be watched a few times during the course of ownership, it didn't become that much of an issue. The direct audio music used for the credit sequence would probably only be seen a couple of times at the most so that became a non-issue as well. The only real difficult connection was between the main menu direct audio cue and the rest of the game music, MIDI files triggering an internal sound bank. These were heard every time the game was played, and because they were of different musical styles, there was noticeable contrast. The developer made a conscious choice to do this, creating a different rhythm for each part of the game, but it still sounded incongruous.

What could we have done to develop some consistency? The first thought would be to develop the sound bank using similar instrumentation as the original direct audio piece and to compose all of the music in the same style. Another idea would be to have a single composer redo all of the direct audio cues utilizing the same instrumentation. Yet another option would be to use MIDI cues and the same sound bank for all of the music. Plenty of ideas, any of which would help.

This example helps illustrate many points. Music is a highly personalized experience and composers will always create with their particular "sound." As mentioned in an earlier chapter, every element a composer uses — from their instruments, samples, and talent, to the microphones, signal processors, and recording mediums — contributes to this sound. As you become familiar with an artist, you can recognize their work. I remember hearing a new song on the radio the other day. I had never heard it before and by the first measure I had guessed who the artist was without them even singing a note. Their style and sound was obvious. This concept plays out the same with video game composers. Different composers on the same project are obvious. Not that it can't work, it just has a different sound and may distract the player enough to remind them they are just playing a video game.

If all of the music is within the same genre, using the same main instrumentation will tie the experience together. If direct audio will be used, ensure the recording method is the same. If the songs are recorded live, make sure all of the songs are recorded live. If the instruments are all plugged directly into a mixing board and triggered via MIDI in the recording studio, make sure all of the music is done that way. Finally, when the music is implemented into the game, use consistent playback methods. Have all of the music streamed from a CD or have it all trigger a sound bank. The type of music occupying the majority of airtime should set the tone. If there are several cinematic tie-ins, make sure the rest of the music has those same elements. By doing so, the entire production will have a constant audio personality. This is a good thing.

Music Mastering

A game score can take another important lesson from the record industry. Before any CD release is made, the music is taken to the next level with what is known as the *mastering* process. This is where subtle EQ, volume, and compression are used to even out the rough edges and to blend the music into one coherent work. Often times, 10 different songs recorded for an album will end up with 10 slightly different mixes. Some will have more bass, others more high end, and others will have volume mismatches. When a listener plays an entire album, they might have to continuously adjust the volume for each song or turn down the bass which may be perfect in nine songs, but blows out the speakers in one. Mastering takes all of these differences into account and ensures the listener can relax during the playback experience and not have to re-engineer songs on the fly. During this process, all aspects are matched from song to song so that the EQ and volume knobs never have to be touched. It's a process which often gets forgotten in the rush to meet a deadline.

For game music, various pieces are submitted at milestones during game development. Over the course of the month or two a composer is working, the last music cue submitted will have changed in volume and EQ from the first one and will be noticeably different in the game if they were to be played side-by-side. Some composers get around this by comparing each submission to the first piece they've done, but to do it right, a couple of days at the end of the final cycle should be set aside for the mastering process. This helps guarantee a cohesive collection of music. Unfortunately, it won't be appreciated much by the player when done right, but you can bet it will have the opposite effect when done wrong.

10.1.2 Consistency in Sound Effects

Sound designers can naturally benefit from lessons learned in the music world to take their craft up another notch — to bring commonality to the player's experience and increase the chance for audio success in a game.

More so than composing, it is important for sound designers to be able to commit to one project at a time in order to achieve consistency. I can't remember how many times I've tried to work on several sound effects projects at once and ended up losing perspective on all of them. What ended up happening is I began treating it as one big project, even though none were related, using the same sound palette, trying to take shortcuts. At the time, it seemed logical but when I sat back to listen to the four games side-by-side, they sounded the same and none had their own personality. It's a pretty straightforward idea, but difficult when you are busy.

Another step to ensure uniformity across the entire line-up of effects is to process all the game sounds using the same sound processor settings. Using the same EQ, volume, reverb settings, and so on will furnish them with a similar *feel*. Jamey Scott uses this trick with much success in his projects. This type of final mastering gives the sounds an overall commonality.

Sound Effects Mastering

Mastering can also be accomplished on purpose — planned in advance as the final step before delivery. Running all of your sound effects through mastering software to adjust compression, limiting, volume, and equalization is a great idea that many non-musicians don't ever consider. They associate the process with music, but it can be equally valuable with sound effects. A final "mastering" session sees to their overall uniformity and ensures consistent playback quality — giving the final mixed audio a certain characteristic which ties it to the game. Good software can add a pleasant analog warmth, clarity, and presence; allow hard digital clipping; or add a smooth, tape-like saturation to the mixed sounds for a feel that is truly unique. Some sound designers use this process as their secret weapon to give the final polish to their work.

The final step, before submitting finished sound effects, is to listen to them in their entirety back-to-back, one after another. Listen specifically to their volume or perceived loudness with respect to the other effects and make adjustments to those that seem out of place. Be sure this comparison is conducted aurally and not visually. Some sounds can "look" softer than others but will actually be louder when played. Your ears have to be trusted on this one. There will be some sounds which need to be softer or louder by design, such as soft button clicks or thundering explosions, and you can ignore those. The rest will require some consistency and by listening to them as a whole, there won't be any surprises later on. With the myriad of details needed to complete a game project, it is easy to let a sound slip through the cracks. This process will ensure it isn't your fault and keep the game sounding smooth.

Early in my sound design career, I worked on a Bingo game project, initially delivering about 85 sound files for the number/letter calls. I had edited the best takes from the voice talent recordings and just sent them in. It was pretty cut and dried and I didn't think much of it; the calls seemed fairly consistent, plus I was in a hurry to meet the deadline. It wasn't until the following week when they were placed in the game that I noticed the conspicuous volume differences between them. That's when I discovered the little trick of listening to them all back-to-back, as well as randomly, to ensure they were even in volume. Looking at the sound files and using the same normalization and limiter settings didn't work as I had expected, but the time spent listening sure did. The middle frequency range is generally better reproduced by most multimedia playback systems and this all-voice sound effects project required some extra care.

10.1.3 Consistency in Voice-Overs and Speech

After discussing the considerations for music and sound effects, voice-overs, speech, and other narrative sound files would need to show consistency as well. Everything previously mentioned — from using the same equipment and signal processors to the mastering process — should be utilized in this pursuit. Additional factors can also help maintain uniformity when working with voices.

This might sound obvious, but, always use the same voice talent for a specific character. There are exceptions, for instance an alien creature who has the vocal range from the growling lows of James Earl Jones to the high screech of a five-year-old girl, where you might need at least two voice actors to accommodate the requirements. (Unless you can find someone who has that range, of course.) And there are always the times when you need a line at the last minute and you are the only one around to perform the substitution. But, as a whole, using the same voice makes sense. People who play these games aren't dumb and they will notice anything out of place, cheapening their gaming experience. If there is a female voice announcing warnings and malfunctions aboard your spaceship, make sure it's the same voice. Make sure your little gremlin characters start with the same voice, even if it is processed beyond recognition.

Another consistency trick is to record all of the narratives in one session, using the same recording technique, the same microphone, and the same settings. By doing so, there won't be any concerns about the voice actor's tone sounding different either. Human voice qualities can change depending on the time of day, how tired they are, how humid or dry the air is, or whether or not they just drank battery acid. If they have to return later, you may suffer the possibility of them having a cold, for example, which could affect their sound and ruin your efforts. Equipment properties may have changed, and unless you have instant recall available on every piece of gear you use, they too will sound different. It will all add up to the same person sounding conspicuously dissimilar in the game.

Consistent audio qualities is an important issue for everyone on the development team to concern themselves with. Much effort and thought goes into not only the creative aspects of audio production, but how it all fits into the game. By utilizing the forementioned ideas and techniques, it is possible to produce a game with sounds that are enhancements and not distractions.

GAME COMPOSERS AT WORK

Stephen Rippy of Ensemble Studios

How does scoring for a game start for you? "We tend to start with a lot of research. This can involve anything from studying historical, culture-specific music to just trying to get a new drum sound — it all depends on the project. The research phase gradually morphs into production mode. Pieces of music start to trickle in, and before we know it, half of the material is written. I always keep a CD in my car that features the most current version of the soundtrack that we're working on. Not only does this help me to get a better grasp on what shape the music is taking, it also gets me very familiar with the problems that will need to be addressed in the final mix. We mix all of our tracks at once at the end of the project. It's a very tedious process, but the final versions of the songs are always leagues beyond the temporary mixes that we've, by that point, grown accustomed to."

Do you have a particular time when you are most creative? "I'm definitely most creative with a deadline looming. The most extreme example of this occurred with the Conquerors expansion pack for Age of Empires 2. In six months, my partner and I wrote, recorded, and mixed an hour and a half of totally new music. It was a blistering schedule, but we got some great stuff out of it."

Any advice for future game composers? "A game composer should be able to work quickly and regularly. Additionally, since it's very helpful to be able to write in a wide variety of styles, a composer should be willing to listen to and absorb everything. Above all else, though, a composer needs to be able to serve a project; if that means changing or cutting material, then that's what he or she has to do. It all has to fit the vision of the game."

10.2 Quality Control

Video games, though nothing but strings of 1's and 0's, are like any other product and require some form of quality control. As the sound person, there is much to do from your end to ensure the audio portion of the product is up to par. Creating one third of the game experience is a heavy responsibility and it behooves you to not leave this step to the developer entirely. You are the audio expert, you know the intentions behind every piece of music and sound, your name is on the box, and this final product is what might attract your next big, money-making project. There is a lot riding on your sounds and you can't just leave it to fate or some low-level, code programmer who doesn't understand audio.

If the audio was built using top-notch, professional studio equipment, those standards are usually acceptable and odds are it will also sound professional. Using experienced and talented craftsmen along with great gear will increase this chance of success. Starting out with quality will boost you past mediocrity, giving less need for a separate quality control phase. But, regardless of how good you and your sounds are, it is always a good idea to keep track of their progress once they've left your hands.

10.2.1 Check Mixes on Several Systems

Before any final music or sound effects are delivered to the developer, it is a good idea to listen to them on different systems and different speakers. This will check the integrity of the audio across a wide range of possible playback systems — whether it's a cheap set of multimedia speakers bought from a swap meet to a full-on, $10,000 home theater surround sound system. The options are infinite and you want to have the confidence your audio sounds good on all of them. Play back at different volumes, from very soft to as loud as the neighbors can stand. Listen for an even mix in each cue or effect. Make sure the low-end frequencies don't distort and the high end is present and not overpowering at any setting. If all of the audio sounds good on the various systems and settings, they've passed the test. If not, fix them.

10.2.2 Check Your Sounds in the Actual Game

This sounds obvious, but more often than not, the sound person gets left out of this final step. If you're able, listen to the audio in the game. If not, make sure a trusted member of the development team, with audio experience, is there to perform this crucial assessment. Some actually believe this process to be the most vital phase of the production cycle. Most composers, sound designers, and producers insist the audio guru listen to their sounds in the actual game — typically happening around time the game goes into beta. At this point, the effects and music should be in place and the sound team should sit down and study their audio intently. It's not uncommon for the audio to sound great in the studio but not so hot (too loud, too soft, too long, or too short) once they're in the actual game.

While analyzing the audio in the beta version of a game he was working on, Joey Kuras discovered a programmer on the project had taken one of the sound effects (footsteps) and cranked up the volume so they could be heard at the same level as the rest of the sounds. What were intended to be subtle, barely-discernable Foley effects turned into a loud series of crunches which sounded seriously out of place. Thankfully, Joey's screening session caught the problem and it was corrected in time.

Remember, you are the person getting paid for your particular audio expertise. Your opinion and experience is a valued asset in the production process. Often, the developer will be in such a hurry that they attempt to cut corners to make a deadline and your opinions will be left unsolicited instead.

You must insist, prior to releasing your sounds, that you are permitted to test them in the game.

The example with Joey is just one of many stories I've heard where your intentions to make quality audio are thwarted by someone on the team who doesn't have a clue. They don't do it deliberately, it's just they don't know any better. Your job is to stay on it to the very end and make sure your hard work is presented to the game player as intended. Tenacity is a good quality to have.

TOOLS OF THE TRADE

Joey Kuras, Sound Designer, Tommy Tallarico Studios

Even though Joey Kuras insists he's just a guy who found himself in the right place at the right time, he has more than earned his place in the gaming industry as one of the premier sound designers. With credits in over 65 titles and many years of working with Tommy Tallarico Studios, he is the man to watch in the coming years. His quiet and generally reserved demeanor in no way reflects the explosive talent that lurks beneath. He can deliver the goods on time and with an enormous amount of subtle creativity. A short list of recent game titles include: Tomorrow Never Dies, Pac-Man World, Tony Hawk's Skateboarding, Bass Master Classic, Spiderman, Wheel of Time, Knockout Kings 2000, Stunt Copter, Messiah, Demolition Racer, Test Drive 6, March Madness 2000, Sacrifice, Time Crisis, and the cinematics for Army Men: Air Attack.

His home-based studio in Orange County, California, is a no-nonsense, ergonomic space that allows him to function effectively with little wasted motion. A grand piano and friendly feline are both nearby to provide the appropriate distractions when the time arises.

Computers: PC: Pentium II 448 MHz, 128 MB RAM, 68 GB on 3 hard drives, Sound Blaster Live.
Mac: PowerMac 8300, 300 MHz, 128 RAM, 13 GB on 2 hard drives

Software: PC: Sonic Foundry Sound Forge 4.5, Acoustic Modeller plug-in, Cool Edit, GoldWave. Mac: Alchemy 3.0, Hyperprism, Waves Convert, Digital Performer 2.7

Plug-ins: Waves Native Power Pack, Pluggo. "I try to get my hands on every piece of software that makes or alters audio. I have a lot of shareware stuff. Usually once a month or so I search for new programs. If it does only one useful thing I use it for that. I have too many to list here but let's just say if it's even remotely cool, I have it."

Multi-track: Digital Performer and the MOTU 2408. "I also have Cakewalk Pro Audio 9 that does multi-track. Everything is done within the Mac; recording, effects, and mixdown."

Mixing board and monitoring system: Mackie 1604 into a Samson power amp, KRK & EV MS-802 monitors

Keyboards and sound modules: Two sound modules used exclusively. Roland JV-1080 synthesizer and Roland S-760 sampler. Also adding the Roland JP-8080

Instruments: Two guitars available but, "I mainly use the Epiphone Les Paul through a Digitech GSP 2101 Artist Pro. Also have a 6' Weber Baby Grand — black of course!"

Remote recording equipment: Sony TCD-D7 portable DAT with Sennheiser ME-60 shotgun mic

Sound effects libraries: "All of them. Everything by Sound Ideas and almost everything by Hollywood Edge. I would also like to add that just about everything in my house has been used to make sound effects at one point or another, including my cat."

Development systems: "I develop on the Playstation (Mac hardware), N64 (special cartridge), Dreamcast (no hardware needed), Playstation 2 (hardware not available yet), PC (no hardware needed), and all the older systems as well, but not working on them anymore."

10.2.3 Teamwork with the Developer

As an audio contractor, it is sometimes quite tough to build a relationship with a development team who's been together for a year or more. You are the new kid on the block, entering the picture late in the game. And, with your part completed within a month or so, you won't be around for long either. Not having every member of the team present as one cohesive unit can be a serious stumbling block. As the outsider, you must fight this phenomenon and work a little bit harder to show them you are part of the team and are as passionate about the project as they are. Enthusiasm is infectious and if you display a steady stream, you'll score points quickly.

This bond with the team will strengthen the overall quality of a project. When they see you working hard towards making the game better than anything else that's ever been done, they won't resist your ideas and opinions as much. Nobody likes a snooty, self-centered boob concerned only with making the game a showcase for their work. Games, films, and television shows that only seem to serve one actor, artist, or director are often doomed to failure. The public picks up on these things quickly and demands the total experience. They want good artwork, good game play, and good audio with the total package. Working with a unified development team will naturally lead to good quality control, where everyone is interested in the overall picture and not just their own agenda.

10.3 Conclusion

Exercising good quality control is as integral to the process as hiring the best team money can buy. As all of these incredible pieces of the game project come crashing together, this is the time for attention to every little detail to get them to mesh perfectly. It doesn't matter if every component is a masterpiece on its own. What does matter is how all of the individual masterpieces fit together to form the big picture. By maintaining tight control of every aspect, the developers can ensure a great game. By maintaining good control of your audio submissions, the developer will benefit from your valuable knowledge, experience, and talent and have one less issue to concern themselves with at crunch time. Now you can continue on your path to game audio superstardom!

CHAPTER 11
Game Platforms and Their Audio Development Issues

Fortunately, for composers and sound designers today, providing audio content for the myriad of gaming consoles and platforms isn't as difficult as in the recent past. With the relatively simultaneous launch of three new game consoles — the Sony PlayStation 2, Nintendo GameCube, and Microsoft's Xbox — the new era of audio development allows audio creators to utilize familiar tools instead of dealing with often laborious development systems. Previously, a game composer would have to acquire and license one of these development systems and spend time learning it before they could even begin composing. Thankfully, those days have gone the way of the dinosaur and we can now concentrate solely on content creation.

It's not to say there aren't any development systems involved. Each new console has their own proprietary kit that allows developers to create a game title. Audio you create will have to pass through it at some point. The big advantage for us is that we can deliver our music and sound effects as .wav or .aiff files (as we normally save and edit to anyway) or as .mid files — all of which are converted to useable formats after delivery. As an in-house audio specialist, you may be more directly involved with this conversion; outside 3rd-party contractors have less of a chance. Currently, the new console development systems are closely guarded, except to licensed developers. At some point, it may be possible for the content provider to acquire one as well but we'll have to wait and see.

So, the good news is: we can make great audio in a fashion we are accustomed to. The bad news is: there are still many different game platforms and system standards we must conform to. Despite the massive improvements of the new offering of consoles, we are still restricted to some fairly solid boundaries. The game consoles themselves have built-in limitations. The developer's choice of implementation will introduce others, depending on how they use the resources. I plan to address the current known quantity of the hardware limitations. Any further developer restrictions will have to be investigated separately prior to a project, of course. Just be aware they will exist beyond what I've discussed here.

Currently, there are several consoles and platforms that games are being developed for. But as new ones are launched, games for the older generation are obviously no longer produced. Simple economics dictates that once the goldmine is played out, it's time to move on to the next. At the moment this book was published, the Nintendo 64, Sega Dreamcast, and Sony PlayStation 1 were on their way out the door and it's doubtful you would ever do music for one of these platforms. So I won't waste your time discussing historical audio details of how it used to be done. Instead, I shall concentrate on the consoles and platforms you *will* provide content for; PlayStation 2, GameCube, Xbox, Game Boy Advanced, CD-ROM, Java, Flash, and Coin-op.

11.1 Sony PlayStation 2

The Sony PlayStation 2 was the first of the new generation game consoles to hit the streets. While not radically different than the original PlayStation regarding the way that sounds are prepared and used, there are still improvements in quality and storage. Most of the effort, it seems, went towards processor speed and graphics support — bowing to public demand for better "looking" games. The use of the DVD storage medium and streaming capabilities does allow for higher quality audio than in years past, but it ultimately comes down to how the developer utilizes the console resources and what elements take priority.

The main processing unit on the PS2 is known as the Emotion Engine (EE) — a CPU capable of 128 bits and a clock speed of 295 mHz supported by 32 MB of RAM. Graphics capabilities are enhanced by a separate CPU, a "Graphics Synthesizer," and 4 MB of embedded cache VRAM. Sound processing for this console exists on its own, on a processor known as the IOP (Input/Output Processor), to keep from having to share other resources. The IOP has a compliment of 2 SPU2 chips allowing for a combined local sound memory of 2 MB.

The SPU2 chip allows for high quality sounds, up to 48 kHz sample rates, although original source files are not required at this high sample rate. Creative decisions still need to be made regarding file size and quality in order to conserve space. For those files that do use a lower sample rate, they will be upsampled to 48 kHz at the time of output. Generally, most audio will be stored and implemented at a lower sample rate.

As audio is completed, the PS2 requires conversion of audio files to a Sony proprietary format known as VAG (like the original PlayStation). This particular format applies data compression of 3.5:1 which can change the resolution of the sound during output, but overall, it is consistent. Event-based and streamed audio is mixed in the SPU2 using 48 total voices and routed to either analog stereo or digital optical outputs for playback. If the player is using a Pro Logic decoder, they can experience the audio in Dolby Surround instead of standard stereo, a nice feature.

The 2 MB of sound RAM can be utilized many ways, at the developer's discretion. Sound effects can be stored for instantaneous playback, music or background ambience loops can be streamed using RAM as a buffer from the DVD, or sound bank samples can be stored for triggering from MIDI files, or a combination of all three.

This increase in RAM brings many advantages over the original PlayStation. Higher quality audio and longer loops can be stored on the disk and streamed and better quality sound bank samples and sound effects can be stored directly in RAM. It is now also possible to stream continuous music and background ambiance at the same time, both in stereo or surround.

Direct audio falls into two categories on the PS2: PCM and ADPCM. PCM (Pulse Code Modulation) is uncompressed audio (like the .wav or .aiff format) used for music and ambiance, voice-overs, and complex sound sources. This format encourages a higher quality sound that uses software-based effects and is easy to implement, programming-wise. The down side is its need for high storage space on a disk and its limit of only 2 channels. ADPCM (Adaptive Delta Pulse Code Modulation) is a compressed format used specifically for simple sound effects, MIDI triggering, and streaming. This smaller sized file doesn't require as much disk space or processing power but is lower in quality.

If you are an in-house composer or sound designer for a Sony developer, you may be involved in the audio conversion to VAG. These developers are licensed to use the development kit which includes various tools for conversion. Outside audio contractors will more than likely be required to deliver their music and sounds as uncompressed digital audio files like .wav or .aiff. Different developers may request different formats based on their needs, so be sure to check with your project lead to be certain.

Overall, the PS2 console does not limit the process of composing music and designing sound effects. The only real limitation comes when final conversions are made and smaller file sizes are needed, but it won't change your creation process. The exception is if the developer requires a sound bank or instructs you to use one they provide. This will limit you to a 2 MB bank of samples and may change your way of musical thinking. Instead of delivering music in a PCM format, a mutually acceptable sequenced format like .mid will suffice. Both methods are workable and you can still provide excellent work.

On a recent PS2 project, I ended up delivering music cues for direct audio use as .wav, a 2 MB sound bank of my choosing as .wav files, the key groups and mapping specific to our mutual sampling equipment, and the remainder of music as .mid files. The sound bank and direct audio were converted directly to VAG, the .mid files and sampler-specific details were pieced together into a platform-workable format — all done by the developer. As the composer, the direct audio cues were a no-brainer. I was able to create music using standard audio production methods and could go all out using whatever sounds I wanted. The challenge came designing a 2 MB sound bank and composing acceptable cues. In the end, overdubbed percussion and countermelodies helped keep the music interesting and dynamic despite only having drums, bass, piano, organ, and synth to work with. A PlayStation 2 game project can certainly test your compositional abilities.

11.2 Nintendo GameCube

Nintendo's next offering in their successful console lineage is the GameCube. The physical console size may be smaller, but substantial improvements under the hood promise a quality gaming experience. There are improvements in every feature across the board including a proprietary 1.5 GB optical game disk (instead of the previous game cartridge) that allows for larger file sizes and, of course, more audio.

The GameCube's main controlling unit is a 405 mHz, IBM Power PC, 3D enhanced microprocessor unit known as "Gekko." 24 MB of 1T-SRAM, considered the fastest RAM available, acts as the main system memory, with 16 MB of Auxiliary RAM (A-RAM) as the main source for elements such as sample audio data. Associated with the MPU is the system LSI referred to as "Flipper" where graphics, the AI, and audio processing are accomplished. Despite other elements sharing the pipeline, audio is processed as a separate entity on a special audio Digital Sound Processor (DSP) mounted to Flipper without compromise. This chip is a proprietary DSP with an attached "Accelerator" hardware that organizes data flow, decodes PCM samples, and flows audio to the Audio Interface. The Audio Interface is a 2 channel, analog or digital connection capable of 48 kHz, 16 bit, stereo or surround encoded audio.

The basic path of audio begins with data being loaded into A-RAM where it is moved, as needed, to the audio DSP for processing. The DSP manages the information, adds any chorus, reverb, or delay effects and sends the audio through the interface to the playback system. Audio from the optical game disk can be streamed directly to the Audio Interface without expense to the rest of the program, completely independent of the DSP, or can be routed through the DSP for additional processing if needed. It is completely the developer's call.

Audio can be produced as 16- or 8-bit PCM (uncompressed audio like .wav or .aiff) for 2 channel playback or as ADPCM (compressed audio) for a maximum of 64 simultaneous channel playback — all of which are capable of 3D and can be encoded for surround. The Nintendo 64 console used ADPCM exclusively; PCM audio's introduction on the GameCube is a noteworthy enhancement.

The beauty of this platform — at least from a composer or sound designer's perspective — is that no development kit is needed for audio creation. Music and sound effects can be produced as you are accustomed to and delivered to the developer for implementation. There is an audio tool available from Nintendo developer support called MusyX (pronounced Musics) that simplifies implementation, so all the audio creator has to do is deliver the files to the programmer, who then simply inserts them into the game. The advantage is that the final audio mix can be performed by the person with the ears and not by the one who is deep into the code.

The MusyX tool emulates the GameCube audio system on Win9X/2K and can handle all of the audio needs for a game title. Sound effects, sequenced interactive music, and streamed audio are its main function, but it can also provide dynamic voice allocation and programmable audio macros. All 3D surround functions like panning, volume and effects processing, and multiple sequencer instances (including crossfades) can be created using this tool as well.

Sound effects can be randomized and panned easily, without actual loop points. A programmer would only have to make a call to one sound event which triggers the sound designer's bank of sounds established using the macro tool. Where there may be several sounds involved triggered at random moments, the programmer only sees it as one instance. The sound designer becomes completely responsible for when, where, and how loud a sound plays.

The macro function is a powerful part of the MusyX tool, designed to free the programmer from having to make creative decisions. When a game company hires a composer and sound designer, they are paying for their skill in audio and now no longer have to be concerned with involving the programmer. This tool can design macros, using provided templates or by building your own, to be as simple as "start sound, stop sound" or as complex as managing the complete soundscape in an entire level. These macros can even be used in place of MIDI files with better results due to smaller data transfer.

The GameCube console can play streamed audio direct from the game disk or trigger a sound bank via MIDI or programmed macro files. Interestingly, the system has the capability of using different sets of sound samples, much like sound fonts, that can be loaded and used for different occasions. Instead of having to trigger from the same set of sounds for an entire game, this offers the potential of replacing them for different levels or situations, keeping the audio fresh and the player happy.

As the composer or sound designer, you can expect to perform many different functions for the GameCube platform. Ultimately, you could provide music and sound effects as .wav, or other PCM audio formats, and either stream them from the disk or trigger them from MIDI files and macros. Music can be delivered either as direct audio or as sequenced data files, which in turn, would require one or more sound banks to be created as well. Macro programming may be required using the MusyX tool. At the time of this writing, however, this tool was not available to content providers unless they were a licensed GameCube developer. Perhaps, by the time you read this, it will be obtainable. Programming your own macros is said to be relatively easy, linear programming so don't concern yourself too much having to learn something complex.

Sound effects creation will be slightly more complex. Instead of delivering single, one-shot effects, sounds that can be layered will need to be produced for more options and interactivity. If you we creating a sound effect for a big machine for example, instead of layering several other sounds into a single file and then looping it over and over, GameCube audio lets you apply components of the sound separately (like individual hums, whirrs, and clanks) and have them playback randomly without an actual loop point. Be prepared to work with a different mindset; this idea seems to be here to stay.

11.3 Microsoft Xbox

The Xbox is Microsoft's first entry into the game console business and promises to be a winner. Looking past the initial hype, the capabilities of this machine appear to far exceed any previous company's attempt at a home game console. With a Pentium III class, 733 mHz CPU, 64 MB RAM, 250 mHz custom Graphics Processing Unit (GPU), DVD, and 8 GB hard drive (a first in console gaming history), this platform is set up to be a powerhouse. Initially, you get the sense the Xbox is a beefy PC without all of the artery-clogging administrative functions running continuously in the background. Basically, you'd be right except for the added features designed to move enormous amounts of graphic and audio data.

The main processing unit for audio data is the Xbox Media Communications Processor (MCP) which includes four independent audio processors; the set-up engine, Voice Processor (VP), Global Processor (GP), and Encode Processor (EP). Audio data flows from the set-up engine to the VP, to the GP, and finally the EP for connection to the outside world that will give analog or digital outputs in stereo or 3D positional audio.

The set-up engine's main function is the set-up of data transfer for multiple output streams and to expand 16-bit data out to the Xbox format. By doing this in hardware, it relieves the programmers of having to deal with various software issues to achieve the Xbox format. The set-up engine will also accomplish parameter ramping and other housekeeping functions if needed.

The Xbox Voice Processor (VP) is a hard-coded, fixed function DSP. It has a 256 voice synthesizer running at 48 kHz, either mono or stereo, and all running concurrently. Of those 256, 64 can be 3D encoded for surround applications. A single band of EQ, essentially a filter block, is available for specific obstruction/occlusion effects, such as a voice being heard from another room through a wall. A hardware submixer also lies on the VP allowing any number of the 256 voices to be grouped into different sub mixes and rerouted back through to make further use of different filters and EQ settings a second time. The 256 voices use the DLS 2 standard (Down-Loadable Sound) and allow for an incredible array of possible game sounds and instrumentation.

The Global Processor (GP) is a fully programmable DSP designed specifically for effects processing, but can be used for other things as deemed necessary by a developer. Since the goal is to make sound effects and music more interesting and dynamic, the unit ships as an effects processor with preprogrammed settings. Sound processing using modulation, chorus, compression, flanger, reverb, and distortion is possible out of the box and a developer can add additional ones of their own.

The Encode Processor (EP) receives all of the audio data from the GP and creates the final audio output. This EP is capable of real-time, multi-speaker encoding and automatic multi-channel mixdown to stereo. It has been designed to handle all aspects of multi-channel data internally including multi-channel .wav files.

The 8 GB hard drive — new to console gaming — has some very distinct advantages. Because it has a lower seek time and through-put than the DVD drive, the hard drive is used primarily to augment the system RAM. It can serve as a temporary cache or as an audio buffer to reduce hits to the DVD which will allow other information to be accessed unencumbered. How the hard drive is ultimately used is left to the developer.

The software used to create and implement audio for the Xbox is based on DirectX 8 and Windows media software. The basic Application Programming Interface (API), DirectSound, is designed specifically for the Xbox and accomplishes programming direct to the hardware. The DirectMusic API is a complex tool that takes care of most of the audio content design and implementation on a content-driven basis and is created with a program called DirectMusic Producer. With these tools and DirectX audio scripting, the programmer only has to give high-level cues, such as "entered hallway," "fired gun," and "enemy died," and the sound designer decides what audio events will happen. The composer can react to other cues and design various levels of the same music. For example, if a programmer cues two bad guys in a room as the player enters, the composer would dictate music of low intensity to play as opposed to if the room had 20 bad guys waiting in ambush. In that case, the music would more than likely be at its highest level of intensity as decided by the content provider. The programmer sets up the cues; the composer and sound designers decide what audio plays during them.

Creating audio for the Xbox is essentially the same as anything else. Composers and sound designers can utilize their existing audio editors and sequencers and deliver sounds as .wav, .wma, or any sequenced data such as .mid. There is no need to learn any new tools just to create audio. DirectMusic Producer is a tool that Microsoft provides if you want to do any DirectMusic content, DirectX audio scripting, Downloadable Sound (DLS) collections, audio path configuration, or wave table synthesis. Any work done on the PC is compatible and can be cross-platformed to the Xbox.

Be sure to check out the companion CD-ROM for a fully useable copy of the program or download it at http://msdn.microsoft.com

---

However, DirectMusic Producer is not necessary if the developer intends to use strictly linear audio — like a single music cue playing in the background or standard one-shot sound effects.

The greatest challenge a composer may have when creating music for the Xbox is the need for various levels of intensity for the same music. A film composer may be more practiced at this, perhaps we can take a few lessons from them. The ability to take the same music theme and use it in quiet moments, as a soft, minimal piece and then turn the intensity up to 10 during the action sequences makes them perfect for this type of work. Check out any James Bond flick to see what I mean; the familiar theme is *everywhere*.

Music is always in various layers so it won't be as difficult as it may seem. The lowest level of a piece could be a piano playing the simple melody. The next level up would add percussion. The next would add bass, then a counter melody, then strings playing in harmony, then full-on drums and electric guitar. It may be as simple as building the massive score at the start then working backwards, taking tracks out one at a time until you reach the simplest form.

Sound designers will have greater responsibility and creative license when producing sound effects. A programmer will set the cue and the audio provider will simply decide which sound effects to play and when. Various sound effects for the same action will have to be created, a lot of extra work. Creating sound effects in different layers and triggering them as needed will keep you on your toes.

Microsoft has taken a new approach to providing support to the game creators. Besides standard "Developer Support," they are also providing "Artist Support," where content providers (such as composers and sound designers) can contact them directly for answers. If you are an artist working on an Xbox title with questions or ideas, you may contact them at: content@xbox.com.

TOOLS OF THE TRADE

Chance Thomas, Composer, HUGEsound Networks

Chance Thomas is a multiple award-winning composer and music producer honored by the Emmy Awards, Telly Awards, Addy Awards, Aurora Awards, and several industry associations for his outstanding musical creativity. His music is widely recognized — having been broadcast to every television market in the United States and across five continents. A national marketing survey found that individuals from every zip code in America have a copy of Chance's music in their home!

Chance writes and produces music for a wide variety of game, film, television, and commercial projects on an on-going basis — most noted for producing epic orchestral and acoustic scores. His trademark approach balances the power and dynamic of a live film orchestra against the delicate beauty of solo acoustic instruments and human voices. Additional depth and color are often added to his scores by layered synthesizers and digital samples.

As the former Senior Music Producer at Sierra On Line, Chance has as also composed for projects by Electronic Arts and Infogrames. His most ambitious project was Quest for Glory V, where he made grand use of a live film orchestra for a truly provocative score.

Computers: Dell PC Pentium III 450; includes Aark 20/20 digital I/O card and breakout box; Power Mac G3 266; includes MOTU PCI-324 audio card; Quantex PC Pentium II 200; includes Digital Audio Labs Digital Only CarD; Dell PC Pentium 200; includes Creative Labs Sound Blaster Live card; 3COM Office Connect ISDN LAN Modem, and dual ISDN high-speed internet connection. (All computers are enclosed in temperature controlled Iso-boxes.)

Software: MOTU Digital Performer, MOTU AudioDesk, Coda Finale, Cakewalk Pro Audio, Sonic Foundry Sound Forge, Syntrillium Software Cool Edit Pro, Fraunhofer MP3 Producer, Adaptec CD Creator, RealAudio Encoder, Apple QuickTime

Multi-track: MOTU 2408 digital recording system, 2 TASCAM DA-88 eight-track digital tape recording decks, 2 Alesis ADAT XT eight-track digital tape recording decks, Alesis ADAT Black eight-track digital tape recording deck

Mixing board & monitoring system: Two linked Yamaha O2R mixing consoles. Provides 80 channels of fully automated digital mixdown with total recall, multi-band parametric EQ, and active dynamic processing on every channel, upgraded with surround mixing software, set in a solid oak Recording Desk from Custom Consoles of Nashville; four Genelec 1031A monitoring speakers; six Fostex 6301B monitoring speakers, set of Creative Labs EAX surround sound monitoring speakers

Mixdown deck(s): Panasonic SV-3800 DAT, Sony DTC-700 DAT, Digital Audio Labs Digital Only Card

Outboard gear: Lexicon PCM-90 digital effects processor, two Lexicon PCM-80 digital effects processors, Roland SRV-2000 digital effects processor, MOTU Midi Timepiece, Opcode Systems 8 Port SE MIDI interface

Keyboards, samplers, sound modules: Korg Trinity Pro keyboard with memory upgrades and extra sound bank, Korg 01/W fd keyboard, Nemysis Giga Sampler, Kurzweil K-2500 with memory upgrades, Korg Wavestation SR synthesizer module, Roland TD-7 percussion module, three JV-880 synthesizer modules

Microphones: Neumann M-149 tube microphone, AKG C 414 B-ULS condenser microphone

Additional instruments: Live orchestra, from 8 to 36 musicians; assorted individual instruments including classical guitar, harp, udu, saxophone, oboe d'amore, hurdy-gurdy, fiddle, viola di gamba, hi-strung guitar, flute, lute, english horn, rebec, upright bass, mandolin, etc.

11.4 CD-ROM Games

CD-ROM games, for the PC or the Mac, rely on several variables in the scheme of development. Unlike consoles, which have standard and predictable hardware, home computers can have a wide range of processors, graphics cards, sound cards, memory, and peripheral devices that add complexity to the task. Developers must target specific minimum system requirements and hardware standards in order for their game to work as advertised, but always run the risk of surprises and conflicts. They must decide whether or not to take advantage of any new features like surround sound, sound fonts, or on-board effects processing. It's a jungle, one fraught with many twists and turns.

There are many different ways for a CD-ROM game title to deliver sound. Most current titles still make use of standard linear music and sound effects — basically those that are turned on and play from start to finish. Some games are blazing the trail with use of interactive audio tailored specifically to what a player may be experiencing at the time. How this is actually accomplished is left to the developer's imagination.

When a game is first installed on a player's machine, several different things will happen that affect the sound and how it is used. Considerations such as file size and processor speed will first determine what format the audio will be stored in; other data elements, such as graphics or program data, will decide what has to be crammed through those skinny little pipes and how it will be done successfully.

CD-ROM games can make use of PCM (.wav, .aiff, etc.) or ADPCM (.wma, .mp3, etc.) sound files, Red Book audio, sequenced data files (.mid), downloadable sound fonts, or any other proprietary format deemed appropriate by a developer. These sounds can be implemented in as many ways with varied results dependent on the hardware inside a player's computer.

Most game sounds are delivered as an audio data file such as .wav or .aiff. These are then stored on a game CD or loaded to the hard drive during installation. Most sound effects will further be stored in the system's RAM as a game is launched for immediate triggering; those less critical remain on the hard drive. Direct audio such as music (because it is considered as a lower priority and because of storage considerations) usually remains on the CD. Music playback will depend on the system resources — whether it is streamed directly from the CD, bypassing the processor altogether, or buffered onto the hard drive or RAM. It could also be played as Red Book audio as you would do if you put the disk into an audio CD player. It is essential the large file sizes of linear background music not interfere with any other elements of a game. Red Book audio bypasses everything by going from the CD, down a separate wire to the sound card, and directly to the speakers. Unfortunately, this type of audio also takes up a lot of storage space and isn't always an option. It is a delicate balance indeed.

Once all of the audio is set to play, CD-ROM games will normally use a licensed audio development tool or library of pre-written code, often referred to as an API (Application Programming Interface) or SDK (Software Development Kit), such as the Miles Sound System, to make an efficient use of it all. If not, they will budget extra time into their development cycle to reinvent the wheel, but for a relatively cheap licensing fee, the time and energy saved is well worth the expenditure. Embedded audio tools can handle most of a developer's needs. A developer has many different ways to present audio, with

- multiple channel mixing,
- on-the-fly format conversion,
- volume and panning control,
- EQ and effects processing,
- interactive MIDI music with downloadable samples,
- and 3D surround sound support

available in a pre-packaged, drop-in application. You can see why it becomes important that the sound designer and composer know what content is needed, what format, and an idea of how it will be implemented.

Overall, doing work for CD-ROM titles is fairly similar to other game platforms. Music and sound effects will be created in either a linear, one-shot format or as several pieces for interactive or random use. These will typically be delivered as .wav or .aiff, but compressed formats like .mp3 or .wma are rapidly becoming more appealing for their small file sizes and good audio quality. Music can be a bit more complicated with several different variables. Linear music can be performed and delivered much the same as sound effects, but as larger files obviously. In addition, it can be burned as Red Book audio (the standard audio CD format), something you don't normally do with sound effects. They can also be delivered as a sequenced data file, such as .mid, to include customized sound fonts which can be very beneficial for sound effects that repeat often. By storing them in the sound card, they won't take up RAM resources and will make room for other applications. Customized sound fonts can change from level to level or scene to scene providing fresh sounds for both the music and sound effects.

You may also have an opportunity to work with the various formats of 3D audio, interactive music, and many of the latest hardware features of the home computer market. Be sure to keep up with what is happening and you won't be surprised when a developer starts talking about something new. Console game platforms vary little in technology until the next one is developed a few years down the road. Home computers are in a constant state of flux. This type of new technology has a way of subtly creeping into the game market and it behooves you to stay informed.

11.5 Web-based Games — Java and Flash

Doing music and sound effects for games can also mean providing content for the web-based genre as well. The scale is not quite as grand as other types of games, but they do have their advantages. Where else can you knock out a game a day? Where else could you work on games with various themes every week instead of the same large project that spans several months? The pay is the same (except you're doing less sounds so the paycheck *is* smaller, but the fee per sound effect can be billed at your same big game price!) and the variety keeps things fun. I have spent a couple of years contracting for an on-line game company that puts out a new game every couple of weeks and have amassed over 60 games to my credit. I have a blast and always look forward to the next project.

On-line web games are produced as either Java or Flash applications that can be played directly on a web browser. They are generally novelty or casino games with many recently moving towards multi-player action. They are extremely popular with web enthusiasts and to those who don't like the over-complexity of today's brand of video game entertainment. One popular on-line game site's demographics found that 85% of their clientele were actually middle-aged women!

The one huge difference between on-line games and other console games is the need to produce decent quality with very small file sizes. Because developers must take into account the lower bandwidth of the internet and work within those constraints, content size becomes the main issue. Generally, sound effects are very short in nature to keep content size to a minimum. Music is a low priority and normally not considered for these types of games but short loops can be used with acceptable results if sound effects are sparse.

In a world where composers and sound designers strive for high fidelity, this type of work may be considerably frustrating. Web-based games must use every trick in the book to keep file sizes to a minimum which means cutting corners. Where 44.1 kHz was the norm, it now becomes 8 kHz. Where 16-bit resolution once ruled, 8 bit takes over. There is no such thing as stereo; all files are done in mono. Expect to deliver content as 8 kHz, 8-bit mono and like it.

Flash content is converted in its own process with its own compression and can be delivered as .wav or .aiff; some developers will even take .mp3. Java requires the .au format using µ-Law (pronounced "mu-Law") compression. This type of compression is a specific algorithm for voice signals as identified by the Geneva Recommendations (G.711) who defined this method of encoding 16-bit PCM signals into a non-linear 8-bit format commonly used in telecommunications and Java applications. You'll need to become very intimate with this format's idiosyncrasies if you except to work in this particular world.

Creating audio for these types of games takes a little more finesse than other full resolution sound projects. I recommend initially creating all content at the highest possible sample rate and resolution, then convert down to what is needed. The big problem when resampling to a low rate such as 8 kHz, is that most of the higher frequency activity is lost, causing severe loss of definition. Listen to a really bad AM radio broadcast and you'll know what I mean. It is essential to keep the end conversion in mind and construct audio that works effectively. Subtle sounds like "clinking" brass shell casings hitting the ground will sound like small pebbles and that expensive cymbal crash will sound like a cheap child's toy. None of those high frequency sounds will make it so don't be shocked. Do your best to work within the given parameters and make the files as clean and healthy as possible.

11.6 GameBoy Advanced

The most popular game platform in our short video game history is the Nintendo GameBoy. This compact, hand-held device is tremendously popular with our growingly mobile society where adults and children alike take their fun on the road. Millions of games have already been sold with millions more to go with the introduction of the new GameBoy Advanced (GBA). You may even be fortunate enough to do music and sound effects for one of them too.

At the time of this writing, Nintendo was still tight-lipped about many specs on the new GameBoy Advanced platform but we do have some details. The CPU is capable of 32-bit ARM with embedded memory versus the previous 8 bit for the GameBoy Color. The 2.9" TFT screen is capable of 240×160 resolution and 32,768 possible colors (511 of those simultaneously). The audio hardware is basically the same as a normal GameBoy with the addition of two dedicated hardware sample channels and an improved re-definable channel. The upgraded audio capabilities include:

- two pulse wave channels capable of variable-width pulse wave with four settings;
- one variable frequency, white noise channel;
- one re-definable channel switchable between 16 and 32 bytes with four volume settings; and
- two 8-bit sample channels.

It is additionally capable of 32 sampled voices and, believe it or not, is also certified for Dolby Surround Sound!

Music is implemented on the GBA through a dedicated program code known as the *audio driver*. Audio drivers come in several forms; a basic driver ships with the system's development tools. They are normally workable but require extra finesse to operate correctly. Dedicated drivers are available from a few companies, and while often powerful, they are limited in that they are pre-made to suit as many scenarios as possible and often have excessively high processor times. The final option, recommended by GameBoy audio extraordinaire Will Davis, is the best way to get the most out of a limited chip — get your hands dirty and code your own drivers, customizing them to fit your client's requirements. Very few people nowadays actually have both the technical and creative know-how to take this route, so an alternative would be to hire a competent audio programmer to work with you.

The limitations of the GameBoy Advanced system will ultimately define the music. If you're composing music in a certain style, then you are limited to certain sounds, rhythmic patterns, or other factors that govern why certain pieces of music fall into that genre. The key is to find a palette of sounds that fit the style and fit within the constraints of the project. These confines can actually help composition. If you're composing a piece of music to be played by a pianist on a single piano for example, you wouldn't waste time composing parts for guitar, bass, and strings.

Some composers who specialize in GameBoy audio will compose straight to the target platform through a dedicated editor and driver. Their composing rig connects to the GameBoy circuitry to trigger internal sounds so what they compose is what they hear. Final files delivered to a developer will be as .bin files for inclusion in the product's code. Another method is to utilize custom audio tools such as the GameBoy version of MusyX which is much the same as the GameCube version. This program offers macro-based, programmable MIDI and sound effects playback to include a Dolby Surround Sound encoder and 32 mixed sample voices that fully support Programmable Sound Generation (PSG) voices adopted directly from the original GameBoy system. Because this program doesn't offer its own sequencing program, musicians can utilize their current software and save the music as .mid for implementation.

The pitfall to avoid when composing for the GBA console is not knowing the limitations of the machine. Even knowing the limitations, experienced GameBoy composers might go a step further to try and beat the machine, to get it to do things it's not designed to do, even if no one else notices. Getting wrapped up in this endeavor, though, often leads to being surprised by a deadline. Running out of memory, or running out of processor time can be another problem. Customized drivers generally use only 1–2% of the CPU resources as compared with the 15–30% for ready-to-buy drivers.

The GameBoy Advanced console will certainly challenge any composer. It may even be the last true game composer's machine, at least from the old school perspective. Future handhelds will no doubt be powerful enough to stream MP3s (or a future equivalent). But with this one, you'll really need to concentrate and work within the box to make a melody shine. Keep the tunes simple, clean, and tidy. And remember that spaces or silence between sounds are still part of the music.

11.7 Coin-Op Games

I've focused mainly on the home market of video games thus far but there are other systems that we can provide audio for, such as the wonderful world of "coin-op." The highly proprietary games in the big wooden cabinets cover a broad scope and variety of possibilities. Besides the standard coin-op games we all know and love where the player stands in front of the machine mashing a shelf of buttons, the new generation of games take on many shapes and forms — from consoles where you sit in or ride on, to those where you stand on an apparatus and gyrate. The array of audio needed is as diverse as the game platforms available on the market today.

As far as system specs, coin-op machines are generally designed from the ground up depending on their mission. The developer/manufacturer will piece together each component for an explicit purpose, audio parts being no different. Audio sub-systems, playback amplification, multi-speaker placement, and other proprietary hardware and software are all designed to meet the needs of the game and almost no two are alike. There are some coin-op units that use an existing console, such as the Sega games running on their Dreamcast system and Sony's PS2. These units are essentially a home game console with custom peripherals stuck in a cabinet that requires quarters.

There is no one standard for audio generation and playback in coin-op machines; it's all over the map. Composer and sound designer Michael Henry (at Atari Games/Midway Games West) did the music and sound effects for the coin-op game San Francisco Rush 2049. The cabinet featured a five-speaker, fully discreet, surround sound system — all running on proprietary hardware designed in-house for that particular game. There were two main speakers above the video monitor, two speakers located in the molded seat behind the player's head, and a subwoofer in the seat which thumps the player's bottom end. In addition to having a 5-channel surround music mix, Michael was able to pass real-time sound effects to any of the five speakers. If the car hit a curb, a big THUMP from the subwoofer would rattle the seat. If a car approached from behind during a race, you'd hear it in the rear speakers and the sound would pan to the front speakers as the car passed. Sounds in the environment were also fully positional. If the car passed a giant lava lamp in the Haight Ashbury track, the bubbling sound passed from front to back, left to right, depending on where the car traveled.

For the coin-op sequel to Rush 2049, Hot Rod Rebels, Michael designed a patent-pending, audio delivery system that involved actual chrome car exhaust pipes mounted on the cabinet below the seat. Big, rumbly dragster and funny car engine sounds were directed to the pipes to enhance the realism of the driving experience. If you put your hand down near the opening, you could even feel air blowing out the exhaust pipes. There have also been shooting games where speakers were mounted in the gun, so when the gun was fired, the sound actually came from the weapon. There are motorcycle games where you sit on a realistic-looking molded plastic motorcycle that has a subwoofer in the bike for engine sounds.

While many coin-op games may not require such sophisticated audio implementations, it all depends on what the game needs to convince the player they are really "in the game." Therefore, audio systems can often be built from scratch for just one game and then you'd start all over again on the next one.

The original San Francisco Rush and Rush the Rock (Alcatraz edition) had an interactive audio component. The composer who did the music for these, Gunnar Madsen, came up with a clever implementation for the music. When the player sees the screen where they register their name, a tune plays with a vocal that says, "What's your name?". When the player finishes entering their name and selects "END," the music seamlessly goes on to a tag that says "That's your name!". Just one example of crafty implementation. The interactive music component required a custom-designed audio system, not just involving custom hardware, but audio programming resources as well and some of the lead game programmer's time.

In the case of San Francisco Rush 2049, the developer had a proprietary system to deliver five channels of discreet sound. Michael would make a surround mix of music tracks using Pro Tools and then save out and convert individual tracks. These were then interleaved or multiplexed using a proprietary tool. After he converted the music tracks to this format, a game programmer would add them to the game, and then Michael would go back and audition it in the actual game cabinet and make changes if necessary. In the end, if you want to implement anything in a coin-op situation, it will mean working closely with a programmer — either a game or audio programmer. This goes whether it is music or sound effects or any in-game, real-time effects processing like panning, reverb, Doppler, volume adjustments, and so on.

Composing and creating sound effects for coin-op games is like everything else in coin-op, it depends on the game. In the case of the interactive music for the original Rush, Gunnar needed to set up sample banks with instruments and score the music using these. At some point, the samples would be transferred to the coin-op, burned into ROM, and played back in the cabinet for testing, after which additional adjustments would be made.

For most coin-op titles, you'd approach composing just as you would for any other consumer platform. There are some differences. For example, play times for a level are usually shorter in coin-op than in a typical consumer game, so long, drawn-out compositions are usually unnecessary. The player will almost never hear the end of the music track because the game will be over. Remember, coin-op games are designed to suck the quarters from a player's pocket and several dollars is usually needed just to complete a level.

Unless the game has some specific requirements such as interactivity or another proprietary format, you will most likely deliver audio to the developer as Red Book, 44.1 kHz, stereo audio via CD or DAT. Other uncompressed audio formats such as .wav or .aiff might also be acceptable.

As far as a development kit, there are no commercially available audio tools specific to coin-op because most developers design their own. A developer may provide the composer or sound designer with a PC card that emulates their proprietary audio subsystem or some software tools to generate content. Generally, all you will need is the usual assortment of audio and music software. In the case of console-based arcade games (cabinets with a PS2, Dreamcast, or Xbox inside), the developers will normally provide the audio tools, conversion utilities, and so forth.

These are obtainable directly from the companies or through the licensed developer you are working with.

Coin-op is certainly unique. If you walk into any busy arcade and listen for a few minutes, you'll meet the biggest challenge when creating audio for these types of games: simply getting your sound effects, voice, and music heard intelligibly over the general din. Any subtlety in a music track or sound effect will be lost in a busy arcade. Most coin-op audio providers will make sure their audio sounds brighter — either through EQ or some sort of effects processing — to help the audio cut through the noise level in a typical arcade. If you happen to be involved in the cabinet design, clever speaker placement will also help solve this audio nightmare. You don't want speakers that are too far away from the player or amplifiers that are underpowered. Use your ears and listen from the player's perspective. Get out of the studio and into the field. Michael Henry often hits an arcade when one of his games is out on test to hear what it sounds like in the noisy, real-life situation.

11.8 Conclusion

Without going into too much technical detail and losing the audio production issues, this is the basic state of today's game consoles. Researching these platforms simultaneously is enough to cause the lines to blur, but I can assure you, once you get into a project on a specific console, it will make better sense. The beauty of music and sound production in this day and age is that most audio can be created using techniques and programs familiar to you without the arduous task of having to adapt to a whole new process. It can get quite involved when the various audio tools like MusyX or DirectMusic Producer come into play, but at least these run on the PC and don't require new and expensive hardware.

Sound is becoming more involved with many of the 3D surround options, interactivity, and an increase in overall quality. These advances are what will drive audio production for the next generation and it behooves you to become familiar, if not an expert, on the properties of the latest incarnation.

CHAPTER 12
For the Developer

If you are a game developer, or happen to play one on TV, this chapter is specifically designed with you in mind. There are many aspects of "all things sound" that musicians and sound designers have gathered over years in the trenches — most of which are never fully understood by the non-musical artisans. The intention of this chapter is to shed some light on these invisible subtleties and to talk about audio issues in general.

As a developer, audio often tends to be the misunderstood entity in creating a game. There is a certain psychology that can be applied to enhance the gaming experience in regards to audio content providers. It's not merely adding music, sound effects, and narration and hoping it works. There has to be a definitive plan to make it work right. More times than I care to remember, I've heard game players complain about a game — not about the graphics, not about the game play, but about the sound. Why is that? Were their expectations too high? Was there too much audio bombarding their senses? Was the audio just bad?

There are other audio issues to deal with in conjunction with making the content pieces fit.

What if you need to hire a game composer, a sound designer, or some voice talent for your latest and greatest?   How would you go about finding them and the one that fits perfectly? Game composers don't normally advertise in the local phone book, that's for sure.

What actually goes on with a composer/sound designer after you've made the order for audio content?   Music and sound effects don't magically appear. There is some serious work involved. By having a general idea about what goes on behind the scenes, your expectations will closer match your requests.

What can you do as a developer to make dealing with an audio contractor a fruitful experience?   Certain guidance and motivation is needed. A developer can certainly influence the quality of the audio content by their interactions with the contractor.

These are all valid concerns, ones which, in my conversations with many developers, appear to be the "questions of the day." Answering and understanding them will help make the process of game creation easier for all of us.

12.1   Understanding Sound

Video games are pure entertainment that can stimulate our senses. The ability to provide quality sound happens to be one of the most recent technological advancements to game evolution. We've had graphics drawn with millions of colors and worthy artificial intelligence for many years, but decent audio implementation and playback systems have not caught up with our expectations until recently. With these new advancements, we are discovering the need to be skillful and in control of what the player hears and feels on an emotional level.

The games industry is experiencing what the film industry encountered when sound was first introduced into movies. Technology has advanced to the point where those simple "bleeps and bloops" have given way to 6-channel surround sound, full orchestral scores, Hollywood sound effects for every tiny thing, narration, character voices, and now multi-player voice interaction — all competing for a player's attention. The aural experience has gotten literally insane!

Our goal is to use the music and sound to enhance the player's gaming encounter, not distract them. We want the players to enjoy the audio, not turn it off. We want them to become totally consumed by the sights and sounds of our creation. We want them to tell their friends! Before that can happen, though, we must understand what sound can and cannot do for us.

12.1.1   The Psychology of Sound

There is a certain psychology associated with what we hear and what we experience. Throughout our lifetimes, on an individual basis, we have each encountered sound — our reactions to it vary depending on the events associated with those sounds and the context of which those sounds are presented.

For instance, the sound of tires squealing can have a wide range of emotions attached to it. If I'm sitting at a stoplight and hear a tire screech close by, my first reaction is fear, an accelerated heart rate, and a quick look around to make sure I'm not about to get hit. Once I see it's a car of teenagers peeling out around a corner, my emotion turns to anger at their recklessness. But, as the light turns green and, all alone at the intersection, I mash my foot on the accelerator and smile as the tires fight to grip the pavement, I feel exalted as I return to my younger years. The same sound, three different emotions.

Sound effects in games serve many functions. Primarily, they are a method of aural feedback that simulates what you would hear if you were actually in the game. If I shoot my weapon and it's not empty, it goes "bang" instead of "click." If I hit something with it, it goes "thwack-oomph-thud." If I depress a button and it opens a door, it goes "whoosh." Every direct action has a corresponding sound reaction.

Sound effects can lend believability to an otherwise unbelievable place. Ambiance and general Foley sounds bring a scene to life and lend an air of realism. For example, a good driving game will use sounds of city life, wind, scenery ambience, and even animals — all of which we have heard ourselves in our travels. We expect to hear them and are satisfied when we do, even on a subconscious level. These sounds don't have to be "in your face" to do the job, they just need to be there somewhere in the background.

Guttural satisfaction cannot be discounted either. Sound effects are also designed to entertain and wow the player. Hollywood goes with bigger than life sounds, and games can too. After spending five minutes in a battle with the big bad guy, you want to hear something to make the effort worthwhile. This little sonic reward can bring a smile to the player's face and keep them coming back for more.

Music has an equal effect on us as well. A fast tempo raises our heart rate; a slow tempo makes us relax. The choice of instrumentation, whether soothing or obnoxious, will have an effect. Events associated with certain music can trigger flashbacks whether they are pleasant or not. Music can set the stage and place us in a different world, a different country, or a different time. Music can make you laugh, make you cry, make you aggressive, make you docile, make you fall in love, or make you hate. It is a powerful force and when used properly, can bring an entirely new dimension to a gamer's experience.

Music is primarily designed to create a certain atmosphere or feeling for the player while in the game world. It can create a dark and mysterious world, adding tension and desperation to reinforce the seriousness of a situation. It can be silly and fun, clowning around to keep the mood light and upbeat. Music, like sound effects, can also add a sense of realism. Whether the scene takes the player to the Wild West or to India, the musical accompaniment helps put them within that setting. If it is done correctly, it will not only provide a hint to their location but serve another purpose: to give the game experience a pulse. Driving games usually have tracks throughout the world a player can test their skill on. Most of these types of games will have an upbeat, fast tempo which keeps the game moving. Techno or rock serves this purpose well and by adding an instrument native to that particular locale, it provides an obvious personality to the scene. Creating a rhythm — whether slow and thought-provoking or fast and out of control — can be done through the use of appropriate music.

By understanding the effect and exploiting the deep-rooted psychological aspects of music and sound, video games can be taken to the next level of believability and entertainment. It's not a difficult prospect, just one that requires some thought and proper planning. Remember the power, then turn it on.

12.1.2 Soundscapes

Chapter 10 discussed the concept of a soundscape in more detail, but I want to reiterate the importance of this useful philosophy just in case this is the only chapter you dive into. Basically, the game soundscape is every element that makes sound: the music, the sound effects, and the narratives. It is the purposeful blend of these elements that form an organized presentation known as a "soundscape." Without this type of order, there is audio chaos.

As a developer, you must concern yourself with the overall balance of graphics, gameplay, and audio. Before you can do that in earnest, though, you must treat the audio features as a single entity, as the soundscape. Some developers have dedicated audio directors or producers whose sole function is the coordination of the project's sound. Others utilize a single person or audio company for the music and sound effects and rely on their expertise to harmonize the efforts. Both are steps in the right direction and I applaud those who are serious enough to pursue these routes.

The complexity and density of any music will first be determined by its purpose. If it serves as an opening sequence, a cinematic score, or menu screen music, it can be busier. If it is to play as background ambience, extra care should be taken to make the music simple, using less counter-melodies and percussive elements. If the music serves its purpose, it won't compete with other audio.

Sound effects should normally take priority in the soundscape and not be buried in the music. Music with a lot of mid-frequency activity will encourage the design of sound effects that stick more to the high- or low-frequency ranges. If sounds are created with the music in mind, they can be designed to compliment the sonic activity already in progress.

Narratives, or voice-overs, are primarily located in the middle of the frequency spectrum. Instruments such as piano, organ, guitar, and saxophone have a dominance here too. A concerted effort must be made to prevent a blazing guitar solo to play over important narration; a game winning clue could be lost in the melee.

When the final audio pieces are assembled, take some time to ensure a equitable mix. The first instinct is to reduce volume levels of offending audio in order to hear those with priority. If there is time before the project deadline, resist that urge and look for other solutions instead. All it might take is an equalization adjustment to make the one stand out or to produce a hole in the spectrum. You want all of the audio to be heard clearly. Pulling a sound out of the mix is like casting it aside; why was it created in the first place? All of the audio serves a purpose and it is extremely important that it be heard as intended.

12.1.3 Size Versus Quality

Composers and sound designers normally create their audio product with excellence in mind. Music and sound effects are saved to digital files that can be quite large in order to preserve their sonic integrity and high quality. The typical standard is:

- 44 kHz sample rate
- 16-bit resolution
- 2-channel stereo

Each minute of this format produces a file size of roughly 11 MB and an hour of this audio can almost completely consume the space on a CD, leaving little room for anything else. As a developer, the amount of storage space and processing speed available is of great concern. In order for all elements of a title to fit into a nice, tidy package, priorities are made and file sizes are economized.

In the end, only two aspects of a game have the ability to be resized to conserve valuable storage: graphics and audio. Smaller graphic files with less colors and pixels equal a grainy, unrealistic visual presentation. Graphic artists can balance their artistic vision and file sizes by adjusting parameters to an acceptable conclusion. Sound artists face similar considerations.

In order to make a smaller sound file, the sound quality must be degraded in such a way that less information will be stored. We can do this by lowering the sample rate, the resolution, or the number of channels to a size which is more palatable. The following table from Chapter 7 has been reprinted here for reference. When asked to reduce a file's size, I will first decide how important the stereo or surround image is. If converting to mono doesn't make an appreciable difference, I do this first — cutting the file size in half. Or, for slightly less audio quality but maintaining the stereo field, I could reduce the sample rate to 22 kHz. Either way, the quality of the sound is less affected by a higher sample rate. Frequency degradation becomes obvious as sample rates are lowered and the sound quality starts to collapse. The very last choice I would consider would be a change in resolution. 16-bit audio resolution is better than 8 bit, but it is also twice as large in size. 8-bit resolution is prone to excess noise and care should be taken to ensure the audio volume level is louder than any noise by-product associated with the loss of resolution.

Memory storage requirements for one minute of sound.

Type:	Mono	Mono	Stereo	Stereo	Encoded Dolby Surround	Encoded Dolby Surround
Resolution:	8 bit	16 bit	8 bit	16 bit	8 bit	16 bit
Sample Rate						
44.1 kHz	2,646k	5,292k	5,292k	10,584k	5,292k	10,584k
22.05 kHz	1,323k	2,646k	2,646k	5,292k	2,646k	5,292k
11.025 kHz	661.5k	1,323k	1,323k	2,646k	1,323k	2,646k
8 kHz	480k	960k	960k	1,920k	960k	1,920k

Each year, the quality of video game music and sound effects gets closer and closer to that of movies. As the sound quality increases, so does its file size, and the trade-off between size and quality must be debated.

Always specify that you want your sound effects created in the highest quality possible.

Because new technology is now becoming more mainstream, some development teams may soon opt to go even higher, to 96 kHz, 24-bit audio. Why? Because you want to develop the sounds in the highest fidelity then convert down to what is needed for the game. If a game needs 22 kHz, 16-bit stereo audio and it is discovered later that it can fit 44.1 kHz, 16-bit stereo, it may already be too late for the content provider. Attempting to convert up almost always adds unacceptable noise to a recording — you can't do it. You usually have to start the whole recording process again from scratch.

One company decided to do a television commercial for its game and wanted to use original effects. They contacted the sound designer who worked on the project and requested their sounds in CD-quality format (44 kHz, 16-bit stereo). Unfortunately, he didn't have them at that sample rate and proceeded to spend a few sleepless nights recreating them. It would have been just a few minutes of work had they already been available. Nowadays, computer storage space is inexpensive and larger file sizes aren't a burden. Encourage your contractor to use the highest quality, for the game's sake *and* for future possibilities.

This quality versus size issue basically comes down to a final trade-off, what quality of sound is acceptable for its affected file size. Be sure to discuss with your sound person what they recommend, if there is a choice involved. Their expertise and quest for high standards are a perfect source for advice. Sometimes, especially with Java and Flash games, 8 kHz, 8 bit, mono files are about all you are going to get and you'll just have to make the most of them — there won't be any options. But, overall, the higher the sample rate and resolution, the better the sound quality, and this is what we should all be pushing for.

12.2 Working with Contractors

The process of determining the appropriate audio content, creating it, then implementing it isn't always a painless experience. Game producers and contractors alike need to understand each other's professional needs and responsibilities so the audio creation process becomes less grueling to both. This section describes the process of determining what you will need from a third-party audio expert and what that person will need from you.

Early concepts of art and gameplay have a tendency to change and continuously evolve, so music and sound design at the outset of a project is usually a grand waste of time. Producers have the difficult task of trying to determine the audio needs of the game early in the development cycle, and if a contracted sound person is used, the producer must find someone whose skills and credits match those of the game being developed and negotiate a contract. When you are spending up to $30,000 for sound effects or $75,000 for music, you want to get your money's worth.

Take a long-range look at what sort of sounds the game may need such as general Foley sounds, imaginative or "far out" sound effects, music, and narratives. Specify whether or not your game will have a wide range of settings and characters. It's important to bring the development team together to begin thinking at least conceptually about the game audio as early as possible. If you've decided on a composer and/or sound designer, bring them in on the discussions and listen to what their experience has to say. Much time can be saved and the process will have more grease for a smooth ride. Don't be tempted to wait on the audio implementation details until later. However, as mentioned previously in section 9.4, starting work on the actual game audio too early in the process often leads to major headaches down the line.

When a game is far enough along (for example, at the point when characters, movements, and a defined gameplay model are present), the composer and sound designer should enter the picture. By allowing them to meet with the development team, view some rough game levels, and perhaps see some animation sketches, their idea machine will begin to churn out possible routes to take. A few specific questions will bring direction and needed information together to start off smartly.

12.2.1 Reconnaissance and Homework

The actual task of finding a 3rd-party contractor can be as arduous as creating the game itself. Unless you've worked with a particular audio team in the past and are comfortable using them again, you'll need to take care of some advance work. This type of investigation can be done painlessly if done during downtime or between projects and not at the last minute.

Even before the project is put out for bid, the media buyer can do his homework. Investigating various audio companies and individuals beforehand is a good idea to help stay ahead of the game. Web search engines can help, developer resource web sites are prevalent, and the numerous unsolicited emails, inquiries, and resumes can be (finally) taken advantage of. Because everybody knows everyone in the games business, you could also touch base with your counterparts at other game companies and find out who they use. Word of mouth and networking is a powerful resource so be sure to use it to its fullest. I've gotten most of my jobs that way. Request a current demo reel, references, and past work examples and retain on file until the time comes.

As of publication, the web sites listed below and in the table on page 88 (section 4.2.1) were available for industry talent — not just sound artists, but programmers and graphic artists as well — many also serving as general development resources.

Web links to investigate for gaming project help:

Gamasutra.com	http://www.gamasutra.com
Music 4 Games	http://www.music4games.net/directory.html
Dungeon Crawl	http://developer.dungeon-crawl.com

Web links to investigate for gaming project help:

Black Sheep Journal	http://members.aol.com/blaksheepj
GameDev.Net	http://www.gamedev.net/info/about
Games Link Central	http://www.geocities.com/SiliconValley/Park/2745/glc-select.html

When that time does come, the producer alone (or with several of the team members) should sit down to evaluate the submissions. Generally, you are looking for:

- great work,
- creativity,
- a shared vision,
- reliability,
- experience, and
- someone who you feel can work with the team for length of the project.

After the field has been narrowed to a couple of choices, pick up the phone or invite them over. It's a good idea to actually *talk* to the candidates. Check their production schedules (some busier sound guys are booked two to three months in advance), ensure they will be available, see which one you feel is best at communicating and receiving ideas, and who you can get along with. A gut feeling will tell you the one who is right for the job.

So, now we've moved from the courting stage of our business relationship to engagement and the possible commitment of marriage. Both parties bring their interests (and sometimes lawyers) to the table and work out an agreement both feel comfortable with. Overall, negotiations for sound design are fairly simple. More complicated negotiations come up when music creation is involved, such as hashing out ancillary rights, payment for different SKUs, bonuses, property rights for soundtrack releases, and so on. Spend a little time working out an equitable agreement, that is, get the business out of the way so you can focus on the creative aspects of making a great game.

The key contract point is the cost the developer will incur for the audio services. Price varies per contractor; each has a different overhead to meet and costs that need to be covered. Some, with more experience, can demand more, which will definitely be worth the price for the maturity, experience, and hassle-free production. Other factors can increase the price too, such as:

- rush jobs,
- special requests,
- processing pre-recorded narration,
- auditioning, hiring, and producing voice talent, and
- abnormal amounts of revisions or change orders.

So do your best to plan ahead. When it comes to the bottom line, the final costs are negotiable, of course, but don't expect the contractor to work for free or below their expenses. It costs money to be in business and we want to support those who work hard for our cause.

12.2.2 Questions Composers and Sound Designers Will Ask

When a developer has made the final contract negotiations and the documents are signed, the other details regarding the project are released to the audio provider. This is the point where "clear and concise" means the difference between complete audio bliss or a sound disaster. Words have a way of meaning different things to different people and the sound guy will ask for the specifics in order to make it crystal clear. (For more information, also see section 5.3, "Asking the Right Questions" on page 97 and section 7.2, "Meetings with the Game Development Team" on page 169.)

What is the intended genre for the game? You want the music and sound effects to follow the spirit of the game. Make sure you give your sound contractor a feel of what the game is about, what genre it falls into, what similar games are available.

What sample rate, bit size, stereo/mono, file format is desired? The development team will have done all of their math to determine how much space and processing power will be allotted for graphics and sound. This will help decide how high the sound quality can be and what parameters the audio will be created within.

Will sound effects be altered by any software or hardware processors? Driving games are one example where the reverb effect is used quite frequently. This is the kind of information the sound designer needs to know. Additional processing by a game engine will determine to what extent certain sounds are processed beforehand by the sound designer. (If a sound designer applies reverb to a sound the developer had planned on applying reverb to in the game, that could be a problem). Decide as soon as possible if there are plans for this type of processing and communicate them. That way, the sound designer is sure to not over-process any files. Music is normally left untreated, but be sure to let the composer know if their music will change in any way also.

Are any ambient sounds or music tracks needed? We don't want to have the player distracted by silence. This question may jog memories or give you ideas not thought of previously. If you intend for music to play instead of ambient sounds, communicate it. This will prevent a phone call late in the production cycle for forgotten pieces.

Will certain audio have priority during playback? There can be instances during gameplay when one single sound or musical cue punctuates the moment. All other sounds become irrelevant and this one bit of audio takes the priority. Because other sounds won't be drowning them out or playing over them, you won't have to make considerations for other effects or music being heard at the same time. By pointing to them, the sound designer or composer will know which ones to make shine.

Will there be any voice-overs or speech commands that need to be heard? A composer or sound designer can also be involved with processing speech via EQ or volume to ensure they can be heard and understood. This is a similar process to having the vocals stand out in a song mix. It will also give the audio contractor indications if room is needed in the soundscape for speech and they can leave frequency holes for them to be better heard.

Are any narratives needed? Will there be background sounds or music to accompany narration? Narratives fit into the sound recording category and generally, anyone capable of music and sound design can also record narration. If you already have narratives recorded, the sound artist can often provide the service of transferring to digital file, maximizing the sound, cutting them to length, and adding any additional background or Foley sounds. If narratives are to be recorded, they would need to know if they will be providing the voice talent and budget accordingly. A good question to ask your perspective sound artist is if they have any experience directing narrative sessions. Or make it clear the games producer will fill that role.

Any special sound considerations? Is the game intended to be a trendsetter with Dolby Surround Sound, DTS, studio quality speakers or subwoofers? Are you planning to advertise the game's cinema-quality sound?

What platform are they creating audio for? This information will suggest what type of playback system the consumer will likely use, therefore the confines for the final music and sound effects. As sound people, our interest is to make submissions work well with all audio systems — from dime-store speakers to high-end studio monitors — but the main focus is on the system the majority of players will be using.

What type of music, if any, will play as the sounds are triggered? This would give the sound designer an indication of what other sonic activity will be happening during gameplay. If the music intends to be a soft, orchestral score, the sound effects can be geared to that mood and not sound obtrusive. If a rock soundtrack is to play, then harsher sounds and careful manipulation of an effects higher and lower frequencies will ensure these stand out. The sounds should all work together to enhance gameplay and not fight for attention. The composer could also leave room in the frequency spectrum for certain sound effects if they know about them ahead of time.

Are any sound resources available to the composer or sound designer for licensed materials? Some games are based on film or television properties produced under licensing agreements. If you have secured use of the *actual* sounds or music from these works, does the composer and sound designer have them at their disposal to manipulate for the game or are they expected to recreate them? While the sound designer may not have an actual hand at creating any sound effects originally, they are equipped to convert them to the proper formats and sample rates and need to know if this service is desired too.

12.3.2 Working with Composers

A developer can convey music needs to a composer in a manner much like you do for a sound designer. A list of requested music can be made, highlighting specific details such as the length of each cue, whether it needs to loop continuously, and what format it should be delivered. Or you can forward a beta copy or video tape of the game and leave it up to the composer completely. A list is generally the best approach, but be sure to leave the door open to other suggestions from the music guy just in case.

A composer will need to have plenty of details and care should be taken that your vision is conveyed. I don't recommend telling them exactly what to play and how to play it. Unless your musical background is substantial, this will not guarantee their best work. But, if you point them in the right direction and trust their expertise and musical judgment, the results will be dramatic.

Timelines and milestones in a development project can be critical. Resist the temptation to procrastinate and don't wait until the last minute to bring a composer on scene. For truly inspired performances, musicians and composer need time to let ideas surface. If your game is something special and can benefit from a brilliant score, use your time wisely and share schedules and expectations with the artisan. Professional music people are not primadonnas; they just need for room to let the music grow. Capitalize on this phenomenon and make your game great.

To learn more about the game composer's world, also see Chapter 8.

Music Creation Example

When a composer receives the call for music, the developer, without even knowing it, has set a massive creative wheel in motion. Music in our culture is taken for granted and most do not understand the often monumental effort it takes to create something out of thin air. When all you hear is the end result, it is easy to discount the behind the scenes effort.

This example will illustrate what a composer goes through when creating a short musical piece for a game. This particular one is a music cue from a recent PlayStation 2 project. The developer requested a 30-second, loopable cue to be delivered as a .mid file and a 2 MB sound bank of instrumentation which would be triggered by the .mid file. The game was of the sports genre and this music was for the main menu screen.

Before any music was composed, time was spent viewing video tapes of actual gameplay, the menu screen itself, and a tape of an actual live event. I took copious notes of initial thoughts, ideas for instrumentation and direction of the piece. I listened to audio examples of licensed music that would also appear in the game and additional ideas the audio director had in mind. After a few hours of concentration, I put everything aside until the next day. The intention was to let my mind process the information and to form ideas that I could pursue during the composition phase.

The next morning, I began the arduous task of assembling instrumentation and other sounds which would form my basic "sound palette." We had decided on a hip-hop theme with piano

Are any special filenaming conventions required for final delivery of audio? If th
development team is overly organized or if they waited until late in production to bring a
audio provider on board, they may already have filenames embedded into the code. Whil
renaming files is not a big deal, it may help cut down on any confusion when delivery is mad
if they are already named appropriately.

12.3 Getting to Work

The contractor has been hired, the previous questions have all been answered, and we are off to
a good start. This is a good point for you to assign the one or two individuals to act as the liaison
to the composer and/or sound designer — someone responsible for communicating specs, signing off on the work, and so on. This will prevent mixed signals, ensuring clear and effective communication, *the* key to obtaining sounds that match your vision.

This is the point where the audio creation process begins in earnest. If it is a locally-based contractor, have them stop by, meet the rest of the creation team, and discuss the game's intention. If
they are unavailable to visit, consider sending copies of artwork, storyboards, and any story text
that may have been written. If there are any animation ideas, movie promos, or even a rough version of the game available, send those along too. Now is not the time to keep secrets. The contractor has signed a non-disclosure agreement so there should be no fear. They are part of the
team and on your side.

12.3.1 Working with Sound Designers

There are several ways sound effect needs are conveyed to the sound designer. A sound list could
be delivered, specifying a description of the sound, what it is used for in the game, and the
requested duration. I refer to this as a "wish list" because often enough it never gets totally fulfilled. Numerous changes in the game see to that and what initially seems like a good idea at the
time becomes something different later on. For more information, see section 9.6.1, "Sound
Effects Lists" on page 248.

An alpha or beta version of the game can be delivered with placeholder sound effects already
in place. General library sounds or effects taken from other games can be inserted giving life to
soundless artwork and to show the sound designer where new effects are needed. Other placeholders can be words instead of sounds such as "click," "explode," or "shot." As the designer plays
the game, they create a sound to match the action.

For a better idea of what it takes for a sound designer to craft audio,
see Chapter 9 and the example in section 9.7.3.

---

and organ as the primary instruments and I started with those, a bass sound, a synthesizer, a pad, and percussions. After spending hours sifting through sample and keyboard libraries, I narrowed the choices to 10 patches and 2–3 possibilities for each drum sound. I initially started with 7–8 note samples of each instrument — enough to cover most of the keyboard range — with the further intent of discarding those that didn't get used. I didn't want to limit myself and this gave plenty of options if I decided to play an instrument higher or lower than its normal range. I also chose drum and percussion sounds that would blend well with the musical style and the other instruments. At the end of this process, I felt confident there were plenty of sounds to work with and began the next step.

With only 2 MB of space available for the sound bank, I had to make tough decisions early on that would affect the musical output. Composers don't normally work well within tiny restraints and I was attempting to make it as painless as possible. How long should the percussion sounds ring? How much sustain should the keyboard instruments have? The idea was to make the sounds as short as possible without using loop points, but long enough so the instrument doesn't fade too quickly. I chose to work with each sample and estimate the music needs, making each sample slightly longer than I would probably need. After composing, I planned to come back and re-edit the samples to save space and figured it easier to shorten them later rather than to make them longer.

Each sample was imported into an audio editing program, in this case Sound Forge. One by one, I adjusted each sample to maximize the file. Samples from the same instrument where sized similarly and all were saved as separate .wav files. These files were then imported into a dedicated hardware sampler, that is, a piece of musical equipment that allows playback as notes are triggered from a keyboard or other MIDI device.

Inside the sampler, each individual sample was assigned an instrument patch and a range of notes to be played over (technical terms such as *key grouping* and *key mapping* describe this process more accurately). Discrete MIDI channels are assigned to each instrument group, organizing separate patches for easy sequencing and manipulation. Much time is spent testing these sounds to ensure there are no dead spots and that all of the notes blend together naturally. Simple adjustments and tweaks are made to make the digital files sound musical. Once everything is set, the samples and key groups are uploaded back into the computer, burned to CDR, and tested a final time in the sampler. Sample selection, editing, and the loading process ended up taking the better part of the day and, after two days, a note has yet to be composed. We'll remedy that shortly.

A lesson developers can learn from this is that, technically, a lot of work has to be accomplished before actual music creation can begin. In this case, we are creating a sound bank for a Playstation 2 game, but similar processes are involved for "standard" music creation as well. The composer must choose, from their array of sounds, the ones that fit together and belong in a specific game. They must set up keyboard rigs, samplers, and other instruments. Some composers will try to leave their studio set-ups plugged in and ready to go, but because different types of music require different processes, preparation time is always a necessity.

After the technical aspects are dealt with, the composition phase can begin. I started early the next morning by firing up the keyboard rig, loading samples and key groups, and opening a sequencing program on the PC. The software would become the canvas, where separate, layered performances would trigger sampled instrumentation to be saved in the final requested .mid format.

There is no one way music composition begins — each composer has their own methods that can even change from project to project, depending upon their resources. In this case, the hip-hop style dictated a solid groove as the foundation, so I began with drums. The electronic drum kit was maneuvered center stage and I spent about a half an hour beating out ideas. Another 15 minutes and a drum take I could live with was recorded to the sequencer. In the sequencing program, I spent some time cleaning and tightening up the performance and setting a good loop point as close to the 30-second mark as practical. The beauty of a sequencer is the ability to move drum hits around and to add parts that a human couldn't possibly play. Next, a half hour was spent creating percussions: bongos, woodblocks, tambourine and such to complement the drum pattern and give inspiration for the performances to come. These were also cleaned up in the sequencer and saved to the working file.

With a solid groove established, I tried a couple different approaches in search of the music. I started with the bass then moved to the piano to see how these ideas were fitting together. After about an hour, a legitimate idea was forming and I pushed to flesh it out. Another half hour later, the main piano and bass line were recorded with acceptable results and it was into the sequencer again to clean them up.

Next came the organ, with some arpeggio riffs and spark of a melody; another hour had these recorded. Some synth counterpoints and exclamations came to mind and these were recorded next. This was a good point to step back and listen to the piece as a whole because most of the elements were in place.

After some lunch and fresh air, I came back to the studio for a clean look at what I'd been up to. A few minor tweaks were made here and there, adding chords instead of single notes and making volume adjustments. Just for fun, I threw in some subtle bongo rolls and other punctuations and spent the remainder of the day fine-tuning the piece. It was sounding great and I was thoroughly convinced it would fit the bill. Now that I was happy, it was time to get the opinion that really mattered. An audio .mp3 version was made and sent off to the producer and I shut down for the night, waiting for the thumbs up.

The next day, I received the blissful word that all content providers long to hear — the client accepted the cue! And off I went to work on the next in the series of contracted cues. After the music was completed, the final step was to whittle the sound bank from the 5 MB I was using to the 2 MB required for the PS2 console. The sounds were all recorded as 44 kHz, 16-bit mono audio and the goal was to keep the quality as high as possible. I first threw out sounds that didn't get used and then shortened long sounds that weren't sustained. This narrowed the collective size down to 4 MB. I looked at what instruments could possibly be combined, desperate for any space at all. Even after dumping one instrument, the savings was inconsequential and I decided to resample instead. In the audio editor, the sound files were resampled to 22 kHz, leaving them at 16-bit resolution, and burned to CD.

The final phase was to test them in the sampler and in the cues. Some very minor adjustments needed to be made, mostly volume parameters, but overall, the music remained as intended. I shipped out the new sound bank disk and the updated .mid files and that was that.

The total amount of effort for this one 30-second music cue came to four days. Two days were spent in preparation, getting organized and readying the sounds; the last two days spent composing, tweaking, and delivering the final sound bank. A lot of work; basically, 96 hours for a 30-second return on the investment. This is a great example of the "behind the scenes" efforts most developers never see, so be sure to keep this in the back of your mind when asking for music with a short deadline.

Soapbox time

Pardon me for a moment while I get up on my soapbox, but this is worthwhile. Producers and developers who know nothing about how music creation and sound design is accomplished tend to place undo demands on the composer and sound designer and/or ask for the impossible and in the process, kill any inspiration. It is tremendously frustrating to negotiate and work with those who don't know the basic concepts of our processes. One original sound can take two hours on up to create — it is not just taking something from an effects library disc and converting it to the needed format. One minute of original music can take eight hours to compose and record, depending on the style. A lot of hard work, creativity, and several days preparation can go into creation. An entire game can be done in two weeks — with much pressure on the audio content provider — but it can take a month or two easily.

The art of music and sound design is just that: art. Composers and sound designers are artists complete with egos, emotions, and insecurities. Great music and sounds can not be regurgitated on command. Please keep this is mind when making requests. Thanks. I'll get down now.

12.4 The Next Step

After the music and sound effects are created, other matters should be focused on to guarantee the audio will fit the game like a glove. Maintaining consistency is the first issue a sound designer and composer must apply. All sounds need the same character; that is, the element that cements it to this, and only this game. Having a sound distract the player during gameplay because it sounds out-of-place breaks that spell.

The best way to ensure consistent game audio is to have the audio provider devote time to *only* your game for the duration of the project. Ask prospective contractors up front whether they can commit solely to one project at a time. Often this focus alone will obtain the consistency you are pursuing. For instance, Joey Kuras had to revisit the sounds he created for Tomorrow Never Dies many months after he had completed the initial sound list. After designing the new sounds, the old ones didn't sound right. He ended up spending extra time EQ'ing and adjusting the volume of the other sounds to bring them up to the new level. Although he used the same equipment as the first time around, his mixing board and equipment settings had changed enough in the interim to make the new effects sound different. By adjusting all the effects at once, the chance of this is more remote, and more consistency results.

An additional step to ensure consistency across your audio is to process all the game sounds using the same sound processor settings. Using the same EQ, volume, reverb settings, and so on will furnish them with a similar feel. Jamey Scott uses this trick with much success in his projects.

Another concern to address with your composer and sound designer is that of quality assurance. Some believe this process does the most to guarantee the sounds work perfectly in a game. Every composer, sound designer, and many producers I've talked with insist the audio experts listen to their sounds in the *actual* game. Typically this happens around the time the game goes into beta. The music and effects should be in place. The sound team should sit down and study their audio intently. It's not uncommon for audio to sound great in the studio but not so hot (too loud, too soft, too long, or too short) once it is synchronized with the action in the game. While analyzing the audio in the beta version of a game he was working on, Joey Kuras discovered that a programmer on the project had taken one of the effects, the sound of footsteps, and bumped up the volume. What was intended to be subtle, barely discernable Foley effects turned into a loud series of crunches. Thankfully, Joey's screening session caught the problem and it was corrected in time.

12.5 Production Nightmares

In a perfect world, the audio creation process would go off without a hitch. The audio would come in on time, on budget, and would be precisely what your game needs to make it a hit. But we all know there is no such place. We strive, instead, to keep the pain of the process at a tolerance level and just deal with it.

So many variables can come into play as the laws of Mr. Murphy blossom exponentially. The producers may not choose the proper adjectives to describe the game and, in turn, the description may not mean the same to the content provider. The production could go through so many changes the composer or sound designer loses interest. The audio guy could suddenly become a monk. We've all had our own experiences to share. Many, I'm sure, we'd rather forget altogether. But, I'd rather we all learn from them and not be doomed to repeat history.

I once ended up replacing a sound designer late in the production of a fantasy game because the producer was becoming ever dissatisfied with him. It seemed the milestone work was being submitted later and later and the overall creative quality was rapidly declining. He became unpredictable to the point where weeks would go by without ever hearing from him and then the work he did submit, stunk. An example was some magical spells used by various wizards in the game. It seems he was recording profanity and simply playing it backwards. While it wasn't recognizable, someone with audio editing software could reverse it and a possible lawsuit could develop.

That was something this small developer couldn't afford. I was able to step in late in the game and help out. The other guy? He was never heard from again.

Lee Moyer, Executive Producer at Digital Addiction, related this story: "As we are working solely in on-line games, we need only the shortest of sound effects so as not to blow our 'bit budget.' We have two spells in our game, Sanctum, that provide the only noise as effects, Elven Piper and Organ Grinder. These spells are given only to beta testers and are therefore valuable due to their scarcity. Some players will go months before first encountering the drone of Elven Pipes.

Since we desired short, almost existential, sound bites to score some of the 375 spells in Sanctum, there was a need for sound help. The first sounds we got back were created by a contractor. They all sounded OK, but did not seem to match the actual effect within the game. Our contractor's taste did not match our own understanding of the virtual world we'd created. Conveying our needs to an outsider was almost impossible, and so we turned inward. We've a musically talented staff, and the sound libraries we needed. Company founder and Lead Programmer, Ethan Ham, and QA lead, Matt Hulan, did the lion's share of sampling, playing, and editing."

Mark Temple, Owner and Executive Producer of Enemy Technology, has many games to his individual credit and is currently at work on the company's first game title. One of his biggest pet peeves is trying to work with composers and sound designers who are not computer literate. Yes, believe it or not, even in this day and age, there are still some out there who don't know much beyond their immediate sound applications. He has made several treks during hectic schedules to visit a contractor just to get a copy of the game running. He's also had to instruct them how to zip and unzip files, attach sound files to email, or use a modem to connect to the company BBS. It gets a little frustrating when your efforts should to be focused on producing the game — not troubleshooting someone else's lack of knowledge. He makes it a point when hiring anyone that they know their way around a computer.

Here are some other situations Mark has faced and ideas we discussed to avoid them.

While in the middle of a contract, his sound designer left the project with half of the milestones complete and half of the sound effects' budget. A new sound artist was quickly brought in but the effects had a different quality and it became difficult to match the previous work — not to mention the time spent to "spool up" the new guy. Reluctantly, they opted to start from scratch, thus going over the sound budget and past their time schedule. People leave in the middle of projects all the time; sometimes for creative differences, sometimes because they don't get along with the development team, or sometimes because a bigger carrot has been dangled in front of them. There are as many different ways to prevent this as there are reasons to leave. Honest communication and understanding of the creative processes involved is a good start. Contract points, that give the proper incentive (such as increasing the milestone payments with the largest at the completion of all work), are another option, but overly aggressive ones will spoil the relationship early. Find the balance.

A potential contract sound designer, whose work was outstanding, wanted to do the job but didn't have the right equipment or money to buy it. He didn't get the job in this case because neither party had the resources to make it happen. Developers in the past have been known to either loan or buy equipment for the contractor. It depends heavily on the need for the contractor and the cash flow of the developer. In this case, though, it was seen as a lack of commitment from the sound designer. Talk about it together and see what solutions are available before passing up the deal.

Attempting to "one-stop shop," Mark found few sound designers who could also compose and produce music. The idea was to bring one less member onto the team to save time and money. Looking in the right place may have helped this situation. (No offense, Mark.) If they had done previous research, they could have had a list of names and demos at their disposal. But since that didn't appear to be the case, there are plenty of on-line sites that cater to this very thing. (See the web site resources listed on page 295 of this chapter.)

12.6 Conclusion

There tends to be a stigma attached to hiring any outside, 3rd-party contractor. It seems a highly unnatural act to search beyond company walls after you've spent a tremendous amount of time and effort collecting and nurturing your own talent. But, even these companies need to look elsewhere on occasion — when a flood of work drowns your staff or when everybody goes on vacation at the same time.

Much argument can be made regarding in-house audio talent and contractors. If you have the financial resources to pay someone to staff your audio department, despite not having enough work to keep them busy, these particular bragging rights might become expensive. Hiring outside help only when there is work to be done can actually make good sense. Some very large game developers have recently let their in-house staff go for this very reason. It is often cheaper to hire a contractor as they are needed rather than have someone collecting a paycheck with no work on their plate.

Artists are more creative in the worlds they have designed for themselves. Avoiding a rigid 9-to-5 schedule lets them budget their own time and work when they are at their best. Their happiness and security can be heard in their much inspired work.

Working with these types of people is no different than coaxing excellence from your other team members. Graphic artists, programmers, composers, sound designers, actors, and voice talent are all looking to you for the proper motivation and mothering and, though the audio contractor is not immediately within the corporate view, they respond to the same positive stimulus as well.

Even though there are no hard and fast rules, no secret formulas, and no prescribed methods for creating the consummate assemblage of audio for a game, it can happen. It takes fluid communication and a firm vision from the development team, coupled with an audio contractor who shows no bounds to their creativity and patience. Together we can take on the gaming world and keep them lining up at the stores. I'll see you there.

CHAPTER 13
Game Over? Not Hardly

Audio for the video game industry is a continuous pursuit. For the composer, musician, and sound designer, it's a quest to be heard, to create noteworthy compositions, to sell them, to make a living, and maybe gain a little notoriety in the process. For the developer, it is the aspiration to take their game to the next level with the ideal audio enhancement, to create a truly entertaining experience, and entice consumers to spend money on their product. It's by no means a simple proposition for anyone, but when it does work, it is a thing of beauty!

Getting into the game industry will be easy for some and very difficult for others, but whatever way it happens for you, don't take it at face value. You need to also be able to sustain yourself. Some will get a job with the first phone call they make, others will get 100 "no's" before they ever get a nibble. The ultimate trick now is to use that momentum to get the next job and the next and the next. Be sure to look in the right places, make yourself known, and use every bit of talent and skill you were born with. You will need all of it every day of your new career to establish a solid foothold in the industry. It can be done and you can do it!

Once you do become involved in the games industry and begin pumping out massive quantities of killer audio, be sure to also take care of yourself, your family, and your industry. Always do your best work and what's best for the project. The optimal way to attract new clients is to offer superior workmanship on every project. This keeps you in demand and the standards high throughout the industry. Never give your music or sound effects away for free or below cost — this only cheapens your work and other game audio creators' worth. By charging rates similar to everyone else, the people who make a living at this endeavor won't have to lower prices to match those who are giving it away. Don't let yourself be taken advantage of. While most game developers are part of honest, hard working companies, there are a few without scruples who will sway you into poor decisions that will cost you money. Always protect your interests and remember you are in business to make a profit, not take it in the shorts.

You've read all about the in's and out's of game audio — from the composer and sound designer's side to the developer's side. You know what tools you need, how to get organized for business, where to look for work, how to make the deals, and that ever important skill of actually doing audio for the various game platforms. It's been an enlightening tour, one that I hope has given you the insight to fulfill your personal and professional goals. Many game composers and sound designers are incredibly happy in the games industry; there is no other place they'd rather be. There is so much to offer the skilled artisan and anyone of you with the ambition can be quite successful at it.

But, don't let it stop there. This book was originally conceived by the surprising feedback I received from my articles in *Game Developer Magazine* and Gamasutra.com — by the many people who typed in my email address (aaron@onyourmarkmusic.com) and told me what they thought. Their questions and concerns are what became the basis of this project and I've incorporated every one of them here.

So, let me know what you think. Did this book help you? Did you learn the skills to thrive in the games industry? Did I accomplish my goal? Let me know how you used this information, what it did for you, and most of all, please share your successes and the experiences you have in the business. I'd really like to hear them. And if you ever see me wandering the aisles of GDC, E3, or any of those glorious trade shows, be sure to come over and say "hi." I'd enjoy meeting you. Take care, work hard, and make us proud!

APPENDIX A

The Grammy's and Other Game Audio Awards

So, fame, fortune, and the satisfaction of a job well done isn't quite enough motivation for you, huh? Well then, how would you like a Grammy Award for your troubles? Beginning with the 42nd Grammy Award Ceremony in 2000, game scores were, at last, able to compete for one of those enviable golden gramophones.

The National Academy of Recording Arts & Sciences (NARAS) Board of Trustees approved three categories to include music written for video games:

- Best Soundtrack Album for Motion Picture, Television, or Other Visual Media
- Best Song for a Motion Picture, Television, or Other Visual Media
- Best Instrumental Composition for Motion Picture, Television, or Other Visual Media

"Other Visual Media" is the term designed to encompass video and computer games, multimedia, and the future possibilities of the internet into one tidy, little package. Although no game music was nominated during the first year, the ball has begun its roll. Our very own game industry music notables, led by powerhouse Chance Thomas (Quest for Glory V, Middle Earth) and supporting cast (Tommy Tallarico, Mark Miller, Ron Hubbard, Brian Schmidt, George Sanger, Bobby Prince, Tom White, Michael Land, Alexander Brandon, Murray Allen, Greg Rahn, and others) presented a persuasive case to the Awards Committee.

And to think this all started by accident. Chance Thomas had met one of the key leaders of the academy and during a conversation, mentioned composing for video games. This man of great stature and influence scoffed, wrinkled his nose, and said, "You mean like Pac Man and Donkey Kong?". If only outwardly unaffected by the situation, Chance explained he had just completed a game soundtrack using a live orchestra and other high-brow instrumentation like classical guitars and layered voices. The nose became unwrinkled and eyebrows raised in pleasant surprise. Now that he had his attention, he casually asked if there could ever be a Grammy category for game scores. The answer even surprised Chance, who was to write up a formal proposal and send it to the address on the business card being thrust into his hand.

Thus began a two year journey into what Chance has described as "like getting a bill passed through Congress." Endless letters, emails, phone calls, faxes, meetings, and an ever-growing number of allies on the inside led the Awards and Nominations Committee to eventually review the proposal. Their interest became evident when they scheduled a Game Music Summit in December 1998 with a dozen of the game industry's top music professionals. This "Working Group on Game Music Awards and Membership" opened the eyes of the committee, giving them clear insight into the quality of game music. On May 6, 1999, NARAS made the announcement many had eagerly anticipated: game scores would be allowed to compete for Grammy Awards beginning with the year's 42nd awards ceremony.

This new attention can only be positive to gaming and to the music makers within the industry. There is no better advertisement that putting "*Musical Score by Grammy Award Winner…* " on the box cover.

A.1 Who's Eligible?

Because the Grammy's are awarded to honor excellence in recorded music and the music is judged on its own merits, not just any game soundtrack is eligible. Many past and current games have an outstanding score, but unless the music is available in its own stand-alone format, it won't be considered.

To make the eligibility requirements, a game score has to be commercially available as either its own separate music CD or stored in Red Book audio format on the game CD-ROM or "enhanced" CD (able to play on a standard CD player). NARAS has the exact definition of a commercial release, but for our purposes, it must be a serious commercial distribution and not from our own "vanity" label, i.e., not burned on our CD-R and available only through our personal web site.

Figure A.1 This is where it all began for game scores — the 42nd Annual Grammy Awards. While no game scores where nominated for a Grammy, the long road to eligibility had finally come to fruition.

A.2 NARAS Details

Are you interested? Let's talk about how to become a part of it all, shall we? There are three categories an individual may join for the Recording Academy:

1. Voting Member.   This is where everyone wants to be — an actual voting member of the Academy. You and your peers determine who will be nominated and who will win a Grammy by two separate rounds of voting. Professionals with creative or technical credits on six commercially-released tracks (or their equivalents) and those who have had credits as either a vocalist, producer, songwriter, composer, engineer, instrumentalist, arranger, conductor, art director, album notes writer, narrator, music video artist, or technicians are eligible in this category. Proof, such as photocopies of album jackets or liner notes, are required.

As a game composer, most of us will be eligible in several categories — everything from songwriter, arranger, engineer, musician, and producer. And if you have at least six tracks on a single game, or on a combination of others, you are eligible for this category.

2. Associate Member.   This non-voting membership is open to creative and technical professionals with fewer than six credits and other recording industry professionals such as writers, publishers, attorneys, label staff, and artist managers who are directly involved, on a professional basis, in the music business.

By joining this category, you are getting involved and showing your support for the process. And after you have your six credits, it's an easy transition to Voting Membership status.

3. Affiliate Member.   This category of supporting members is made up of music students, music educators, music merchants, music therapists, and others whose professional interests are closely aligned with the goals of the Academy.

A.3 Applying

The applications process is fairly easy.

- Go to: www.grammy.com/academy and download the latest Adobe Acrobat file
- Email: memservices@grammy.com
- Call: (310) 392-3777 for an application

There is also an application in Adobe Acrobat format on the companion CD-ROM. Fill it out, mail or even fax it back, along with any proof of participation and membership fee and you are set. After the Academy's membership committee reviews your application and verifies your eligibility, you will receive notification of their decision.

If applying for Voting Membership, you must list your credits and show proof by way of a copy of the album jacket or liner notes. Associate membership also requires proof of credits (if you have less than the six credits for voting status) or send a business card and detailed description on your company letterhead outlining any professional affiliation to the music industry for consideration.

A.4 Other Game Music Award Possibilities

While NARAS is the most prestigious organization to recognize musical achievement, they are not the only ones who acknowledge excellence in our work. The Academy of Interactive Arts and Sciences (AIAS) offers the Interactive Achievement Award in the Best Sound Design and Best Original Score categories at their yearly presentation. This previously combined category was split after a proposal, considerable lobbying, and follow up by a now familiar name, Chance Thomas. Awards are usually presented at E3 or at GDC. This is also a superb way to show your support for continued industry excellence. "If we will support and nurture this, our own Academy," Chance Thomas adds, "it will become meaningful to our careers in offering education, networking opportunities, legislative support, and of course, an award that means something to our peers." An application, for those of you who are interested, can also be found on the companion CD-ROM.

More information and membership information on this growing organization is available on their web site, www.interactive.org

---

Additionally, there are also several industry- and magazine-sponsored events that hold their own yearly awards competitions. The Electronic Entertainment Expo (E3), the Game Developers Conference (GDC), Independent Games Festival (IGF), and *PC Gamer* Magazine are among some that recognize achievement in various categories including music and sound design.

And you thought nobody would care about all your hard work. Granted, it wasn't always that way, but thanks to many of our long-established colleagues in the games business, we now can have something to show for it besides a paycheck.

INDEX

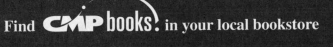

What's on the CD-ROM?

The companion CD-ROM for *The Complete Guide to Game Audio* includes:

- music and sound effects samples,
- game trailers,
- demo reel samples,
- demo versions of sound editing and sequencing programs from companies such as Sonic Foundry, Cakewalk, Goldwave, DirectMusic, Propellerhead, and others,
- information from Dolby Laboratories on surround sound for games and PC usage and the original Dolby SDK,
- interviews with composers and sound designers,
- sample business contracts and talent releases,
- applications for the National Academy of Recording Arts & Sciences (NARAS) and the Academy of Interactive Arts and Sciences (AIAS),
- and more!